Praise for C++ *Software Design*

Even after knowing design patterns for a long time, this book showed me
a surprisingly large number of new aspects on how to use them properly in
the context of C++ and the SOLID principles.

—*Matthias Dörfel, CTO at INCHRON AG*

I really enjoyed reading the book! Studying the guidelines made me reconsider
my code and improve it by applying them. Can you ask for more?

—*Daniela Engert, senior software engineer*
at GMH Prüftechnik GmbH

One of the most entertaining and useful software design books I've read in a long while.

—*Patrice Roy, professeur, Collège Lionel-Groulx*

It has been over 25 years since the Gang of Four's Design Patterns
changed the way programmers think about software. This book changed
the way I think about Design Patterns.

—*Stephan Weller, Siemens Digital Industries Software*

C++ Software Design
Design Principles and Patterns
for High-Quality Software

Klaus Iglberger

Beijing · Boston · Farnham · Sebastopol · Tokyo

C++ Software Design

by Klaus Iglberger

Published by O'Reilly Media, Inc., 1005 Gravenstein Highway North, Sebastopol, CA 95472.

O'Reilly books may be purchased for educational, business, or sales promotional use. Online editions are also available for most titles (*http://oreilly.com*). For more information, contact our corporate/institutional sales department: 800-998-9938 or *corporate@oreilly.com*.

Acquisitions Editor: Amanda Quinn
Development Editor: Shira Evans
Production Editor: Kate Galloway
Copyeditor: Sonia Saruba
Proofreader: Piper Editorial Consulting, LLC

Indexer: Judith McConville
Interior Designer: David Futato
Cover Designer: Karen Montgomery
Illustrator: Kate Dullea

September 2022:   First Edition

Revision History for the First Edition
2022-09-21:   First Release
2023-12-08:   Second Release

See *http://oreilly.com/catalog/errata.csp?isbn=9781098113162* for release details.

978-1-098-11316-2

[LSI]

Table of Contents

Preface

In your hands you're holding the C++ book that I wish I would have had many years ago. Not as one of my first books, no, but as an advanced book, after I had already digested the language mechanics and was able to think beyond the C++ syntax. Yes, this book would have definitely helped me better understand the fundamental aspects of maintainable software, and I'm confident that it will help you too.

Why I Wrote This Book

By the time I was really digging into the language (that was a few years after the first C++ standard had been released), I had read pretty much every C++ book there was. But despite the fact that many of these books were great and definitely paved the way for my current career as a C++ trainer and consultant, they were too focused on the little details and the implementation specifics, and too far away from the bigger picture of maintainable software.

At the time, very few books truly focused on the bigger picture, dealing with the development of large software systems. Among these were John Lakos's *Large Scale C++ Software Design*,[1] a great but literally heavy introduction to dependency management, and the so-called Gang of Four book, which is *the* classic book on software design patterns.[2] Unfortunately, over the years, this situation hasn't really changed: most books, talks, blogs, etc., primarily focus on language mechanics and features—the small details and specifics. Very few, and in my opinion way too few, new releases focus on maintainable software, changeability, extensibility, and testability. And if they try to, they unfortunately quickly fall back into the common habit of explaining language mechanics and demonstrating features.

---

1 John Lakos, *Large-Scale C++ Software Design* (Addison-Wesley, 1996).

2 Erich Gamma et al., *Design Patterns: Elements of Reusable Object-Oriented Software* (Addison-Wesley, 1994).

This is why I've written this book. A book that does not, in contrast to most others, spend time on the mechanics or the many features of the language, but primarily focuses on changeability, extensibility, and testability of software in general. A book that does not pretend that the use of new C++ standards or features will make the difference between good or bad software, but instead clearly shows that it is the management of dependencies that is decisive, that the dependencies in our code decide between it being good or bad. As such, it is a rare kind of book in the world of C++ indeed, as it focuses on the bigger picture: software design.

What This Book Is About

Software Design

From my point of view, good software design is the essence of every successful software project. Yet still, despite its fundamental role, there is so little literature on the topic, and very little advice on what to do and how to do things right. Why? Well, because it's difficult. Very difficult. Probably the most difficult facet of writing software that we have to face. And that's because there is no single "right" solution, no "golden" advice to pass on through the generations of software developers. It always depends.

Despite this limitation, I will give advice on how to design good, high-quality software. I will provide design principles, design guidelines, and design patterns that will help you to better understand how to manage dependencies and turn your software into something you can work with for decades. As stated before, there is no "golden" advice, and this book doesn't hold any ultimate or perfect solution. Instead, I try to show the most fundamental aspects of good software, the most important details, the diversity and the pros and the cons of different designs. I will also formulate intrinsic design goals and demonstrate how to achieve these goals with Modern C++.

Modern C++

For more than a decade, we've been celebrating the advent of Modern C++, applauding the many new features and extensions of the language, and by doing so, creating the impression that Modern C++ will help us solve all software-related problems. Not so in this book. This book does not pretend that throwing a few smart pointers at the code will make the code "Modern" or automatically yield good design. Also, this book won't show Modern C++ as an assortment of new features. Instead, it will show how the philosophy of the language has evolved and the way we implement C++ solutions today.

But of course, we will also see code. Lots of it. And of course this book will make use of the features of newer C++ standards (including C++20). However, it will also make an effort to emphasize that the design is independent of the implementation details and the used features. New features don't change the rules about what is good design or bad design; they merely change the way we implement good design. They make it easier to implement good design. So this book shows and discusses implementation details, but (hopefully) doesn't get lost in them and always remains focused on the big picture: software design and design patterns.

Design Patterns

As soon as you start mentioning design patterns, you inadvertently conjure up the expectation of object-oriented programming and inheritance hierarchies. Yes, this book will show the object-oriented origin of many design patterns. However, it will put a strong emphasis on the fact that there isn't just one way to make good use of a design pattern. I will demonstrate how the implementation of design patterns has evolved and diversified, making use of many different paradigms, including object-oriented programming, generic programming, and functional programming. This book acknowledges the reality that there is no one true paradigm and does not pretend that there is only one single approach, one ever-working solution for all problems. Instead it tries to show Modern C++ for what it truly is: the opportunity to combine all paradigms, weave them into a strong and durable net, and create software design that will last through the decades.

I hope this book proves to be the missing piece in C++ literature. I hope it helps you as much as it would have helped me. I hope that it holds some answers you have been looking for and provides you with a couple of key insights that you were missing. And I also hope that this book keeps you somewhat entertained and motivated to read everything. Most importantly, however, I hope that this book will show you the importance of software design and the role that design patterns play. Because, as you will see, design patterns are everywhere!

Who This Book Is For

This book is of value to every C++ developer. In particular, it is for every C++ developer interested in understanding the usual problems of maintainable software and learning about common solutions to these problems (and I assume that is indeed *every* C++ developer). However, this book is not a C++ beginner's book. In fact, most of the guidelines in this book require some experience with software development in general and C++ in particular. For instance, I assume that you have a firm grasp of the language mechanics of inheritance hierarchies and some experience with templates. Then I can reach for the corresponding features whenever necessary and appropriate. Once in a while, I will even reach for some C++20 features (in particular

C++20 concepts). However, as the focus is on software design, I will rarely dwell on explaining a particular feature, so if a feature is unknown to you, please consult your favorite C++ language reference. Only occasionally will I add some reminders, mostly about common C++ idioms (such as the Rule of 5 (*https://oreil.ly/fzS3f*)).

How This Book Is Structured

This book is organized into chapters, each containing several guidelines. Each guideline focuses on one key aspect of maintainable software or one particular design pattern. Hence, the guidelines represent the major takeaways, the aspects that I hope bring the most value to you. They're written such that you can read all of them from front to back, but since they're only loosely coupled, they enable you to also start with the guideline that attracts your attention. Still, they're not independent. Therefore, each guideline contains the necessary cross-references to other guidelines to show you that everything is connected.

Conventions Used in This Book

The following typographical conventions are used in this book:

Italic
> Indicates new terms, URLs, email addresses, filenames, and file extensions.

`Constant width`
> Used for program listings, as well as within paragraphs to refer to program elements such as variable or function names, databases, data types, environment variables, statements, and keywords.

`Constant width bold`
> Shows commands or other text that should be typed literally by the user.

`Constant width italic`
> Shows text that should be replaced with user-supplied values or by values determined by context.

 This element signifies a tip or suggestion.

This element signifies a general note.

Using Code Examples

Supplemental material (code examples, exercises, etc.) is available for download at *https://github.com/igl42/cpp_software_design*.

If you have a technical question or a problem using the code examples, please send email to *bookquestions@oreilly.com*.

This book is here to help you get your job done. In general, if example code is offered with this book, you may use it in your programs and documentation. You do not need to contact us for permission unless you're reproducing a significant portion of the code. For example, writing a program that uses several chunks of code from this book does not require permission. Selling or distributing examples from O'Reilly books does require permission. Answering a question by citing this book and quoting example code does not require permission. Incorporating a significant amount of example code from this book into your product's documentation does require permission.

We appreciate, but generally do not require, attribution. An attribution usually includes the title, author, publisher, and ISBN. For example: "*C++ Software Design* by Klaus Iglberger (O'Reilly). Copyright 2022 Klaus Iglberger, 978-1-098-11316-2."

If you feel your use of code examples falls outside fair use or the permission given above, feel free to contact us at *permissions@oreilly.com*.

O'Reilly Online Learning

 For more than 40 years, *O'Reilly Media* has provided technology and business training, knowledge, and insight to help companies succeed.

Our unique network of experts and innovators share their knowledge and expertise through books, articles, and our online learning platform. O'Reilly's online learning platform gives you on-demand access to live training courses, in-depth learning paths, interactive coding environments, and a vast collection of text and video from O'Reilly and 200+ other publishers. For more information, visit *http://oreilly.com*.

How to Contact Us

Please address comments and questions concerning this book to the publisher:

O'Reilly Media, Inc.
1005 Gravenstein Highway North
Sebastopol, CA 95472
800-998-9938 (in the United States or Canada)
707-829-0515 (international or local)
707-829-0104 (fax)

We have a web page for this book, where we list errata, examples, and any additional information. You can access this page at *https://oreil.ly/c-plus-plus*.

Email *bookquestions@oreilly.com* to comment or ask technical questions about this book.

For news and information about our books and courses, visit *http://oreilly.com*.

Find us on LinkedIn: *https://linkedin.com/company/oreilly-media*.

Follow us on Twitter: *http://twitter.com/oreillymedia*.

Watch us on YouTube: *http://youtube.com/oreillymedia*.

Acknowledgments

A book such as this is never the achievement of a single individual. On the contrary, I have to explicitly thank many people who helped me in different ways to make this book a reality. First and foremost, I want to express my deep gratitude to my wife, Steffi, who read through the entire book without even knowing C++. And who took care of our two kids to give me the necessary calm to bring all of this information to paper (I am still not sure which of these two was the bigger sacrifice).

A special thank-you goes to my reviewers, Daniela Engert, Patrice Roy, Stefan Weller, Mark Summerfield, and Jacob Bandes-Storch, for investing their valuable time to make this a better book by constantly challenging my explanations and examples.

A big thank-you also goes to Arthur O'Dwyer, Eduardo Madrid, and Julian Schmidt for their input and feedback about the Type Erasure design pattern, and to Johannes Gutekunst for the discussions on software architecture and documentation.

Furthermore, I want to say thank you to my two cold readers, Matthias Dörfel and Vittorio Romeo, who helped catch many last-second mistakes (and indeed they did).

Last, but definitely not least, a big thank-you goes to my editor, Shira Evans, who has spent many hours giving invaluable advice about making the book more consistent and more fun to read.

CHAPTER 1

The Art of Software Design

What is software design? And why should you care about it? In this chapter, I will set the stage for this book on software design. I will explain software design in general, help you understand why it is vitally important for the success of a project, and why it is the one thing you should get right. But you will also see that software design is complicated. Very complicated. In fact, it is the most complicated part of software development. Therefore, I will also explain several software design principles that will help you to stay on the right path.

In "Guideline 1: Understand the Importance of Software Design" on page 2, I will focus on the big picture and explain that software is expected to change. Consequently, software should be able to cope with change. However, that is much easier said than done, since in reality, coupling and dependencies make our life as a developer so much harder. That problem is addressed by software design. I will introduce software design as the art of managing dependencies and abstractions—an essential part of software engineering.

In "Guideline 2: Design for Change" on page 11, I will explicitly address coupling and dependencies and help you understand how to design for change and how to make software more adaptable. For that purpose, I will introduce both the *Single-Responsibility Principle (SRP)* and the *Don't Repeat Yourself (DRY)* principle, which help you to achieve this goal.

In "Guideline 3: Separate Interfaces to Avoid Artificial Coupling" on page 24, I will expand the discussion about coupling and specifically address coupling via interfaces. I will also introduce the *Interface Segregation Principle (ISP)* as a means to reduce artificial coupling induced by interfaces.

In "Guideline 4: Design for Testability" on page 28, I will focus on testability issues that arise as a result of artificial coupling. In particular, I will raise the question of how to test a private member function and demonstrate that the one true solution is a consequent application of separation of concerns.

In "Guideline 5: Design for Extension" on page 35, I will address an important kind of change: extensions. Just as code should be easy to change, it should also be easy to extend. I will give you an idea how to achieve that goal, and I will demonstrate the value of the *Open-Closed Principle (OCP)*.

Guideline 1: Understand the Importance of Software Design

If I were to ask you which code properties are most important to you, you would, after some thinking, probably say things like readability, testability, maintainability, extensibility, reusability, and scalability. And I would completely agree. But now, if I were to ask you how to achieve these goals, there is a good chance that you would start to list some C++ features: RAII, algorithms, lambdas, modules, and so on.

Features Are Not Software Design

Yes, C++ offers a lot of features. A lot! Approximately half of the almost 2,000 pages of the printed C++ standard are devoted to explaining language mechanics and features.[1] And since the release of C++11, there is the explicit promise that there will be more: every three years, the C++ standardization committee blesses us with a new C++ standard that ships with additional, brand-new features. Knowing that, it doesn't come as a big surprise that in the C++ community there's a very strong emphasis on features and language mechanics. Most books, talks, and blogs are focused on features, new libraries, and language details.[2]

It almost feels as if features are the most important thing about programming in C++, and crucial for the success of a C++ project. But honestly, they are not. Neither the knowledge about all the features nor the choice of the C++ standard is responsible for the success of a project. No, you should not expect features to save your project. On the contrary: a project can be very successful even if it uses an older C++

---

1 But of course you would never even try to print the current C++ standard. You would either use a PDF of the official C++ standard (*https://oreil.ly/bZUDd*) or use the current working draft (*https://oreil.ly/r46ta*). For most of your daily work, however, you might want to refer to the C++ reference site (*https://oreil.ly/z0tKS*).

2 Unfortunately, I can't present any numbers, as I can hardly say that I have a complete overview of the vast realm of C++. On the contrary, I might not even have a complete overview of the sources I'm aware of! So please consider this as my personal impression and the way I perceive the C++ community. You may have a different impression.

---

standard, and even if only a subset of the available features are used. Leaving aside the human aspects of software development, much more important for the question about success or failure of a project is the overall *structure* of the software. It is the structure that is ultimately responsible for maintainability: how easy is it to change code, extend code, and test code? Without the ability to easily change code, add new functionality, and have confidence in its correctness due to tests, a project is at the end of its lifecycle. The structure is also responsible for the scalability of a project: how large can the project grow before it collapses under its own weight? How many people can work on realizing the vision of the project before they step on one another's toes?

The overall structure is the design of a project. The design plays a much more central role in the success of a project than any feature could ever do. Good software is not primarily about the proper use of any feature; rather, it is about solid architecture and design. Good software design can tolerate some bad implementation decisions, but bad software design cannot be saved by the heroic use of features (old or new) alone.

Software Design: The Art of Managing Dependencies and Abstractions

Why is software design so important for the quality of a project? Well, assuming everything works perfectly right now, as long as nothing changes in your software and as long as nothing needs to be added, you are fine. However, that state will likely not last for long. It's reasonable to expect that something will change. After all, the one constant in software development is change. Change is the driving force behind all our problems (and also most of our solutions). That's why software is called *soft*ware: because in comparison to hardware, it is soft and malleable. Yes, *soft*ware is expected to be easily adapted to the ever-changing requirements. But as you may know, in reality this expectation might not always be true.

To illustrate this point, let's imagine that you select an issue from your issue tracking system that the team has rated with an expected effort of 2. Whatever a 2 means in your own project(s), it most certainly does not sound like a big task, so you are confident that this will be done quickly. In good faith, you first take some time to understand what is expected, and then you start by making a change in some entity A. Because of immediate feedback from your tests (you are lucky to have tests!), you are quickly reminded that you also have to address the issue in entity B. That is surprising! You did not expect that B was involved at all. Still, you go ahead and adapt B anyway. However, again unexpectedly, the nightly build reveals that this causes C and D to stop working. Before continuing, you now investigate the issue a little deeper and find that the roots of the issue are spread through a large portion of the codebase. The small, initially innocent-looking task has evolved into a large, potentially risky code modification.[3] Your confidence in resolving the issue quickly is gone. And your plans for the rest of the week are as well.

Maybe this story sounds familiar to you. Maybe you can even contribute a few war stories of your own. Indeed, most developers have similar experiences. And most of these experiences have the same source of trouble. Usually the problem can be reduced to a single word: *dependencies*. As Kent Beck has expressed in his book on test-driven development:[4]

> Dependency is the key problem in software development at all scales.

Dependencies are the bane of every software developer's existence. "But of course there are dependencies," you argue. "There will always be dependencies. How else should different pieces of code work together?" And of course, you are correct. Different pieces of code need to work together, and this interaction will always create some form of coupling. However, while there are necessary, unavoidable dependencies, there are also artificial dependencies that we accidentally introduce because we lack an understanding of the underlying problem, don't have a clear idea of the bigger picture, or just don't pay enough attention. Needless to say, these artificial dependencies hurt. They make it harder to understand our software, change software, add new features, and write tests. Therefore, one of the primary tasks, if not *the* primary task, of a software developer is to keep artificial dependencies at a minimum.

This minimization of dependencies is the goal of software architecture and design. To state it in the words of Robert C. Martin:[5]

> The goal of software architecture is to minimize the human resources required to build and maintain the required system.

Architecture and design are the tools needed to minimize the work effort in any project. They deal with dependencies and reduce the complexity via abstractions. In my own words:[6]

> Software design is the art of managing interdependencies between software components. It aims at minimizing artificial (technical) dependencies and introduces the necessary abstractions and compromises.

---

3 Whether or not the code modification is risky may very much depend on your test coverage. A good test coverage may actually absorb some of the damage bad software design may cause.

4 Kent Beck, *Test-Driven Development: By Example* (Addison-Wesley, 2002).

5 Robert C. Martin, *Clean Architecture* (Addison-Wesley, 2017).

6 These are indeed my own words, as there is no single, common definition of software design. Consequently, you may have your own definition of what software design entails and that is perfectly fine. However, note that this book, including the discussion of design patterns, is based on my definition.

Yes, software design is an art. It's not a science, and it doesn't come with a set of easy and clear answers.[7] Too often the big picture of design eludes us, and we are overwhelmed by the complex interdependencies of software entities. But we are trying to deal with this complexity and reduce it by introducing the right kind of abstractions. This way, we keep the level of detail at a reasonable level. However, too often individual developers on the team may have a different idea of the architecture and the design. We might not be able to implement our own vision of a design and be forced to make compromises in order to move forward.

 The term *abstraction* is used in different contexts. It's used for the organization of functionality and data items into data types and functions. But it's also used to describe the modeling of common behavior and the representation of a set of requirements and expectations. In this book on software design, I will primarily use the term for the latter (see in particular Chapter 2).

Note that the words *architecture* and *design* can be interchanged in the preceding quotes, since they're very similar and share the same goals. Yet they aren't the same. The similarities, but also differences, become clear if you take a look at the three levels of software development.

The Three Levels of Software Development

Software Architecture and *Software Design* are just two of the three levels of software development. They are complemented by the level of *Implementation Details*. Figure 1-1 gives an overview of these three levels.

To give you a feeling for these three levels, let's start with a real-world example of the relationship among architecture, design, and implementation details. Consider yourself to be in the role of an architect. And no, please don't picture yourself in a comfy chair in front of a computer with a hot coffee next to you, but picture yourself outside at a construction site. Yes, I'm talking about an architect for buildings.[8] As such an architect, you would be in charge of all the important properties of a house: its integration into the neighborhood, its structural integrity, the arrangement of rooms, plumbing, etc. You would also take care of a pleasing appearance and functional qualities—perhaps a large living room, easy access between the kitchen and the dining room, and so on. In other words, you would be taking care of the overall

---

7 Just to be clear: computer science is a science (it's in the name). Software *engineering* appears to be a hybrid form of science, craft, and art. And one aspect of the latter is software *design*.

8 With this metaphor, I'm not trying to imply that architects for buildings work at the construction site all day. Very likely, such an architect spends as much time in a comfy chair and in front of a computer as people like you and me. But I think you get the point.

architecture, the things that would be hard to change later, but you would also deal with the smaller design aspects concerning the building. However, it's hard to tell the difference between the two: the boundary between architecture and design appears to be fluid and is not clearly separated.

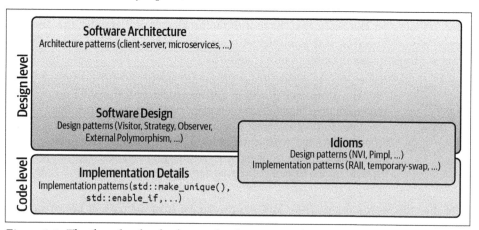

Figure 1-1. The three levels of software development: Software Architecture, Software Design, and Implementation Details. Idioms can be design or implementation patterns.

These decisions would be the end of your responsibility, however. As an architect, you wouldn't worry about where to place the refrigerator, the TV, or other furniture. You wouldn't deal with all the nifty details about where to place pictures and other pieces of decoration. In other words, you wouldn't handle the details; you would just make sure that the homeowner has the necessary structure to live well.

The furniture and other "nifty details" in this metaphor correspond to the lowest and most concrete level of software development, the implementation details. This level handles how a solution is implemented. You choose the necessary (and available) C++ standard or any subset of it, as well as the appropriate features, keywords, and language specifics to use, and deal with aspects such as memory acquisition, exception safety, performance, etc. This is also the level of *implementation patterns*, such as `std::make_unique()` as a *factory function*, `std::enable_if` as a recurring solution to explicitly benefit from SFINAE, etc.[9]

---

9 Substitution Failure Is Not An Error (SFINAE) is a basic template mechanism commonly used as a substitute for C++20 concepts to constrain templates. For an explanation of SFINAE and `std::enable_if` in particular, refer to your favorite textbook about C++ templates. If you don't have any, a great choice is the C++ template bible: David Vandevoorde, Nicolai Josuttis, and Douglas Gregor's *C++ Templates: The Complete Guide* (Addison-Wesley).

In software design, you start to focus on the big picture. Questions about maintainability, changeability, extensibility, testability, and scalability are more pronounced on this level. Software design primarily deals with the interaction of software entities, which in the previous metaphor are represented by the arrangement of rooms, doors, pipes, and cables. At this level, you handle the physical and logical dependencies of components (classes, function, etc.).[10] It's the level of design patterns such as Visitor, Strategy, and Decorator that define a dependency structure among software entities, as explained in Chapter 3. These patterns, which usually are transferable from language to language, help you break down complex things into digestible pieces.

Software Architecture is the fuzziest of the three levels, the hardest to put into words. This is because there is no common, universally accepted definition of software architecture. While there may be many different views on what exactly an architecture is, there is one aspect that everyone seems to agree on: architecture usually entails the big decisions, the aspects of your software that are among the hardest things to change in the future:

> Architecture is the decisions that you wish you could get right early in a project, but that you are not necessarily more likely to get them right than any other.[11]
>
> —Ralph Johnson

In Software Architecture, you use architectural patterns such as *client-server architecture*, *microservices*, and so on.[12] These patterns also deal with the question of how to design systems, where you can change one part without affecting any other parts of your software. Similar to *Software design* patterns, they define and address the structure and interdependencies among software entities. In contrast to design patterns, though, they usually deal with the key players, the big entities of your software (e.g., modules and components instead of classes and functions).

From this perspective, Software Architecture represents the overall strategy of your software approach, whereas Software Design is the tactics to make the strategy work. The problem with this picture is that there is no definition of "big." Especially with the advent of microservices, it becomes more and more difficult to draw a clear line between small and big entities.[13]

---

10 For a lot more information on physical and logical dependency management, see John Lakos's "dam" book, *Large-Scale C++ Software Development: Process and Architecture* (Addison-Wesley).

11 Martin Fowler, "Who Needs an Architect?" *IEEE Software*, 20, no. 5 (2003), 11–13, *https://doi.org/ 10.1109/MS.2003.1231144*.

12 A very good introduction to microservices can be found in Sam Newman's book *Building Microservices: Designing Fine-Grained Systems*, 2nd ed. (O'Reilly).

13 Mark Richards and Neal Ford, *Fundamentals of Software Architecture: An Engineering Approach* (O'Reilly, 2020).

Thus, architecture is often described as what expert developers in a project perceive as the key decisions.

What makes the separation between architecture, design, and details a little more difficult is the concept of an *idiom*. An *idiom* is a commonly used but language-specific solution for a recurring problem. As such, an idiom also represents a pattern, but it could be either an *implementation pattern* or a *design pattern*.[14] More loosely speaking, C++ idioms are the best practices of the C++ community for either design or implementation. In C++, most idioms fall into the category of implementation details. For instance, there is the *copy-and-swap idiom* (*https://oreil.ly/hioCd*) that you may know from the implementation of a copy assignment operator, and the *RAII idiom* (*https://oreil.ly/55blq*) (Resource Acquisition Is Initialization—you should definitely be familiar with this; if not, please see your second-favorite C++ book[15]). None of these idioms introduce an abstraction, and none of them help to decouple. Still, they are indispensable to implement good C++ code.

I hear you ask, "Could you be a little more specific, please? Isn't RAII also providing some form of decoupling? Doesn't it decouple resource management from business logic?" You're correct: RAII separates resource management and business logic. However, it doesn't achieve this by means of decoupling, i.e., abstraction, but by means of encapsulation. Both abstraction and encapsulation help you make complex systems easier to understand and change, but while abstraction solves the problems and issues that arise at the Software Design level, encapsulation solves the problems and issues that arise at the Implementation Details level. To quote Wikipedia (*https://oreil.ly/BeFXr*):

> The advantages of RAII as a resource management technique are that it provides encapsulation, exception safety [...], and locality [...]. Encapsulation is provided because resource management logic is defined once in the class, not at each call site.

While most idioms fall into the category of Implementation Details, there are also idioms that fall into the category of Software Design. Two examples are the *Non-Virtual Interface (NVI) idiom* and the *Pimpl idiom*. These two idioms are based on two classic design patterns: the *Template Method* design pattern and the *Bridge*

---

14 The term *implementation pattern* was first used in Kent Beck's book *Implementation Patterns* (Addison-Wesley). In this book, I'm using that term to provide a clear distinction from the term *design pattern*, since the term *idiom* may refer to a pattern on either the Software Design level or the Implementation Details level. I will use the term consistently to refer to commonly used solutions on the Implementation Details level.

15 Second-favorite after this one, of course. If this is your only book, then you might refer to the classic *Effective C++: 55 Specific Ways to Improve Your Programs and Designs*, 3rd ed., by Scott Meyers (Addison-Wesley).

design pattern, respectively.[16] They introduce an abstraction and help decouple and design for change and extensions.

The Focus on Features

If software architecture and software design are of such importance, then why are we in the C++ community focusing so strongly on features? Why do we create the illusion that C++ standards, language mechanics, and features are decisive for a project? I think there are three strong reasons for that. First, because there are so many features, with sometimes complex details, we need to spend a lot of time talking about how to use all of them properly. We need to create a common understanding on which use is good and which use is bad. We as a community need to develop a sense of idiomatic C++.

The second reason is that we might put the wrong expectations on features. As an example, let's consider C++20 modules. Without going into details, this feature may indeed be considered the biggest technical revolution since the beginning of C++. Modules may at last put the questionable and cumbersome practice of including header files into source files to an end.

Due to this potential, the expectations for that feature are enormous. Some people even expect modules to save their project by fixing their structural issues. Unfortunately, modules will have a hard time satisfying these expectations: modules don't improve the structure or design of your code but can merely represent the current structure and design. Modules don't repair your design issues, but they may be able to make the flaws visible. Thus, modules simply cannot save your project. So indeed, we may be putting too many or the wrong expectations on features.

And last, but not least, the third reason is that despite the huge amount of features and their complexity, in comparison to the complexity of software design, the complexity of C++ features is small. It's much easier to explain a given set of rules for features, regardless of how many special cases they contain, than it is to explain the best way to decouple software entities.

While there is usually a good answer to all feature-related questions, the common answer in software design is "It depends." That answer might not even be evidence of inexperience, but of the realization that the best way to make code more maintainable, changeable, extensible, testable, and scalable heavily depends on many project-

---

16 The Template Method and Bridge design patterns are 2 of the 23 classic design patterns introduced in the so-called Gang of Four (GoF) book by Erich Gamma et al., *Design Patterns: Elements of Reusable Object-Oriented Software*. I won't go into detail about the Template Method in this book, but you'll find good explanations in various textbooks, including the GoF book itself. I will, however, explain the Bridge design pattern in "Guideline 28: Build Bridges to Remove Physical Dependencies" on page 250.

specific factors. The decoupling of the complex interplay between many entities may indeed be one of the most challenging endeavors that mankind has ever faced:

> Design and programming are human activities; forget that and all is lost.[17]

To me, a combination of these three reasons is why we focus on features so much. But please, don't get me wrong. That's not to say that features are not important. On the contrary, features *are* important. And yes, it's necessary to talk about features and learn how to use them correctly, but once again, they alone do not save your project.

The Focus on Software Design and Design Principles

While features are important, and while it is of course good to talk about them, software design is more important. Software design is essential. I would even argue that it's the foundation of the success of our projects. Therefore, in this book I will make the attempt to truly focus on software design and design principles instead of features. Of course I will still show good and up-to-date C++ code, but I won't force the use of the latest and greatest language additions.[18] I *will* make use of some new features when it is reasonable and beneficial, such as C++20 concepts, but I will *not* pay attention to `noexcept`, or use `constexpr` everywhere.[19] Instead I will try to tackle the difficult aspects of software. I will, for the most part, focus on software design, the rationale behind design decisions, design principles, managing dependencies, and dealing with abstractions.

In summary, software design is the critical part of writing software. Software developers should have a good understanding of software design to write good, maintainable software. Because after all, good software is low-cost, and bad software is expensive.

Guideline 1: Understand the Importance of Software Design

- Treat software design as an essential part of writing software.
- Focus less on C++ language details and more on software design.
- Avoid unnecessary coupling and dependencies to make software more adaptable to frequent changes.
- Understand software design as the art of managing dependencies and abstractions.

---

17 Bjarne Stroustrup, *The C++ Programming Language*, 3rd ed. (Addison-Wesley, 2000).

18 Kudos to John Lakos, who argues similarly and uses C++98 in his book, *Large-Scale C++ Software Development: Process and Architecture* (Addison-Wesley).

19 Yes, Ben and Jason, you have read correctly, I will not `constexpr` ALL the things. See Ben Deane and Jason Turner, "constexpr ALL the things" (*https://oreil.ly/Pazfb*), CppCon 2017.

- Consider the boundary between software design and software architecture as fluid.

Guideline 2: Design for Change

One of the essential expectations for good software is its ability to change easily. This expectation is even part of the word *soft*ware. *Soft*ware, in contrast to *hard*ware, is expected to be able to adapt easily to changing requirements (see also "Guideline 1: Understand the Importance of Software Design" on page 2). However, from your own experience you may be able to tell that often it is not easy to change code. On the contrary, sometimes a seemingly simple change turns out to be a week-long endeavor.

Separation of Concerns

One of the best and proven solutions to reduce artificial dependencies and simplify change is to separate concerns. The core of the idea is to split, segregate, or extract pieces of functionality:[20]

> Systems that are broken up into small, well-named, understandable pieces enable faster work.

The intent behind separation of concerns is to better understand and manage complexity and thus design more modular software. This idea is probably as old as software itself and hence has been given many different names. For instance, the same idea is called *orthogonality* by the Pragmatic Programmers.[21] They advise separating orthogonal aspects of software. Tom DeMarco calls it *cohesion*:[22]

> Cohesion is a measure of the strength of association of the elements inside a module. A highly cohesive module is a collection of statements and data items that should be treated as a whole because they are so closely related. Any attempt to divide them up would only result in increased coupling and decreased readability.

In the *SOLID* principles,[23] one of the most established sets of design principles, the idea is known as the *Single-Responsibility Principle (SRP)*:

---

20 Michael Feathers, *Working Effectively with Legacy Code* (Addison-Wesley, 2013).

21 David Thomas and Andrew Hunt, *The Pragmatic Programmer: Your Journey to Mastery*, 20th Anniversary Edition (Addison-Wesley, 2019).

22 Tom DeMarco, *Structured Analysis and System Specification* (Prentice Hall, 1979).

23 SOLID is an acronym of acronyms, an abbreviation of the five principles described in the next few guidelines: SRP, OCP, LSP, ISP, and DIP.

> A class should have only one reason to change.[24]

Although the concept is old and is commonly known under many names, many attempts to explain separation of concerns raise more questions than answers. This is particularly true for the SRP. The name of this design principle alone raises questions: what is a responsibility? And what is a *single* responsibility? A common attempt to clarify the vagueness about SRP is the following:

> Everything should do just one thing.

Unfortunately this explanation is hard to outdo in terms of vagueness. Just as the word *responsibility* doesn't carry a lot of meaning, *just one thing* doesn't help to shed any more light on it.

Irrespective of the name, the idea is always the same: group only those things that truly belong together, and separate everything that does not strictly belong. Or in other words: separate those things that change for different reasons. By doing this, you reduce artificial coupling between different aspects of your code and it helps you make your software more adaptable to change. In the best case, you can change a particular aspect of your software in exactly one place.

An Example of Artificial Coupling

Let's shed some light on separation of concerns by means of a code example. And I do have a great example indeed: I present to you the abstract Document class:

```
//#include <some_json_library.h>  // Potential physical dependency

class Document
{
 public:
   // ...
   virtual ~Document() = default;

   virtual void exportToJSON( /*...*/ ) const = 0;  ❶
   virtual void serialize( ByteStream&, /*...*/ ) const = 0;  ❷
   // ...
};
```

This sounds like a very useful base class for all kinds of documents, doesn't it? First, there is the exportToJSON() function (❶). All deriving classes will have to implement the exportToJSON() function in order to produce a JSON file (*https://oreil.ly/YWrsw*) from the document. That will prove to be pretty useful: without having to know

---

24 The first book on the SOLID principles was Robert C. Martin's *Agile Software Development: Principles, Patterns, and Practices* (Pearson). A newer and much cheaper alternative is *Clean Architecture*, also from Robert C. Martin (Addison-Wesley).

about a particular kind of document (and we can imagine that we will eventually have PDF documents, Word documents, and many more), we can always export in JSON format. Nice! Second, there is a `serialize()` function (❷). This function lets you transform a `Document` into bytes via a `ByteStream`. You can store these bytes in some persistent system, like a file or a database. And of course we can expect that there are many other, useful functions available that will allow us to pretty much use this document for everything.

However, I can see the frown on your face. No, you don't look particularly convinced that this is good software design. It may be because you're just very suspicious about this example (it simply looks too good to be true). Or it may be that you've learned the hard way that this kind of design eventually leads to trouble. You may have experienced that using the common object-oriented design principle to bundle the data and the functions that operate on them may easily lead to unfortunate coupling. And I agree: despite the fact that this base class looks like a great all-in-one package, and even looks like it has everything that we might ever need, this design will soon lead to trouble.

This is bad design because it contains many dependencies. Of course there are the obvious, direct dependencies, as for instance the dependency on the `ByteStream` class. However, this design also favors the introduction of artificial dependencies, which will make subsequent changes harder. In this case, there are three kinds of artificial dependencies. Two of these are introduced by the `exportToJSON()` function, and one by the `serialize()` function.

First, `exportToJSON()` needs to be implemented in the derived classes. And yes, there is no choice, because it is a pure virtual function (*https://oreil.ly/1u9at*) (denoted by the sequence = 0, the so-called *pure specifier*). Since derived classes will very likely not want to carry the burden of implementing JSON exports manually, they will rely on an external, third-party JSON library: *json* (*https://oreil.ly/MqB03*), *rapidjson* (*https://oreil.ly/jNMsz*), or *simdjson* (*https://oreil.ly/5dBzC*). Whatever library you choose for that purpose, because of the `exportToJSON()` member function, deriving documents would suddenly depend on this library. And, very likely, all deriving classes would depend on the same library, for consistency reasons alone. Thus, the deriving classes are not really independent; they are artificially coupled to a particular design decision.[25] Also, the dependency on a specific JSON library would definitely limit the reusability of the hierarchy, because it would no longer be lightweight. And

---

25 Don't forget that the design decisions taken by that external library may impact your own design, which would obviously increase the coupling.

switching to another library would cause a major change because all deriving classes would have to be adapted.[26]

Of course, the same kind of artificial dependency is introduced by the `serialize()` function. It's likely that `serialize()` will also be implemented in terms of a third-party library, such as protobuf (*https://oreil.ly/z6Kgr*) or Boost.serialization (*https://oreil.ly/ySJLk*). This considerably worsens the dependency situation because it introduces a coupling between two orthogonal, unrelated design aspects (i.e., JSON export and serialization). A change to one aspect might result in changes to the other aspect.

In the worst case, the `exportToJSON()` function might introduce a second dependency. The arguments expected in the `exportToJSON()` call might accidentally reflect some of the implementation details of the chosen JSON library. In that case, eventually switching to another library might result in a change of the signature of the `exportToJSON()` function, which would subsequently cause changes in all callers. Thus, the dependency on the chosen JSON library might accidentally be far more widespread than intended.

The third kind of dependency is introduced by the `serialize()` function. Due to this function, the classes deriving from `Document` depend on global decisions on how documents are serialized. What format do we use? Do we use little endian or big endian? Do we have to add the information that the bytes represent a PDF file or a Word file? If yes (and I assume that is very likely), how do we represent such a document? By means of an integral value? For instance, we could use an enumeration for this purpose:[27]

```
enum class DocumentType
{
   pdf,
   word,
   // ... Potentially many more document types
};
```

This approach is very common for serialization. However, if this low-level document representation is used within the implementations of the `Document` classes, we would accidentally couple all the different kinds of documents. Every deriving class would implicitly know about all the other `Document` types. As a result, adding a new kind of document would directly affect all existing document types. That would be a serious design flaw, since, again, it will make change harder.

---

26 That includes the classes that other people may have written, i.e., classes that you do not control. And no, the other people won't be happy about the change. Thus, the change may be *really* difficult.

27 An enumeration seems to be an obvious choice, but of course there are other options as well. In the end, we need an agreed-upon set of values that represent the different document formats in the byte representation.

Unfortunately, the Document class promotes many different kinds of coupling. So no, the Document class is not a great example of good class design, since it isn't easy to change. On the contrary, it is hard to change and thus a great example of a violation of the SRP: the classes deriving from Document and users of the Document class change for many reasons because we have created a strong coupling between several orthogonal, unrelated aspects. To summarize, deriving classes and users of documents may change for any of the following reasons:

- The implementation details of the exportToJSON() function change because of a direct dependency on the used JSON library
- The signature of the exportToJSON() function changes because the underlying implementation changes
- The Document class and the serialize() function change because of a direct dependency on the ByteStream class
- The implementation details of the serialize() function change because of a direct dependency on the implementation details
- All types of documents change because of the direct dependency on the Document Type enumeration

Obviously, this design promotes more changes, and every single change would be harder. And of course, in the general case, there is the danger that additional orthogonal aspects are artificially coupled inside documents, which would further increase the complexity of making a change. In addition, some of these changes are definitely not restricted to a single place in the codebase. In particular, changes to the implementation details of exportToJSON() and serialize() would not be restricted to only one class, but likely all kinds of documents (PDF, Word, and so on). Therefore, a change would affect a significant number of places all over the codebase, which poses a maintenance risk.

Logical Versus Physical Coupling

The coupling isn't limited to logical coupling but also extends to physical coupling. Figure 1-2 illustrates that coupling. Let's assume that there is a User class on the low level of our architecture that needs to use documents that reside on a higher level of the architecture. Of course the User class depends directly on the Document class, which is a necessary dependency—an intrinsic dependency of the given problem. Thus, it should not be a concern for us. However, the (potential) physical dependency of Document on the selected JSON library and the direct dependency on the Byte Stream class cause an indirect, transitive dependency of User to the JSON library and ByteStream, which reside on the highest level of our architecture. In the worst case, this means that changes to the JSON library or the ByteStream class have an effect on

User. Hopefully it's easy to see that this is an artificial, not an intentional, dependency: a User shouldn't have to depend on JSON or serialization.

 I should explicitly state that there is a *potential* physical dependency of Document on the select JSON library. If the <Document.h> header file includes any header from the JSON library of choice (as indicated in the code snippet at the beginning of "An Example of Artificial Coupling" on page 12), for instance because the export ToJSON() function expects some arguments based on that library, then there is a clear dependency on that library. However, if the interface can properly abstract from these details and the <Document.h> header doesn't include anything from the JSON library, the physical dependency might be avoided. Thus, it depends on how well the dependencies can be (and are) abstracted.

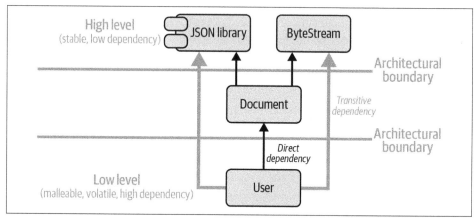

Figure 1-2. The strong transitive, physical coupling between User and orthogonal aspects like JSON and serialization.

"High level, low level—now I'm confused," you complain. Yes, I know that these two terms usually cause some confusion. So before we move on, let's agree on the terminology for high level and low level. The origin of these two terms relates to the way we draw diagrams in the *Unified Modeling Language (UML)* (*https://oreil.ly/s0ID2*): functionality that we consider to be stable appears on the top, on a high level. Functionality that changes more often and is therefore considered to be volatile or malleable appears on the bottom, the low level. Unfortunately, when we draw architectures, we often try to show how things build on one another, so the most stable parts appear at the bottom of an architecture. That, of course, causes some confusion. Independent of how things are drawn, just remember these terms: *high level* refers to stable parts of your architecture, and *low level* refers to the aspects that change more often or are more likely to change.

Back to the problem: the SRP advises that we should separate concerns and the things that do not truly belong, i.e., the noncohesive (adhesive) things. In other words, it advises us to separate the things that change for different reasons into *variation points*. Figure 1-3 shows the coupling situation if we isolate the JSON and serialization aspects into separate concerns.

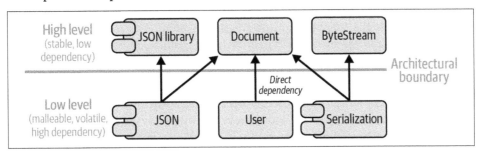

Figure 1-3. Adherence to the SRP resolves the artificial coupling between User *and* JSON *and serialization.*

Based on this advice, the Document class is refactored in the following way:

```
class Document
{
  public:
    // ...
    virtual ~Document() = default;

    // No more 'exportToJSON()' and 'serialize()' functions.
    // Only the very basic document operations, that do not
    // cause strong coupling, remain.
    // ...
};
```

The JSON and serialization aspects are just not part of the fundamental pieces of functionality of a Document class. The Document class should merely represent the very basic operations of different kinds of documents. All orthogonal aspects should be separated. This will make changes considerably easier. For instance, by isolating the JSON aspect into a separate variation point and into the new JSON component, switching from one JSON library to another will affect only this one component. The change could be done in exactly one place and would happen in isolation from all the other, orthogonal aspects. It would also be easier to support the JSON format by means of several JSON libraries. Additionally, any change to how documents are serialized would affect only one component in the code: the new Serialization component. Also, Serialization would act as a variation point that enables isolated, easy change. That would be the optimal situation.

After your initial disappointment with the Document example, I can see you're looking happier again. Perhaps there's even an "I knew it!" smile on your face. However, you're not entirely satisfied yet: "Yes, I agree with the general idea of separating concerns. But how do I have to structure my software to separate concerns? What do I have to do to make it work?" That is an excellent question, but one with many answers that I'll address in the upcoming chapters. The first and most important point, however, is the identification of a variation point, i.e., some aspect in your code where changes are expected. These variation points should be extracted, isolated, and wrapped, such that there are no longer any dependencies on these variations. That will ultimately help make changes easier.

"But that is still only superficial advice!" I hear you say. And you're correct. Unfortunately, there is no single answer and there is no simple answer. It depends. But I promise to give many concrete answers for how to separate concerns in the upcoming chapters. After all, this is a book on software design, i.e., a book on managing dependencies. As a little teaser, in Chapter 3 I will introduce a general and practical approach to this problem: design patterns. With this general idea in mind, I will show you how to separate concerns using different design patterns. For instance, the *Visitor*, *Strategy*, and *External Polymorphism* design patterns come to mind. All of these patterns have different strengths and weaknesses, but they share the property of introducing some kind of abstraction to help you to reduce dependencies. Additionally, I promise to take a close look at how to implement these design patterns in modern C++.

I will introduce the Visitor design pattern in "Guideline 16: Use Visitor to Extend Operations" on page 112, and the Strategy design pattern in "Guideline 19: Use Strategy to Isolate How Things Are Done" on page 140. The External Polymorphism design pattern will be the topic of "Guideline 31: Use External Polymorphism for Nonintrusive Runtime Polymorphism" on page 279.

Don't Repeat Yourself

There is a second, important aspect to changeability. To explain this aspect, I will introduce another example: a hierarchy of items. Figure 1-4 gives an impression of this hierarchy.

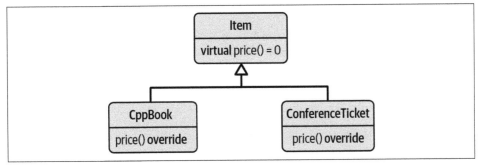

Figure 1-4. The Item class hierarchy.

At the top of that hierarchy is the Item base class:

```
//---- <Money.h> ----------------

class Money { /*...*/ };

Money operator*( Money money, double factor );
Money operator+( Money lhs, Money rhs );


//---- <Item.h> ---------------

#include <Money.h>

class Item
{
 public:
   virtual ~Item() = default;
   virtual Money price() const = 0;
};
```

The Item base class represents an abstraction for any kind of item that has a price tag (represented by the Money class). Via the price() function, you can query for that price. Of course there are many possible items, but for illustration purposes, we restrict ourselves to CppBook and ConferenceTicket:

```
//---- <CppBook.h> ----------------

#include <Item.h>
#include <Money.h>
#include <string>

class CppBook : public Item
{
 public:
   explicit CppBook( std::string title, std::string author, Money price )    ❸
      : title_( std::move(title) )
      , author_( std::move(author) )
```

```
        , priceWithTax_( price * 1.15 )  // 15% tax rate
      {}

      std::string const& title() const { return title_; }     ❹
      std::string const& author() const { return author_; }   ❺

      Money price() const override { return priceWithTax_; }   ❻

   private:
      std::string title_;
      std::string author_;
      Money priceWithTax_;
};
```

The constructor of the CppBook class expects a title and author in the form of strings and a price in the form of Money (❸).[28] Apart from that, it only allows you to access the title, the author, and the price with the title(), author(), and price() functions (❹, ❺, and ❻). However, the price() function is a little special: obviously, books are subject to taxes. Therefore, the original price of the book needs to be adapted according to a given tax rate. In this example, I assume an imaginary tax rate of 15%.

The ConferenceTicket class is the second example of an Item:

```
//---- <ConferenceTicket.h> ----------------

#include <Item.h>
#include <Money.h>
#include <string>

class ConferenceTicket : public Item
{
  public:
    explicit ConferenceTicket( std::string name, Money price )   ❼
      : name_( std::move(name) )
      , priceWithTax_( price * 1.15 )  // 15% tax rate
    {}

    std::string const& name() const { return name_; }

    Money price() const override { return priceWithTax_; }

  private:
    std::string name_;
```

---

28 You might be wondering about the explicit use of the explicit keyword for this constructor. Then you might also be aware that Core Guideline C.46 (*https://oreil.ly/1DPsA*) advises using explicit by default for single-argument constructors. This is really good and highly recommended advice, as it prevents unintentional, potentially undesirable conversions. While not as valuable, the same advice is also reasonable for all the other constructors, except for the copy and move constructors, which don't perform a conversion. At least it doesn't hurt.

```
    Money priceWithTax_;
};
```

ConferenceTicket is very similar to the CppBook class, but expects only the name of the conference and the price in the constructor (❼). Of course, you can access the name and the price with the name() and price() functions, respectively. Most importantly, however, the price for a C++ conference is also subject to taxes. Therefore, we again adapt the original price according to the imaginary tax rate of 15%.

With this functionality available, we can go ahead and create a couple of Items in the main() function:

```cpp
#include <CppBook.h>
#include <ConferenceTicket.h>
#include <algorithm>
#include <cstdlib>
#include <memory>
#include <vector>

int main()
{
   std::vector<std::unique_ptr<Item>> items{};

   items.emplace_back(
      std::make_unique<CppBook>("Effective C++", "Meyers", 19.99) );
   items.emplace_back(
      std::make_unique<CppBook>("C++ Templates", "Josuttis", 49.99) );

   items.emplace_back( std::make_unique<ConferenceTicket>("CppCon", 999.0) );
   items.emplace_back( std::make_unique<ConferenceTicket>("Meeting C++", 699.0) );
   items.emplace_back( std::make_unique<ConferenceTicket>("C++ on Sea", 499.0) );

   Money const total_price =
      std::accumulate( begin(items), end(items), Money{},
         []( Money accu, auto const& item ){
            return accu + item->price();
         } );

   // ...

   return EXIT_SUCCESS;
}
```

In `main()`, we create a couple of items (two books and three conferences) and compute the total price of all items.[29] The total price will, of course, include the imaginary tax rate of 15%.

That sounds like a good design. We have separated the specific kinds of items and are able to change how the price of each item is computed in isolation. It seems that we have fulfilled the SRP and extracted and isolated the variation points. And of course, there are more items. Many more. And all of them will make sure that the applicable tax rate is properly taken into account. Great! Now, while this `Item` hierarchy will make us happy for some time, the design unfortunately has a significant flaw. We might not realize it today, but there's always a looming shadow in the distance, the nemesis of problems in software: change.

What happens if for some reason the tax rate changes? What if the 15% tax rate is lowered to 12%? Or raised to 16%? I can still hear the arguments from the day the initial design was committed into the codebase: "No, that will never happen!" Well, even the most unexpected thing may happen. For instance, in Germany, the tax rate was lowered from 19% to 16% for half a year in 2021. This, of course, would mean that we have to change the tax rate in our codebase. Where do we apply the change? In the current situation, the change would pretty much affect every class deriving from the `Item` class. The change would be all over the codebase!

Just as much as the SRP advises separating variation points, we should take care not to duplicate information throughout the codebase. As much as everything should have a single responsibility (a single reason to change), every responsibility should exist only once in the system. This idea is commonly called the *Don't Repeat Yourself* (DRY) principle. This principle advises us to not duplicate some key information in many places—but to design the system such that we can make the change in only one place. In the optimal case, the tax rate(s) should be represented in exactly one place to enable you to make an easy change.

Usually the SRP and the DRY principles work together very nicely. Adhering the SRP will often lead to adhering to DRY as well, and vice versa. However, sometimes adhering to both requires some extra steps. I know you're eager to learn what these extra steps are and how to solve the problem, but at this point, it's sufficient to point out the general idea of SRP and DRY. I promise to revisit this problem and to show

---

29 You might realize I've picked the names of the three conferences I regularly attend: CppCon (*https://cppcon.org*), Meeting C++ (*http://meetingcpp.com*), and C++ on Sea (*https://cpponsea.uk*). There are many more C++ conferences, though. To give a few examples: ACCU (*https://accu.org/conf-main/main*), Core C++ (*https://corecpp.org*), pacific++ (*https://www.pacificplusplus.com*), CppNorth (*https://cppnorth.ca*), emBO++ (*https://www.embo.io*), and CPPP (*https://cppp.fr*). Conferences are a great and fun way to stay up to date with C++. Make sure to check out the Standard C++ Foundation home page (*https://isocpp.org*) for any upcoming conferences.

you how to solve it (see "Guideline 35: Use Decorators to Add Customization Hierarchically" on page 348).

Avoid Premature Separation of Concerns

At this point, I've hopefully convinced you that adhering to SRP and DRY is a very reasonable idea. You might even be so committed that you plan to separate everything—all classes and functions—into the most tiny units of functionality. After all, that's the goal, right? If this is what you're thinking right now, please stop! Take a deep breath. And one more. And then please listen carefully to the wisdom of Katerina Trajchevska:[30]

> Don't try to achieve SOLID, use SOLID to achieve maintainability.

Both SRP and DRY are your tools for achieving better maintainability and simplifying change. They are not your goals. While both are of utmost importance in the long run, it can be very counterproductive to separate entities without a clear idea about what kind of change will affect you. Designing for change usually favors one specific kind of change but might unfortunately make other kinds of change harder. This philosophy is part of the commonly known *YAGNI* principle (*https://oreil.ly/Gu7u9*) (You Aren't Gonna Need It), which warns you about overengineering (see also "Guideline 5: Design for Extension" on page 35). If you have a clear plan, if you know what kind of change to expect, then apply SRP and DRY to make that kind of change simple. However, if you don't know what kind of change to expect, then don't guess—just wait. Wait until you have a clear idea about what kind of change to expect and then refactor to make the change as easy as possible.

 Just don't forget that one aspect of easily changing things is having unit tests in place that give you confirmation that the change did not break the expected behavior.

In summary, change is expected in *soft*ware and therefore it's vital to design for change. Separate concerns and minimize duplication to enable you to easily change things without being afraid to break other, orthogonal aspects.

---

30 Katerina Trajchevska, "Becoming a Better Developer by Using the SOLID Design Principles" (*https://oreil.ly/cwo8Y*), Laracon EU, August 30–31, 2018.

Guideline 3: Separate Interfaces to Avoid Artificial Coupling

Let's revisit the Document example from "Guideline 2: Design for Change" on page 11. I know, by now you probably feel like you've seen enough documents, but believe me, we're not done yet. There's still an important coupling aspect to address. This time we don't focus on the individual functions in the Document class but on the interface as a whole:

```cpp
class Document
{
 public:
   // ...
   virtual ~Document() = default;

   virtual void exportToJSON( /*...*/ ) const = 0;
   virtual void serialize( ByteStream& bs, /*...*/ ) const = 0;
   // ...
};
```

Segregate Interfaces to Separate Concerns

The Document requires deriving classes to handle both JSON exports and serialization. While, from the point of view of a document, this may seem reasonable (after all, *all* documents should be exportable into JSON and serializable), it unfortunately causes another kind of coupling. Imagine the following user code:

```cpp
void exportDocument( Document const& doc )
{
   // ...
   doc.exportToJSON( /* pass necessary arguments */ );
```

```
    // ...
  }
```

The exportDocument() function is solely interested in exporting a given document to JSON. In other words, the exportDocument() function is *not* concerned with serializing a document or with any other aspect that Document has to offer. Still, as a result of the definition of the Document interface, due to coupling many orthogonal aspects together, the exportDocument() function depends on much more than just the JSON export. All of these dependencies are unnecessary and artificial. Changing any of these—for instance, the ByteStream class or the signature of the serialize() function—has an effect on *all* users of Document, even those that do not require serialization. For any change, *all* the users, including the exportDocument() function, would need to be recompiled, retested, and, in the worst case, redeployed (for instance, if delivered in a separate library). The same thing happens, however, if the Document class is extended by another function—for instance, an export to another document type. The problem gets bigger the more orthogonal functionality is coupled in Document: any change carries the risk of causing a rippling effect throughout the codebase. Which is sad indeed, as interfaces should help to decouple, not introduce artificial coupling.

This coupling is caused by a violation of the Interface Segregation Principle (ISP), which is the *I* in the *SOLID* acronym:

> Clients should not be forced to depend on methods that they do not use.[31]

The ISP advises separating concerns by segregating (decoupling) interfaces. In our case, there should be two separate interfaces representing the two orthogonal aspects of JSON export and serialization:

```
class JSONExportable
{
 public:
   // ...
   virtual ~JSONExportable() = default;

   virtual void exportToJSON( /*...*/ ) const = 0;
   // ...
};

class Serializable
{
 public:
   // ...
   virtual ~Serializable() = default;
```

---

31 Robert C. Martin, *Agile Software Development: Principles, Patterns, and Practices.*

```
    virtual void serialize( ByteStream& bs, /*...*/ ) const = 0;
    // ...
};

class Document
    : public JSONExportable
    , public Serializable
{
 public:
    // ...
};
```

This separation does not make the `Document` class obsolete. On the contrary, the `Document` class still represents the requirements posed on all documents. However, this separation of concerns now enables you to minimize dependencies to only the set of functions that is actually required:

```
void exportDocument( JSONExportable const& exportable )
{
    // ...
    exportable.exportToJSON( /* pass necessary arguments */ );
    // ...
}
```

In this form, by depending only on the segregated `JSONExportable` interface, the `exportDocument()` function no longer depends on the serialization functionality and thus no longer depends on the `ByteStream` class. Thus, the segregation of interfaces has helped to reduce coupling.

"But isn't that just a separation of concerns?" you ask. "Isn't that just another example of the SRP?" Yes, indeed it is. I agree that we've essentially identified two orthogonal aspects, separated them, and thus applied the SRP to the `Document` interface. Therefore, we could say that ISP and SRP are the same. Or at least that ISP is a special case of the SRP because of the focus of the ISP on interfaces. This attitude seems to be the common opinion in the community, and I agree. However, I still consider it valuable to talk about ISP. Despite the fact that ISP may only be a special case, I would argue that it's an important special case. Unfortunately, it is often very tempting to aggregate unrelated, orthogonal aspects into an interface. It might even happen to *you* that you couple separate aspects into an interface. Of course, I would never imply that you did this on purpose, but unintentionally, accidentally. We often do not pay enough attention to these details. Of course, you argue, "I would never do that." However, in "Guideline 19: Use Strategy to Isolate How Things Are Done" on page 140, you'll see an example that might convince you how easily this can happen. Since changing interfaces later may be extremely difficult, I believe it pays off to raise awareness of this problem with interfaces. For that reason, I didn't drop the ISP but included it as an important and noteworthy case of the SRP.

Minimizing Requirements of Template Arguments

Although it appears as if the ISP is applicable only to base classes, and although the ISP is mostly introduced by means of object-oriented programming, the general idea of minimizing the dependencies introduced by interfaces can also be applied to templates. Consider the `std::copy()` function, for instance:

```
template< typename InputIt, typename OutputIt >
OutputIt copy( InputIt first, InputIt last, OutputIt d_first );
```

In C++20, we could apply *concepts* to express the requirements:

```
template< std::input_iterator InputIt, std::output_iterator OutputIt >
OutputIt copy( InputIt first, InputIt last, OutputIt d_first );
```

`std::copy()` expects a pair of input iterators as the range to copy from, and an output iterator to the target range. It explicitly requires input iterators and output iterators, since it does not need any other operation. Thus, it minimizes the requirements on the passed arguments.

Let's assume that `std::copy()` requires `std::forward_iterator` instead of `std::input_iterator` and `std::output_iterator`:

```
template< std::forward_iterator ForwardIt >
ForwardIt copy( ForwardIt first, ForwardIt last, ForwardIt d_first );
```

This would unfortunately limit the usefulness of the `std::copy()` algorithm. We would no longer be able to copy from input streams, since they don't generally provide the multipass guarantee and do not enable us to write. That would be unfortunate. However, focusing on dependencies, `std::copy()` would now depend on operations and requirements it doesn't need. And iterators passed to `std::copy()` would be forced to provide additional operations, so `std::copy()` would force dependencies on them.

This is only a hypothetical example, but it illustrates how important the separation of concerns in interfaces is. Obviously, the solution is the realization that input and output capabilities are separate aspects. Thus, after separating concerns and after applying the ISP, the dependencies are significantly reduced.

Guideline 3: Separate Interfaces to Avoid Artificial Coupling

- Be aware that coupling also affects interfaces.
- Adhere to the Interface Segregation Principle (ISP) to separate concerns in interfaces.
- Consider the ISP as a special case of the Single-Responsibility Principle (SRP).
- Understand that the ISP helps for both inheritance hierarchies and templates.

Guideline 4: Design for Testability

As discussed in "Guideline 1: Understand the Importance of Software Design" on page 2, *soft*ware changes. It's expected to change. But every time you change something in your software, you run the risk of breaking something. Of course, not intentionally but accidentally, despite your best efforts. The risk is always there. As an experienced developer, however, you don't lose any sleep over that. Let there be risk—you don't care. You have something that protects you from accidentally breaking things, something that keeps the risk at a minimum: your tests.

The purpose of having tests is to be able to assert that all of your software functionality still works, despite constantly changing things. So obviously, tests are your protection layer, your life vest. Tests are essential! However, first of all, you have to write the tests. And in order to write tests and set up this protective layer, your software needs to be testable: your software must be written in a way that it is possible, and in the best case even *easily* possible, to add tests. Which brings us to the heart of this guideline: software should be designed for testability.

How to Test a Private Member Function

"Of course I have tests," you argue. "Everyone should have tests. That's common knowledge, isn't it?" I completely agree. And I believe you that your codebase is equipped with a reasonable test suite.[32] But surprisingly, despite everyone agreeing to the need for tests, not every piece of software is written with this awareness in mind.[33] In fact, a lot of code is hard to test. And sometimes this is simply because the code is not designed to be tested.

To give you an idea, I have a challenge for you. Take a look at the following `Widget` class. `Widget` holds a collection of `Blob` objects, which once in a while need to be updated. For that purpose, `Widget` provides the `updateCollection()` member function, which we now assume is so important that we need to write a test for it. And this is my challenge: how would you test the `updateCollection()` member function?

```
class Widget
{
    // ...
```

---

[32] If you don't have a test suite in place, then you have work to do. Seriously. A very coherent reference to get started is Ben Saks's talk on unit tests, "Back to Basics: Unit Tests" (*https://oreil.ly/VBo9X*), from CppCon 2020. A second, very good reference to wrap your mind around the whole topic of testing and test-driven development in particular is Jeff Langr's book, *Modern C{plus}{plus} Programming with Test-Driven Development* (O'Reilly).

[33] I know, "everyone agrees" is unfortunately far from reality. If you need proof that the seriousness of tests has not yet reached every project and every developer, take a look at this issue (*https://oreil.ly/NuEua*) from the OpenFOAM issue tracker.

```
  private:
    void updateCollection( /* some arguments needed to update the collection */ );

    std::vector<Blob> blobs_;
    /* Potentially other data members */
};
```

I assume that you immediately see the real challenge: the `updateCollection()` member function is declared in the private section of the class. This means that there is no direct access from the outside and therefore no direct way of testing it. So take a few seconds to think about this...

"It's private, yes, but this is still not much of a challenge. There are multiple ways I can do that," you say. I agree, there are multiple ways you could try. So please, go ahead. You weigh your options, then you come up with your first idea: "Well, the easiest approach would be to test the function via some other, public member function that internally calls the `updateCollection()` function." That sounds like an interesting first idea. Let's assume that the collection needs to be updated when a new `Blob` is added to it. Calling the `addBlob()` member function would trigger the `updateCollection()` function:

```
class Widget
{
 public:
   // ...
   void addBlob( Blob const& blob, /*...*/ )
   {
      // ...
      updateCollection( /*...*/ );
      // ...
   }

 private:
   void updateCollection( /* some arguments needed to update the collection */ );

   std::vector<Blob> blobs_;
   /* Potentially other data members */
};
```

Although this sounds like a reasonable thing to do, it's also something you should avoid if possible. What you are suggesting is a so-called *white box test*. A white box test knows about the internal implementation details of some function and tests based on that knowledge. This introduces a dependency of the test code on the implementation details of your production code. The problem with this approach is that software changes. Code changes. Details change. For instance, at some point in the future, the `addBlob()` function might be rewritten so it does not have to update the collection anymore. If this happens, your test no longer performs the task it was written to do. You would lose your `updateCollection()` test, potentially without even realizing it. Therefore, a white box test poses a risk. Just as much as you should avoid and reduce dependencies in your production code (see "Guideline 1: Understand the Importance of Software Design" on page 2), you should also avoid dependencies between your tests and the details of your production code.

What we really need is a *black box test*. A black box test does not make any assumptions about internal implementation details, but tests only for expected behavior. Of course, this kind of test can also break if you change something, but it shouldn't break if some implementation details change—only if the expected behavior changes.

"OK, I get your point," you say. "But you don't suggest making the update Collection() function public, do you?" No, rest assured that isn't what I'm suggesting. Of course, sometimes this may be a reasonable approach. But in our case, I doubt that this would be a wise move. The updateCollection() function should not be called just for fun. It should be called only for a good reason, only at the right time, and probably to preserve some kind of invariant. This is something we should not entrust a user with. So no, I don't think that the function would be a good candidate for the public section.

"OK, good, just checking. Then let's simply make the test a friend of the Widget class. This way it would have full access and could call the private member function unhindered":

```
class Widget
{
   // ...
 private:
   friend class TestWidget;

   void updateCollection( /* some arguments needed to update the collection */ );

   std::vector<Blob> blobs_;
   /* Potentially other data members */
};
```

Yes, we could add a friend. Let's assume that there is the TestWidget test fixture, containing all the tests for the Widget class. We could make this test fixture a friend of the Widget class. Although this may sound like another reasonable approach, I unfortunately have to be the spoilsport again. Yes, technically this would solve the problem, but from a design perspective, we've just introduced an artificial dependency again. By actively changing the production code to introduce the friend declaration, the production code now knows about the test code. And while the test code should of course know about the production code (that's the point of the test code), the production code should not have to know about the test code. This introduces a cyclic dependency, which is an unfortunate and artificial dependency.

"You sound like this is the worst thing in the world. Is it really that bad?" Well, sometimes this may actually be a reasonable solution. It definitely is a simple and quick solution. However, since right now we have the time to discuss all of our options, there definitely must be something better than adding a friend.

 I don't want to make things worse, but in C++ we don't have a lot of friends. Yes, I know, this sounds sad and lonely, but of course I mean the keyword friend: in C++, friend is not your friend. The reason is that friends introduce coupling, mostly artificial coupling, and we should avoid coupling. Of course, exceptions can be made for the good friends, the ones you cannot live without, such as hidden friends (*https://oreil.ly/Lu6rq*), or idiomatic uses of friend, such as the *Passkey idiom* (*https://oreil.ly/qEN0m*). A test is more like a friend on social media, so declaring a test a friend does not sound like a good choice.

"OK, then let's switch from private to protected and make the test derive from the Widget class," you suggest. "This way, the test would gain full access to the updateCollection() function":

```
class Widget
{
   // ...
 protected:
   void updateCollection( /* some arguments needed to update the collection */ );

   std::vector<Blob> blobs_;
   /* Potentially other data members */
};

class TestWidget : private Widget
{
   // ...
};
```

Well, I have to admit that technically this approach would work. However, the fact that you're suggesting inheritance to solve this issue tells me that we definitely have to talk about the meaning of inheritance and how to use it properly. To quote the two pragmatic programmers:[34]

> Inheritance is rarely the answer.

Since we'll be focusing on this topic fairly soon, let me just say that it feels like we're abusing inheritance for the sole reason of gaining access to nonpublic member

---

34 David Thomas and Andrew Hunt, *The Pragmatic Programmer: Your Journey to Mastery.*

functions. I'm pretty certain this isn't why inheritance was invented. Using inheritance to gain access to the protected section of a class is like the bazooka approach to something that should be very simple. It is, after all, almost identical to making the function public, because everyone can easily gain access. It seems we really haven't designed the class to be easily testable.

"Come on, what else could we do? Or do you really want me to use the preprocessor and define all private labels as public?":

```
#define private public

class Widget
{
   // ...
  private:
    void updateCollection( /* some arguments needed to update the collection */ );

    std::vector<Blob> blobs_;
    /* Potentially other data members */
};
```

OK, let's take a deep breath. Although this last approach may seem funny, keep in mind that we have now left the range of reasonable arguments.[35] If we seriously consider using the preprocessor to hack our way into the private section of the Widget class, then all is lost.

The True Solution: Separate Concerns

"OK then, what *should* I do to test the private member function? You have already discarded all the options." No, not all the options. We have not yet discussed the one design approach that I highlighted in "Guideline 2: Design for Change" on page 11: separation of concerns. My approach would be to extract the private member function from the class and make it a separate entity in our codebase. My preferred solution in this case is to extract the member function as a free function:

```
void updateCollection( std::vector<Blob>& blobs
                             , /* some arguments needed to update the collection */ );

class Widget
{
   // ...
  private:
    std::vector<Blob> blobs_;
    /* Potentially other data members */
};
```

---

35 We may even have entered the scary realm of undefined behavior.

All calls to the previous member function could be replaced with a call to the free updateCollection() function by just adding blobs_ as the first function argument. Alternatively, if there is some state attached to the function, we extract it in the form of another class. Either way, we design the resulting code such that it's easy, perhaps even trivial, to test:

```
namespace widgetDetails {

class BlobCollection
{
 public:
   void updateCollection( /* some arguments needed to update the collection */ );

 private:
   std::vector<Blob> blobs_;
};

} // namespace widgetDetails

class Widget
{
   // ...
 private:
   widgetDetails::BlobCollection blobs_;
   /* Other data members */
};
```

"You cannot be serious!" you exclaim. "Isn't this the worst of all options? Aren't we artificially separating two things that belong together? And isn't the SRP telling us that we should keep the things that belong together close to one another?" Well, I don't think so. On the contrary, I firmly believe that only now are we adhering to the SRP: the SRP states that we should isolate the things that do not belong together, the things that can change for different reasons. Admittedly, at first sight, it may appear as if Widget and updateCollection() belong together, since after all, the blob_ data member needs to be updated once in a while. However, the fact that the update Collection() function isn't properly testable is a clear indication that the design does not fit yet: if anything that needs explicit testing can't be tested, something is amiss. Why make our lives so much harder and hide the function to test in the private section of the Widget class? Since testing plays a vital role in the presence of change, testing represents just another way to help decide which things belong together. If the updateCollection() function is important enough that we want to test it in isolation, then apparently it changes for a reason other than Widget. This indicates that Widget and updateCollection() do not belong together. Based on the SRP, the updateCollection() function should be extracted from the class.

"But isn't this against the idea of encapsulation?" you ask. "And don't you dare wave away encapsulation. I consider encapsulation to be very important!" I agree, it is very important, fundamentally so! However, encapsulation is just one more reason to separate concerns. As Scott Meyers claims in his book, *Effective C++*, extracting functions from a class is a step toward increasing encapsulation. According to Meyers, you should generally prefer nonmember non-friend functions to member functions.[36] This is because every member function has full access to every member of a class, even the `private` members. However, in the extracted form, the `updateCollection()` function is restricted to just the `public` interface of the `Widget` class and is not able to access the `private` members. Therefore, these `private` members become a little more encapsulated. Note that the same argument holds true for extracting the `BlobCollection` class: the `BlobCollection` class is not able to touch the nonpublic members of the `Widget` class, and therefore `Widget` also becomes a little more encapsulated.

By separating concerns and extracting this piece of functionality, you now gain several advantages. First, as just discussed, the `Widget` class becomes more encapsulated. Fewer members can access the `private` members. Second, the extracted `update Collection()` function is easily, even trivially, testable. You don't even need a `Widget` for that but instead can either pass `std::vector<Blob>` as the first argument (not the implicit first argument of any member function, the `this` pointer) or call the `public` member function. Third, you don't have to change any other aspect in the `Widget` class: you simply pass the `blobs_` member to the `updateCollection()` function whenever you need to update the collection. No need to add any other `public` getter. And, probably most importantly, you can now change the function in isolation, without having to deal with `Widget`. This indicates that you have reduced dependencies. While in the initial setup the `updateCollection()` function was tightly coupled to the `Widget` class (yes, the `this` pointer), we have now severed these ties. The `updateCollection()` function is now a separate service that might even be reused.

I can see that you still have questions. Maybe you're concerned that this means you shouldn't have any member functions anymore. No, to be clear, I did not suggest that you should extract each and every member function from your classes. I merely suggested you take a closer look at those functions that need to be tested but are placed in the `private` section of your class. Also, you might wonder how this works with virtual functions, which cannot be extracted in the form of a free function. Well, there's no quick answer for that, but it's something that we will deal with in many different ways throughout this book. My objective will always be to reduce coupling and to increase testability, even by separating virtual functions.

In summary, do not hinder your design and testability with artificial coupling and artificial boundaries. Design for testability. Separate concerns. Free your functions!

---

36 You can find this compelling argument in item 23 of Scott Meyers's *Effective C++*.

Guideline 5: Design for Extension

There is an important aspect about changing software that I haven't highlighted yet: extensibility. Extensibility should be one of the primary goals of your design. Because, frankly speaking, if you're no longer able to add new functionality to your code then your code has reached the end of its lifetime. Thus, adding new functionality— extending the codebase—is of fundamental interest. For that reason, extensibility should indeed be one of your primary goals and a driving factor for good software design.

The Open-Closed Principle

Design for extension is unfortunately not something that just falls into your lap or magically materializes. No, you will have to explicitly take extensibility into account when designing software. We've already seen an example of a naive approach of serializing documents in "Guideline 2: Design for Change" on page 11. In that context, we used a `Document` base class with a pure virtual `serialize()` function:

```
class Document
{
 public:
   // ...
   virtual ~Document() = default;

   virtual void serialize( ByteStream& bs, /*...*/ ) const = 0;
   // ...
};
```

Since `serialize()` is a pure virtual function, it needs to be implemented by all deriv-ing classes, including the PDF class:

```
class PDF : public Document
{
 public:
   // ...
```

```
    void serialize( ByteStream& bs, /*...*/ ) const override;
    // ...
};
```

So far, so good. The interesting question is: how do we implement the serialize()
member function? One requirement is that at a later point in time we are able to convert the bytes back into a PDF instance (we want to deserialize bytes back to a PDF).
For that purpose, it is essential to store the information that the bytes represent. In
"Guideline 2: Design for Change" on page 11, we accomplished this with an
enumeration:

```
enum class DocumentType
{
    pdf,
    word,
    // ... Potentially many more document types
};
```

This enumeration can now be used by all derived classes to put the type of the document at the beginning of the byte stream. This way, during deserialization, it's easy to
detect which kind of document is stored. Sadly, this design choice turns out to be an
unfortunate decision. With that enumeration, we have accidentally coupled all kinds
of document: the PDF class knows about the Word format. And of course the corresponding Word class would know about the PDF format. Yes, you are correct—they
don't know about the implementation details, but they are still aware of each other.

This coupling situation is illustrated in Figure 1-5. From an architectural point of
view, the DocumentType enumeration resides on the same level as the PDF and Word
classes. Both types of documents use (and thus depend on) the DocumentType
enumeration.

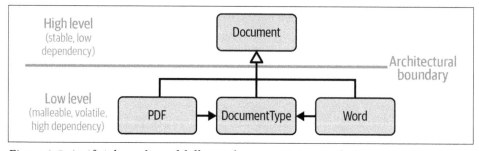

*Figure 1-5. Artificial coupling of different document types via the DocumentType
enumeration.*

The problem with this becomes obvious if we try to extend the functionality. Next to
PDF and Word, we now also want to support a plain XML format. Ideally, all we
should have to do is add the XML class as deriving from the Document class. But,
unfortunately, we also have to adapt the DocumentType enumeration:

```
enum class DocumentType
{
    pdf,
    word,
    xml,    // The new type of document
    // ... Potentially many more document types
};
```

This change will at least cause all the other document types (PDF, Word, etc.) to recompile. Now you may just shrug your shoulders and think, "Oh well! It just needs to recompile." Well, note that I said *at least*. In the worst case, this design has significantly limited others to extend the code—i.e., to add new kinds of documents—because not everyone is able to extend the DocumentType enumeration. No, this kind of coupling just doesn't feel right: PDF and Word should be entirely unaware of the new XML format. They shouldn't see or feel a thing, not even a recompilation.

The problem in this example can be explained as a violation of the Open-Closed Principle (OCP). The OCP is the second of the SOLID principles. It advises us to design software such that it is easy to make the necessary extensions:[37]

> Software artifacts (classes, modules, functions, etc.) should be open for extension, but closed for modification.

The OCP tells us that we should be able to extend our software (open for extension). However, the extension should be easy and, in the best case, possible by just adding new code. In other words, we shouldn't have to modify existing code (closed for modification).

In theory, the extension should be easy: we should only have to add the new derived class XML. This new class alone would not require any modifications in any other piece of code. Unfortunately, the serialize() function artificially couples the different kinds of documents and requires a modification of the DocumentType enumeration. This modification, in turn, has an impact on the other types of Document, which is exactly what the OCP advises against.

Luckily, we've already seen a solution for how to achieve that for the Document example. In this case, the right thing to do is to separate concerns (see Figure 1-6).

By separating concerns, by grouping the things that truly belong together, the accidental coupling between different kinds of documents is gone. All code dealing with serialization is now properly grouped inside the Serialization component, which can logically reside on another level of the architecture. Serialization depends on all types of documents (PDF, Word, XML, etc.), but none of the document types

---

37 Bertrand Meyer, *Object-Oriented Software Construction*, 2nd ed. (Pearson, 2000).

depend on `Serialization`. In addition, none of the documents are aware of any other type of document (as it should be).

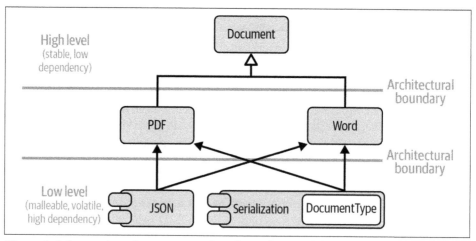

Figure 1-6. Separation of concerns resolves the violation of the OCP

"Wait a second!" you say. "In the code for the serialization, we still need the enumeration, don't we? How else would I store the information about what the stored bytes represent?" I'm glad you're making this observation. Yes, inside the `Serialization` component we will still (very likely) need something like the `DocumentType` enumeration. However, by separating concerns, we have properly resolved this dependency problem. None of the different types of documents depends on the `DocumentType` enumeration anymore. All dependency arrows now go from the low level (the `Serialization` component) to the high level (`PDF` and `Word`). And that property is essential for a proper, good architecture.

"But what about adding a new type of document? Doesn't that require a modification in the `Serialization` component?" Again, you are absolutely correct. Still, this is not a violation of OCP, which advises that we should not have to modify existing code on the same architectural level or on higher levels. However, there is no way you can control or prevent modifications on the lower levels. `Serialization` *must* depend on all types of documents and therefore *must* be adapted for every new type of document. For that reason, `Serialization` must reside on a lower level (think *depending* level) of our architecture.

As also discussed in "Guideline 2: Design for Change" on page 11, the solution in this example is the separation of concerns. Thus, it appears as if the real solution is to adhere to the SRP. For that reason, there are some critical voices that don't consider the OCP a separate principle but the same as the SRP. I admit that I understand this reasoning. Very often the separation of concerns already leads to the desired extensibility. It's something we will experience multiple times throughout this book, in particular when we talk about design patterns. Thus, it stands to reason that SRP and OCP are related or even the same.

On the other hand, in this example we have seen that there are some specific, architectural considerations about the OCP that we didn't take into account while talking about the SRP. Also, as we will experience in "Guideline 15: Design for the Addition of Types or Operations" on page 102, we will often have to make explicit decisions about what we want to extend and how we want to extend it. That decision can significantly influence how we apply the SRP and the way we design our software. Therefore, the OCP seems to be more about the awareness of extensions and conscious decisions about extensions than the SRP. As such, it is perhaps a little more than just an afterthought of the SRP. Or perhaps it just depends.[38]

Either way, this example indisputably demonstrates that extensibility should be explicitly considered during software design, and that the desire for extending our software in a specific way is an excellent indication for the need to separate concerns. It is important to understand how software will be extended, to identify such *customization points*, and to design so that this kind of extension can be performed easily.

Compile-Time Extensibility

The Document example may give the impression that all of these design considerations apply to runtime polymorphism. No, absolutely not: the same considerations and the same arguments also apply to compile-time problems. To illustrate this, I now reach for a couple of examples from the Standard Library. Of course, it is of utmost interest that you're able to extend the Standard Library. Yes, you're supposed to *use* the Standard Library, but you are also encouraged to build on it and add your own pieces of functionality. For that reason, the Standard Library is designed for extensibility. But interestingly, it isn't using base classes for that purpose, but primarily builds on function overloading, templates, and (class) template specialization.

An excellent example of extension by function overloading is the std::swap() algorithm. Since C++11, std::swap() has been defined in this way:

```
namespace std {

template< typename T >
void swap( T& a, T& b )
{
   T tmp( std::move(a) );
   a = std::move(b);
   b = std::move(tmp);
}
```

---

38 The answer "It depends!" will of course satisfy even the strongest critics of the OCP.

```
} // namespace std
```

Due to the fact that `std::swap()` is defined as a function template, you can use it for any type: fundamental types like `int` and `double`, Standard Library types like `std::string`, and, of course, your own types. However, there may be some types that require special attention, some types that cannot or should not be swapped by means of `std::swap()` (for instance, because they cannot be efficiently moved) but could still be swapped efficiently by different means. But still, it's expected that value types can be swapped, as it is also expressed by Core Guideline C.83 (*https://oreil.ly/ Peqhm*):[39]

> For value-like types, consider providing a noexcept swap function.

In such a case, you can overload `std::swap()` for your own type:

```
namespace custom {

class CustomType
{
    /* Implementation that requires a special form of swap */
};

void swap( CustomType& a, CustomType& b )
{
    /* Special implementation for swapping two instances of type 'CustomType' */
}

} // namespace custom
```

If `swap()` is used correctly, this custom function will perform a special kind of swap operation on two instances of `CustomType`:[40]

```
template< typename T >
void some_function( T& value )
{
    // ...
    T tmp( /*...*/ );

    using std::swap;        // Enable the compiler to consider std::swap for the
                            // subsequent call
    swap( tmp, value );     // Swap the two values; thanks to the unqualified call
                            // and thanks to ADL this would call 'custom::swap()'
```

---

39 The C++ Core Guidelines (*https://oreil.ly/PGze4*) are a community effort to collect and agree on a set of guidelines for writing good C++ code. They best represent the common sense of what idiomatic C++ is. You can find these guidelines on GitHub (*https://oreil.ly/PGze4*).

40 The abbreviation ADL refers to Argument Dependent Lookup. See the CppReference (*https://oreil.ly/lRSZD*) or my CppCon 2020 talk (*https://oreil.ly/3f7Zo*) for an introduction.

```
    // ...                    // in case 'T' is 'CustomType'
}
```

Obviously, `std::swap()` is designed as a *customization point*, allowing you to plug in new custom types and behavior. The same is true of all algorithms in the Standard Library. Consider, for instance, `std::find()` and `std::find_if()`:

```
template< typename InputIt, typename T >
constexpr InputIt find( InputIt first, InputIt last, T const& value );

template< typename InputIt, typename UnaryPredicate >
constexpr InputIt find_if( InputIt first, InputIt last, UnaryPredicate p );
```

By means of the template parameters, and implicitly, the corresponding concepts, `std::find()` and `std::find_if()` (just as all other algorithms) enable you to use your own (iterator) types to perform a search. In addition, `std::find_if()` allows you to customize how the comparison of elements is handled. Thus, these functions are definitely designed for extension and customization.

The last kind of *customization point* is template specialization. This approach is, for instance, used by the `std::hash` class template. Assuming the `CustomType` from the `std::swap()` example, we can specialize `std::hash` explicitly:

```
template<>
struct std::hash<CustomType>
{
    std::size_t operator()( CustomType const& v ) const noexcept
    {
        return /*...*/;
    }
};
```

The design of `std::hash` puts you in a position to adapt its behavior for any custom type. Most noteworthy, you are not required to modify any existing code; it's enough to provide this separate specialization to adapt to special requirements.

Almost the entire Standard Library is designed for extension and customization. This shouldn't come as a surprise, however, because the Standard Library is supposed to represent one of the highest levels in your architecture. Thus, the Standard Library cannot depend on anything in your code, but you depend entirely on the Standard Library.

Avoid Premature Design for Extension

The C++ Standard Library is a great example of designing for extension. Hopefully it gives you a feeling for how important extensibility really is. However, although extensibility is important, this doesn't mean that you should automatically, without reflection, reach for either base classes or templates for every possible implementation detail just to guarantee extensibility in the future. Just as you shouldn't prematurely separate concerns, you should also not prematurely design for extension. Of course, if you have a good idea about how your code will evolve, then by all means, go ahead and design it accordingly. However, remember the YAGNI principle: if you do not know how the code will evolve, then it may be wise to wait, instead of anticipating an extension that will never happen. Perhaps the next extension will give you an idea about future extensions, which puts you in a position to refactor the code such that subsequent extensions are easy. Otherwise you might run into the problem that favoring one kind of extension makes other kinds of extensions much more difficult (see, for instance, "Guideline 15: Design for the Addition of Types or Operations" on page 102). That is something you should avoid, if possible.

In summary, designing for extension is an important part of design for change. Therefore, explicitly keep an eye out for pieces of functionality that are expected to be extended and design the code so that extension is easy.

Guideline 5: Design for Extension

- Favor design that makes it easy to extend code.
- Adhere to the Open-Closed Principle (OCP) to keep code open for extension but closed for modification.
- Design for code additions by means of base classes, templates, function overloading, or template specialization.
- Avoid premature abstraction if you are not sure about the next addition.

CHAPTER 2

The Art of Building Abstractions

Abstractions play a vital role in software design and software architecture. In other words, good abstractions are the key to managing complexity. Without them, good design and proper architecture are hard to imagine. Still, building good abstractions and using them well is surprisingly difficult. As it turns out, building and using abstractions comes with a lot of subtleties, and therefore feels more like an art than a science. This chapter goes into detail about the meaning of abstractions and the art of building them.

In "Guideline 6: Adhere to the Expected Behavior of Abstractions" on page 44, we will talk about the purpose of abstractions. We will also talk about the fact that abstractions represent a set of requirements and expectations and why it is so important to adhere to the expected behavior of abstractions. In that context I will introduce another design principle, the *Liskov Substitution Principle* (LSP).

In "Guideline 7: Understand the Similarities Between Base Classes and Concepts" on page 52, we will compare the two most commonly used abstractions: base classes and concepts. You will understand that from a semantic point of view both approaches are very similar since both are able to express expected behavior.

In "Guideline 8: Understand the Semantic Requirements of Overload Sets" on page 56, I will extend the discussion about semantic requirements and talk about a third kind of abstraction: function overloading. You will understand that all functions, being part of an overload set, also have an expected behavior and thus also have to adhere to the LSP.

In "Guideline 9: Pay Attention to the Ownership of Abstractions" on page 62, I will focus on the architectural meaning of abstractions. I will explain what an architecture is and what we expect from the high and low levels of an architecture. I will also show you that from an architectural point of view, it is not enough to *just* introduce an abstraction to resolve dependencies. To explain this, I will introduce the *Dependency Inversion Principle* (DIP), vital advice on how to build an architecture by means of abstractions.

In "Guideline 10: Consider Creating an Architectural Document" on page 74, we will talk about the benefits of an architectural document. Hopefully, this will be an incentive to create one in case this wasn't already on your radar.

Guideline 6: Adhere to the Expected Behavior of Abstractions

One of the key aspects of decoupling software, and thus one of the key aspects of software design, is the introduction of abstractions. For that reason, you would expect that this is a relatively straightforward, easy thing to do. Unfortunately, as it turns out, building abstractions is difficult.

To demonstrate what I mean, let's take a look at an example. I have selected *the* classic example for that purpose. Chances are, you might already know this example. If so, please feel free to skip it. However, if you're not familiar with the example, then this may serve as an eye-opener.

An Example of Violating Expectations

Let's start with a `Rectangle` base class:

```
class Rectangle
{
 public:
   // ...
   virtual ~Rectangle() = default;   ❶

   int getWidth() const;   ❸
   int getHeight() const;

   virtual void setWidth(int);   ❹
   virtual void setHeight(int);

   virtual int getArea() const;   ❺
   // ...

 private:
   int width;   ❷
   int height;
};
```

First of all, this class is designed as a base class, since it provides a virtual destructor (❶). Semantically, a `Rectangle` represents an abstraction for different kinds of rectangles. And technically, you can properly destroy an object of derived type via a pointer to `Rectangle`.

Second, the `Rectangle` class comes with two data members: `width` and `height` (❷). That is to be expected, since a rectangle has two side lengths, which are represented by `width` and `height`. The `getWidth()` and `getHeight()` member functions can be used to query the two side lengths (❸), and via the `setWidth()` and `setHeight()` member functions, we can set the `width` and `height` (❹). It's important to note that I can set these two independently; i.e., I can set the `width` without having to modify the `height`.

Finally, there is a `getArea()` member function (❺). `getArea()` computes the area of the rectangle, which is of course implemented by returning the product of `width` and `height`.

Of course there may be more functionality, but the given members are the ones that are important for this example. As it is, this seems to be a pretty nice `Rectangle` class. Obviously, we're off to a good start. But, of course there's more. For instance, there is the `Square` class:

```cpp
class Square : public Rectangle   ❻
{
 public:
   // ...
   void setWidth(int) override;    ❼
   void setHeight(int) override;   ❽

   int getArea() const override;   ❾
   // ...
};
```

The `Square` class publicly inherits from the `Rectangle` class (❻). And that seems pretty reasonable: from a mathematical perspective, a square appears to be a special kind of rectangle.[1]

A `Square` is special, in the sense that it has only one side length. But the `Rectangle` base class comes with two lengths: `width` and `height`. For that reason, we have to make sure that the invariants of the `Square` are always preserved. In this given implementation with two data members and two getter functions, we have to make sure

---

1 In one of my training classes several years ago, I was "gently" reminded that from a mathematical perspective, a square is not a rectangle but a rhombus. My knees still shake when I think about that lecture. Therefore, I specifically say "appears to be" instead of "is" to denote the naive impression that unaware people like me might have had.

that both data members always have the same value. Therefore, we override the setWidth() member function to set both width and height (❼). We also override the setHeight() member function to set both width and height (❽).

Once we have done that, a Square will always have equal side lengths, and the getArea() function will always return the correct area of a Square (❾). Nice!

Let's put these two classes to good use. For instance, we could think about a function that transforms different kinds of rectangles:

```cpp
void transform( Rectangle& rectangle )   ❿
{
   rectangle.setWidth ( 7 );   ⓫
   rectangle.setHeight( 4 );   ⓬

   assert( rectangle.getArea() == 28 );   ⓭

   // ...
}
```

The transform() function takes any kind of Rectangle by means of a reference to non-const (❿). That's reasonable, because we want to change the given rectangle. A first possible way to change the rectangle is to set the width via the setWidth() member function to 7 (⓫). Then we could change the height of the rectangle to 4 via the setHeight() member function (⓬).

At this point, I would argue that you have an implicit assumption. I am pretty certain that you assume that the area of the rectangle is 28, because, of course, 7 times 4 is 28. That is an assumption we can test via an assertion (⓭).

The only thing missing is to actually call the transform() function. That's what we do in the main() function:

```cpp
int main()
{
   Square s{};   ⓮
   s.setWidth( 6 );

   transform( s );   ⓯

   return EXIT_SUCCESS;
}
```

In the main() function, we create a special kind of rectangle: a Square (⓮).[2] This square is passed to the transform() function, which of course works, since a reference to a Square can be implicitly converted to a reference to a Rectangle (⓯).

---

2 Not mathematically, but in this implementation.

If I were to ask you, "What happens?" I'm pretty sure you would answer, "The assert() fails!" Yes, indeed, the assert() will fail. The expression passed to the assert() will evaluate to false, and assert() will crash the process with a SIGKILL signal. Well, that's certainly unfortunate. So let's do a postmortem analysis: why does the assert() fail? Our expectation in the transform() function is that we can change the width and height of a rectangle independently. This expectation is explicitly expressed with the two function calls to setWidth() and setHeight(). However, unexpectedly, this special kind of rectangle does not allow that: to preserve its own invariants, the Square class must always make sure that both side lengths are equal. Thus, the Square class has to violate this expectation. This violation of the expectation in an abstraction is a violation of the LSP.

The Liskov Substitution Principle

The LSP is the third of the SOLID principles and is concerned with *behavioral subtyping*, i.e., with the expected behavior of an abstraction. This design principle is named after Barbara Liskov (*https://oreil.ly/XkNi4*), who initially introduced it in 1988 and clarified it with Jeannette Wing in 1994:[3]

> Subtype Requirement: Let $\varphi(x)$ be a property provable about objects x of type T. Then $\varphi(y)$ should be true for objects y of type S where S is a subtype of T.

This principle formulates what we commonly call an *IS-A* (*https://oreil.ly/isoda*) relationship. This relationship, i.e., the expectations in an abstraction, *must* be adhered to in a subtype. That includes the following properties:

- Preconditions cannot be strengthened in a subtype: a subtype cannot expect more in a function than what the super type expresses. That would violate the expectations in the abstraction:

```
struct X
{
   virtual ~X() = default;

   // Precondition: the function accepts all 'i' greater than 0
   virtual void f( int i ) const
   {
      assert( i > 0 );
      // ...
   }
};
```

---

3 The LSP was first introduced by Barbara Liskov in the paper "Data Abstraction and Hierarchy" (*https://oreil.ly/Z9lu1*) in 1988. In 1994, it was reformulated in the paper "A Behavioral Notion of Subtyping" (*https://oreil.ly/ic7N3*) by Barbara Liskov and Jeannette Wing. For her work, Barbara Liskov received the Turing Award in 2008.

```
struct Y : public X
{
   // Precondition: the function accepts all 'i' greater than 10.
   // This would strengthen the precondition; numbers between 1 and 10
   // would no longer be allowed. This is a LSP violation!
   void f( int i ) const override
   {
      assert( i > 10 );
      // ...
   }
};
```

- Postconditions cannot be weakened in a subtype: a subtype cannot promise less when leaving a function than the super type promises. Again, that would violate the expectations in the abstraction:

```
struct X
{
   virtual ~X() = default;

   // Postcondition: the function will only return values larger than 0
   virtual int f() const
   {
      int i;
      // ...
      assert( i > 0 );
      return i;
   }
};

struct Y : public X
{
   // Postcondition: the function may return any value.
   // This would weaken the postcondition; negative numbers and 0 would
   // be allowed. This is a LSP violation!
   int f() const override
   {
      int i;
      // ...
      return i;
   }
};
```

- Function return types in a subtype must be *covariant*: member functions of the subtype can return a type that is itself a subtype of the return type of the corresponding member function in the super type. This property has direct language support in C++. However, the subtype cannot return any super type of the return type of the corresponding function in the super type:

```
struct Base { /*...some virtual functions, including destructor...*/ };
struct Derived : public Base { /*...*/ };

struct X
{
   virtual ~X() = default;
   virtual Base* f();
};

struct Y : public X
{
   Derived* f() override;   // Covariant return type
};
```

- Function parameters in a subtype must be *contravariant*: in a member function, the subtype can accept a super type of the function parameter in the corresponding member function of the super type. This property does *not* have direct language support in C++:

```
struct Base { /*...some virtual functions, including destructor...*/ };
struct Derived : public Base { /*...*/ };

struct X
{
   virtual ~X() = default;
   virtual void f( Derived* );
};

struct Y : public X
{
   void f( Base* ) override;   // Contravariant function parameter; Not
                               // supported in C++. Therefore the function
                               // does not override, but fails to compile.
};
```

- Invariants of the super type must be preserved in a subtype: any expectation about the state of a super type must always be valid before and after all calls to any member function, including the member functions of the subtype:

```
struct X
{
   explicit X( int v = 1 )
     : value_(v)
   {
      if( v < 1 || v > 10 ) throw std::invalid_argument( /*...*/ );
   }

   virtual ~X() = default;

   int get() const { return value_; }
```

```
  protected:
    int value_;   // Invariant: must be within the range [1..10]
};

struct Y : public X
{
 public:
   Y()
      : X()
   {
       value_ = 11;   // Broken invariant: After the constructor, 'value_'
                      // is out of expected range. One good reason to
                      // properly encapsulate invariants and to follow
                      // Core Guideline C.133: Avoid protected data.
   }
};
```

In our example, the expectation in a Rectangle is that we can change the two side
lengths independently, or, more formally, that the result of getWidth() does not
change after setHeight() is called. This expectation is intuitive for any kind of rectangle. However, the Square class itself introduces the invariant that all sides must
always be equal, or else the Square would not properly express our idea of a square.
But by protecting its own invariants, the Square unfortunately violates the expectations in the base class. Thus, the Square class doesn't fulfill the expectations in the
Rectangle class, and the hierarchy in this example doesn't express an IS-A relationship. Therefore, a Square cannot be used in all the places a Rectangle is expected.

"But isn't a square a rectangle?" you ask. "Isn't that properly expressing the geometrical relation?"[4] Yes, there may be a geometrical relation between squares and rectangles, but in this example the inheritance relationship is broken. This example
demonstrates that the mathematical IS-A relationship is indeed different from the
LSP IS-A relationship. While in geometry a square is always a rectangle, in computer
science it really depends on the actual interface and thus the expectations. As long as
there are the two independent setWidth() and setHeight() functions, a Square will
always violate the expectations. "I understand," you say. "Nobody would claim that,
geometrically, a square is still a square after changing its width, right?" Exactly.

The example also demonstrates that inheritance is not a natural or intuitive feature,
but a hard feature. As stated in the beginning, building abstractions is hard. Whenever you use inheritance, you *must* make sure that all expectations in the base class
are fulfilled and that the derived type behaves as expected.

---

4 If you have a strong opinion about a square being a rhombus, please forgive me!

Criticism of the Liskov Substitution Principle

Some people argue that the LSP, as explained earlier, is in fact not what is described in the conference paper "Data Abstraction and Hierarchy" by Barbara Liskov and that the notion of subtyping is flawed. And that is correct: we usually do not substitute derived objects for base objects, but we use a derived object as a base object. However, this literal and strict interpretation of Liskov's statements does not play any role in the kinds of abstractions that we build on a daily basis. In their 1994 paper "A Behavioral Notion of Subtyping," Barbara Liskov and Jeannette Wing proposed the term *behavioral subtyping*, which is the common understanding of the LSP today.

Other people argue that because of potential violations of the LSP, a base class does not serve the purpose of an abstraction. The rationale is that using code would also depend on the (mis-)behavior of derived types. This argument unfortunately turns the world upside down. A base class *does* represent an abstraction, because calling code can and should only and exclusively depend on the *expected* behavior of this abstraction. It's that dependency that makes LSP violations programming errors. Unfortunately, sometimes people try to fix LSP violations by introducing special workarounds:

```
class Base { /*...*/ };
class Derived : public Base { /*...*/ };
class Special : public Base { /*...*/ };
// ... Potentially more derived classes

void f( Base const& b )
{
   if( dynamic_cast<Special const*>(&b) )
   {
      // ... do something "special," knowing that 'Special' behaves differently
   }
   else
   {
      // ... do the expected thing
   }
}
```

This kind of workaround will indeed introduce a dependency in the behavior of the derived types. And a very unfortunate dependency, indeed! This should always be considered an LSP violation and very bad practice.[5] It doesn't serve as a general argument against the abstracting properties of a base class.

---

5 And yet, in a sufficiently large codebase, there's a good chance that you'll find at least one example of this kind of malpractice. In my experience, it's often the result of too little time to rethink and adapt the abstraction.

The Need for Good and Meaningful Abstractions

To properly decouple software entities, it is fundamentally important that we can count on our abstractions. Without meaningful abstractions that we, the human readers of code, *fully* understand, we cannot write robust and reliable software. Therefore, adherence to the LSP is essential for the purpose of software design. However, a vital part is also the clear and unambiguous communication of the expectations of an abstraction. In the best case, this happens by means of software itself (*self-documenting code*), but it also entails a proper documentation of abstractions. As a good example, I recommend the iterator concepts documentation (*https://oreil.ly/OBpAg*) in the C++ standard, which clearly lists the expected behavior, including pre- and post-conditions.

Guideline 6: Adhere to the Expected Behavior of Abstractions

- Understand that an abstraction represents a set of requirements and expectations.

- Follow the Liskov Substitution Principle (LSP) to adhere to the expected behavior of abstractions.

- Make sure that derived classes adhere to the expected behavior of their base classes.

- Communicate the expectations of an abstraction.

Guideline 7: Understand the Similarities Between Base Classes and Concepts

In "Guideline 6: Adhere to the Expected Behavior of Abstractions" on page 44, I may have created the impression that the LSP is concerned only with inheritance hierarchies and base classes. To make sure that this impression doesn't stick, allow me to explicitly state that the LSP is *not* limited to dynamic (runtime) polymorphism and inheritance hierarchies. On the contrary, we can apply the LSP just as well to static (compile-time) polymorphism and templated code.

To make the point, let me ask you a question: what's the difference between the following two code snippets?

```
//==== Code Snippet 1 ====

class Document
{
 public:
   // ...
   virtual ~Document() = default;
```

```
    virtual void exportToJSON( /*...*/ ) const = 0;
    virtual void serialize( ByteStream&, /*...*/ ) const = 0;
    // ...
};

void useDocument( Document const& doc )
{
    // ...
    doc.exportToJSON( /*...*/ );
    // ...
}


//==== Code Snippet 2 ====

template< typename T >
concept Document =
    requires( T t, ByteStream b ) {
        t.exportToJSON( /*...*/ );
        t.serialize( b, /*...*/ );
    };

template< Document T >
void useDocument( T const& doc )
{
    // ...
    doc.exportToJSON( /*...*/ );
    // ...
}
```

I'm pretty sure your first answer is that the first code snippet shows a solution using dynamic polymorphism, and the second one shows static polymorphism. Yes, great! What else? OK, yes, of course, the syntax is different, too. OK, I see, I should ask my question a little more precisely: in which way do these two solutions differ *semantically*?

Well, if you think about it, then you might find that from a semantic point of view the two solutions are very similar indeed. In the first code snippet, the useDocument() function works only with classes derived from the Document base class. Thus, we can say that the function works only with classes adhering to the expectations of the Document abstraction. In the second code snippet, the use Document() function works only with classes that implement the Document concept. In other words, the function works only with classes adhering to the expectations of the Document abstraction.

If you now have the feeling of déjà vu, then my choice of words hopefully struck a chord. Yes, in both code snippets, the useDocument() function works only with classes adhering to the expectations of the Document abstraction. So despite the fact that the first code snippet is based on a runtime abstraction and the second function represents a compile-time abstraction, these two functions are very similar from a semantic point of view.

Both the base class and the concept represent a set of requirements (syntactic requirements, but also semantic requirements). As such, both represent a formal description of the expected behavior and thus are the means to express and communicate expectations for calling code. Thus, concepts can be considered the equivalent, the static counterpart, of base classes. And from this point of view, it makes perfect sense to also consider the LSP for template code.

"I'm not buying that," you say. "I've heard that C++20 concepts cannot express semantics!"[6] Well, to this I can only respond with a definitive yes and no. Yes, C++20 concepts cannot fully express semantics, that's correct. But on the other hand, concepts still express expected behavior. Consider, for instance, the C++20 form of the std::copy() algorithm:[7]

```
template< typename InputIt, typename OutputIt >
constexpr OutputIt copy( InputIt first, InputIt last, OutputIt d_first )
{
   while( first != last ) {
      *d_first++ = *first++;
   }
   return d_first;
}
```

The std::copy() algorithm expects three arguments. The first two arguments represent the range of elements that need to be copied (the *input range*). The third argument represents the first element we need to copy to (the *output range*). A general expectation is that the *output range* is big enough that all the elements from the *input range* can be copied to it.

There are more expectations that are implicitly expressed via the names for the iterator types: InputIt and OutputIt. InputIt represents a type of *input iterator*. The C++ standard states all the expectations of such iterator types, such as the availability of an (in-)equality comparison, the ability to traverse a range with a prefix and postfix increment (operator++() and operator++(int)), and the ability to access elements with the dereference operator (operator*()). OutputIt, on the other hand,

---

6 This is indeed a very often discussed topic. You'll find a very good summary of this in foonathan's blog (*https://oreil.ly/HiJP9*).

7 In C++20, std::copy() is finally constexpr but does not yet use the std::input_iterator and std::output_iterator concepts. It is still based on the formal description of input and output iterators; see LegacyInputIterator (*https://oreil.ly/9vsvC*) and LegacyOutputIterator (*https://oreil.ly/ZcJeU*).

---

represents a type of *output iterator*. Here, the C++ standard also explicitly states all expected operations.

`InputIt` and `OutputIt` may not be C++20 concepts, but they represent the same idea: these named template parameters don't just give you an idea about what kind of type is required; they also express expected behavior. For instance, we expect that subsequent increments of `first` will eventually yield `last`. If any given concrete iterator type does not behave this way, `std::copy()` will not work as expected. This would be a violation of the expected behavior, and as such, a violation of the LSP.[8] Therefore, both `InputIt` and `OutputIt` represent LSP abstractions.

Note that since concepts represent an LSP abstraction, i.e., a set of requirements and expectations, they are subject to the *Interface Segregation Principle* (ISP) as well (see "Guideline 3: Separate Interfaces to Avoid Artificial Coupling" on page 24). Just as you should separate concerns in the definition of requirements in the form of base classes (say, "interface" classes), you should separate concerns when defining a concept. The Standard Library iterators do that by building on one another, thus allowing you to select the desired level of requirements:

```
template< typename I >
concept input_or_output_iterator =
  /* ... */;

template< typename I >
concept input_iterator =
   std::input_or_output_iterator<I> &&
   /* ... */;

template< typename I >
concept forward_iterator =
   std::input_iterator<I> &&
   /* ... */;
```

Since both named template parameters and C++20 concepts serve the same purpose and since both represent LSP abstractions, from now on, in all subsequent guidelines, I will use the term *concept* to refer to both of them. Thus, with the term *concept*, I will refer to any way to represent a set of requirements (in most cases for template arguments, but sometimes even more generally). If I want to refer to either of these two specifically, I will make it explicitly clear.

In summary, any kind of abstraction (dynamic and static) represents a set of requirements with that expected behavior. These expectations need to be fulfilled by concrete implementations. Thus, the LSP clearly represents essential guidance for all kinds of IS-A relationships.

---

8 And no, it wouldn't be a compile-time error, unfortunately.

> ## Guideline 7: Understand the Similarities Between Base Classes and Concepts
>
> - Apply the Liskov Substitution Principle (LSP) to both dynamic and static polymorphism.
> - Consider concepts (both the C++20 feature and pre-C++20 named template arguments) as the static equivalent of base classes.
> - Adhere to the expected behavior of concepts when using templates.
> - Communicate the expectations of a concept (in particular for pre-C++20 named template arguments).

Guideline 8: Understand the Semantic Requirements of Overload Sets

In "Guideline 6: Adhere to the Expected Behavior of Abstractions" on page 44, I introduced you to the LSP and hopefully made a strong argument: *every* abstraction represents a set of semantic requirements! In other words, an abstraction expresses expected behavior, which needs to be fulfilled. Otherwise, you (very likely) will have a problem. In "Guideline 7: Understand the Similarities Between Base Classes and Concepts" on page 52, I extended the LSP discussion to concepts and demonstrated that the LSP can and *should* also be applied to static abstractions.

That's not the end of the story, though. As stated before: *every* abstraction represents a set of requirements. There is one more kind of abstraction that we have not yet taken into account, one that's unfortunately often overlooked, despite its power, and hence one that we should not forget in the discussion: function overloading. "Function overloading? You mean the fact that a class can have several functions with the same name?" Yes, absolutely. You probably have experienced that this is indeed a pretty powerful feature. Think, for instance, about the two overloads of the begin() member function inside the std::vector: depending on whether you have a const or a non-const vector, the corresponding overload is picked. Without you even noticing. Pretty powerful! But honestly, this isn't really much of an abstraction. While it's convenient and helpful to overload member functions, I have a different kind of function overloading in mind, the kind that truly represents a form of abstraction: free functions.

The Power of Free Functions: A Compile-Time Abstraction Mechanism

Next to concepts, function overloading by means of free functions represents a second compile-time abstraction: based on some given types, the compiler figures out which function to call from a set of identically named functions. This is what we call an *overload set*. This is an extremely versatile and powerful abstraction mechanism with many, many great design characteristics. First of all, you can add a free function to any type: you can add one to an `int`, to `std::string`, and to any other type. Non-intrusively. Try that with a member function, and you will realize that this just does not work. Adding a member function is intrusive. You can't add anything to a type that cannot have a member function or to a type that you cannot modify. Thus, a free function perfectly lives up to the spirit of the Open-Closed Principle (OCP): you can extend the functionality by simply adding code, without the need to modify already existing code.

This gives you a significant design advantage. Consider, for instance, the following code example:

```
template< typename Range >
void traverseRange( Range const& range )
{
    for( auto pos=range.begin(); pos!=range.end(); ++pos ) {
        // ...
    }
}
```

The `traverseRange()` function performs a traditional, iterator-based loop over the given `range`. To acquire iterators, it calls the `begin()` and `end()` member functions on the `range`. While this code will work for a large number of container types, it will not work for a built-in array:

```
#include <cstdlib>

int main()
{
    int array[6] = { 4, 8, 15, 16, 23, 42 };

    traverseRange( array );  // Compilation error!

    return EXIT_SUCCESS;
}
```

This code will not compile, as the compiler will complain about the missing `begin()` and `end()` member functions for the given array type. "Isn't that why we should avoid using built-in arrays and use `std::array` instead?" I completely agree: you should use `std::array` instead. This is also very nicely explained by Core Guideline SL.con.1 (*https://oreil.ly/FRrfz*):

> Prefer using STL `array` or `vector` instead of a C array.

However, while this is good practice, let's not lose sight of the design issues of the `traverseRange()` function: `traverseRange()` is restricting itself by depending on the `begin()` and `end()` member functions. Thus, it creates an artificial requirement on the `Range` type to support a member `begin()` and a member `end()` function and, by that, limits its own applicability. There is a simple solution, however, a simple way to make the function much more widely applicable: build on the overload set of free `begin()` and `end()` functions:[9]

```
template< typename Range >
void traverseRange( Range const& range )
{
    using std::begin;   // using declarations for the purpose of calling
    using std::end;     //   'begin()' and 'end()' unqualified to enable ADL

    for( auto pos=begin(range); pos!=end(range); ++pos ) {
        // ...
    }
}
```

This function is still doing the same thing as before, but in this form it doesn't restrict itself by any artificial requirement. And indeed, there is no restriction: *any* type can have a free `begin()` and `end()` function or, if it is missing, can be equipped with one. Nonintrusively. Thus, this function works with any kind of `Range` and doesn't have to be modified or overloaded if some type does not meet the requirement. It is more widely applicable. It is truly generic.[10]

Free functions have more advantages, though. As already discussed in "Guideline 4: Design for Testability" on page 28, free functions are a very elegant technique to separate concerns, fulfilling the Single-Responsibility Principle (SRP). By implementing an operation outside a class, you automatically reduce the dependencies of that class to the operation. Technically, this becomes immediately clear, since in contrast to member functions, free functions don't have an implicit first argument, the `this` pointer. At the same time, this promotes the function to become a separate, isolated service, which can be used by many other classes as well. Thus, you promote reuse and reduce duplication. This very, very nicely adheres to the idea of the Don't Repeat Yourself (DRY) principle.

The beauty of this is wonderfully demonstrated in Alexander Stepanov's brainchild, the Standard Template Library (STL).[11] One part of the STL philosophy is to loosely couple the different pieces of functionality and promote reuse by separating concerns as free functions. That's why containers and algorithms are two separate concepts within the STL: conceptually, containers don't know about the algorithms, and algorithms don't know about containers. The abstraction between them is accomplished

---

9 The free `begin()` and `end()` functions are an example of the *Adapter* design pattern; see "Guideline 24: Use Adapters to Standardize Interfaces" on page 198 for more details.

10 That is why range-based for loops build on the free `begin()` and `end()` functions.

11 Alexander Stepanov and Meng Lee, "The Standard Template Library" (*https://oreil.ly/vgm61*), October 1995.

via iterators that allow you to combine the two in seemingly endless ways. A truly remarkable design. Or to say it in the words of Scott Meyers:[12]

> There was never any question that the [standard template] library represented a breakthrough in efficient and extensible design.

"But what about `std::string`? `std::string` comes with dozens of member functions, including many algorithms." You're making a good point, but more in the sense of a counter example. Today the community agrees that the design of `std::string` is not great. Its design promotes coupling, duplication, and growth: in every new C++ standard, there are a couple of new, additional member functions. And growth means modifications and subsequently the risk of accidentally changing something. This is a risk that you want to avoid in your design. However, in its defense, `std::string` was not part of the original STL. It was not designed alongside the STL containers (`std::vector`, `std::list`, `std::set`, etc.) and was adapted to the STL design only later. That explains why it's different from the other STL containers and does not completely share their beautiful design goal.

The Problem of Free Functions: Expectations on the Behavior

Apparently, free functions are remarkably powerful and seriously important for generic programming. They play a vital role in the design of the STL and the design of the C++ Standard Library as a whole, which builds on the power of this abstraction mechanism.[13] However, all of this power can only work if a set of overload functions adheres to a set of rules and certain expectations. It can only work if it adheres to the LSP.

For instance, let's imagine that you have written your own `Widget` type and want to provide a custom `swap()` operation for it:

```
//---- <Widget.h> ----------------

struct Widget
{
```

---

12 Scott Meyers, *Effective STL: 50 Specific Ways to Improve Your Use of the Standard Template Library* (Addison-Wesley Professional, 2001).

13 Free functions are indeed a seriously valuable design tool. To give one example of this, allow me to tell a short war story. You might know Martin Fowler's book *Refactoring: Improving the Design of Existing Code* (Addison-Wesley), which may be considered one of *the* classics for professional software development. The first edition of the book was published in 1999 and provided programming examples in Java. The second edition of the book was released in 2018, but interestingly rewritten with JavaScript. One of the reasons for that choice was the fact that any language having a C-like syntax was considered easier to digest for a majority of readers. However, another important reason was the fact that JavaScript, unlike Java, provides free functions, which Martin Fowler considers a very important tool for decoupling and separating concerns. Without this feature, you would be limited in your flexibility to achieve the refactoring goal.

```
    int i;
    int j;
};

void swap( Widget& w1, Widget& w2 )
{
    using std::swap;
    swap( w1.i, w2.i );
}
```

Your Widget only needs to be a simple wrapper for int values, called i and j. You provide the corresponding swap() function as an accompanying free function. And you implement swap() by swapping only the i value, not the j value. Further imagine that your Widget type is used by some other developer, maybe a kind coworker. At some point, this coworker calls the swap() function:

```
#include <Widget.h>
#include <cstdlib>

int main()
{
    Widget w1{ 1, 11 };
    Widget w2{ 2, 22 };

    swap( w1, w2 );

    // Widget w1 contains (2,11)
    // Widget w2 contains (1,22)

    return EXIT_SUCCESS;
}
```

Can you imagine the surprise of your coworker when after the swap() operation the content of w1 is not (2,22) but (2,11) instead? How unexpected is it that only part of the object is swapped? Can you imagine how frustrated your coworker must be after an hour of debugging? And what would happen if this wasn't a *kind* coworker?

Clearly, the implementation of swap() doesn't fulfill the expectations of a swap() function. Clearly, anyone would expect that the entire observable state of the object is swapped. Clearly, there are behavioral expectations. Thus, if you buy into an overload set, you're immediately and inevitably subject to fulfill the expected behavior of the overload set. In other words, you have to adhere to the LSP.

"I see the problem, I get that. I promise to adhere to the LSP," you say. That's great, and this is an honorable intention. The problem is that it might not always be entirely clear what the expected behavior is, especially for an overload set that is scattered across a big codebase. You might not know about all the expectations and all the details. Thus sometimes, even if you're aware of this problem and pay attention, you might still not do the "right" thing. This is what several people in the community are worried about: the unrestricted ability to add potentially LSP-violating functionality into an overload set.[14] And as stated before, it's easy to do. Anyone, anywhere, can add free functions.

As always, every approach and every solution has advantages, and also disadvantages. On the one hand, it is enormously beneficial to exploit the power of overload sets, but on the other hand, it is potentially very difficult to do the right thing. These two sides of the same coin are also expressed by Core Guideline C.162 (*https://oreil.ly/IyZwR*) and Core Guideline C.163 (*https://oreil.ly/8VWH1*):

> Overload operations that are roughly equivalent.
>
> —Core Guideline C.162

> Overload only for operations that are roughly equivalent.
>
> —Core Guideline C.163

Whereas C.162 expresses the advantages of having the same name for semantically equivalent functions, C.163 expresses the problem of having the same name for semantically different functions. Every C++ developer should be aware of the tension between these two guidelines. Additionally, to adhere to the expected behavior, every C++ developer is well advised to be aware of existing overload sets (`std::swap()`, `std::begin()`, `std::cbegin()`, `std::end()`, `std::cend()`, `std::data()`, `std::size()`, etc.) and to know about common naming conventions. For instance, the name `find()` should be used only for a function that performs a linear search over a range of elements. For any function that performs a binary search, the name `find()` would raise the wrong expectations and would not communicate the precondition that the range needs to be sorted. And then, of course, the names `begin()` and `end()` should always fulfill the expectation to return a pair of iterators that can be used to traverse a range. They should not start or end some kind of process. This task would be better performed by a `start()` and a `stop()` function.[15]

"Well, I agree with all these points," you say. "However, I'm primarily using virtual functions, and since these cannot be implemented in terms of free functions, I can't really use all of this advice on overload sets, right?" It may surprise you, but this advice still applies to you. Since the ultimate goal is to reduce dependencies, and since virtual functions may cause quite a significant amount of coupling, one of the goals will be to "free" these, too. In fact, in many of the subsequent guidelines, and perhaps most prominently in "Guideline 19: Use Strategy to Isolate How Things Are

---

14 A great discussion of this can be found in episode 83 of *Cpp.Chat* (*https://cpp.chat/83*), where Jon Kalb, Phil Nash, and Dave Abrahams discuss the lessons learned from C++ and how they were applied in the development of the Swift programming language.

15 As Kate Gregory would say, "Naming Is Hard: Let's Do Better." This is the title of her highly recommended talk from CppCon 2019 (*https://oreil.ly/TLuqb*).

Done" on page 140 and "Guideline 31: Use External Polymorphism for Nonintrusive Runtime Polymorphism" on page 279, I will tell the story of how to extract and separate virtual functions in the form of, but not limited to, free functions.

In summary, function overloading is a powerful compile-time abstraction mechanism that you should not underestimate. In particular, generic programming heavily exploits this power. However, don't take this power too lightly: remember that just as with base classes and concepts, an overload set represents a set of semantic requirements and thus is subject to the LSP. The expected behavior of an overload set must be adhered to, or things will not work well.

Guideline 8: Understand the Semantic Requirements of Overload Sets

- Be aware that function overloading is a compile-time abstraction mechanism.
- Keep in mind that there are expectations on the behavior of functions within an overload set.
- Pay attention to existing names and conventions.

Guideline 9: Pay Attention to the Ownership of Abstractions

As stated in "Guideline 2: Design for Change" on page 11, change is the one constant in software development. Your software should be prepared for change. One of the essential ingredients for dealing with change is the introduction of abstractions (see also "Guideline 6: Adhere to the Expected Behavior of Abstractions" on page 44). Abstractions help reduce dependencies and thus make it easier to change details in isolation. However, there is more to introducing abstractions than just adding base classes or templates.

The Dependency Inversion Principle

The need for abstractions is also expressed by Robert Martin:[16]

> The most flexible systems are those in which source code dependencies refer only to abstractions, not to concretions.

---

16 Robert C. Martin, *Clean Architecture* (Addison-Wesley, 2017).

This piece of wisdom is commonly known as the Dependency Inversion Principle (DIP), which is the fifth of the SOLID principles. Simply stated, it advises that for the sake of dependencies, you should depend on abstractions instead of concrete types or implementation details. Note that this statement doesn't say anything about inheritance hierarchies but only mentions abstractions in general.

Let's take a look at the situation illustrated in Figure 2-1.[17] Imagine you are implementing the logic for an automated teller machine (ATM). An ATM provides several kinds of operations: you can withdraw money, deposit money, and transfer money. Since all of these operations deal with real money, they should either run to full completion or, in case of any kind of error, be aborted and all changes rolled back. This kind of behavior (either 100% success or a complete rollback) is what we commonly call a *transaction*. Consequently, we can introduce an abstraction named `Transaction`. All abstractions (`Deposit`, `Withdrawal`, and `Transfer`) inherit from the `Transaction` class (depicted by the UML inheritance arrow).

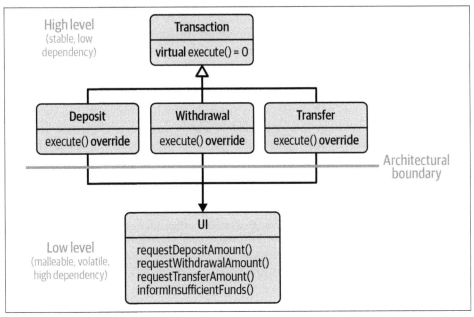

Figure 2-1. Initial strong dependency relationship between several transactions and a UI

---

17 This example is taken from Robert Martin's book *Agile Software Development: Principles, Patterns, and Practices* (Prentice Hall, 2002). Martin used this example to explain the Interface Segregation Principle (ISP), and for that reason, he didn't go into detail about the question of ownership of abstractions. I will try to fill this gap.

All transactions are in need of input data entered by a bank customer via the user interface. This user interface is provided by the UI class, which provides many different functions to query for the entered data: requestDepositAmount(), request WithdrawalAmount(), requestTransferAmount(), informInsufficientFunds(), and potentially more functions. All three abstractions directly call these functions whenever they need information. This relationship is depicted by the little solid arrow, which indicates that the abstractions depend on the UI class.

While this setup may work for some time, your trained eye might have already spotted a potential problem: what happens if something changes? For instance, what happens if a new transaction is added to the system?

Let's assume that we must add a SpeedTransfer transaction for VIP customers. This might require us to change and extend the UI class with a couple of new functions (for instance, requestSpeedTransferAmount() and requestVIPNumber()). That, in turn, also affects all of the other transactions, since they directly depend on the UI class. In the best case, these transactions simply have to be recompiled and retested (still, this takes time!); in the worst case, they might have to be redeployed in case they are delivered in separate shared libraries.

The underlying reason for all of that extra effort is a broken architecture. All transactions indirectly depend on one another via the concrete dependency on the UI class. And that is a very unfortunate situation from an architectural point of view: the transaction classes reside at the high level of our architecture, while the UI class resides at the low level. In this example, the high level depends on the low level. And that is just wrong: in a proper architecture, this dependency should be inverted.[18]

All transactions indirectly depend on one another due to the dependency on the UI class. Furthermore, the high level of our architecture depends on the low level. This is a pretty unfortunate situation indeed, a situation that we should resolve properly. "But that's simple!" you say. "We just introduce an abstraction!" That's exactly what Robert Martin expressed in his statement: we need to introduce an abstraction in order not to depend on the concrete implementation in the UI class.

---

18 If you argue that the Transaction base class could be on an even higher level, you are correct. You've earned yourself a bonus point! But for the remainder of the example we won't need this extra level, and therefore I will ignore it.

However, a single abstraction wouldn't solve the problem. The three kinds of transactions would still be indirectly coupled. No, as Figure 2-2 illustrates, we need three abstractions: one for each transaction.[19]

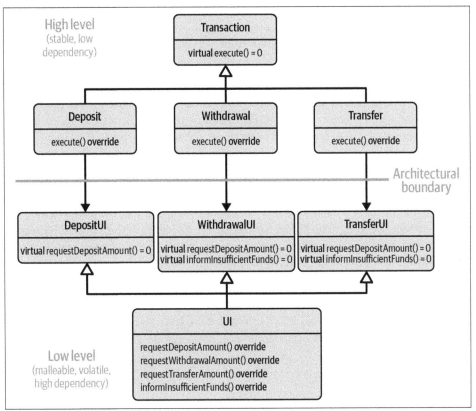

Figure 2-2. The relaxed dependency relationship between several transactions and a UI

---

19 If you're wondering about the two informInsufficientFunds() functions: yes, it is possible to implement *both* virtual functions (i.e., the one from the WithdrawalUI and the one from the TransferUI) by means of a single implementation in the UI class. Of course, this works well only as long as these two functions represent the same expectations and thus can be implemented as one. However, if they represent different expectations, then you're facing a *Siamese Twin Problem* (see Item 26 in Herb Sutter's *More Exceptional C++: 40 New Engineering Puzzles, Programming Problems, and Solutions* (Addison-Wesley). For our example, let's assume that we can deal with these two virtual functions the easy way.

By introducing the `DepositUI`, `WithdrawalUI`, and `TransferUI` classes, we've broken the dependency among the three transactions. The three transactions are no longer dependent on the concrete `UI` class, but on a lightweight abstraction that represents only those operations that the relevant transaction truly requires. If we now introduce the `SpeedTransfer` transaction, we can also introduce the `SpeedTransferUI` abstraction, so none of the other transactions will be affected by the changes introduced in the `UI` class.

"Oh, yes, I get it! This way we have fulfilled three design principles!" You sound impressed. "We've introduced an abstraction to cut the dependency on the implementation details of the user interface. That must be the DIP. And we've followed the ISP and removed the dependencies among the different transactions. And as a bonus, we have also nicely grouped the things that truly belong together. That's the SRP, right? That's amazing! Let's celebrate!"

Wait, wait, wait…Before you go off to uncork your best bottle of champagne to celebrate solving this dependency problem, let's take a closer look at the problem. So yes, you are correct, we follow the ISP by separating the concerns of the `UI` class. By segregating it into three client-specific interfaces, we've resolved the dependency situation among the three transactions. This is indeed the ISP. Very nice!

Unfortunately, we haven't resolved our architectural problem yet, so no, we do not follow the DIP (yet). But I get the misunderstanding: it does appear as if we have inverted the dependencies. Figure 2-3 shows that we have really introduced an inversion of dependencies: instead of depending on the concrete `UI` class, we now depend on abstractions.

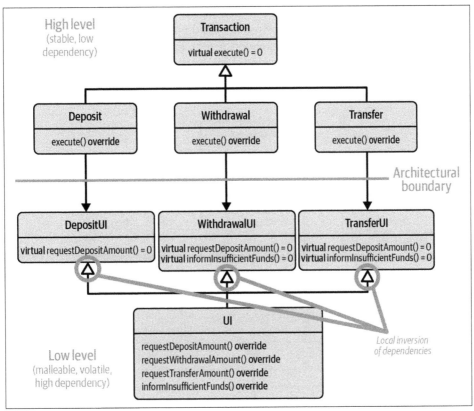

Figure 2-3. The local inversion of dependencies by introduction of three abstract UI classes

However, what we have introduced is a *local* inversion of dependencies. Yes, a local inversion only, not a global inversion. From an architectural point of view, we still have a dependency from the high level (our transaction classes) to the low level (our UI functionality). So no, it is not enough to *just* introduce an abstraction. It's also important to consider *where* to introduce the abstraction. Robert Martin expressed this with the following two points:[20]

1. High-level modules should not depend on low-level modules. Both should depend on abstractions.

2. Abstractions should not depend on details. Details should depend on abstractions.

---

20 Martin, *Clean Architecture*.

The first point clearly expresses an essential property of an architecture: the high level, i.e., the stable part(s) of our software, should not depend on the low level, i.e., the implementation details. That dependency should be inverted, meaning that the low level should depend on the high level. Luckily, the second point gives us an idea how to achieve that: we assign the three abstractions to the high level. Figure 2-4 illustrates the dependencies when we consider abstractions part of the high level.

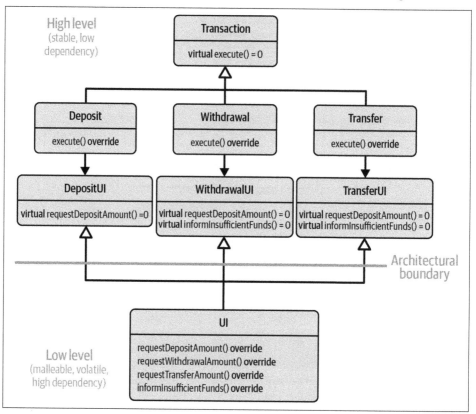

Figure 2-4. Inversion of dependencies by assigning the abstractions to the high level

By assigning the abstractions to the high level and by making the high level the owner of the abstractions, we truly follow the DIP: all arrows now run from the low level to the high level. Now we do have a proper architecture.

"Wait a second!" You look a little confused. "That's it? All we need is to perform a mental shift of the architectural boundary?" Well, it may very well be more than just a mental shift. This may result in moving the dependent header files for the UI classes from one module to another and also completely rearranging the dependent include statements. It's not just a mental shift—it is a reassignment of ownership.

"But now we no longer group the things that belong together," you argue. "The user interface functionality is now spread across both levels. Isn't that a violation of the SRP?" No, it isn't. On the contrary, only after assigning the abstractions to the high level do we now properly follow the SRP. It's not the UI classes that belong together; it's the transaction classes and the dependent UI abstractions that should be grouped together. Only in this way can we steer the dependency in the right direction; only in this way do we have an architecture. Thus, for a proper dependency inversion, the abstraction *must* be owned by the high level.

Dependency Inversion in a Plug-In Architecture

Perhaps this fact makes more sense if we consider the situation depicted in Figure 2-5. Imagine you have created the next-generation text editor. The core of this new text editor is represented by the Editor class on the lefthand side. To ensure that this text editor will be successful, you want to make sure that the fan community can participate in the development. Therefore, one vital ingredient for your success is the ability of the community to add new functionality in the form of plug-ins. However, the initial setting is pretty flawed from an architectural point of view and will hardly satisfy your fan community: the Editor directly depends on the concrete VimMode Plugin class. Since the Editor class is part of the high level of the architecture, which you should consider as your own realm, the VimModePlugin is part of the low level of the architecture, which is the realm of your fan community. Since the Editor directly depends on the VimModePlugin, and because that essentially means that your community can define their interfaces as they please, you would have to change the editor for every new plug-in. As much as you love to work on your brainchild, there's only so much time you can devote to adapting to different kinds of plug-ins. Unfortunately, your fan community will soon be disappointed and move on to another text editor.

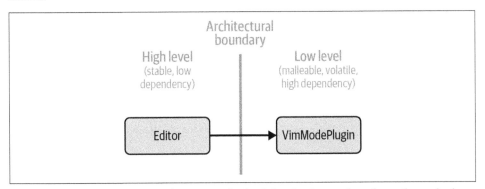

Figure 2-5. Broken plug-in architecture: the high-level Editor class depends on the low-level VimModePlugin class

Of course, that shouldn't happen. In the given `Editor` example, it certainly isn't a good idea to make the `Editor` class depend on all the concrete plug-ins. Instead, you should reach for an abstraction, for instance, in the form of a `Plugin` base class. The `Plugin` class now represents the abstraction for all kinds of plug-ins. However, it doesn't make sense to introduce the abstraction in the low level of the architecture (see Figure 2-6). Your `Editor` would still depend on the whims of your fan community.

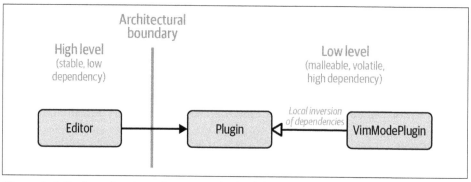

Figure 2-6. Broken plug-in architecture: the high-level `Editor` *class depends on the low-level* `Plugin` *class*

This misdirected dependency also becomes apparent when looking at the source code:

```
//---- <thirdparty/Plugin.h> ----------------

class Plugin { /*...*/ };  // Defines the requirements for plugins


//---- <thirdparty/VimModePlugin.h> ----------------

#include <thirdparty/Plugin.h>

class VimModePlugin : public Plugin { /*...*/ };


//---- <yourcode/Editor.h> ----------------

#include <thirdparty/Plugin.h>  // Wrong direction of dependencies!

class Editor { /*...*/ };
```

The only way to build a proper plug-in architecture is to assign the abstraction to the high level. The abstraction *must* belong to *you*, not to your fan community. Figure 2-7 demonstrates that this resolves the architectural dependency and frees your `Editor` class from the dependencies on plug-ins. This resolves both the DIP, because the dependency is properly inverted, and the SRP, because the abstraction belongs to the high level.

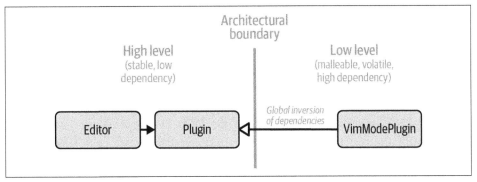

Figure 2-7. Correct plug-in architecture: the low-level VimModePlugin class depends on the high-level Plugin class

A look at the source code reveals that the direction of dependencies has been fixed: the VimModePlugin depends on your code, and not vice versa:

```
//---- <yourcode/Plugin.h> ----------------

class Plugin { /*...*/ };  // Defines the requirements for plugins


//---- <yourcode/Editor.h> ----------------

#include <yourcode/Plugin.h>

class Editor { /*...*/ };


//---- <thirdparty/VimModePlugin.h> ---------------

#include <yourcode/Plugin.h>  // Correct direction of dependencies

class VimModePlugin : public Plugin { /*...*/ };
```

Again, to get a proper dependency inversion, the abstraction must be owned by the high level. In this context, the Plugin class represents the set of requirements that needs to be fulfilled by all plug-ins (see again "Guideline 6: Adhere to the Expected Behavior of Abstractions" on page 44). The Editor defines and thus owns these requirements. It doesn't depend on them. Instead, the different plug-ins depend on the requirements. That is dependency inversion. Hence, the DIP is not just about the introduction of an abstraction but also about the ownership of that abstraction.

Dependency Inversion via Templates

So far I might have given you the impression that the DIP is concerned with only inheritance hierarchies and base classes. However, dependency inversion is also achieved with templates. In that context, however, the question of ownership is resolved automatically. As an example, let's consider the `std::copy_if()` algorithm:

```
template< typename InputIt, typename OutputIt, typename UnaryPredicate >
OutputIt copy_if( InputIt first, InputIt last, OutputIt d_first,
                  UnaryPredicate pred );
```

This `copy_if()` algorithm also adheres to the DIP. The dependency inversion is achieved with the concepts `InputIt`, `OutputIt`, and `UnaryPredicate`. These three concepts represent the requirements on the passed iterators and predicates that need to be fulfilled by calling code. By specifying these requirements through concepts, i.e., by owning these concepts, `std::copy_if()` makes other code depend on itself and does not itself depend on other code. This dependency structure is depicted in Figure 2-8: both containers and predicates depend on the requirements expressed by the corresponding algorithm. Thus, if we consider the architecture within the Standard Library, then `std::copy_if()` is part of the high level of the architecture, and containers and predicates (function objects, lambdas, etc.) are part of the low level of the architecture.

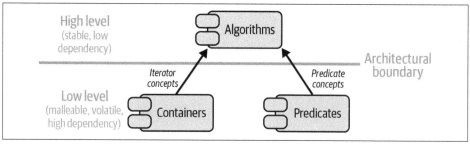

Figure 2-8. Dependency structure of the STL algorithms

Dependency Inversion via Overload Sets

Inheritance hierarchies and concepts are not the only means to invert dependencies. Any kind of abstraction is able to do so. Therefore, it shouldn't come as a surprise that overload sets also enable you to follow the DIP. As you have seen in "Guideline 8: Understand the Semantic Requirements of Overload Sets" on page 56, overload sets represent an abstraction and, as such, a set of semantic requirements and expectations. In comparison to base classes and concepts, though, there is unfortunately no code that explicitly describes the requirements. But if these requirements are owned by a higher level in your architecture, you can achieve dependency inversion. Consider, for instance, the following `Widget` class template:

```
//---- <Widget.h> ----------------

#include <utility>

template< typename T >
struct Widget
{
   T value;
};

template< typename T >
void swap( Widget<T>& lhs, Widget<T>& rhs )
{
   using std::swap;
   swap( lhs.value, rhs.value );
}
```

Widget owns a data member of an unknown type T. Despite the fact that T is unknown, it is possible to implement a custom swap() function for Widget by building on the semantic expectations of the swap() function. This implementation works, as long as the swap() function for T adheres to all expectations for swap() and follows the LSP:[21]

```
#include <Widget.h>
#include <assert>
#include <cstdlib>
#include <string>

int main()
{
   Widget<std::string> w1{ "Hello" };
   Widget<std::string> w2{ "World" };

   swap( w1, w2 );

   assert( w1.value == "World" );
   assert( w2.value == "Hello" );

   return EXIT_SUCCESS;
}
```

In consequence, the Widget swap() function itself follows the expectations and adds to the overload set, similar to what a derived class would do. The dependency structure for the swap() overload set is shown in Figure 2-9. Since the requirements, or the expectations, for the overload set are part of the high level of the architecture, and since any implementation of swap() depends on these expectations, the dependency

---

21 I know what you're thinking. However, it was just a matter of time until you encountered a "Hello World" example.

runs from the low level toward the high level. The dependency is therefore properly inverted.

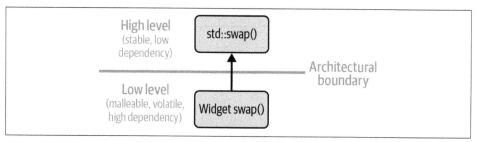

Figure 2-9. Dependency structure of the `swap()` *overload set*

Dependency Inversion Principle Versus Single-Responsibility Principle

As we have seen, the DIP is fulfilled by properly assigning ownership and by properly grouping the things that truly belong. From that perspective, it sounds plausible to consider the DIP as just another special case of the SRP (similar to the ISP). However, hopefully you see that the DIP is more than that. As the DIP, in contrast to the SRP, is very much concerned with the architectural point of view, I consider it a vital piece of advice to build proper global dependency structures.

To summarize, in order to build a proper architecture with a proper dependency structure, it's essential to pay attention to the ownership of abstractions. Since abstractions represent requirements on the implementations, they should be part of the high level to steer all dependencies toward the high level.

> ## Guideline 9: Pay Attention to the Ownership of Abstractions
>
> - Keep in mind that in a proper architecture, low-level implementation details depend on high-level abstractions.
> - Adhere to the Dependency Inversion Principle (DIP), and assign abstractions to the high level of an architecture.
> - Make sure abstractions are *owned* by the high level, not by the low level.

Guideline 10: Consider Creating an Architectural Document

Let's chat a little about your architecture. Let me start with a very simple question: do you have an architectural document? Any plan or description that summarizes the major points and fundamental decisions of your architecture and that shows the high levels, the low levels, and the dependencies between them? If your answer is yes, then you're free to skip this guideline and continue with the next one. If your answer is no, however, then let me ask a few follow-up questions. Do you have a *Continuous Integration* (CI) environment? Do you use automated tests? Do you apply static code analysis tools? All yes? Good, there's still hope. The only remaining question is: why don't you have an architectural document?

"Oh, come on, don't turn a mosquito into an elephant. A missing architectural document is not the end of the world! After all, we are Agile, we can change things quickly!" Imagine my completely blank expression, followed by a long sigh. Well, honestly, I was afraid this would be your explanation. It's unfortunately what I hear far too often. There may be a misunderstanding: the ability to quickly change things is not the point of an Agile methodology. Sadly, I also have to tell you that your answer doesn't make any sense. You could just as well have answered with "After all, we like chocolate!" or "After all, we wear carrots around our necks!" To explain what I mean, I will quickly summarize the point of the Agile methodology and then subsequently explain why you should invest in an architectural document.

The expectation that Agile methods help to change things quickly is pretty widespread. However, as several authors in the recent past have clarified, the major, and probably only, point of the Agile methodology is to get quick feedback.[22] In Agile methods, the entire software development process is built around it: quick feedback due to business practices (such as planning, small releases, and acceptance tests), quick feedback due to team practices (e.g., collective ownership, CI, and stand-up meetings), and quick feedback due to technical practices (such as test-driven development, refactoring, and pair programming). However, contrary to popular belief, the quick feedback does not mean that you can change your software quickly and easily. Though quick feedback is, of course, key to quickly knowing that something has to be done, you gain the ability to quickly change your software only with good software design and architecture. These two save you the Herculean effort to change things; quick feedback only tells you something is broken.

"OK, you're right. I get your point—it is important to pay attention to good software design and architecture. But what's the point of an architectural document?" I'm glad we agree. And that is an excellent question. I see we are making progress. To explain the purpose of an architectural document, let me give you another definition of architecture:[23]

---

22 The point is, for instance, made by Robert C. Martin, one of the signees of the Agile manifesto, in his book *Clean Agile: Back to Basics* (Pearson). A second good summary is given by Bertrand Meyer in *Agile! The Good, the Hype and the Ugly* (Springer). Finally, you can also consult the second edition of James Shore's book *The Art of Agile Development* (O'Reilly). A good talk on the misuse of the term *Agile* is Dave Thomas's "Agile Is Dead" presentation (*https://oreil.ly/LJZN1*) from GOTO 2015.

23 Quoted in Martin Fowler, "Who Needs an Architect?" *IEEE Software* 20, no. 5 (2003), 11–13, *https://doi.org/10.1109/MS.2003.1231144.*

In most successful software projects, the expert developers working on that project have a shared understanding of the system design. This shared understanding is called 'architecture.'

—Ralph Johnson

Ralph Johnson describes *architecture* as the shared understanding of a codebase—the global vision. Let's assume that there is no architectural document, nothing that summarizes the global picture—the global vision of your codebase. Let's also assume that you believe you have a very clear idea of the architecture of your codebase. Then here are a few more questions: how many developers are on your team? Are you certain that all of these developers are familiar with the architecture in your head? Are you certain that all of them share the same vision? Are you certain that they all help you move forward *in the same direction*?

If your answers are yes, then you might not have gotten the point yet. It is fairly certain that every developer has different experiences and a slightly different terminology. It is also fairly certain that every developer sees the code differently and has a slightly different idea of the current architecture. And this slightly different view of the current state of affairs may lead to a slightly different vision for the future. While this might not be immediately evident over a short period of time, there is a good chance that surprises will happen in the long run. Misunderstandings. Misinterpretations. This is exactly the point of an architectural document: one common document that unifies the ideas, visions, and essential decisions in one place; helps maintain and communicate the state of the architecture; and helps avoid any misunderstandings.

This document also preserves ideas, visions, and decisions. Imagine that one of your leading software architects, one of the brains behind the architecture of your codebase, leaves the organization. Without a document with the fundamental decisions, this loss of manpower will also cause a loss of essential information about your codebase. As a consequence, you will lose consistency in the vision of your architecture and also, more importantly, some confidence to adapt or change architectural decisions. No new hire will ever be able to replace that knowledge and experience, and no one will be able to extract all that information from the code. Thus, the code will become more rigid, more "legacy." This promotes decisions to rewrite large parts of the code, with questionable outcomes, as the new code will initially lack a lot of the wisdom of the old code.[24] Thus, without an architectural document, your long-term success is at stake.

---

24 Joel Spolsky, whom you may know as the author of the *Joel on Software* blog (*https://www.joelonsoft ware.com*), and also as one of the creators of Stack Overflow, named the decision to rewrite a large piece of code from scratch "the single worst strategic mistake that any company can make" (*https://oreil.ly/ndLhY*).

The value in such an architectural document becomes obvious if we take a look at how seriously architecture is taken at construction sites. Construction is not even going to start without a plan. A plan that everyone agrees to. Or let's imagine what would happen if there was no plan: "Hey, I said the garage should be to the left of the house!" "But I built it to the left of the house." "Yes, but I meant my left, not your left!"

This is exactly the kind of problem that can be avoided by investing time in an architectural document. "Yes, yes, you're right," you admit, "but such a document is *soooo* much work. And all of this information is in the code anyway. It adapts with the code, while the document goes out of date *soooo* quickly!" Well, not if you're doing it properly. An architectural document shouldn't go out of date quickly because it should primarily reflect the big picture of your codebase. It shouldn't contain the little details that indeed can change very often; instead, it should contain the overall structure, the connections between key players, and the major technological decisions. All these things are not expected to change (although we all agree that "not expected to change" doesn't mean that they won't change; after all, *soft*ware is expected to change). And yes, you are correct: these details are, of course, also part of the code. After all, the code contains all the details and thus can be said to represent the ultimate truth. However, it doesn't help if the information is not easy to come by, is hidden from plain sight, and requires an archaeological effort to extract.

I am also aware that, in the beginning, the endeavor to create an architectural document does sound like a lot of work. An enormous amount of work. All I can do is encourage you to get started somehow. Initially, you do not have to document your architecture in all its glory, but maybe you start with only the most fundamental structural decisions. Some tools can already use this information to compare your assumed architectural state and its actual state.[25] Over time, more and more architectural information can be added, documented, and maybe even tested by tools, which leads to more and more commonly available, established wisdom for your entire team.

"But how do I keep this document up to date?" you ask. Of course, you'll have to maintain this document, integrate new decisions, update old decisions, etc. However, since this document should only contain information about the aspects that do not often change, there should be no need to constantly touch and refactor it. It should be enough to schedule a short meeting of the senior developers every one or two weeks to discuss if and how the architecture has evolved. Thus, it is hard to imagine this

---

25 One possible tool for this purpose is the Axivion Suite (*https://oreil.ly/32kue*). You start by defining architectural boundaries between your modules, which can be used by the tool to check if the architectural dependencies are upheld. Another tool with such capabilities is the Sparx Systems Enterprise Architect (*https://oreil.ly/1oC3Y*).

document becoming a bottleneck in the development process. In this regard, consider this document a bank deposit safe: it is invaluable to have all of the accumulated decisions of the past when you need them and to keep the information secure, but you wouldn't open it every single day.

In summary, the benefits of having an architectural document by far outweigh the risks and efforts. The architectural document should be considered an essential part of any project and an integral part of the maintenance and communication efforts. It should be considered equally important as a CI environment or automated tests.

Guideline 10: Consider Creating an Architectural Document

- Understand that an architectural document serves the purpose of maintaining and communicating the current state of the architecture.
- Use tools to support and help you test the current state of your architecture against the expected state.

CHAPTER 3

The Purpose of Design Patterns

Visitor, *Strategy*, *Decorator*. These are all names of design patterns that we'll deal with in the upcoming chapters. However, before taking a detailed look at each of these design patterns, I should give you an idea about the general purpose of a design pattern. Thus in this chapter, we will first take a look at the fundamental properties of design patterns, why you would want to know about them and use them.

In "Guideline 1: Understand the Importance of Software Design" on page 2, I already used the term *design pattern* and explained on which level of software development you use them. However, I have not yet explained in detail what a design pattern *is*. That will be the topic of "Guideline 11: Understand the Purpose of Design Patterns" on page 80: you will understand that a design pattern has a name that expresses an intent, introduces an abstraction that helps to decouple software entities, and has been proven over the years.

In "Guideline 12: Beware of Design Pattern Misconceptions" on page 85, I will focus on several misconceptions about design patterns and explain what a design pattern *is not*. I will try to convince you that design patterns are not about implementation details and do not represent language-specific solutions to common problems. I will also do my best to show you that they are not limited to object-oriented programming nor to dynamic polymorphism.

In "Guideline 13: Design Patterns Are Everywhere" on page 92, I will demonstrate that it's hard to avoid design patterns. They are everywhere! You will realize that the C++ Standard Library in particular is full of design patterns and makes good use of their strengths.

In "Guideline 14: Use a Design Pattern's Name to Communicate Intent" on page 97, I will make the point that part of the strength of a design pattern is the ability to communicate intent by using its name. Thus I will show you how much more information and meaning you can add to your code by using the name of a design pattern.

Guideline 11: Understand the Purpose of Design Patterns

There's a good chance that you have heard about design patterns before and a fairly good chance that you've used some of them in your programming career. Design patterns are nothing new: they have been around at least since the Gang of Four (GoF) released their book on design patterns in 1994.[1] And while there are always critics, their special value has been acknowledged throughout the software industry. Yet, despite the long existence and importance of design patterns, despite all the knowledge and accumulated wisdom, there are many misconceptions about them, especially in the C++ community.

To use design patterns productively, as a first step you need to understand what design patterns are. A design pattern:

- Has a name
- Carries an intent
- Introduces an abstraction
- Has been proven

A Design Pattern Has a Name

First of all, a design pattern has a name. While this sounds very obvious and necessary, it is indeed a fundamental property of a design pattern. Let's assume that the two of us are working on a project together and are tasked with finding a solution to a problem. Imagine I told you, "I would use a *Visitor* for that."[2] Not only would this tell you what I understand to be the real problem, but it would also give you a precise idea about the kind of solution I'm proposing.

---

1 The Gang of Four, or simply GoF, is a commonly used reference to the four authors Erich Gamma, Richard Helm, Ralph E. Johnson, and John Vlissides and their book on design patterns: *Design Patterns: Elements of Reusable Object-Oriented Software* (Prentice Hall). The GoF book still is, after several decades, *the* reference on design patterns. Throughout the rest of this book, I will refer to either the GoF book, the GoF patterns, or the characteristic, object-oriented GoF style.

2 If you do not know the *Visitor* design pattern yet, don't worry. I will introduce the pattern in Chapter 4.

The name of a design pattern allows us to communicate on a very high level and to exchange a lot of information with very few words:

> ME: I would use a Visitor for that.
>
> YOU: I don't know. I thought of using a Strategy.
>
> ME: Yes, you may have a point there. But since we'll have to extend operations fairly often, we probably should consider a Decorator as well.

By just using the names *Visitor*, *Strategy*, and *Decorator*, we've discussed the evolution of the codebase, and described how we expect things to change and to be extended in years to come.[3] Without these names, we would have a much harder time expressing our ideas:

> ME: I think we should create a system that allows us to extend the operations without the need to modify existing types again and again.
>
> YOU: I don't know. Rather than new operations, I would expect new types to be added frequently. So I prefer a solution that allows me to add types easily. But to reduce coupling to the implementation details, which is to be expected, I would suggest a way to extract implementation details from existing types by introducing a variation point.
>
> ME: Yes, you may have a point there. But since we'll have to extend operations fairly often, we probably should consider designing the system in such a way that we can build on and reuse a given implementation easily.

Do you see the difference? Do you *feel* the difference? Without names, we have to talk about a lot more details explicitly. Obviously this kind of precise communication is possible only if we share the same understanding of design patterns. That is why it's so important to know about design patterns and to talk about them.

A Design Pattern Carries an Intent

By using the name of a design pattern, you can express your intent concisely and limit possible misunderstandings. This leads to the second property of a design pattern: an intent. The *name* of a design pattern conveys its *intent*. If you use the name of a design pattern, you implicitly state what you consider to be the problem and what you see as a solution.

Hopefully you realized that in our little conversion, we weren't talking about any kind of implementation. We didn't talk about implementation details, any features, or any particular C++ standard. We didn't even talk about any particular programming language. And please don't assume that by giving you the name of a design pattern I have implicitly told you how to implement the solution. That is not what a design pattern is about. On the contrary: the name should tell you about the structure

---

3 The Strategy design pattern will be explained in detail in Chapter 5, the Decorator design pattern in Chapter 9.

that I propose, about how I plan to manage dependencies and about how I expect the system to evolve. That is the intent.

In fact, many design patterns have a similar structure. In the GoF book, many of the design patterns look very much alike, which, of course, raises a lot of confusion and questions. For instance, structurally, there appears to be almost no difference between the Strategy, the *Command*, and the *Bridge* design patterns.[4] However, their intent is very different and you would therefore use them to solve different problems. As you will see in various examples in the following chapters, there are almost always many different implementations you can choose from.

A Design Pattern Introduces an Abstraction

A design pattern always provides some way to reduce dependencies by introducing some kind of abstraction. This means that a design pattern is always concerned with managing the interaction between software entities and decoupling pieces of your software. For example, consider the Strategy design pattern, one of the original GoF design patterns, in Figure 3-1. Without going into too much detail, the Strategy design pattern introduces an abstraction in the form of the Strategy base class. This base class decouples the Strategy user (the Context class in the high level of your architecture) from the implementation details of the concrete strategies (Concrete StrategyA and ConcreteStrategyB in the low level of your architecture). As such, Strategy fulfills the properties of a design pattern.[5]

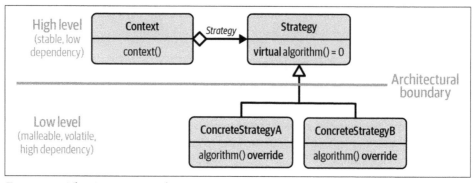

Figure 3-1. The GoF Strategy design pattern

---

4 I mention only the design patterns that I will explain in later chapters (see the Strategy and *Command* design patterns in Chapter 5 and the *Bridge* design pattern in "Guideline 28: Build Bridges to Remove Physical Dependencies" on page 250). There are a few more design patterns that share the same structure.

5 If you are unfamiliar with the Strategy design pattern, rest assured that Chapter 5 will provide much more information, including several code examples.

A similar example is the *Factory Method* design pattern (yet another GoF design pattern; see Figure 3-2). The intent of *Factory Method* is to decouple from the creation of specific products. For that purpose, it introduces two abstractions in the form of the `Product` and `Creator` base classes, which architecturally reside in the high level. The implementation details, given by means of the `ConcreteProduct` and `Concrete Creator` classes, reside on the low level of the architecture. With this architectural structure, *Factory Method* also qualifies as a design pattern: it has a name, the intent to decouple, and it introduces abstractions.

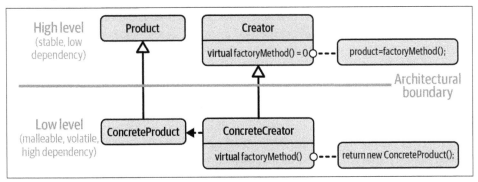

Figure 3-2. The GoF Factory Method design pattern

Note that the abstraction introduced by a design pattern is not necessarily introduced by means of a base class. As I will show you in the following sections and chapters, this abstraction can be introduced in many different ways, for instance, by means of templates or simply by function overloading. Again, a design pattern does not imply any specific implementation.

As a counter example, let us consider the `std::make_unique()` function:

```
namespace std {

template< typename T, typename... Args >
unique_ptr<T> make_unique( Args&&... args );

} // namespace std
```

In the C++ community, we often talk about the `std::make_unique()` function as a *factory function*. It's important to note that although the term *factory function* gives the impression that `std::make_unique()` is one example of the *Factory Method* design pattern, this impression is incorrect. A design pattern helps you to decouple by introducing an abstraction, which allows you to customize and defer implementation details. In particular, the intent of the *Factory Method* design pattern is to introduce a *customization point* for the purpose of object instantiation. `std::make_unique()` does not provide such a *customization point*: if you use `std::make_unique()`, you know that you will get a `std::unique_ptr` to the type you are asking for and that the instance will be created by means of `new`:

```
// This will create a 'Widget' by means of calling 'new'
auto ptr = std::make_unique<Widget>( /* some Widget arguments */ );
```

Since `std::make_unique()` doesn't provide you with any way to customize that behavior, it can't help to reduce coupling between entities, and thus it cannot serve the purpose of a design pattern.[6] Still, `std::make_unique()` is a recurring solution for a specific problem. In other words, it is a pattern. However, it isn't a *design pattern* but an *implementation pattern*. It is a popular solution to encapsulate implementation details (in this case, the generation of an instance of `Widget`), but it does not abstract from what you get or how it will be created. As such, it is part of the *Implementation Details* level but not the *Software Design* level (refer back to Figure 1-1).

The introduction of abstractions is the key to decoupling software entities from one another and to designing for change and extension. There is no abstraction in the `std::make_unique()` function template, and thus no way for you to extend the functionality (you cannot even properly overload or specialize). In contrast, the *Factory Method* design pattern *does* provide an abstraction from *what* is created and *how* this something is created (including actions before and after the instantiation). Due to that abstraction you'll be able to write new factories at a later point, without having to change existing code. Therefore, the design pattern helps you decouple and extend your software, while `std::make_unique()` is only an *implementation pattern*.

A Design Pattern Has Been Proven

Last but not least, a design pattern has been proven over the years. The Gang of Four did not collect all possible solutions, only solutions that were commonly used in different codebases to solve the same problem (although potentially with different implementations). Thus a solution has to demonstrate its value several times before it emerges as a pattern.

To summarize: a design pattern is a proven, named solution, which expresses a very specific intent. It introduces some kind of abstraction, which helps to decouple software entities and thus helps to manage the interaction between software entities. Just as we should use the term *Design* to denote the art of managing dependencies and decoupling (see "Guideline 1: Understand the Importance of Software Design" on page 2), we should use the term *Design Pattern* accurately and on purpose.

---

6 This may be a controversial example. Since I know the C++ community, I know that you may have a different opinion. However, I stand by mine: due to its definition, `std::make_unique()` is incapable of decoupling software entities and therefore does not play a role on the level of software design. It's merely an implementation detail (but a valuable and useful one).

> ## Guideline 11: Understand the Purpose of Design Patterns
>
> - Understand that design patterns are proven, named solutions with an intent to decouple.
> - Realize that design patterns introduce some kind of abstraction.
> - Keep in mind that design patterns are targeted at software design, i.e., help to manage dependencies.
> - Be aware of the difference between design patterns and implementation patterns.

Guideline 12: Beware of Design Pattern Misconceptions

The last section focused on explaining the purpose of a design pattern: the combination of a name, an intent, and some form of abstraction to decouple software entities. However, just as it's important to understand what a design pattern *is*, it's important to understand what a design pattern *is not*. Unfortunately, there are several common misconceptions about design patterns:

- Some consider design patterns as a goal and as a guarantee for achieving good software quality.
- Some argue that design patterns are based on a particular implementation and thus are language-specific idioms.
- Some say that design patterns are limited to object-oriented programming and dynamic polymorphism.
- Some consider design patterns outdated or even obsolete.

These misconceptions come as no surprise since we rarely talk about design but instead focus on features and language mechanics (see "Guideline 1: Understand the Importance of Software Design" on page 2). For that reason, I will debunk the first three misconceptions in this guideline and will deal with the fourth one in the next section.

Design Patterns Are Not a Goal

Some developers love design patterns. They are so infatuated with them that they try to solve all their problems by means of design patterns, whether it is reasonable or not. Of course, this way of thinking potentially increases the complexity of code and decreases comprehensibility, which may prove to be counterproductive. Consequently, this overuse of design patterns may result in frustration in other developers, in a bad reputation of design patterns in general, or even in rejection of the general idea of patterns.

To spell it out: design patterns are *not* a goal. They are a means to achieve a goal. They may be part of the solution. But they are not a goal. As Venkat Subramaniam would say: if you get up in the morning, thinking "What design pattern will I use today?", then this is a telltale sign that you are missing the purpose of design patterns.[7] There is no reward, no medal, for using as many design patterns as possible. The use of a design pattern shouldn't create complexity but, on the contrary, decrease complexity. The code should become simpler, more comprehensible, and easier to change and maintain, simply because the design pattern should help to resolve dependencies and create a better structure. If using a design pattern leads to higher complexity and creates problems for other developers, it apparently isn't the right solution.

Just to be clear: I'm not telling you not to use design patterns. I'm merely telling you not to overuse them, just as I would tell you not to overuse any other tool. It always depends on the problem. For instance, a hammer is a great tool, as long as your problem is nails. As soon as your problem changes to screws, a hammer becomes a somewhat inelegant tool.[8] To properly use design patterns, to know when to use them and when *not* to use them, it's so important to have a firm grasp of them, to understand their intent and structural properties, and to apply them wisely.

Design Patterns Are Not About Implementation Details

One of the most common misconceptions about design patterns is that they are based on a specific implementation. This includes the opinion that design patterns are more or less language-specific idioms. This misconception is easy to understand, as many design patterns, in particular the GoF patterns, are usually presented in an object-oriented setting and explained by means of object-oriented examples. In such a context, it's easy to mistake the implementation details for a specific pattern and to assume that both are the same.

Fortunately, it's also easy to demonstrate that design patterns are *not* about implementation details, any particular language feature, or any C++ standard. Let's take a look at different implementations of the same design pattern. And yes, we will start with the classic, object-oriented version of the design pattern.

---

7 Venkat Subramaniam and Andrew Hunt, *Practices of an Agile Developer* (The Pragmatic Programmers, LLC, 2017).

8 Well, it works, in some definition of "works."

Consider the following scenario: we want to draw a given shape.[9] The code snippet demonstrates this by means of a circle, but of course it could be any other kind of shape, like a square or a triangle. For the purpose of drawing, the `Circle` class provides the `draw()` member function:

```
class Circle
{
 public:
   void draw( /*...*/ );  // Implemented in terms of some graphics library
   // ...
};
```

It now appears self-evident that you need to implement the `draw()` function. Without further thought, you might do this by means of a common graphics library such as OpenGL, Metal, Vulcan, or any other graphics library. However, it would be a big design flaw if the `Circle` class provides an implementation of the `draw()` functionality itself: by implementing the `draw()` function directly, you would introduce a strong coupling to your chosen graphics library. This comes with a couple of downsides:

- For every possible application of `Circle`, you would always need the graphics library to be available, even though you might not be interested in graphics but only need it as a geometric primitive.

- Every change to the graphics library might have an effect on the `Circle` class, resulting in necessary modifications, retesting, redeployment, etc.

- Switching to another library in the future would mean everything but a smooth transition.

These problems all have a common source: implementing the `draw()` function directly within the `Circle` class violates the *Single-Responsibility Principle* (SRP; see "Guideline 2: Design for Change" on page 11). The class wouldn't change for a single reason anymore and would strongly depend on that design decision.

The classic object-oriented solution for this problem is to extract the decision about how to draw the circle and introduce an abstraction for that by means of a base class. Introducing such a *variation point* is the effect of the Strategy design pattern (see Figure 3-3).[10]

---

9 I know what you're thinking: "You cannot be serious! There is so many interesting examples out there, but you select the oldest and most boring example in the book!" OK, I admit that might not be the most exciting example to pick. But, still, I have two good reasons to use this example. First, the scenario is so well known that I can assume that no one has trouble understanding it. That means that everyone should be able to follow my arguments about software design. And second, let's agree that it's kind of a tradition in computer science to start with a shape or an animal example. And, of course, I do not want to disappoint traditionalists.

10 Chapter 5 will provide a complete and thorough introduction of the *Strategy* design pattern.

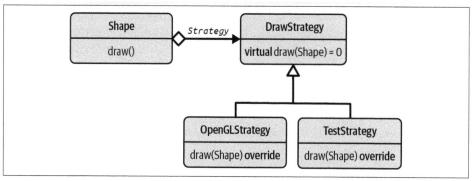

Figure 3-3. The Strategy design pattern applied to drawing circles

The intent of the Strategy design pattern is to define a family of algorithms and encapsulate each one, therefore making them interchangeable. Strategy lets the algorithm vary independently from clients that use it. By introducing the DrawStrategy base class, it becomes possible to easily vary the draw() implementation of the given Circle. This also enables everyone, not just you, to implement a new drawing behavior without modifying existing code and to inject it from the outside into the Circle. This is what we commonly call *dependency injection*:

```cpp
#include <Circle.h>
#include <OpenGLStrategy.h>
#include <cstdlib>
#include <utility>

int main()
{
   // ...

   // Creating the desired drawing strategy for a circle.
   auto strategy =
      std::make_unique<OpenGLStrategy>( /* OpenGL-specific arguments */ );

   // Injecting the strategy into the circle; the circle does not have to know
   // about the specific kind of strategy, but can with blissful ignorance use
   // it via the 'DrawStrategy' abstraction.
   Circle circle( 4.2, std::move(strategy) );
   circle.draw( /*...*/ );

   // ...

   return EXIT_SUCCESS;
}
```

This approach vastly increases the flexibility with respect to different drawing behavior: it factors out all dependencies on specific libraries and other implementation details and thus makes the code more changeable and extensible. For instance, it's now easily possible to provide a special implementation for testing purposes (i.e., a TestStrategy). This demonstrates that the improved flexibility has a very positive impact on the testability of the design.

The Strategy design pattern is one of the classic GoF design patterns. As such, it is often referred to as an object-oriented design pattern and is often considered to require a base class. However, the intent of Strategy is not limited to object-oriented programming. Just as it's possible to use a base class for the abstraction, it is just as easily possible to rely on a template parameter:

```
template< typename DrawStrategy >
class Circle
{
 public:
   void draw( /*...*/ );
};
```

In this form, deciding how to draw the circle happens at compile time: instead of writing a base class DrawStrategy and passing a pointer to a DrawStrategy at run-time, the implementation details for drawing are provided by means of the Draw Strategy template argument. Note that while the template parameter allows you to inject the implementation details from the outside, the Circle is still not depending on any implementation details. Therefore you have still decoupled the Circle class from the used graphics library. In comparison to the runtime approach, though, you will have to recompile every time the DrawStrategy changes.

While it's true that the template-based solution fundamentally changes the properties of the example (i.e., no base class and no virtual functions, no runtime decisions, no single Circle class, but one Circle type for every concrete DrawStrategy), it still implements the intent of the Strategy design pattern perfectly. Thus this demonstrates that a design pattern is not restricted to a particular implementation or a specific form of abstraction.

Design Patterns Are Not Limited to Object-Oriented Programming or Dynamic Polymorphism

Let's consider another use case for the Strategy design pattern: the Standard Library accumulate() function template from the <numeric> header:

```
std::vector<int> v{ 1, 2, 3, 4, 5 };
auto const sum =
   std::accumulate( begin(v), end(v), int{0} );
```

By default, std::accumulate() sums up all elements in the given range. The third argument specifies the initial value for the sum. Since std::accumulate() uses the type of that argument as the return type, the type of the argument is explicitly highlighted as int{0} instead of just 0 to prevent subtle misunderstandings. However, summing up elements is only the tip of the iceberg: if you need to, you can specify how elements are accumulated by providing a fourth argument to `std::accumulate()`. For instance, you could use `std::plus` or `std::multiplies` from the `<functional>` header:

```
std::vector<int> v{ 1, 2, 3, 4, 5 };
auto const sum =
   std::accumulate( begin(v), end(v), int{0}, std::plus<>{} );
auto const product =
   std::accumulate( begin(v), end(v), int{1}, std::multiplies<>{} );
```

By means of the fourth argument, `std::accumulate()` can be used for any kind of reduction operation, and thus the fourth argument represents the implementation of the reduction operation. As such, it enables us to vary the implementation by injecting the details of how the reduction should work from the outside. `std::accumulate()` therefore does not depend on a single, specific implementation but can be customized by anyone to a specific purpose. This represents exactly the intent of the Strategy design pattern.[11]

`std::accumulate()` draws its power from a generic form of the Strategy design pattern. Without the ability to change this behavior, it would be useful in only a very limited number of use cases. Due to the Strategy design pattern, the number of possible uses is endless.[12]

The example of `std::accumulate()` demonstrates that design patterns, even the classic GoF patterns, are not tied to one particular implementation and additionally are not limited to object-oriented programming. Clearly the intent of many of these patterns is also useful for other paradigms like functional or generic programming.[13] Therefore, design patterns are not limited to dynamic polymorphism, either. On the contrary: design patterns work equally well for static polymorphism and can therefore be used in combination with C++ templates.

---

11 You may (correctly) observe that even without the fourth argument you could change how the accumulation works by providing a custom addition operator (i.e., `operator+()`) for the given type. However, that is only of limited use. While you can provide a custom addition operator for user-defined types, you cannot provide a custom addition operator for fundamental types (such as the `int` in the example). Also, it's very questionable to define `operator+()` for anything other than an addition operation (or related operations like the concatenation of strings). Thus, relying on the addition operator would be limiting technically and semantically.

12 In his CppCon 2016 talk "std::accumulate: Exploring an Algorithmic Empire" (*https://oreil.ly/P8qpA*), Ben Deane has impressively demonstrated how powerful `std::accumulate()` is thanks to that fourth argument.

13 For more information about STL algorithms and their functional programming heritage, see Ivan Cukic's excellent introduction to *Functional Programming in C++* (Manning).

To further emphasize the point and to show you an additional example of the Strategy design pattern, consider the declarations for the std::vector and std::set class templates:

```
namespace std {

template< class T
        , class Allocator = std::allocator<T> >
class vector;

template< class Key
        , class Compare = std::less<Key>
        , class Allocator = std::allocator<Key> >
class set;

} // namespace std
```

All containers in the Standard Library (with the exception of std::array) provide you with the opportunity to specify a custom allocator. In the case of std::vector it's the second template argument, and for std::set it's the third argument. All memory requests from the container are handled via the given allocator.

By exposing a template argument for the allocator, the Standard Library containers give you the opportunity to customize memory allocation from the outside. They enable you to define a family of algorithms (in earlier case, an algorithm for the memory acquisition) and encapsulate each one and therefore make them interchangeable. Consequently you're able to vary this algorithm independently from clients (in this case, the containers) that use it.[14]

Having read that description, you should recognize the Strategy design pattern. In this example, Strategy is again based on static polymorphism and implemented by means of a template argument. Clearly, Strategy is not limited to dynamic polymorphism.

While it's obviously true that design patterns in general aren't limited to object-oriented programming or dynamic polymorphism, I should still explicitly state that there are some design patterns whose intent is targeted to alleviate the usual problems in object-oriented programming (e.g., the *Visitor* and *Prototype* design patterns).[15] And of course there are also design patterns focused on functional programming or generic programming (e.g., the *Curiously Recurring Template Pattern*

---

14 Another commonly used name for that form of the Strategy design pattern is *Policy-Based Design*; see "Guideline 19: Use Strategy to Isolate How Things Are Done" on page 140.

15 I will explain the *Visitor* design pattern in Chapter 4 and the *Prototype* design pattern in "Guideline 30: Apply Prototype for Abstract Copy Operations" on page 272.

[CRTP] and *Expression Templates*).[16] While most design patterns are not paradigm centric and their intention can be used in a variety of implementations, some are more specific.

In the upcoming chapters, you'll see examples for both categories. You will see design patterns that have a very general intent and are consequently of general usefulness. Additionally, you will see some design patterns that are more paradigm-specific and, due to that, will fail to be useful outside of their target domain. Still, they all have the main characteristics of design patterns in common: a name, an intent, and some form of abstraction.

In summary: design patterns are not limited to object-oriented programming, nor are they limited to dynamic polymorphism. More specifically, design patterns are not about a particular implementation and they are not language-specific idioms. Instead, they are focused entirely on the intent to decouple software entities in a specific way.

Guideline 12: Beware of Design Pattern Misconceptions

- Consider design patterns as a tool to solve a design problem, not as a goal.
- Be aware that design patterns are not limited to object-oriented programming.
- Bear in mind that design patterns are not limited to dynamic polymorphism.
- Understand that design patterns are not language-specific idioms.

Guideline 13: Design Patterns Are Everywhere

The previous section has demonstrated that design patterns are not limited to object-oriented programming or dynamic polymorphism, that they are not language-specific idioms, and that they are not about a particular implementation. Still, due to these common misconceptions and because we don't consider C++ as solely object-oriented programming language anymore, some people even claim that design patterns are outdated or obsolete.[17]

---

16 Again, I'm referring you to Ivan Cukic's introduction to *Functional Programming in C++*. The *CRTP* design pattern will be the topic of "Guideline 26: Use CRTP to Introduce Static Type Categories" on page 225. For information on *Expression Templates*, a template-based pattern, refer to *the* C++ template reference: David Vandevoorde, Nicolai Josuttis, and Douglas Gregor's *C++ Templates: The Complete Guide* (Addison-Wesley).

17 I would argue that C++ has been a multiparadigm programming language since the moment the first implementation of templates was added to the language in 1989. The impact of templates on the language became clear with the addition of part of the Standard Template Library (STL) to the Standard Library in 1994. Since then, C++ has provided object-oriented, functional, and generic capabilities.

I imagine you're now looking a little skeptical. "Obsolete? Isn't that a little exaggerated?" you ask. Well, unfortunately not. To tell a little war story, in early 2021 I had the honor of giving a virtual talk about design patterns in a German C++ user group. My main objective was to explain what design patterns are and that they are very much in use today. During the talk, I felt good, invigorated in my mission to help people see all the benefits of design patterns, and I sure gave my best to make everybody see the light that knowledge about design patterns brings. Still, a few days after the publication of the talk on YouTube, a user commented on the talk with "Really? Design Patterns in 2021?"

I very much hope that you are now shaking your head in disbelief. Yes, I could not believe it either, especially after having shown that there are hundreds of examples for design patterns in the C++ Standard Library. No, design patterns are neither outdated nor obsolete. Nothing could be further from the truth. To prove that design patterns are still very much alive and relevant, let's consider the updated allocators facility in the C++ Standard Library. Take a look at the following code example that uses allocators from the `std::pmr` (*polymorphic memory resource*) namespace:

```cpp
#include <array>
#include <cstddef>
#include <cstdlib>
#include <memory_resource>
#include <string>
#include <vector>

int main()
{
   std::array<std::byte,1000> raw;  // Note: not initialized!  ❶

   std::pmr::monotonic_buffer_resource
      buffer{ raw.data(), raw.size(), std::pmr::null_memory_resource() };  ❷

   std::pmr::vector<std::pmr::string> strings{ &buffer };  ❸

   strings.emplace_back( "String longer than what SSO can handle" );
   strings.emplace_back( "Another long string that goes beyond SSO" );
   strings.emplace_back( "A third long string that cannot be handled by SSO" );

   // ...

   return EXIT_SUCCESS;
}
```

This example demonstrates how to use a `std::pmr::monotonic_buffer_resource` (*https://oreil.ly/E40Dn*) as allocator to redirect all memory allocations into a predefined byte buffer. Initially we are creating a buffer of 1,000 bytes in the form of a `std::array` (❶). This buffer is provided as a source of memory to a `std::pmr::monotonic_buffer_resource` by means of passing a pointer to the first element (via `raw.data()`) and the size of the buffer (via `raw.size()`) (❷).

The third argument to the `monotonic_buffer_resource` represents a backup allocator, which is used in case the `monotonic_buffer_resource` runs out of memory. Since we don't need additional memory in this case, we use the `std::pmr::null_memory_resource()` function, which gives us a pointer to the standard allocator that always fails to allocate. That means that you can ask as nicely as you want, but the allocator returned by `std::pmr::null_memory_resource()` will always throw an exception when you ask for memory.

The created buffer is passed as allocator to the `strings` vector, which will now acquire all its memory from the initial byte buffer (❸). Furthermore, since the vector forwards the allocator to its elements, even the three strings, which we add by means of the `emplace_back()` function and which are all too long to rely on the *Small String Optimization (SSO)*, will acquire all their memory from the byte buffer. Thus, no dynamic memory is used in the entire example; all memory will be taken from the byte array.[18]

At first glance, this example doesn't look like it requires any design pattern to work. However, the allocator functionality used in this example uses at least four different design patterns: the Template Method design pattern, the Decorator design pattern, the Adapter design pattern, and (again) the Strategy design pattern.

There are even five design patterns if you count the *Singleton* pattern: the `null_memory_resource()` function (❷) is implemented in terms of the *Singleton* pattern:[19] it returns a pointer to a static storage duration object, which is used to guarantee that there is at most one instance of this allocator.

All C++ allocators from the `pmr` namespace, including the allocator returned by `null_memory_resource()` and the `monotonic_buffer_resource`, are derived from the `std::pmr::memory_resource` base class. The first design pattern becomes visible if you look at the `memory_resource` class definition:

---

18 The *Small String Optimization (SSO)* is a common optimization for small strings. Instead of allocating dynamic memory on the heap via the provided allocator, the string would store the small number of characters directly into the stack part of the string. Since a string usually occupies between 24 and 32 bytes on the stack (which is not a C++ standard requirement but a property of common implementations of `std::string`), anything beyond 32 bytes will require a heap allocation. That is the case with the three given strings.

19 *Singleton* is one of the original 23 GoF design patterns. But I will do my best in "Guideline 37: Treat Singleton as an Implementation Pattern, Not a Design Pattern" on page 380 to convince you that *Singleton* is not actually a design pattern but an implementation detail. For that reason, I will refer to *Singleton* not as a design pattern but simply as an implementation pattern.

```
namespace std::pmr {

class memory_resource
{
 public:
   // ... a virtual destructor, some constructors and assignment operators

   [[nodiscard]] void* allocate(size_t bytes, size_t alignment);
   void deallocate(void* p, size_t bytes, size_t alignment);
   bool is_equal(memory_resource const& other) const noexcept;

 private:
   virtual void* do_allocate(size_t bytes, size_t alignment) = 0;
   virtual void do_deallocate(void* p, size_t bytes, size_t alignment) = 0;
   virtual bool do_is_equal(memory_resource const& other) const noexcept = 0;
};

} // namespace std::pmr
```

You may notice that the three functions in the public section of the class have a virtual counterpart in the private section of the class. Whereas the public allocate(), deallocate(), and is_equal() functions represent the user-facing interface of the class, the do_allocate(), do_deallocate(), and do_is_equal() functions represent the interface for derived classes. This separation of concerns is an example of the *Non-Virtual Interface (NVI)* idiom, which itself is an example of the *Template Method* design pattern.[20]

The second design pattern we implicitly use is the Decorator design pattern.[21] Decorator helps you to build a hierarchical layer of allocators and to wrap and extend the functionality of one allocator to another. This idea becomes clearer in this line:

```
std::pmr::monotonic_buffer_resource
    buffer{ raw.data(), raw.size(), std::pmr::null_memory_resource() };
```

By passing the allocator returned by the null_memory_resource() function to the monotonic_buffer_resource, we decorate its functionality. Whenever we ask the monotonic_buffer_resource for memory via the allocate() function, it may forward the call to its backup allocator. This way, we can implement many different kinds of allocators, which in turn can be easily assembled to form a complete memory subsystem with different layers of allocation strategies. This kind of combining and reusing pieces of functionality is the strength of the Decorator design pattern.

---

20 Unfortunately, I won't cover the *Template Method* design pattern in this book. This isn't because it's not important but simply due to a lack of available pages. Please refer to the GoF book for more details.

21 I will give a complete introduction of the Decorator design pattern in Chapter 9.

You may have noticed that in the example code we have used `std::pmr::vector` and `std::pmr::string`. I assume you remember that `std::string` is just a type alias to `std::basic_string<char>`. Knowing that, it probably comes as no surprise that the two types in the `pmr` namespace are also just type aliases:

```
namespace std::pmr {

template< class CharT, class Traits = std::char_traits<CharT> >
using basic_string =
   std::basic_string< CharT, Traits,
                      std::pmr::polymorphic_allocator<CharT> >;

template <class T>
using vector =
   std::vector< T, std::pmr::polymorphic_allocator<T> >;

} // namespace std::pmr
```

These type aliases still refer to the regular `std::vector` and `std::basic_string` classes but do not expose a template parameter for an allocator anymore. Instead, they employ a `std::pmr::polymorphic_allocator` as allocator. This is an example of the Adapter design pattern.[22] The intent of an Adapter is to help you to glue two non-fitting interfaces together. In this case, the `polymorphic_allocator` helps to transmit between the classic, static interface required from the classic C++ allocators and the new, dynamic allocator interface required by `std::pmr::memory_resource`.

The fourth and last design pattern used in our example is, again, the Strategy design pattern. By exposing a template argument for the allocator, Standard Library containers like `std::vector` and `std::string` give you the opportunity to customize memory allocation from outside. This is a static form of the Strategy design pattern and has the same intent as customizing algorithms (see also "Guideline 12: Beware of Design Pattern Misconceptions" on page 85).

This example impressively demonstrates, that design patterns are far from being obsolete. On closer examination, we see them everywhere: any kind of abstraction and any attempt to decouple software entities and introduce flexibility and extensibility is very likely based on some design pattern. For that reason, it definitely helps to know about the different design patterns and to understand their intent to recognize them and apply them whenever it is necessary and appropriate.

---

22 The Adapter design pattern will be the topic of "Guideline 24: Use Adapters to Standardize Interfaces" on page 198.

Guideline 13: Design Patterns Are Everywhere

- Understand that any kind of abstraction and any attempt to decouple likely represents a known design pattern.

- Learn about the different design patterns and understand their intent to decouple.

- Apply design patterns based on their intent whenever necessary.

Guideline 14: Use a Design Pattern's Name to Communicate Intent

In the last two sections, you learned what a design pattern is, what it's not, and that design patterns are everywhere. You also learned that every design pattern has a name, which expresses a clear, concise, and unambiguous intent. Hence, the name carries meaning.[23] By using the name of a design pattern you can express what the problem is and which solution you've chosen to solve the problem, and you can describe how the code is expected to evolve.

Consider, for instance, the Standard Library `accumulate()` function:

```
template< class InputIt, class T, class BinaryOperation >
constexpr T accumulate( InputIt first, InputIt last, T init,
                        BinaryOperation op );
```

The third template parameter is named `BinaryOperation`. While this does communicate the fact that the passed callable is required to take two arguments, the name does not communicate the intent of the parameter. To express the intent more clearly, consider calling it `BinaryReductionStrategy`:

```
template< class InputIt, class T, class BinaryReductionStrategy >
constexpr T accumulate( InputIt first, InputIt last, T init,
                        BinaryReductionStrategy op );
```

Both the term *Reduction* and the name *Strategy* carry meaning for every C++ programmer. Therefore, you've now captured and expressed your intent much more clearly: the parameter enables *dependency injection* of a binary operation, which allows you to specify how the reduction operation works. Therefore, the parameter solves the problem of customization. Still, as you will see in Chapter 5, the Strategy design pattern communicates that there are certain expectations for the operation. You can only specify how the reduction operation works; you cannot redefine what

---

23 Good names always carry meaning. This is why they are so fundamentally important.

accumulate() does. If that's what you want to express, you should use the name of the *Command* design pattern:[24]

```
template< class InputIt, class UnaryCommand >
constexpr UnaryCommand
    for_each( InputIt first, InputIt last, UnaryCommand f );
```

The std::for_each() algorithm allows you to apply any kind of unary operation to a range of elements. To express this intent, the second template parameter could be named UnaryCommand, which unambiguously expresses that there are (nearly) no expectations for the operation.

Another example from the Standard Library shows how much value the name of a design pattern can bring to a piece of code:

```
#include <cstdlib>
#include <iostream>
#include <string>
#include <variant>

struct Print
{
   void operator()(int i) const {
      std::cout << "int: " << i << '\n';
   }
   void operator()(double d) const {
      std::cout << "double: " << d << '\n';
   }
   void operator()(std::string const& s) const {
      std::cout << "string: " << s << '\n';
   }
};

int main()
{
   std::variant<int,double,std::string> v{};   ❶

   v = "C++ Variant example";   ❷

   std::visit(Print{}, v);   ❸

   return EXIT_SUCCESS;
}
```

In the main() function, we create a std::variant for the three alternatives int, double, and std::string (❶). In the next line, we assign a C-style string literal, which will be converted to a std::string inside the variant (❷). Then we print the

---

24 I will explain the *Command* design pattern alongside the Strategy design pattern in Chapter 5.

content of the variant via the `std::visit()` function and the `Print` function object
(❸).

Notice the name of the `std::visit()` function. The name directly refers to the *Visitor* design pattern and therefore clearly expresses its intent: you're able to apply any operation to the closed set of types contained in the variant instance.[25] Also, you can extend the set of operations nonintrusively.

You see that using the name of a design pattern carries more information than using an arbitrary name. Still, this shouldn't imply that naming is easy.[26] A name should primarily help you understand the code in a specific context. If the name of a design pattern can help with that, then consider including the design pattern name to express your intent.

Guideline 14: Use a Design Pattern's Name to Communicate Intent

- Use the name of a design pattern to communicate the intent of a solution.
- Use the name of a design pattern to improve readability.

---

25 The *Visitor* design pattern, including the modern implementation with `std::variant`, will be our focus in Chapter 4.

26 Naming is hard, as Kate Gregory aptly remarks in her highly recommended talk "Naming Is Hard: Let's Do Better" (*https://oreil.ly/nyeOv*) at CppCon 2019.

The Visitor Design Pattern

This entire chapter is focused on the *Visitor* design pattern. If you've already heard about the Visitor design pattern or even used it in your own designs, you might be wondering why I have chosen Visitor as the first design pattern to explain in detail. Yes, Visitor is definitely not one of the most glamorous design patterns. However, it will definitely serve as a great example to demonstrate the many options you have when implementing a design pattern and how different these implementations can be. It will also serve as an effective example of advertising the advantages of modern C++.

In "Guideline 15: Design for the Addition of Types or Operations" on page 102, we first talk about the fundamental design decision you'll need to make when walking in the realm of dynamic polymorphism: focus on either types or operations. In that guideline, we will also talk about the intrinsic strengths and weaknesses of programming paradigms.

In "Guideline 16: Use Visitor to Extend Operations" on page 112, I will introduce you to the Visitor design pattern. I will explain its intent to extend operations instead of types, and show you both the advantages and the shortcomings of the classic Visitor pattern.

In "Guideline 17: Consider std::variant for Implementing Visitor" on page 122, you will make the acquaintance of the modern implementation of the Visitor design pattern. I will introduce you to `std::variant` and explain the many advantages of that particular implementation.

In "Guideline 18: Beware the Performance of Acyclic Visitor" on page 133, I will introduce you to the *Acyclic Visitor*. At first glance, this approach appears to resolve some fundamental problems of the Visitor pattern, but on closer inspection we will find that the runtime overhead may disqualify this implementation.

Guideline 15: Design for the Addition of Types or Operations

To you, the term *dynamic polymorphism* may sound like a lot of freedom. It may feel similar to when you were still a kid: endless possibilities, no limitations! Well, you have grown older and faced reality: you can't have everything, and there is always a choice to be made. Unfortunately, it's similar with dynamic polymorphism. Despite the fact that it sounds like complete freedom, there is a limiting choice: do you want to extend types or operations?

To see what I mean, let's return to the scenario from Chapter 3: we want to draw a given shape.[1] We stick to dynamic polymorphism, and for our initial try, we implement this problem with good old procedural programming.

A Procedural Solution

The first header file `Point.h` provides a fairly simple `Point` class. This will mainly serve to make the code complete, but also gives us the idea that we're dealing with 2D shapes:

```
//---- <Point.h> ----------------

struct Point
{
   double x;
   double y;
};
```

The second conceptual header file `Shape.h` proves to be much more interesting:

```
//---- <Shape.h> ----------------

enum ShapeType     ❶
{
   circle,
   square
};

class Shape     ❷
{
 protected:
   explicit Shape( ShapeType type )
      : type_( type )     ❺
   {}
```

---

1 I can see you rolling your eyes! "Oh, that boring example again!" But do consider readers who skipped Chapter 3. They're now happy that they can read this section without a lengthy explanation about the scenario.

```
  public:
    virtual ~Shape() = default;   ❸

    ShapeType getType() const { return type_; }   ❻

  private:
    ShapeType type_;   ❹
};
```

First, we introduce the enumeration ShapeType, which currently lists the two enumerators, circle and square (❶). Apparently, we are initially dealing with only circles and squares. Second, we introduce the class Shape (❷). Given the protected constructor and the virtual destructor (❸), you can anticipate that Shape is supposed to work as a base class. But that's not the surprising detail about Shape: Shape has a data member of type ShapeType (❹). This data member is initialized via the constructor (❺) and can be queried via the getType() member function (❻). Apparently, a Shape stores its type in the form of the ShapeType enumeration.

One example of the use of the Shape base class is the Circle class:

```
//---- <Circle.h> ----------------

#include <Point.h>
#include <Shape.h>

class Circle : public Shape   ❼
{
 public:
   explicit Circle( double radius )
      : Shape( circle )   ❽
      , radius_( radius )
   {
       /* Checking that the given radius is valid */
   }

   double radius() const { return radius_; }
   Point  center() const { return center_; }

 private:
   double radius_;
   Point center_{};
};
```

Circle publicly inherits from Shape (❼), and for that reason, and due to the lack of a default constructor in Shape, needs to initialize the base class (❽). Since it's a circle, it uses the circle enumerator as an argument to the base class constructor.

As stated before, we want to draw shapes. We therefore introduce the draw() function for circles. Since we don't want to couple too strongly to any implementation details of drawing, the `draw()` function is declared in the conceptual header file `DrawCircle.h` and defined in the corresponding source file:

```
//---- <DrawCircle.h> ----------------

class Circle;

void draw( Circle const& );


//---- <DrawCircle.cpp> ----------------

#include <DrawCircle.h>
#include <Circle.h>
#include /* some graphics library */

void draw( Circle const& c )
{
    // ... Implementing the logic for drawing a circle
}
```

Of course, there are not only circles. As indicated by the `square` enumerator, there is also a `Square` class:

```
//---- <Square.h> ----------------

#include <Point.h>
#include <Shape.h>

class Square : public Shape    ❾
{
 public:
   explicit Square( double side )
      : Shape( square )    ❿
      , side_( side )
   {
       /* Checking that the given side length is valid */
   }

   double side  () const { return side_; }
   Point  center() const { return center_; }

 private:
   double side_;
   Point center_{};   // Or any corner, if you prefer
};


//---- <DrawSquare.h> ----------------

class Square;
```

```
void draw( Square const& );


//---- <DrawSquare.cpp> ----------------

#include <DrawSquare.h>
#include <Square.h>
#include /* some graphics library */

void draw( Square const& s )
{
   // ... Implementing the logic for drawing a square
}
```

The Square class looks very similar to the Circle class (❾). The major difference is that a Square initializes its base class with the square enumerator (❿).

With both circles and squares available, we now want to draw an entire vector of different shapes. For that reason, we introduce the drawAllShapes() function:

```
//---- <DrawAllShapes.h> ----------------

#include <memory>
#include <vector>
class Shape;

void drawAllShapes( std::vector<std::unique_ptr<Shape>> const& shapes );  ⓫


//---- <DrawAllShapes.cpp> ----------------

#include <DrawAllShapes.h>
#include <Circle.h>
#include <Square.h>

void drawAllShapes( std::vector<std::unique_ptr<Shape>> const& shapes )
{
   for( auto const& shape : shapes )
   {
      switch( shape->getType() )  ⓬
      {
        case circle:
           draw( static_cast<Circle const&>( *shape ) );
           break;
        case square:
           draw( static_cast<Square const&>( *shape ) );
           break;
      }
   }
}
```

drawAllShapes() takes a vector of shapes in the form of std::unique_ptr<Shape>
(❶). The pointer to the base class is necessary to hold different kinds of concrete
shapes, and the std::unique_ptr in particular to automatically manage the shapes
via the *RAII idiom*. Inside the function, we start by traversing the vector in order to
draw every shape. Unfortunately, all we have at this point are Shape pointers. Therefore, we have to ask every shape nicely by means of the getType() function (❷): what
kind of shape are you? If the shape replies with circle, we know that we have to
draw it as a Circle and perform the corresponding static_cast. If the shape replies
with square, we draw it as a Square.

I can feel that you're not particularly happy about this solution. But before talking
about the shortcomings, let's consider the main() function:

```
//---- <Main.cpp> ----------------

#include <Circle.h>
#include <Square.h>
#include <DrawAllShapes.h>
#include <memory>
#include <vector>

int main()
{
   using Shapes = std::vector<std::unique_ptr<Shape>>;

   // Creating some shapes
   Shapes shapes;
   shapes.emplace_back( std::make_unique<Circle>( 2.3 ) );
   shapes.emplace_back( std::make_unique<Square>( 1.2 ) );
   shapes.emplace_back( std::make_unique<Circle>( 4.1 ) );

   // Drawing all shapes
   drawAllShapes( shapes );

   return EXIT_SUCCESS;
}
```

It works! With this main() function, the code compiles and draws three shapes (two
circles and a square). Isn't that great? It is, but it won't stop you from going into a
rant: "What a primitive solution! Not only is the switch a bad choice for distinguishing between different kinds of shapes, but it also doesn't have a default case! And who
had this crazy idea to encode the type of the shapes by means of an unscoped enumeration?"[2] You're looking suspiciously in my direction…

---

2 Since C++11, we have scoped enumerations (*https://oreil.ly/EP4eR*), sometimes also called *class enumerations*
  because of the syntax enum class, at our disposal. This would, for instance, help the compiler to better warn
  about incomplete switch statements. If you spotted this imperfection, you've earned yourself a bonus point!

Well, I can understand your reaction. But let's analyze the problem in a little more detail. Let me guess: you remember "Guideline 5: Design for Extension" on page 35. And you now imagine what you would have to do to add a third kind of shape. First, you would have to extend the enumeration. For instance, we would have to add the new enumerator `triangle` (⑬):

```
enum ShapeType
{
   circle,
   square,
   triangle   ⑬
};
```

Note that this addition would have an impact not only on the `switch` statement in the `drawAllShapes()` function (it is now truly incomplete), but also on all classes derived from `Shape` (`Circle` and `Square`). These classes depend on the enumeration since they depend on the `Shape` base class and also use the enumeration directly. Therefore, changing the enumeration would result in a recompilation of *all* your source files.

That should strike you as a serious issue. And it is indeed. The heart of the problem is the direct dependency of all shape classes and functions on the enumeration. Any change to the enumeration results in a ripple effect that requires the dependent files to be recompiled. Obviously, this directly violates the Open-Closed Principle (OCP) (see "Guideline 5: Design for Extension" on page 35). This doesn't seem right: adding a `Triangle` shouldn't result in a recompilation of the `Circle` and `Square` classes.

There is more, though. In addition to actually writing a `Triangle` class (something that I leave to your imagination), you have to update the `switch` statement to handle triangles (⑭):

```
void drawAllShapes( std::vector<std::unique_ptr<Shape>> const& shapes )
{
   for( auto const& shape : shapes )
   {
      switch( shape->getType() )
      {
         case circle:
            draw( static_cast<Circle const&>( *shape ) );
            break;
         case square:
            draw( static_cast<Square const&>( *shape ) );
            break;
         case triangle:   ⑭
            draw( static_cast<Triangle const&>( *shape ) );
            break;
      }
   }
}
```

I can imagine your outcry: "Copy-and-paste! Duplication!" Yes, in this situation it is very likely that a developer will use copy-and-paste to implement the new logic. It's just so convenient because the new case is so similar to the previous two cases. And indeed, this is an indication that the design could be improved. However, I see a far more serious flaw: I would assume that in a larger codebase, this is not the only switch statement. On the contrary, there will be others that need to be updated as well. How many are there? A dozen? Fifty? Over a hundred? And how do you find all of these? OK, so you argue that the compiler would help you with this task. Perhaps with the switches, yes, but what if there are also if-else-if cascades? And then, after this update marathon, when you think you are done, how do you guarantee that you have truly updated all the necessary sections?

Yes, I can understand your reaction and why you prefer not to have this kind of code: this explicit handling of types is a maintenance nightmare. To quote Scott Meyers:[3]

> This kind of type-based programming has a long history in C, and one of the things we know about it is that it yields programs that are essentially unmaintainable.

An Object-Oriented Solution

So let me ask: what would you have done? How would you have implemented the drawing of shapes? Well, I can imagine you would have used an object-oriented approach. That means you would scratch the enumeration and add a pure virtual draw() function to the Shape base class. This way, Shape doesn't have to remember its type anymore:

```
//---- <Shape.h> ----------------

class Shape
{
 public:
   Shape() = default;

   virtual ~Shape() = default;

   virtual void draw() const = 0;
};
```

Given this base class, derived classes now would have to implement only the draw() member function (❶❺):

```
//---- <Circle.h> ----------------

#include <Point.h>
```

_____

3 Scott Meyers, *More Effective C++: 35 New Ways to Improve Your Programs and Designs*, Item 31 (Addison-Wesley, 1995).

```
#include <Shape.h>

class Circle : public Shape
{
 public:
   explicit Circle( double radius )
      : radius_( radius )
   {
      /* Checking that the given radius is valid */
   }

   double radius() const { return radius_; }
   Point  center() const { return center_; }

   void draw() const override;  ⑮

 private:
   double radius_;
   Point center_{};
};


//---- <Circle.cpp> ----------------

#include <Circle.h>
#include /* some graphics library */

void Circle::draw() const
{
   // ... Implementing the logic for drawing a circle
}


//---- <Square.h> ----------------

#include <Point.h>
#include <Shape.h>

class Square : public Shape
{
 public:
   explicit Square( double side )
      : side_( side )
   {
      /* Checking that the given side length is valid */
   }

   double side  () const { return side_; }
   Point  center() const { return center_; }

   void draw() const override;  ⑮
```

```
  private:
    double side_;
    Point center_{};
};


//---- <Square.cpp> ---------------

#include <Square.h>
#include /* some graphics library */

void Square::draw() const
{
    // ... Implementing the logic for drawing a square
}
```

Once the virtual draw() function is in place and implemented by all derived classes, it can be used to refactor the drawAllShapes() function:

```
//---- <DrawAllShapes.h> ---------------

#include <memory>
#include <vector>
class Shape;

void drawAllShapes( std::vector< std::unique_ptr<Shape> > const& shapes );


//---- <DrawAllShapes.cpp> ---------------

#include <DrawAllShapes.h>
#include <Shape.h>

void drawAllShapes( std::vector< std::unique_ptr<Shape> > const& shapes )
{
    for( auto const& shape : shapes )
    {
        shape->draw();
    }
}
```

I can see you relax and start smiling again. This is so much nicer, so much cleaner. While I understand that you prefer this solution and that you would like to stay in this comfort zone a little while longer, I unfortunately have to point out a flaw. Yes, this solution might also come with a disadvantage.

As indicated in the introduction to this section, with an object-oriented approach, we are now able to add new types very easily. All we have to do is write a new derived class. We don't have to modify or recompile any existing code (with the exception of the main() function). That perfectly fulfills the OCP. However, did you notice that we are not able to easily add operations anymore? For instance, let's assume we need a virtual `serialize()` function to convert a `Shape` into bytes. How can we add this without modifying existing code? How can anyone easily add this operation without having to touch the `Shape` base class?

Unfortunately, that isn't possible anymore. We are now dealing with a *closed set* of operations, which means that we violate the OCP in relation to addition operations. To add a virtual function, the base class needs to be modified, and all derived classes (circles, squares, etc.) need to implement the new function, even though the function might never be called. In summary, the object-oriented solution fulfills the OCP with respect to adding types but violates it in relation to operations.

I know you thought we left the procedural solution behind for good, but let's take a second look. In the procedural approach, adding a new operation was actually very simple. New operations could be added in the form of free functions or separate classes, for instance. It wasn't necessary to modify the `Shape` base class or any of the derived classes. Thus in the procedural solution, we have fulfilled the OCP with respect to adding operations. But as we've seen, the procedural solution violates the OCP in relation to adding types. Thus, it appears to be an inversion of the object-oriented solution, which is the other way around.

Be Aware of the Design Choice in Dynamic Polymorphism

The takeaway of this example is that there is a design choice when using dynamic polymorphism: either you can add types easily by fixing the number of operations or you can add operations easily by fixing the number of types. Thus, the OCP has two dimensions: when designing software, you have to make a conscious decision about which kind of extension you expect.

The strength of object-oriented programming is the easy addition of new types, but its weakness is that the addition of operations becomes much more difficult. The strength of procedural programming is the easy addition of operations, but adding types is a real pain (Table 4-1). It depends on your project: if you expect new types will be added frequently, rather than operations, you should strive for an OOP solution, which treats operations as a *closed set* and types as an *open set*. If you expect operations will be added, you should strive for a procedural solution, which treats types as a *closed set* and operations as an *open set*. If you make the right choice, you will economize your time and the time of your colleagues, and extensions will feel natural and easy.[4]

---

4 Note that the mathematical notion of open and closed sets (*https://oreil.ly/nt4f4*) is something completely different.

Table 4-1. Strengths and weaknesses of different programming paradigms

Programming paradigm	Strength	Weakness
Procedural programming	Addition of operations	Addition of (polymorphic) types
Object-oriented programming	Addition of (polymorphic) types	Addition of operations

Be aware of these strengths: based on your expectation on how a codebase will evolve, choose the right approach to design for extensions. Do not ignore the weaknesses, and do not put yourself in an unfortunate maintenance hell.

I assume that at this point you're wondering if it's possible to have two *open sets*. Well, to the best of my knowledge, this is not impossible but it's usually impractical. As an example, in "Guideline 18: Beware the Performance of Acyclic Visitor" on page 133, I will show you that performance might take a significant hit.

Since you might be a fan of template-based programming and similar compile time endeavors, I should also make the explicit note that static polymorphism does not have the same limitations. While in dynamic polymorphism, one of the design axes (types and operations) needs to be fixed, in static polymorphism, both pieces of information are available at compile-time. Therefore, both aspects can be extended easily (if you do it properly).[5]

Guideline 15: Design for the Addition of Types or Operations

- Be aware of the strengths and weaknesses of different programming paradigms.
- Exploit the strengths of a paradigm, but avoid the weaknesses.
- Understand the choice between the addition of types or operations in dynamic polymorphism.
- Prefer an object-oriented solution when you primarily want to add types.
- Prefer a procedural/functional solution when you primarily want to add operations.

Guideline 16: Use Visitor to Extend Operations

In the previous section, you saw that the strength of object-oriented programming (OOP) is the addition of types and its weakness is the addition of operations. Of course, OOP has an answer to that weakness: the Visitor design pattern.

---

5 As an example of design with static polymorphism, consider the algorithms from the Standard Template Library (STL). You can easily add new operations, i.e., algorithms, but also easily add new types that can be copied, sorted, etc.

The Visitor design pattern is one of the classic design patterns described by the Gang of Four (GoF). Its focus is on allowing you to frequently add operations instead of types. Allow me to explain the Visitor design pattern using the previous toy example: the drawing of shapes.

In Figure 4-1, you see the Shape hierarchy. The Shape class is again the base class for a certain number of concrete shapes. In this example, there are only the two classes, Circle and Square, but of course it's possible to have more shapes. In addition, you might imagine Triangle, Rectangle, or Ellipse classes.

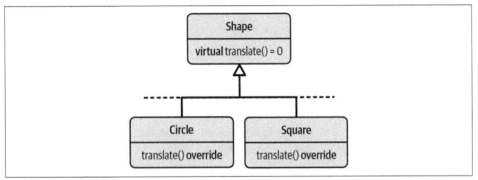

Figure 4-1. The UML representation of a shape hierarchy with two derived classes (Circle and Square)

Analyzing the Design Issues

Let's assume you are certain that you already have all the shapes you'll ever need. That is, you consider the set of shapes a *closed set*. What you are missing, though, are additional operations. For instance, you're missing an operation to rotate the shapes. Also, you would like to serialize shapes, i.e., you would like to convert the instance of a shape into bytes. And of course, you want to draw shapes. In addition, you want to enable anybody to add new operations. Therefore, you expect an *open set* of operations.[6]

Every new operation now requires you to insert a new virtual function into the base class. Unfortunately, that can be troublesome in different ways. Most obviously, not everyone is able to add a virtual function to the Shape base class. I, for instance, can't simply go ahead and change your code. Therefore, this approach would not meet the

---

6 It's always hard to make predictions. But we usually have a pretty good idea about how our codebase will evolve. In case you have no idea how things will move along, you should wait for the first change or extension, learn from that, and make a more informed decision. This philosophy is part of the commonly known YAGNI principle (*https://oreil.ly/stXoI*), which warns you about overengineering; see also "Guideline 2: Design for Change" on page 11.

expectation that everyone can add operations. While you can already see this as a final negative verdict, let's still analyze the problem of virtual functions in more detail.

If you decide to use a pure virtual function, you would have to implement the function in every derived class. For your own derived types, you could shrug this off as just a little bit of extra effort. But you might also cause extra work for other people who have created a shape by inheriting from the Shape base class.[7] And that is very much expected, since this is the strength of OOP: anyone can add new types easily. Since this is to be expected, it may be a reason to not use a pure virtual function.

As an alternative, you could introduce a regular virtual function, i.e., a virtual function with a default implementation. While a default behavior for a rotate() function sounds like a very reasonable idea, a default implementation for a serialize() function doesn't sound easy at all. I admit that I would have to think hard about how to implement such a function. You might now suggest just throwing an exception as the default. However, this means that derived classes must again implement the missing behavior, and it would be a pure virtual function in disguise, or a clear violation of the Liskov Substitution Principle (see "Guideline 6: Adhere to the Expected Behavior of Abstractions" on page 44).

Either way, adding a new operation into the Shape base class is difficult or not even possible at all. The underlying reason is that adding virtual functions violates the OCP. If you really need to add new operations frequently, then you should design so that the extension of operations is easy. That is what the Visitor design pattern tries to achieve.

The Visitor Design Pattern Explained

The intent of the Visitor design pattern is to enable the addition of operations.

The Visitor Design Pattern

Intent: "Represent an operation to be performed on the elements of an object structure. Visitor lets you define a new operation without changing the classes of the elements on which it operates."[8]

In addition to the Shape hierarchy, I now introduce the ShapeVisitor hierarchy on the lefthand side of Figure 4-2. The ShapeVisitor base class represents an

---

7 I wouldn't be happy about it—perhaps I would even be seriously unhappy—but I probably wouldn't get angry. But your other colleagues? Worst case, you might be excluded from the next team barbecue.

8 Erich Gamma et al., *Design Patterns: Elements of Reusable Object-Oriented Software*.

abstraction of shape operations. For that reason, you could argue that ShapeOpera
tion might be a better name for that class. It is beneficial, however, to apply "Guideline 14: Use a Design Pattern's Name to Communicate Intent" on page 97. The name
Visitor will help others understand the design.

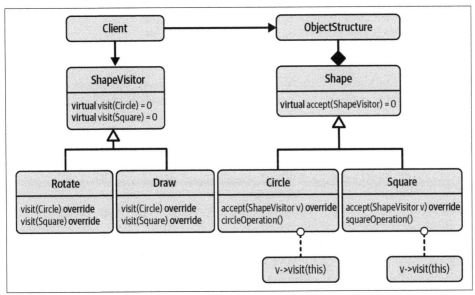

Figure 4-2. The UML representation of the Visitor design pattern

The ShapeVisitor base class comes with one pure virtual visit() function for every
concrete shape in the Shape hierarchy:

```
class ShapeVisitor
{
  public:
    virtual ~ShapeVisitor() = default;

    virtual void visit( Circle const&, /*...*/ ) const = 0;  ❶
    virtual void visit( Square const&, /*...*/ ) const = 0;  ❷
    // Possibly more visit() functions, one for each concrete shape
};
```

In this example, there is one visit() function for Circle (❶) and one for Square
(❷). Of course, there could be more visit() functions—for instance, one for
Triangle, one for Rectangle, and one for Ellipse—given that these are also classes
derived from the Shape base class.

With the ShapeVisitor base class in place, you can now add new operations easily.
All you have to do to add an operation is add a new derived class. For instance, to
enable rotating shapes, you can introduce the Rotate class and implement all

visit() functions. To enable drawing shapes, all you have to do is introduce a Draw class:

```
class Draw : public ShapeVisitor
{
 public:
   void visit( Circle const& c, /*...*/ ) const override;
   void visit( Square const& s, /*...*/ ) const override;
   // Possibly more visit() functions, one for each concrete shape
};
```

And you can think about introducing multiple Draw classes, one for each graphics library you need to support. You can do that easily, because you don't have to modify any *existing code*. It is only necessary to extend the ShapeVisitor hierarchy by adding *new code*. Therefore, this design fulfills the OCP with respect to adding operations.

To completely understand the software design characteristics of Visitor, it is important to understand why the Visitor design pattern is able to fulfill the OCP. The initial problem was that every new operation required a change to the Shape base class. Visitor identifies the addition of operations as a *variation point*. By extracting this variation point, i.e., by making this a separate class, you follow the Single-Responsibility Principle (SRP): Shape does not have to change for every new operation. This avoids frequent modifications of the Shape hierarchy and enables the easy addition of new operations. The SRP therefore acts as an enabler for the OCP.

To use visitors (classes derived from the ShapeVisitor base class) on shapes, you now have to add one last function to the Shape hierarchy: the accept() function (❸):[9]

```
class Shape
{
 public:
   virtual ~Shape() = default;
   virtual void accept( ShapeVisitor const& v ) = 0;   ❸
   // ...
};
```

The accept() function is introduced as a pure virtual function in the base class and therefore has to be implemented in every derived class (❹ and ❺):

```
class Circle : public Shape
{
 public:
```

---

9 accept() is the name used in the GoF book. It is the traditional name in the context of the Visitor design pattern. Of course, you are free to use any other name, such as apply(). But before you rename, consider the advice from "Guideline 14: Use a Design Pattern's Name to Communicate Intent" on page 97.

```
    explicit Circle( double radius )
        : radius_( radius )
    {
        /* Checking that the given radius is valid */
    }

    void accept( ShapeVisitor const& v ) override { v.visit( *this ); }  ❹

    double radius() const { return radius_; }

 private:
    double radius_;
};


class Square : public Shape
{
 public:
    explicit Square( double side )
        : side_( side )
    {
        /* Checking that the given side length is valid */
    }

    void accept( ShapeVisitor const& v ) override { v.visit( *this ); }  ❺

    double side() const { return side_; }

 private:
    double side_;
};
```

The implementation of accept() is easy; however, it merely needs to call the corresponding visit() function on the given visitor based on the type of the concrete Shape. This is achieved by passing the this pointer as an argument to visit(). Thus, the implementation of accept() is the same in each derived class, but due to a different type of the this pointer, it will trigger a different overload of the visit() function in the given visitor. Therefore, the Shape base class cannot provide a default implementation.

This accept() function can now be used where you need to perform an operation. For instance, the drawAllShapes() function uses accept() to draw all shapes in a given vector of shapes:

```
void drawAllShapes( std::vector<std::unique_ptr<Shape>> const& shapes )
{
    for( auto const& shape : shapes )
    {
        shape->accept( Draw{} );
    }
}
```

With the addition of the `accept()` function, you are now able to extend your `Shape` hierarchy easily with operations. You have now designed for an *open set* of operations. Amazing! However, there is no silver bullet, and there is no design that always works. Every design comes with advantages, but also disadvantages. So before you start to celebrate, I should tell you about the shortcomings of the Visitor design pattern to give you the complete picture.

Analyzing the Shortcomings of the Visitor Design Pattern

The Visitor design pattern is unfortunately far from perfect. This should be expected, considering Visitor is a workaround for an intrinsic OOP weakness, instead of building on OOP strengths.

The first disadvantage is a low implementation flexibility. It becomes obvious if you consider the implementation of a `Translate` visitor. The `Translate` visitor needs to move the center point of each shape by a given offset. For that, `Translate` needs to implement a `visit()` function for every concrete `Shape`. Especially for `Translate`, you can imagine that the implementation of these `visit()` functions would be very similar, if not identical: there is nothing different about translating a `Circle` from translating a `Square`. Still, you will need to write all `visit()` functions. Of course, you would extract the logic from the `visit()` functions and implement this in a third, separate function to minimize duplication according to the DRY principle.[10] But unfortunately, the strict requirements imposed by the base class do not give you the freedom to implement these `visit()` functions as one. The result is some boilerplate code:

```
class Translate : public ShapeVisitor
{
 public:
   // Where is the difference between translating a circle and translating
   // a square? Still you have to implement all virtual functions...
   void visit( Circle const& c, /*...*/ ) const override;
   void visit( Square const& s, /*...*/ ) const override;
   // Possibly more visit() functions, one for each concrete shape
};
```

A similar implementation inflexibility is the return type of the `visit()` functions. The decision on what the function returns is made in the `ShapeVisitor` base class. Derived classes cannot change that. The usual approach is to store the result in the visitor and access it later.

---

10 It really is advisable to extract the logic into a single function. The reason is change: if you have to update the implementation later, you don't want to perform the change multiple times. That is the idea of the DRY (Don't Repeat Yourself) principle. So please remember "Guideline 2: Design for Change" on page 11.

The second disadvantage is that with the Visitor design pattern in place, it becomes difficult to add new types. Previously, we made the assumption that you're certain you have all the shapes you will ever need. This assumption has now become a restriction. Adding a new shape in the Shape hierarchy would require the entire ShapeVisitor hierarchy to be updated: you would have to add a new pure virtual function to the ShapeVisitor base class, and this virtual function would have to be implemented by all derived classes. Of course, this comes with all the disadvantages we've discussed before. In particular, you would force other developers to update their operations.[11] Thus, the Visitor design pattern requires a *closed set* of types and in exchange provides an *open set* of operations.

The underlying reason for this restriction is that there is a cyclic dependency among the ShapeVisitor base class, the concrete shapes (Circle, Square, etc.), and the Shape base class (see Figure 4-3).

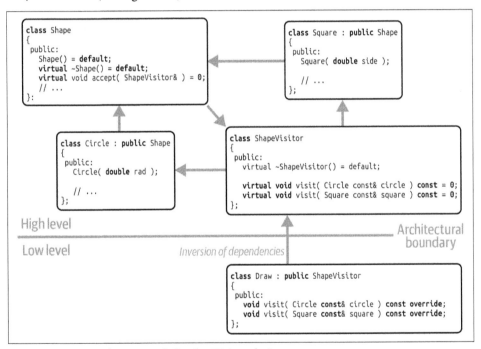

Figure 4-3. Dependency graph for the Visitor design pattern

The ShapeVisitor base class depends on the concrete shapes, since it provides a visit() function for each of these shapes. The concrete shapes depend on the Shape base class, since they have to fulfill all the expectations and requirements of the base

---

11 Consider the risk: this might exclude you from team barbecues for life!

class. And the `Shape` base class depends on the `ShapeVisitor` base class due to the `accept()` function. Because of this cyclic dependency, we are now able to add new operations easily (on a lower level of our architecture because of a dependency inversion), but we cannot add types easily anymore (because that would have to happen on the high level of our architecture). For that reason, we call the classic Visitor design pattern *Cyclic Visitor*.

The third disadvantage is the intrusive nature of a visitor. To add a visitor to an existing hierarchy, you need to add the virtual `accept()` to the base class of that hierarchy. While this is often possible, it still suffers from the usual problem of adding a pure virtual function to an existing hierarchy (see "Guideline 15: Design for the Addition of Types or Operations" on page 102). If, however, it's not possible to add the `accept()` function, this form of Visitor is not an option. If that's the case, don't worry: we will see another, nonintrusive form of the Visitor design pattern in "Guideline 17: Consider std::variant for Implementing Visitor" on page 122.

A fourth, albeit admittedly more obscure, disadvantage is that the `accept()` function is inherited by deriving classes. If someone later adds another layer of derived classes (and that someone might be you) and forgets to override the `accept()` function, the visitor will be applied to the wrong type. And unfortunately, you would not get any warning about this. This is just more evidence that adding new types has become more difficult. A possible solution for this would be to declare the `Circle` and `Square` classes as `final`, which would, however, limit future extensions.

"Wow, that's a lot of disadvantages. Are there any more?" Yes, unfortunately there are two more. The fifth disadvantage is obvious when we consider that for every operation, we're now required to call two virtual functions. Initially, we don't know about either the type of operation or the type of shape. The first virtual function is the `accept()` function, which is passed an abstract `ShapeVisitor`. The `accept()` function now resolves the concrete type of shape. The second virtual function is the `visit()` function, which is passed a concrete type of `Shape`. The `visit()` function now resolves the concrete type of the operation. This so-called *double dispatch* is unfortunately not free. On the contrary, performance-wise, you should consider the Visitor design pattern as rather slow. I will provide some performance numbers in the next guideline.

While talking about performance, I should also mention two other aspects that have a negative impact on performance. First, we usually allocate every single shape and visitor individually. Consider the following `main()` function:

```
int main()
{
    using Shapes = std::vector< std::unique_ptr<Shape> >;

    Shapes shapes;
```

```
shapes.emplace_back( std::make_unique<Circle>( 2.3 ) );   ❻
shapes.emplace_back( std::make_unique<Square>( 1.2 ) );   ❼
shapes.emplace_back( std::make_unique<Circle>( 4.1 ) );   ❽

drawAllShapes( shapes );

// ...

return EXIT_SUCCESS;
}
```

In this `main()` function, all allocations happen by means of `std::make_unique()` (❻, ❼, and ❽). These many, small allocations cost runtime on their own and will in the long run cause memory fragmentation.[12] Also, the memory may be laid out in an unfavorable, cache-unfriendly way. As a consequence, we usually use pointers to work with the resulting shapes and visitors. The resulting indirections make it much harder for a compiler to perform any kind of optimization and will show up in performance benchmarks. However, to be honest, this is not a Visitor-specific problem, but these two aspects are quite common to OOP in general.

The last disadvantage of the Visitor design pattern is that experience has proven this design pattern to be rather hard to fully understand and maintain. This is a rather subjective disadvantage, but the complexity of the intricate interplay of the two hierarchies often feels more like a burden than a real solution.

In summary, the Visitor design pattern is the OOP solution to allow for the easy extension of operations instead of types. That is achieved by introducing an abstraction in the form of the `ShapeVisitor` base class, which enables you to add operations on another set of types. While this is a unique strength of Visitor, it unfortunately comes with several deficiencies: implementation inflexibilities in both inheritance hierarchies due to a strong coupling to the requirements of the base classes, rather bad performance, and the intrinsic complexity of Visitor make it a rather unpopular design pattern.

If you're now undecided whether or not to use a classic Visitor, take the time to read the next section. I will show you a different way to implement a Visitor—a solution that will much more likely be to your satisfaction.

---

12 Memory fragmentation is much more likely when you use `std::make_unique()`, which encapsulates a call to new, instead of some special-purpose allocation schemes.

Guideline 17: Consider std::variant for Implementing Visitor

In "Guideline 16: Use Visitor to Extend Operations" on page 112, I introduced you to the Visitor design pattern. I imagine that you did not immediately fall in love: while Visitor most certainly has a couple of unique properties, it is also a rather complex design pattern with some strong internal coupling and performance deficiencies. No, definitely not love! However, don't worry, the classic form is not the only way you can implement the Visitor design pattern. In this section, I would like to introduce you to a different way to implement Visitor. And I am certain that this approach will be much more to your liking.

Introduction to std::variant

At the beginning of this chapter, we talked about the strengths and weaknesses of the different paradigms (OOP versus procedural programming). In particular, we talked about the fact that procedural programming was particularly good at adding new operations to an existing set of types. So instead of trying to find workarounds in OOP, how about we exploit the strength of procedural programming? No, don't worry; of course I'm not suggesting a return to our initial solution. That approach was just too error prone. Instead I'm talking about std::variant:

```cpp
#include <cstdlib>
#include <iostream>
#include <string>
#include <variant>

struct Print  ❿
{
   void operator()( int value ) const
      { std::cout << "int: " << value << '\n'; }
   void operator()( double value ) const
      { std::cout << "double: " << value << '\n'; }
   void operator()( std::string const& value ) const
      { std::cout << "string: " << value << '\n'; }
};
```

```
int main()
{
    // Creates a default variant that contains an 'int' initialized to 0
    std::variant<int,double,std::string> v{};   ❶

    v = 42;         // Assigns the 'int' 42 to the variant   ❷
    v = 3.14;       // Assigns the 'double' 3.14 to the variant   ❸
    v = 2.71F;      // Assigns a 'float', which is promoted to 'double'   ❹
    v = "Bjarne";   // Assigns the string literal 'Bjarne' to the variant   ❺
    v = 43;         // Assigns the 'int' 43 to the variant   ❻

    int const i = std::get<int>(v);   // Direct access to the value   ❼

    int* const pi = std::get_if<int>(&v);   // Direct access to the value   ❽

    std::visit( Print{}, v );   // Applying the Print visitor   ❾

    return EXIT_SUCCESS;
}
```

Since you might not have had the pleasure of being introduced to the C++17 std::variant yet, allow me to give you an introduction in a nutshell, just in case. A variant represents one of several alternatives. The variant at the beginning of the main() function in the code example can contain an int, a double, or an std::string (❶). Note that I said *or*: a variant can contain only one of these three alternatives. It is never several of them, and under usual circumstances, it should never contain nothing. For that reason, we call a variant a *sum type*: the set of possible states is the sum of possible states of the alternatives.

A default variant is also not empty. It is initialized to the default value of the first alternative. In the example, a default variant contains an integer of value 0. Changing the value of a variant is simple: you can just assign new values. For instance, we can assign the value 42, which now means that the variant stores an integer of value 42 (❷). If we subsequently assign the double 3.14, then the variant will store a double of value 3.14 (❸). If you ever want to assign a value of a type that is not one of the possible alternatives, the usual conversion rules apply. For instance, if you want to assign a float, based on the regular conversion rules it would be promoted to a double (❹).

To store the alternatives, the variant provides just enough internal buffer to hold the largest of the alternatives. In our case, the largest alternative is the std::string, which is usually between 24 and 32 bytes (depending on the used implementation of the Standard Library). Thus, when you assign the string literal "Bjarne", the variant will first clean up the previous value (there isn't much to do; it's just a double) and then, since it is the only alternative that works, construct the std::string in place inside its own buffer (❺). When you change your mind and assign the integer 43 (❻), the variant will properly destroy the std::string by means of its destructor and reuse the internal buffer for the integer. Marvelous, is it not? The variant is type safe and always properly initialized. What more could we ask for?

Well, of course you want to do something with the values inside the variant. It would not be of any use if we just store the value. Unfortunately, you cannot simply assign a variant to any other value, e.g., an int, to get your value back. No, accessing the value is a little more complicated. There are several ways to access the stored values, the most direct approach being std::get() (❼). With std::get() you can query for a value of a particular type. If the variant contains a value of that type, it returns a reference to it. If it does not, it throws the std::bad_variant_exception. That seems to be a pretty rude response, given that you have asked nicely. But we should probably be happy that the variant does not pretend to hold some value when it indeed does not. At least it is honest. There is a nicer way in the form of std::get_if() (❽). In comparison to std::get(), std::get_if() does not return a reference but a pointer. If you request a type that the std::variant currently does not hold, it doesn't throw an exception but instead returns a nullptr. However, there is a third way, a way that is particularly interesting for our purposes: std::visit() (❾). std::visit() allows you to perform any operation on the stored value. Or more precisely, it allows you to pass a custom visitor to perform any operation on the stored value of a *closed set* of types. Sound familiar?

The Print visitor (❿) that we pass as the first argument must provide a function call operator (operator()) for every possible alternative. In this example, that is fulfilled by providing three operator()s: one for int, one for double, and one for std::string. It is particularly noteworthy that Print does not have to inherit from any base class, and it does not have any virtual functions. Therefore, there is no strong coupling to any requirements. If we wanted to, we could also collapse the function call operators for int and double into one, since an int can be converted to a double:

```
struct Print
{
   void operator()( double value ) const
      { std::cout << "int or double: " << value << '\n'; }
   void operator()( std::string const& value ) const
      { std::cout << "string: " << value << '\n'; }
};
```

While the question about which version we should prefer is not of particular interest for us at this moment, you'll notice that we have a lot of implementation flexibility. There is only a very loose coupling based on the convention that for every alternative there needs to be an operator(), regardless of the exact form. We do not have a Visitor base class anymore that forces us to do things in a very specific way. We also do not have any base class for the alternatives: we are free to use fundamental types such as int and double, as well as arbitrary class types such as std::string. And perhaps most importantly, anyone can easily add new operations. No existing code needs to be modified. With this, we can argue that this is a procedural solution, just much more elegant than the initial enum-based approach, which used a base class to hold a discriminator.

Refactoring the Drawing of Shapes as a Value-Based, Nonintrusive Solution

With these properties, std::variant is perfectly suited for our drawing example. Let's re-implement the drawing of shapes with std::variant. First, we refactor the Circle and Square classes:

```
//---- <Circle.h> ----------------

#include <Point.h>

class Circle
{
 public:
   explicit Circle( double radius )
      : radius_( radius )
   {
      /* Checking that the given radius is valid */
   }

   double radius() const { return radius_; }
   Point  center() const { return center_; }

 private:
   double radius_;
   Point center_{};
};
```

```
//---- <Square.h> ----------------

#include <Point.h>

class Square
{
 public:
   explicit Square( double side )
      : side_( side )
   {
      /* Checking that the given side length is valid */
   }

   double side  () const { return side_; }
   Point  center() const { return center_; }
```

```
  private:
    double side_;
    Point center_{};
};
```

Both `Circle` and `Square` are significantly simplified: no more `Shape` base class, no more need to implement any virtual functions—in particular the `accept()` function. Thus, this Visitor approach is nonintrusive: this form of Visitor can be easily added to existing types! And there is no need to prepare these classes for any upcoming operations. We can focus entirely on implementing these two classes as what they are: geometric primitives.

The most beautiful part of the refactoring, however, is the actual use of `std::variant`:

```
//---- <Shape.h> ----------------

#include <variant>
#include <Circle.h>
#include <Square.h>

using Shape = std::variant<Circle,Square>;   ⓫
```

```
//---- <Shapes.h> ---------------

#include <vector>
#include <Shape.h>

using Shapes = std::vector<Shape>;   ⓬
```

Since our *closed set* of types is a set of shapes, variant will now contain either a `Circle` or `Square`. And what is a good name for an abstraction of a set of types that represent shapes? Well...`Shape` (⓫). Instead of a base class that abstracts from the actual type of shape, `std::variant` now acquires this task. If this is the first time you've seen that, you are probably completely amazed. But wait, there is more: this also means that we can now turn our back on `std::unique_ptr`. Remember: the only reason we used (smart) pointers was to enable us to store different kinds of shapes in the same vector. But now that `std::variant` enables us to do the same, we can simply store variant objects inside a single vector (⓬).

With this functionality in place, we can write custom operations on shapes. We're still interested in drawing shapes. For that purpose, we now implement the `Draw` visitor:

```
//---- <Draw.h> ----------------

#include <Shape.h>
#include /* some graphics library */
```

```
struct Draw
{
   void operator()( Circle const& c ) const
      { /* ... Implementing the logic for drawing a circle ... */ }
   void operator()( Square const& s ) const
      { /* ... Implementing the logic for drawing a square ... */ }
};
```

Again, we are following the expectation to implement one `operator()` for every alternative: one for `Circle` and one for `Square`. But this time we have a choice. There is no need to implement any base class, and for that reason, no need to override any virtual function. Therefore, there is no need to implement exactly one `operator()` for every alternative. While in this example it feels reasonable to have two functions, we have the option to combine the two `operator()`s into one function. We also have a choice with respect to the return type of the operation. We can locally decide what we should return, and it is not a base class that, independent from the specific operation, makes a global decision. Implementation flexibility. Loose coupling. Amazing!

The last piece of the puzzle is the `drawAllShapes()` function:

```
//---- <DrawAllShapes.h> ----------------

#include <Shapes.h>

void drawAllShapes( Shapes const& shapes );


//---- <DrawAllShapes.cpp> ----------------

#include <DrawAllShapes.h>

void drawAllShapes( Shapes const& shapes )
{
   for( auto const& shape : shapes )
   {
      std::visit( Draw{}, shape );
   }
}
```

The `drawAllShapes()` function is refactored to make use of `std::visit()`. In this function, we now apply the `Draw` visitor onto all variants stored in a vector.

The job of `std::visit()` is to perform the necessary type dispatch for you. If the given `std::variant` contains a `Circle`, it will call the `Draw::operator()` for circles. Otherwise it will call the `Draw::operator()` for squares. If you wanted to, you could manually implement the same dispatch with `std::get_if()`:

```
void drawAllShapes( Shapes const& shapes )
{
```

```
        for( auto const& shape : shapes )
        {
           if( Circle* circle = std::get_if<Circle>(&shape) ) {
              // ... Drawing a circle
           }
           else if( Square* square = std::get_if<Square>(&shape) ) {
              // ... Drawing a square
           }
        }
     }
```

I know what you're thinking: "Nonsense! Why would I ever want to do that? That would result in the same maintenance nightmare as an enum-based solution." I completely agree with you: from a software design perspective, this would be a terrible idea. Still, and I have to say that this is difficult to admit in the context of this book, there may be a good reason to do that (sometimes): performance. I know, now I've piqued your interest, but since we are almost ready to talk about performance anyway, allow me to defer this discussion for just a few paragraphs. I will come back to this, I promise!

With all of these details in place, we can finally refactor the main() function. But there isn't a lot of work to do: instead of creating circles and squares by means of std::make_unique(), we simply create circles and squares directly, and add them to the vector. This works thanks to the nonexplicit constructor of variant, which allows implicit conversion of any of the alternatives:

```
//---- <Main.cpp> ----------------

#include <Circle.h>
#include <Square.h>
#include <Shapes.h>
#include <DrawAllShapes.h>

int main()
{
   Shapes shapes;

   shapes.emplace_back( Circle{ 2.3 } );
   shapes.emplace_back( Square{ 1.2 } );
   shapes.emplace_back( Circle{ 4.1 } );

   drawAllShapes( shapes );

   return EXIT_SUCCESS;
}
```

The end result of this value-based solution is stunningly fascinating: no base classes anywhere. No virtual functions. No pointers. No manual memory allocations. Things are as straightforward as they could be, and there is very little boilerplate code. Additionally, despite the fact that the code looks very different from the previous

---

solutions, the architectural properties are identical: everyone is able to add new operations without the need to modify existing code (see Figure 4-4). Therefore, we still fulfill the OCP in respect to adding operations.

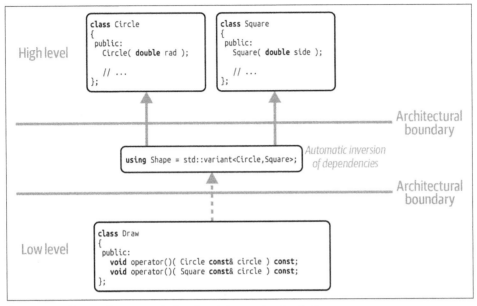

Figure 4-4. Dependency graph for the `std::variant` solution

As already mentioned, this Visitor approach is nonintrusive. From an architectural point of view, this gives you another, significant advantage compared to the classic Visitor. If you compare the dependency graph of the classic Visitor (see Figure 4-3) to the dependency graph of the `std::variant` solution (see Figure 4-4), you will see that the dependency graph for the `std::variant` solution has a second architectural boundary. This means that there is no cyclic dependency between `std::variant` and its alternatives. I should repeat that to emphasize its significance: there is *no* cyclic dependency between `std::variant` and its alternatives! What may look like a little detail is actually a huge architectural advantage. HUGE! As an example, you could create an abstraction based on `std::variant` on the fly:

```
//---- <Shape.h> ----------------

#include <variant>
#include <Circle.h>
#include <Square.h>

using Shape = std::variant<Circle,Square>;   ❸


//---- <SomeHeader.h> ---------------
```

```
#include <Circle.h>
#include <Ellipse.h>
#include <variant>

using RoundShapes = std::variant<Circle,Ellipse>;   ⑭


//---- <SomeOtherHeader.h> ---------------

#include <Square.h>
#include <Rectangle.h>
#include <variant>

using AngularShapes = std::variant<Square,Rectangle>;   ⑮
```

In addition to the Shape abstraction we have already created (⑬), you can create the std::variant for all round shapes (⑭), and you can create a std::variant for all angular shapes (⑮), both possibly far away from the Shape abstraction. You can easily do this because there is no need to derive from multiple Visitor base classes. On the contrary, the shape classes would be unaffected. Thus, the fact that the std::variant solution is nonintrusive is of the highest architectural value!

Performance Benchmarks

I know how you feel right now. Yes, that's what love at first sight feels like. But believe it or not, there's more. There is one topic that we haven't discussed yet, a topic that is dear to every C++ developer, and that is, of course, performance. While this is not really a book about performance, it's still worth mentioning that you do not have to worry about the performance of std::variant. I can already promise you that it's fast.

Before I show you the benchmark results, however, allow me a couple of comments about the benchmarks. Performance—*sigh*. Unfortunately, performance is always a difficult topic. There is always someone who complains about performance. For that reason, I would gladly just skip this topic entirely. But then there are other people who complain about the missing performance numbers. *Sigh*. Well, as it appears that there will always be some complaints, and since the results are just too good to miss, I will show you a couple of benchmark results. But there are two conditions: first, you will not consider them to be quantitative values that represent the absolute truth but only qualitative values that point in the right direction. And second, you will not launch a protest in front of my house because I didn't use your favorite compiler, or compilation flag, or IDE. Promise?

You: nodding and vowing to not complain about trivial things!

OK, great, then Table 4-2 gives you the benchmark results.

Table 4-2. Benchmark results for different Visitor implementations

Visitor implementation	GCC 11.1	Clang 11.1
Classic Visitor design pattern	1.6161 s	1.8015 s
Object-oriented solution	1.5205 s	1.1480 s
Enum solution	1.2179 s	1.1200 s
`std::variant` (with `std::visit()`)	1.1992 s	1.2279 s
`std::variant` (with `std::get_if()`)	1.0252 s	0.6998 s

To make sense of these numbers, I should give you a little more background. To make the scenario a little more realistic, I used not only circles and squares but also rectangles and ellipses. Then I ran 25,000 operations on 10,000 randomly created shapes. Instead of drawing these shapes, I updated the center point by random vectors.[13] This is because this translate operation is very cheap and allows me to better show the intrinsic overhead of all these solutions (such as indirections and the overhead of virtual function calls). An expensive operation, such as draw(), would obscure these details and might give the impression that all approaches are pretty similar. I used both GCC 11.1 and Clang 11.1, and for both compilers I added only the -O3 and -DNDEBUG compilation flags. The platform I used was macOS Big Sur (version 11.4) on an 8-Core Intel Core i7 with 3.8 GHz and 64 GB of main memory.

The most obvious takeaway from the benchmark results is that the variant solution is far more efficient than the classic Visitor solution. This should not come as a surprise: due to the double dispatch, the classic Visitor implementation contains a lot of indirection and therefore is also hard to optimize. Also, the memory layout of the shape objects is perfect: in comparison to all other solutions, including the enum-based solution, all shapes are stored contiguously in memory, which is the most cache-friendly layout you could choose. The second takeaway is that std::variant is indeed pretty efficient, if not surprisingly efficient. However, it is surprising that efficiency heavily depends on whether we use std::get_if() or std::visit() (I promised to get back to this). Both GCC and Clang produce much slower code when using std::visit(). I assume that std::visit() is not perfectly implemented and optimized at that point. But, as I said before, performance is always difficult, and I don't try to venture any deeper into this mystery.[14]

---

13 I am indeed using random vectors, created by means of std::mt19937 and std::uniform_real_distribu tion, but only after proving to myself that the performance does not change for GCC 11.1, and only slightly for Clang 11.1. Apparently, creating random numbers is not particularly expensive in itself (at least on my machine). Since you promised to consider these as qualitative results, we should be good.

14 There are other open source alternative implementations of variant. The Boost library (*https://www.boost.org*) provides two implementations: Abseil (*https://oreil.ly/FTtxY*) provides a variant implementation, and it pays to take a look at the implementation of Michael Park (*https://oreil.ly/EXCYj*).

Most importantly, the beauty of std::variant is not messed up by bad performance numbers. On the contrary: the performance results help intensify your newfound relationship with std::variant.

Analyzing the Shortcomings of the std::variant Solution

While I don't want to endanger this relationship, I consider it my duty to also point out a couple of disadvantages that you will have to deal with if you use the solution based on std::variant.

First, I should again point out the obvious: as a solution similar to the Visitor design pattern and based on procedural programming, std::variant is also focused on providing an *open set* of operations. The downside is that you will have to deal with a *closed set* of types. Adding new types will cause problems very similar to the problems we experienced with the enum-based solution in "Guideline 15: Design for the Addition of Types or Operations" on page 102. First of all, you would have to update the variant itself, which might trigger a recompilation of all code using the variant type (remember updating the enum?). Also, you would have to update all operations and add the potentially missing operator() for the new alternative(s). The good thing is that the compiler would complain if one of these operators is missing. The bad thing is that the compiler will not produce a nice, legible error message, but something that is a little closer to the mother of all template-related error messages. Altogether it really feels pretty much like our previous experience with the enum-based solution.

A second potential problem that you should keep in mind is that you should avoid putting types of very different sizes inside a variant. If at least one of the alternatives is much bigger than the others, you might waste a lot of space storing many of the small alternatives. This would negatively affect performance. A solution would be to not store large alternatives directly but to store them behind pointers, via *Proxy* objects, or by using the *Bridge* design pattern.[15] Of course, this would introduce an indirection, which also costs performance. Whether this is a disadvantage in terms of performance in comparison to storing values of different size is something that you will have to benchmark.

Last but not least, you should always be aware of the fact that a variant can reveal a lot of information. While it represents a runtime abstraction, the contained types are still plainly visible. This can create physical dependencies on the variant, i.e., when modifying one of the alternative types, you might have to recompile any depending code. The solution would, again, be to store pointers or *Proxy* objects instead, which

---

15 The *Proxy* pattern is another one of the GoF design patterns, which I unfortunately do not cover in this book because of limited pages. I will, however, go into detail about the *Bridge* design pattern; see "Guideline 28: Build Bridges to Remove Physical Dependencies" on page 250.

---

would hide implementation details. Unfortunately, that would also impact performance, since a lot of the performance gains come from the compiler knowing about the details and optimizing for them accordingly. Thus, there is always a compromise between performance and encapsulation.

Despite these shortcomings, in summary, `std::variant` proves to be a wonderful replacement for the OOP-based Visitor design pattern. It simplifies the code a lot, removes almost all boilerplate code and encapsulates the ugly and maintenance-intensive parts, and comes with superior performance. In addition, `std::variant` proves to be another great example of the fact that a design pattern is about an intent, not about implementation details.

Guideline 17: Consider std::variant for Implementing Visitor

- Understand the architectural similarity between the classic Visitor and `std::variant`.

- Be aware of the advantages of `std::variant` in comparison to an object-oriented Visitor solution.

- Use the nonintrusive nature of `std::variant` to create abstractions on the fly.

- Keep in mind the shortcomings of `std::variant` and avoid it when it's not appropriate.

Guideline 18: Beware the Performance of Acyclic Visitor

As you saw in "Guideline 15: Design for the Addition of Types or Operations" on page 102, you have to make a decision when using dynamic polymorphism: you can support an open set of *types* or an open set of *operations*. You cannot have both. Well, I specifically said that, to my best knowledge, having both is not actually impossible but usually impractical. To demonstrate, allow me to introduce you to yet another variation of the Visitor design pattern: the *Acyclic Visitor*.[16]

In "Guideline 16: Use Visitor to Extend Operations" on page 112, you saw that there is a cyclic dependency among the key players of the Visitor design pattern: the `Visitor` base class depends on the concrete types of shapes (`Circle`, `Square`, etc.), the concrete types of shapes depend on the `Shape` base class, and the `Shape` base class depends on the `Visitor` base class. Due to that cyclic dependency, which locks all

---

16 For more information on the Acyclic Visitor pattern by its inventor, see Robert C. Martin, *Agile Software Development: Principles, Patterns, and Practices* (Pearson).

those key players onto one level in the architecture, it is hard to add new types to a Visitor. The idea of the Acyclic Visitor is to break this dependency.

Figure 4-5 shows a UML diagram for the Acyclic Visitor. In comparison to the GoF Visitor, while there are only small differences on the righthand side of the picture, there are some fundamental changes on the lefthand side. Most importantly, the Visitor base class has been split into several base classes: the AbstractVisitor base class and one base class for each concrete type of shape (in this example, Circle Visitor and SquareVisitor). All visitors have to inherit from the AbstractVisitor base class but now also have the option to inherit from the shape-specific visitor base classes. If an operation wants to support circles, it inherits from the CircleVisitor base class and implements the visit() function for Circle. If it does not want to support circles, it simply does not inherit from CircleVisitor.

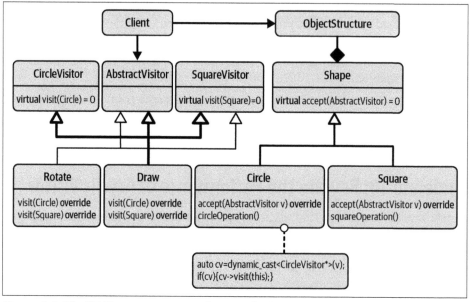

Figure 4-5. The UML representation of an Acyclic Visitor

The following code snippet shows a possible implementation of the Visitor base classes:

```
//---- <AbstractVisitor.h> ---------------

class AbstractVisitor   ❶
{
 public:
    virtual ~AbstractVisitor() = default;
};
```

```
//---- <Visitor.h> ----------------

template< typename T >
class Visitor   ❷
{
 protected:
   ~Visitor() = default;

 public:
   virtual void visit( T const& ) const = 0;
};
```

The `AbstractVisitor` base class is nothing but an empty base class with a virtual destructor (❶). No other function is necessary. As you will see, `AbstractVisitor` serves only as a general tag to identify visitors and doesn't have to provide any operation itself. In C++ we tend to implement the shape-specific visitor base classes in the form of a class template (❷). The `Visitor` class template is parameterized on a specific shape type and introduces the pure virtual `visit()` for that particular shape.

In the implementation of our `Draw` visitor, we would now inherit from three base classes: the `AbstractVisitor`, from `Visitor<Circle>` and `Visitor<Square>`, since we want to support both `Circle` and `Square`:

```
class Draw : public AbstractVisitor
           , public Visitor<Circle>
           , public Visitor<Square>
{
 public:
   void visit( Circle const& c ) const override
     { /* ... Implementing the logic for drawing a circle ... */ }
   void visit( Square const& s ) const override
     { /* ... Implementing the logic for drawing a square ... */ }
};
```

This choice of implementation breaks the cyclic dependency. As Figure 4-6 demonstrates, the high level of the architecture does not depend on the concrete shape types anymore. Both the shapes (`Circle` and `Square`) and the operations are now on the low level of the architectural boundary. We can now add both types and operations.

At this point, you're looking very suspiciously, almost accusingly, in my direction. Didn't I say that having both would not be possible? Obviously, it is possible, right? Well, once again, I didn't claim that it was impossible. I rather said that this might be impractical. Now that you've seen the advantage of an Acyclic Visitor, let me show you the downsides of this approach.

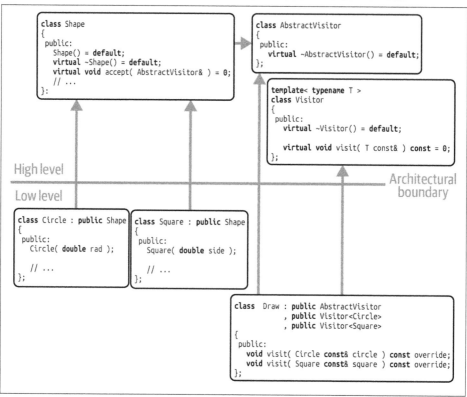

Figure 4-6. Dependency graph for the Acyclic Visitor

First, let's take a look at the implementation of the `accept()` function in `Circle`:

```
//---- <Circle.h> ----------------

class Circle : public Shape
{
 public:
   explicit Circle( double radius )
      : radius_( radius )
   {
      /* Checking that the given radius is valid */
   }

   void accept( AbstractVisitor const& v ) override {  ❸
      if( auto const* cv = dynamic_cast<Visitor<Circle> const*>(&v) ) {  ❹
         cv->visit( *this );  ❺
      }
   }

   double radius() const { return radius_; }
   Point  center() const { return center_; }
```

```
private:
  double radius_;
  Point center_{};
};
```

You might have noticed the one small change in the Shape hierarchy: the virtual accept() function now accepts an AbstractVisitor (❸). You also remember that the AbstractVisitor does not implement any operation on its own. Therefore, instead of calling a visit() function on the AbstractVisitor, the Circle determines if the given visitor supports circles by performing a dynamic_cast to Visitor<Circle> (❹). Note that it performs a pointer conversion, which means that the dynamic_cast returns either a valid pointer to a Visitor<Circle> or a nullptr. If it returns a valid pointer to a Visitor<Circle>, it calls the corresponding visit() function (❺).

While this approach most certainly works and is part of breaking the cyclic dependency of the Visitor design pattern, a dynamic_cast always leaves a bad feeling. A dynamic_cast should always feel a little suspicious, because, if used badly, it can break an architecture. That would happen if we perform a cast from within the high level of the architecture to something that resides in the low level of the architecture.[17] In our case, it's actually OK to use it, since the use happens on the low level of our architecture. Thus, we do not break the architecture by inserting knowledge about a lower level into the high level.

The real deficiency lies in the runtime penalty. When running the same benchmark as in "Guideline 17: Consider std::variant for Implementing Visitor" on page 122 for an Acyclic Visitor, you realize that the runtime is almost one order of magnitude above the runtime of a Cyclic Visitor (see Table 4-3). The reason is that a dynamic_cast is slow. Very slow. And it is particularly slow for this application. What we're doing here is a cross-cast. We aren't simply casting down to a particular derived class, but we are casting into another branch of the inheritance hierarchy. This cross cast, followed by a virtual function call, is significantly more costly than a simple downcast.

Table 4-3. Performance results for different Visitor implementations

Visitor implementation	GCC 11.1	Clang 11.1
Acyclic Visitor	14.3423 s	7.3445 s
Cyclic Visitor	1.6161 s	1.8015 s
Object-oriented solution	1.5205 s	1.1480 s

---

17 Please refer to "Guideline 9: Pay Attention to the Ownership of Abstractions" on page 62 for a definition of the terms *high level* and *low level*.

Visitor implementation	GCC 11.1	Clang 11.1
Enum solution	1.2179 s	1.1200 s
`std::variant` (with `std::visit()`)	1.1992 s	1.2279 s
`std::variant` (with `std::get_if()`)	1.0252 s	0.6998 s

While architecturally, an Acylic Visitor is a very interesting alternative, from a practical point of view, these performance results might disqualify it. This does not mean that you shouldn't use it, but at least be aware that the bad performance might be a very strong argument for another solution.

Guideline 18: Beware the Performance of Acyclic Visitor

- Understand the architectural advantages of an Acyclic Visitor.
- Be aware of the significant performance disadvantages of that solution.

The Strategy and Command
Design Patterns

This chapter is devoted to two of the most commonly used design patterns: the Strategy design pattern and the *Command* design pattern. Most commonly used indeed: the C++ Standard Library itself uses both of them dozens of times, and it's very likely that you have used them many times yourself. Both of these can be considered fundamental tools for every developer.

In "Guideline 19: Use Strategy to Isolate How Things Are Done" on page 140, I will introduce you to the Strategy design pattern. I will demonstrate why this is one of the most useful and most important design patterns and why you will find it useful in many situations.

In "Guideline 20: Favor Composition over Inheritance" on page 162, we will take a look at inheritance and why so many people complain about it. You will see that it's not bad per se, but like everything else, it has its benefits as well as limitations. Most importantly, however, I will explain that many of the classic design patterns do not draw their power from inheritance but rather from composition.

In "Guideline 21: Use Command to Isolate What Things Are Done" on page 165, I will introduce you to the Command design pattern. I will show you how to use that design pattern productively, and also give you an idea of how Command and Strategy compare.

In "Guideline 22: Prefer Value Semantics over Reference Semantics" on page 176, we take a trip into the realm of *reference semantics*. However, we will find that this realm is not particularly friendly and hospitable and makes us worry about the quality of our code. Thus, we will resettle into the realm of *value semantics*, which will welcome us with many benefits for our codebase.

In "Guideline 23: Prefer a Value-Based Implementation of Strategy and Command" on page 186, we will revisit the Strategy and Command patterns. I will demonstrate how we can apply the insight we gained in the realm of value semantics and implement both design patterns based on `std::function`.

Guideline 19: Use Strategy to Isolate How Things Are Done

Let's imagine that you and your team are about to implement a new 2D graphics tool. Among other requirements, it needs to deal with simple geometric primitives, such as circles, squares, and so on, which need to be drawn (see Figure 5-1).

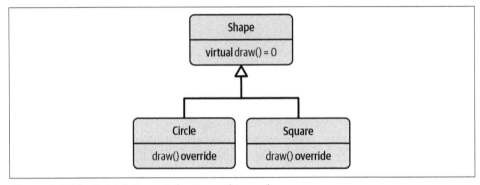

Figure 5-1. The initial Shape inheritance hierarchy

A couple of classes have already been implemented, such as a `Shape` base class, a `Circle` class, and a `Square` class:

```
//---- <Shape.h> ----------------

class Shape
{
 public:
   virtual ~Shape() = default;

   virtual void draw( /*some arguments*/ ) const = 0;  ❶
};


//---- <Circle.h> ----------------

#include <Point.h>
#include <Shape.h>

class Circle : public Shape
{
 public:
   explicit Circle( double radius )
      : radius_( radius )
```

```
  {
     /* Checking that the given radius is valid */
  }

  double radius() const { return radius_; }
  Point  center() const { return center_; }

  void draw( /*some arguments*/ ) const override;  ❷

 private:
   double radius_;
   Point center_{};
};


//---- <Circle.cpp> ----------------

#include <Circle.h>
#include /* some graphics library */

void Circle::draw( /*some arguments*/ ) const
{
   // ... Implementing the logic for drawing a circle
}


//---- <Square.h> ----------------

#include <Point.h>
#include <Shape.h>

class Square : public Shape
{
 public:
   explicit Square( double side )
      : side_( side )
   {
      /* Checking that the given side length is valid */
   }

   double side  () const { return side_; }
   Point  center() const { return center_; }

   void draw( /*some arguments*/ ) const override;  ❸

 private:
   double side_;
   Point center_{};
};


//---- <Square.cpp> ----------------
```

```
#include <Square.h>
#include /* some graphics library */

void Square::draw( /*some arguments*/ ) const
{
    // ... Implementing the logic for drawing a square
}
```

The most important aspect is the pure virtual draw() member function of the Shape base class (❶). While you were on vacation, one of your team members already implemented this draw() member function for both the Circle and the Square classes using OpenGL (❷ and ❸). The tool is already able to draw circles and squares, and the entire team agrees that the resulting graphics look pretty neat. Everyone is happy!

Analyzing the Design Issues

Everyone, except you, that is. Returning from your vacation, you of course immediately realize that the implemented solution violates the Single-Responsibility Principle (SRP).[1] As it is, the Shape hierarchy is not designed for change. First, it's not easy to change the way a shape is drawn. In the current implementation, there is only one fixed way of drawing shapes, and it's not possible to change these details nonintrusively. Since you already predict that the tool will have to support multiple graphic libraries, this is definitely a problem.[2] And second, if you eventually perform the change, you need to change the behavior in multiple, unrelated places.

But there is more. Since the drawing functionality is implemented inside Circle and Square, the Circle and Square classes depend on the implementation details of draw(), meaning they depend on OpenGL. Despite the fact that circles and squares should primarily be some simple geometric primitives, these two classes now carry the burden of having to use OpenGL everywhere they are used.

When pointing this out to your colleagues, they are, at first, a little dumbfounded. And also a little annoyed, since they didn't expect you to point out any flaws in their beautiful solution. However, you have a very nice way of explaining the problem, and eventually they agree with you and start to think about a better solution.

---

1 See "Guideline 2: Design for Change" on page 11.

2 You may correctly argue that there are multiple solutions for this problem: you could have one source file per graphics library, you could rely on the preprocessor by sprinkling a couple of #ifdefs across the code, or you could implement an abstraction layer around the graphics libraries. The first two options feel like technical workarounds to a flawed design. The latter option, however, is a reasonable, alternative solution to the one that I will propose. It's a solution based on the *Facade* design pattern, which, unfortunately, I don't cover in this book.

It doesn't take them long to come up with a better approach. In the next team meeting a few days later, they present their new idea: another layer in the inheritance hierarchy (see Figure 5-2).

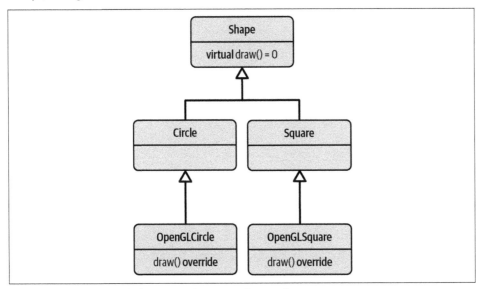

Figure 5-2. The extended Shape inheritance hierarchy

To demonstrate the idea, they have already implemented the OpenGLCircle and OpenGLSquare classes:

```
//---- <Circle.h> ----------------

#include <Shape.h>

class Circle : public Shape
{
 public:
   // ... No implementation of the draw() member function anymore
};


//---- <OpenGLCircle.h> ----------------

#include <Circle.h>

class OpenGLCircle : public Circle
{
 public:
   explicit OpenGLCircle( double radius )
      : Circle( radius )
   {}
```

```
    void draw( /*some arguments*/ ) const override;
};


//---- <OpenGLCircle.cpp> ---------------

#include <OpenGLCircle.h>
#include /* OpenGL graphics library headers */

void OpenGLCircle::draw( /*some arguments*/ ) const
{
   // ... Implementing the logic for drawing a circle by means of OpenGL
}


//---- <Square.h> ---------------

#include <Shape.h>

class Square : public Shape
{
 public:
   // ... No implementation of the draw() member function anymore
};


//---- <OpenGLSquare.h> ---------------

#include <Square.h>

class OpenGLSquare : public Square
{
 public:
   explicit OpenGLSquare( double side )
      : Square( side )
   {}

   void draw( /*some arguments*/ ) const override;
};


//---- <OpenGLSquare.cpp> ---------------

#include <OpenGLSquare.h>
#include /* OpenGL graphics library headers */

void OpenGLSquare::draw( /*some arguments*/ ) const
{
   // ... Implementing the logic for drawing a square by means of OpenGL
}
```

Inheritance! Of course! By simply deriving from `Circle` and `Square`, and by moving the implementation of the `draw()` function further down the hierarchy, it is easily possible to implement the drawing in different ways. For instance, there could be a `MetalCircle` and a `VulkanCircle`, assuming that the Metal (*https://devel oper.apple.com/metal*) and Vulkan (*https://www.vulkan.org*) libraries need to be supported. Suddenly, change is easy, right?

While your colleagues are still very proud about their new solution, you already realize that this approach will not work well for long. And it is easy to demonstrate the shortcomings: all you have to do is consider another requirement, for instance, a `serialize()` member function:

```
class Shape
{
 public:
   virtual ~Shape() = default;

   virtual void draw( /*some arguments*/ ) const = 0;
   virtual void serialize( /*some arguments*/ ) const = 0;   ❹
};
```

The `serialize()` member function (❹) is supposed to transform a shape into a byte sequence, which can be stored in a file or a database. From there, it's possible to deserialize the byte sequence to re-create the exact same shape. And just like the `draw()` member function, the `serialize()` member function can be implemented in various ways. For instance, you could reach for the protobuf (*https://oreil.ly/Q71oF*) or Boost.serialization (*https://oreil.ly/1m84h*) libraries.

Using the same strategy of moving the implementation details down the inheritance hierarchy, this will quickly lead to a pretty complex and rather artificial hierarchy (see Figure 5-3). Consider the class names: `OpenGLProtobufCircle`, `MetalBoostSerial Square`, and so on. Ridiculous, right? And how should we structure this: should we add another layer in the hierarchy (see the `Square` branch)? That approach would quickly lead to a deep and complex hierarchy. Or should we rather flatten the hierarchy out (as in the `Circle` branch of the hierarchy)? And what about reusing implementation details? For instance, how would it be possible to reuse the OpenGL code between the `OpenGLProtobufCircle` and the `OpenGLBoostSerialCircle` classes?

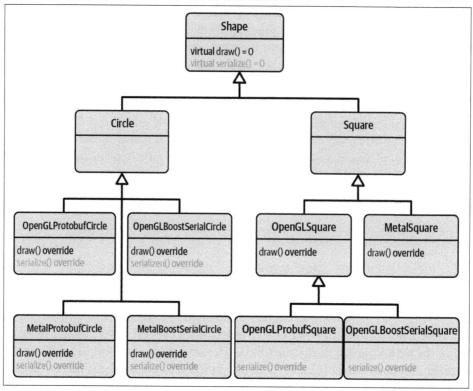

Figure 5-3. Adding the `serialize()` *member function results in a deep and complex inheritance hierarchy*

The Strategy Design Pattern Explained

You realize that your colleagues are just too enamored with inheritance, and that it's up to you to save the day. They appear to need someone to show them how to properly design for this kind of change and present them a proper solution to the problem. As the two pragmatic programmers remarked:[3]

> Inheritance is rarely the answer.

The problem is still the violation of the SRP. Since you have to plan for changing how the different shapes are drawn, you should identify the drawing aspect as a *variation point*. With this realization, the correct approach is to design for change, follow the SRP, and thus extract the variation point. That is the intent of the Strategy design pattern, one of the classic GoF design patterns.

---

3 David Thomas and Andrew Hunt, *The Pragmatic Programmer*.

The Strategy Design Pattern

Intent: "Define a family of algorithms, encapsulate each one, and make them interchangeable. Strategy lets the algorithm vary independently from clients that use it."[4]

Instead of implementing the virtual `draw()` function in a derived class, you introduce another class for the purpose of drawing shapes. In the case of the classic, object-oriented (OO) form of the Strategy design pattern, this is achieved by introducing the `DrawStrategy` base class (see Figure 5-4).

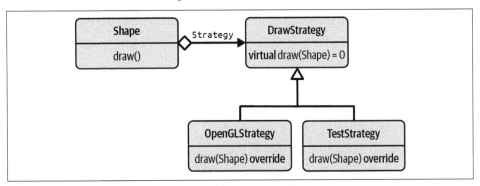

Figure 5-4. The UML representation of the Strategy design pattern

The isolation of the drawing aspect now allows us to change the implementation of drawing without having to modify the shape classes. This fulfills the idea of the SRP. You are now also able to introduce new implementations of `draw()` without modification of any other code. That fulfills the Open-Closed Principle (OCP). Once again, in this OO setting, SRP is the enabler of the OCP.

The following code snippet shows a naive implementation of the `DrawStrategy` base class:[5]

```
//---- <DrawStrategy.h> ----------------

class Circle;
class Square;

class DrawStrategy
{
  public:
```

---

4 Erich Gamma et al., *Design Patterns: Elements of Reusable Object-Oriented Software*.

5 Please explicitly note that I said *naive*. Although the code example is didactically a little questionable, I will show a common misconception before showing a proper implementation. My hope is that this way you will never fall into this common trap.

```cpp
      virtual ~DrawStrategy() = default;

      virtual void draw( Circle const& circle, /*some arguments*/ ) const = 0;  ❺
      virtual void draw( Square const& square, /*some arguments*/ ) const = 0;  ❻
   };
```

The DrawStrategy class comes with a virtual destructor and two pure virtual draw() functions, one for circles (❺) and one for squares (❻). For this base class to compile, you need to forward declare the Circle and the Square classes.

The Shape base class does not change due to the Strategy design pattern. It still represents an abstraction for all shapes and thus offers a pure virtual draw() member function. Strategy aims at extracting implementation details and thus affects only the derived classes:[6]

```cpp
//---- <Shape.h> ----------------

class Shape
{
 public:
   virtual ~Shape() = default;

   virtual void draw( /*some arguments*/ ) const = 0;
   // ... Potentially other functions, e.g. a 'serialize()' member function
};
```

While the Shape base class does not change due to Strategy, the Circle and Square classes are affected:

```cpp
//---- <Circle.h> ----------------

#include <Shape.h>
#include <DrawStrategy.h>
#include <memory>
#include <utility>

class Circle : public Shape
{
 public:
   explicit Circle( double radius, std::unique_ptr<DrawStrategy> drawer )  ❼
      : radius_( radius )
      , drawer_( std::move(drawer) )  ❽
   {
```

---

6 Although this is not a book about implementation details, please allow me to highlight one implementation detail that I find to be the source of many questions in my training classes. I'm certain you've heard about the Rule of 5—if not, please see the C++ Core Guidelines (*https://oreil.ly/fzS3f*). Hence, you realize that the declaration of a virtual destructor disables the move operations. Strictly speaking, this is a violation of the Rule of 5. However, as Core Guideline C.21 (*https://oreil.ly/fzS3f*) explains, for base classes this is not considered to be a problem, as long as the base class does not contain any data members.

```
        /* Checking that the given radius is valid and that
           the given std::unique_ptr instance is not nullptr */
   }

   void draw( /*some arguments*/ ) const override
   {
      drawer_->draw( *this, /*some arguments*/ );   ❿
   }

   double radius() const { return radius_; }

 private:
   double radius_;
   std::unique_ptr<DrawStrategy> drawer_;   ❾
};


//---- <Square.h> ----------------

#include <Shape.h>
#include <DrawStrategy.h>
#include <memory>
#include <utility>

class Square : public Shape
{
 public:
   explicit Square( double side, std::unique_ptr<DrawStrategy> drawer )   ❼
      : side_( side )
      , drawer_( std::move(drawer) )   ❽
   {
      /* Checking that the given side length is valid and that
         the given std::unique_ptr instance is not nullptr */
   }

   void draw( /*some arguments*/ ) const override
   {
      drawer_->draw( *this, /*some arguments*/ );   ❿
   }

   double side() const { return side_; }

 private:
   double side_;
   std::unique_ptr<DrawStrategy> drawer_;   ❾
};
```

Both Circle and Square are now expecting a unique_ptr to a DrawStrategy in their constructors (❼). This allows us to configure the drawing behavior from the outside, commonly called *dependency injection*. The unique_ptr is moved (❽) into a new data member of the same type (❾). It is also possible to provide corresponding setter functions, which would allow you to change the drawing behavior at a later point. The draw() member function now doesn't have to implement the drawing itself but simply has to call the draw() function for the given DrawStrategy (❿).[7]

Analyzing the Shortcomings of the Naive Solution

Wonderful! With this implementation in place, you are now able to locally, in isolation, change the behavior of how shapes are drawn, and you enable everyone to implement the new drawing behavior. However, as it is right now, our Strategy implementation has a serious design flaw. To analyze this flaw, let's assume that you have to add a new kind of shape, maybe a Triangle. This should be easy, because, as we have discussed in "Guideline 15: Design for the Addition of Types or Operations" on page 102, the strength of OOP is the addition of new types.

As you're starting to introduce this Triangle, you realize that it's not as easy to add the new kind of shape as expected. First, you need to write the new class. That is to be expected and not a problem at all. But then you have to update the DrawStrategy base class to also enable the drawing of triangles. This, in turn, will have an unfortunate impact on circles and squares: both the Circle and Square classes need to be recompiled, retested, and potentially redeployed. More generally speaking, *all* shapes are affected in this way. And that should strike you as problematic. Why should circles and squares have to recompile if you add a Triangle class?

The technical reason is that via the DrawStrategy base class, all shapes implicitly know about one another. Adding a new shape therefore affects all other shapes. The underlying design reason is a violation of the Interface Segregation Principle (ISP) (see "Guideline 3: Separate Interfaces to Avoid Artificial Coupling" on page 24). By defining a single DrawStrategy base class, you have artificially coupled circles, squares, and triangles together. Due to this coupling, you have made it more difficult to add new types and thus have limited the strength of OOP. In comparison, you have created a very similar situation as we had when we talked about a procedural solution for the drawing of shapes (see "Guideline 15: Design for the Addition of Types or Operations" on page 102).

"Didn't we unintentionally reimplement the Visitor design pattern?" you are wondering. I see your point: the DrawStrategy looks very similar to a Visitor indeed. But unfortunately, it does not fulfill the intent of a Visitor, since you cannot easily add other operations. To do so, you would have to intrusively add a virtual member

---

[7] As I have referenced Core Guideline C.21 before, it is also worth mentioning that both the Circle and Square classes fulfill the *Rule of 0*; see Core Guideline C.20 (*https://oreil.ly/Gt5Sz*). By not falling into the habit of adding a destructor, the compiler itself generates all special member functions for both classes. And yes, worry not—the destructor is still virtual since the base class destructor is virtual.

function in the Shape hierarchy. "And it is not a Strategy either, because we cannot add types, right?" Yes, correct. You see, from a design perspective, this is the worst kind of situation.

To properly implement the Strategy design pattern, you have to extract the implementation details of each shape separately. You have to introduce one DrawStrategy class for each kind of shape:

```
//---- <DrawCircleStrategy.h> ----------------

class Circle;

class DrawCircleStrategy   ⓫
{
 public:
   virtual ~DrawCircleStrategy() = default;

   virtual void draw( Circle const& circle, /*some arguments*/ ) const = 0;
};


//---- <Circle.h> ----------------

#include <Shape.h>
#include <DrawCircleStrategy.h>
#include <memory>
#include <utility>

class Circle : public Shape
{
 public:
   explicit Circle( double radius, std::unique_ptr<DrawCircleStrategy> drawer )
      : radius_( radius )
      , drawer_( std::move(drawer) )
   {
      /* Checking that the given radius is valid and that
         the given 'std::unique_ptr' is not a nullptr */
   }

   void draw( /*some arguments*/ ) const override
   {
      drawer_->draw( *this, /*some arguments*/ );
   }

   double radius() const { return radius_; }

 private:
   double radius_;
   std::unique_ptr<DrawCircleStrategy> drawer_;
};
```

```
//---- <DrawSquareStrategy.h> ---------------

class Square;

class DrawSquareStrategy  ⓬
{
 public:
   virtual ~DrawSquareStrategy() = default;

   virtual void draw( Square const& square, /*some arguments*/ ) const = 0;
};


//---- <Square.h> ---------------

#include <Shape.h>
#include <DrawSquareStrategy.h>
#include <memory>
#include <utility>

class Square : public Shape
{
 public:
   explicit Square( double side, std::unique_ptr<DrawSquareStrategy> drawer )
      : side_( side )
      , drawer_( std::move(drawer) )
   {
      /* Checking that the given side length is valid and that
         the given 'std::unique_ptr' is not a nullptr */
   }

   void draw( /*some arguments*/ ) const override
   {
      drawer_->draw( *this, /*some arguments*/ );
   }

   double side() const { return side_; }

 private:
   double side_;
   std::unique_ptr<DrawSquareStrategy> drawer_;
};
```

For the Circle class, you have to introduce the DrawCircleStrategy base class (⓫), and for the Square class, it is the DrawSquareStrategy (⓬) base class. And with the addition of a Triangle class, you will also have to add a DrawTriangleStrategy base class. Only in this way can you properly separate concerns and still allow everyone to add new types and new implementations for the drawing of shapes.

With this functionality in place, you can easily implement new Strategy classes for drawing circles, squares, and eventually triangles. As an example, consider the OpenGLCircleStrategy, which implements the DrawCircleStrategy interface:

```
//---- <OpenGLCircleStrategy.h> ----------------

#include <Circle.h>
#include <DrawCircleStrategy.h>
#include /* OpenGL graphics library */

class OpenGLCircleStrategy : public DrawCircleStrategy
{
 public:
   explicit OpenGLCircleStrategy( /* Drawing related arguments */ );

   void draw( Circle const& circle, /*...*/ ) const override;

 private:
   /* Drawing related data members, e.g. colors, textures, ... */
};
```

In Figure 5-5 you can see the dependency graph for the Circle class. Note that the Circle and DrawCircleStrategy classes are on the same architectural level. Even more noteworthy is the cyclic dependency between them: Circle depends on the DrawCircleStrategy, but the DrawCircleStrategy also depends on Circle. But don't worry: although this may look like a problem at first sight, it isn't. It is a necessary relationship that shows that Circle really owns the DrawCircleStrategy and by that creates the desired dependency inversion, as discussed in "Guideline 9: Pay Attention to the Ownership of Abstractions" on page 62.

"Wouldn't it be possible to implement the different draw Strategy classes using a class template? I'm imagining something similar to the Visitor class used for the Acyclic Visitor":[8]

```
//---- <DrawStrategy.h> ----------------

template< typename T >
class DrawStrategy
{
 public:
   virtual ~DrawStrategy() = default;
   virtual void draw( T const& ) const = 0;
};
```

---

8 See "Guideline 18: Beware the Performance of Acyclic Visitor" on page 133 for a discussion about the Acyclic Visitor design pattern.

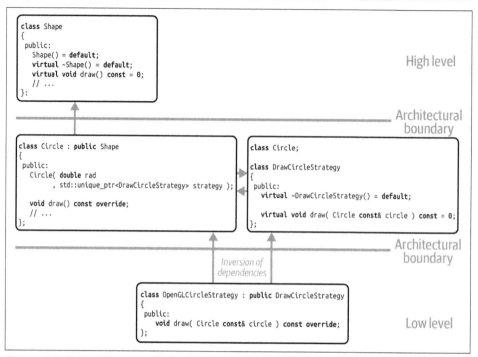

Figure 5-5. Dependency graph for the Strategy design pattern

This is a great idea and exactly what you should do. By means of this class template, you can lift the `DrawStrategy` up into a higher architectural level, reuse code, and follow the DRY principle (see Figure 5-6). Additionally, if we would have used this approach from the start, we would not have fallen into the trap of artificially coupling the different shape types. Yes, I really like that!

Although this is how we would implement such a Strategy class, you still should not expect that this will reduce the number of base classes (it's still the same, just generated) or that it will save you a lot of work. The implementations of `DrawStrategy`, such as the `OpenGLCircleStrategy` class, represent most of the work and will hardly change:

```
//---- <OpenGLCircleStrategy.h> ----------------

#include <Circle.h>
#include <DrawStrategy.h>
#include /* OpenGL graphics library */

class OpenGLCircleStrategy : public DrawStrategy<Circle>
{
   // ...
};
```

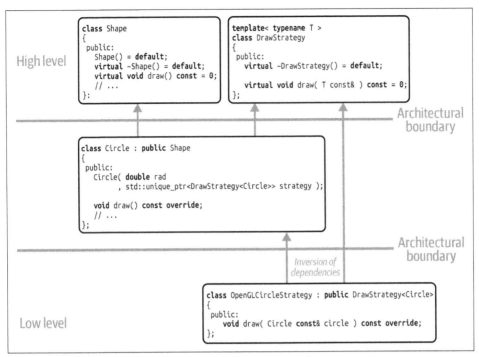

Figure 5-6. Updated dependency graph for the Strategy design pattern

Assuming a similar implementation for the `OpenGLSquareStrategy`, we can now put everything together and draw shapes again but this time properly decoupled with the Strategy design pattern:

```cpp
#include <Circle.h>
#include <Square.h>
#include <OpenGLCircleStrategy.h>
#include <OpenGLSquareStrategy.h>
#include <memory>
#include <vector>

int main()
{
   using Shapes = std::vector<std::unique_ptr<Shape>>;

   Shapes shapes{};

   // Creating some shapes, each one
   //    equipped with the corresponding OpenGL drawing strategy
   shapes.emplace_back(
      std::make_unique<Circle>(
         2.3, std::make_unique<OpenGLCircleStrategy>(/*...red...*/) ) );
   shapes.emplace_back(
      std::make_unique<Square>(
```

```
        1.2, std::make_unique<OpenGLSquareStrategy>(/*...green...*/) ) );
    shapes.emplace_back(
      std::make_unique<Circle>(
        4.1, std::make_unique<OpenGLCircleStrategy>(/*...blue...*/) ) );

    // Drawing all shapes
    for( auto const& shape : shapes )
    {
      shape->draw( /*some arguments*/ );
    }

    return EXIT_SUCCESS;
}
```

Comparison Between Visitor and Strategy

As you have now learned about both the Visitor and Strategy design patterns, you might wonder what the difference between the two is. After all, the implementation looks fairly similar. But while there are parallels in implementation, the properties of the two design patterns are very different. With the Visitor design pattern, we have identified the *general* addition of operations as the *variation point*. Therefore, we created an abstraction for operations in general, which in turn allowed everyone to add operations. The unfortunate side effect was that it was no longer easy to add new shape types.

With the Strategy design pattern, we have identified the implementation details of a *single* function as a *variation point*. After introducing an abstraction for these implementation details, we're still able to easily add new types of shapes, but we are not able to easily add new operations. Adding an operation would still require you to intrusively add a virtual member function. Hence, the intent of the Strategy design pattern is the opposite of the intent of the Visitor design pattern.

It may sound promising to combine the two design patterns to gain the advantages of both ideas (making it easy to add both types *and* operations). Unfortunately, this does not work: whichever of the two design patterns you apply first will fix one of the two axes of freedom.[9] Therefore, you should just remember the strengths and weaknesses of these two design patterns and apply them based on your expectations of how your codebase will evolve.

---

9 I should explicitly state that it does not work in dynamic polymorphism. It does work in static polymorphism, even quite well. Consider, for instance, templates and function overloading.

Analyzing the Shortcomings of the Strategy Design Pattern

I have shown you the advantages of the Strategy design pattern: it allows you to reduce the dependencies on a particular implementation detail by introducing an abstraction for that detail. However, there is no silver bullet in software design, and every design comes with a number of drawbacks. The Strategy design pattern is no exception, and it's important to also take potential disadvantages into account.

First, while the implementation details of a certain operation have been extracted and isolated, the operation itself is still part of the concrete type. This fact is evidence of the aforementioned limitation that we are still not able to easily add operations. Strategy, in contrast to Visitor, preserves the strength of OOP and enables you to easily add new types.

Second, it pays off to identify such variation points early. Otherwise a large refactoring is required. Of course, this doesn't mean you should implement everything with Strategy up front, just in case, to avoid a refactoring. This could quickly result in overengineering. But at the first indication that an implementation detail might change, or that there is a desire to have multiple implementations, you should rather quickly implement the necessary modifications. The best, but of course a little insubstantial, advice is to keep things as simple as possible (the *KISS* principle (*https://oreil.ly/YVUhD*); Keep It Simple, Stupid).

Third, if you implement Strategy by means of a base class, the performance will certainly take a hit by the additional runtime indirection. The performance is also affected by the many manual allocations (the `std::make_unique()` calls), the resulting memory fragmentation, and the various indirections due to numerous pointers. This is to be expected, yet the flexibility of your implementation and the opportunity for everyone to add new implementations may outweigh this performance penalty. Of course, it depends, and you will have to decide on a case-by-case basis. If you implement Strategy using templates (see the discussion about "Policy-Based Design" on page 159), this disadvantage is of no concern.

Last but not least, the major disadvantage of the Strategy design pattern is that a single Strategy should deal with either a single operation or a small group of cohesive functions. Otherwise you would again violate the SRP. If the implementation details of multiple operations need to be extracted, there will have to be multiple Strategy base classes and multiple data members, which can be set via *dependency injection*. Consider, for instance, the situation with an additional `serialize()` member function:

```
//---- <DrawCircleStrategy.h> ----------------

class Circle;

class DrawCircleStrategy
```

```cpp
{
 public:
   virtual ~DrawCircleStrategy() = default;

   virtual void draw( Circle const& circle, /*some arguments*/ ) const = 0;
};


//---- <SerializeCircleStrategy.h> ---------------

class Circle;

class SerializeCircleStrategy
{
 public:
   virtual ~SerializeCircleStrategy() = default;

   virtual void serialize( Circle const& circle, /*some arguments*/ ) const = 0;
};


//---- <Circle.h> ---------------

#include <Shape.h>
#include <DrawCircleStrategy.h>
#include <SerializeCircleStrategy.h>
#include <memory>
#include <utility>

class Circle : public Shape
{
 public:
   explicit Circle( double radius
                  , std::unique_ptr<DrawCircleStrategy> drawer
                  , std::unique_ptr<SerializeCircleStrategy> serializer
                  /* potentially more strategy-related arguments */ )
      : radius_( radius )
      , drawer_( std::move(drawer) )
      , serializer_( std::move(serializer) )
      // ...
   {
      /* Checking that the given radius is valid and that
         the given std::unique_ptrs are not nullptrs */
   }

   void draw( /*some arguments*/ ) const override
   {
      drawer_->draw( *this, /*some arguments*/ );
   }

   void serialize( /*some arguments*/ ) const override
   {
```

```
      serializer_->serialize( *this, /*some arguments*/ );
   }

   double radius() const { return radius_; }

 private:
   double radius_;
   std::unique_ptr<DrawCircleStrategy> drawer_;
   std::unique_ptr<SerializeCircleStrategy> serializer_;
   // ... Potentially more strategy-related data members
};
```

While this leads to a very unfortunate proliferation of base classes and larger instances due to multiple pointers, it also raises the question of how to design the class so that it's possible to conveniently assign multiple different strategies. Therefore, the Strategy design pattern appears to be strongest in situations where you need to isolate a small number of implementation details. If you encounter a situation where you need to extract the details of many operations, it might be better to consider other approaches (see, for instance, the External Polymorphism design pattern in Chapter 7 or the Type Erasure design pattern in Chapter 8).

Policy-Based Design

As already demonstrated in previous chapters, the Strategy design pattern is not limited to dynamic polymorphism. On the contrary, the intent of Strategy can be implemented perfectly in static polymorphism using templates. Consider, for instance, the following two algorithms from the Standard Library:

```
namespace std {

template< typename ForwardIt, typename UnaryPredicate >
constexpr ForwardIt
   partition( ForwardIt first, ForwardIt last, UnaryPredicate p );  ⓭

template< typename RandomIt, typename Compare >
constexpr void
   sort( RandomIt first, RandomIt last, Compare comp );  ⓮

} // namespace std
```

Both the std::partition() and the std::sort() algorithm make use of the Strategy design pattern. The UnaryPredicate argument of std::partition() (⓭) and the Compare argument of std::sort() (⓮) represent a means to inject part of the behavior from outside. More specifically, both arguments allow you to specify how elements are ordered. Hence, both algorithms extract a specific part of their behavior and provide an abstraction for it in the form of a concept (see "Guideline 7: Understand the Similarities Between Base Classes and Concepts" on page 52). This, in contrast to the OO form of Strategy, does not incur any runtime performance penalty.

A similar approach can be seen in the std::unique_ptr class template:

```
namespace std {

template< typename T, typename Deleter = std::default_delete<T> >  ⑮
class unique_ptr;

template< typename T, typename Deleter >  ⑯
class unique_ptr<T[], Deleter>;

} // namespace std
```

For both the base template (⑮) and its specialization for arrays (⑯), it is possible to specify an explicit Deleter as the second template argument. With this argument, you can decide whether you want to free the resource by means of delete, free(), or any other deallocation function. It's even possible to "abuse" std::unique_ptr to perform a completely different kind of cleanup.

This flexibility is also evidence for the Strategy design pattern. The template argument allows you to inject some cleanup behavior into the class. This form of Strategy is also called *policy-based design*, based on a design philosophy introduced by Andrei Alexandrescu in 2001.[10] The idea is the same: extract and isolate specific behavior of class templates to improve changeability, extensibility, testability, and reusability. Thus, policy-based design can be considered the static polymorphism form of the Strategy design pattern. And evidently, the design works really well, as the many applications of this idea in the Standard Library demonstrate.

You can also apply policy-based design to the shape-drawing example. Consider the following implementation of the Circle class:

```
//---- <Circle.h> ----------------

#include <Shape.h>
#include <DrawCircleStrategy.h>
#include <memory>
#include <utility>

template< typename DrawCircleStrategy >  ⑰
class Circle : public Shape
{
 public:
   explicit Circle( double radius, DrawCircleStrategy drawer )
      : radius_( radius )
      , drawer_( std::move(drawer) )
   {
      /* Checking that the given radius is valid */
```

---

10 Andrei Alexandrescu, *Modern C++ Design: Generic Programming and Design Patterns Applied* (Addison-Wesley, 2001).

```
    }

    void draw( /*some arguments*/ ) const override
    {
        drawer_( *this, /*some arguments*/ );  ❶❽
    }

    double radius() const { return radius_; }

  private:
    double radius_;
    DrawCircleStrategy drawer_;  // Could possibly be omitted, if the given
                                 // strategy is presumed to be stateless.
};
```

Instead of passing `std::unique_ptr` to a `DrawCircleStrategy` base class in the constructor, you could specify the Strategy with a template argument (❶❼). The biggest advantage would be the performance improvement due to fewer pointer indirections: instead of calling through `std::unique_ptr`, you could directly call to the concrete implementation provided by the `DrawCircleStrategy` (❶❽). On the downside, you would lose the flexibility to adapt the drawing Strategy of a specific `Circle` instance at runtime. Also, you wouldn't have a single `Circle` class anymore. You would have one instantiation of `Circle` for every drawing strategy. And last but not least, you should keep in mind that class templates usually completely reside in header files. You could therefore lose the opportunity to hide implementation details in a source file. As always, there is no perfect solution, and the choice of the "right" solution depends on the actual context.

In summary, the Strategy design pattern is one of the most versatile examples in the catalog of design patterns. You will find it useful in many situations in the realm of dynamic as well as static polymorphism. However, it is not the ultimate solution for every problem—be aware of its potential disadvantages.

Guideline 19: Use Strategy to Isolate How Things Are Done

- Understand that inheritance is rarely the answer.
- Apply the Strategy design pattern with the intent to extract the implementation details of a cohesive set of functions.
- Implement one Strategy for each operation to avoid artificial coupling.
- Consider policy-based design as the compile-time form of the Strategy design pattern.

Guideline 20: Favor Composition over Inheritance

After the enormous surge of enthusiasm for OOP in the 90s and early 2000s, OOP today is on the defensive. The voices that argue against OOP and highlight its disadvantages grow stronger and louder. This is not limited to the C++ communities but is also in other programming language communities. While OOP in its entirety indeed has some limitations, let's focus on the one feature that appears to generate most of the heat: inheritance. As Sean Parent remarked:[11]

> Inheritance is the base class of evil.

While inheritance is sold as a very natural and intuitive way of modeling real-world relations, it turns out to be much harder to use than promised. You have already seen the subtle failures of using inheritance when we talked about the Liskov Substitution Principle (LSP) in "Guideline 6: Adhere to the Expected Behavior of Abstractions" on page 44. But there are other aspects of inheritance that are often misunderstood.

First and foremost, inheritance is always described as simplifying reusability. This seems intuitive, since it appears obvious that you can reuse code easily if you just inherit from another class. Unfortunately, that's not the kind of reuse inheritance brings to you. Inheritance is not about reusing code in a base class; instead, it is about being reused by other code that uses the base class polymorphically. For instance, assuming a slightly extended Shape base class, the following functions work for all kinds of shapes and thus can be reused by all implementations of the Shape base class:

```cpp
class Shape
{
 public:
   virtual ~Shape() = default;

   virtual void translate( /*some arguments*/ ) = 0;
   virtual void rotate( /*some arguments*/ ) = 0;

   virtual void draw( /*some arguments*/ ) const = 0;
   virtual void serialize( /*some arguments*/ ) const = 0;

   // ... Potentially other member functions ...
};

void rotateAroundPoint( Shape& shape );      ❶
void mergeShapes( Shape& s1, Shape& s2 );    ❷
void writeToFile( Shape const& shape );       ❸
void sendViaRPC( Shape const& shape );        ❹
// ...
```

---

11 Sean Parent, "Inheritance Is the Base Class Of Evil" (*https://oreil.ly/F8FDL*), GoingNative, 2013.

All four functions (❶, ❷, ❸, and ❹) are built on the Shape abstraction. All of these functions are coupled only to the common interface of all kinds of shapes but not to any specific shape. All kinds of shapes can be rotated around a point, merged, written to file, and sent via RPC. Every shape "reuses" this functionality.

It is the ability to express functionality by means of an abstraction that creates the opportunity to reuse code. This functionality is expected to create a vast amount of code, in comparison to the small amount of code the base class contains. Real reusability, therefore, is created by the polymorphic use of a type, not by polymorphic types.[12]

Second, inheritance is said to help in decoupling software entities. While that is most certainly true (remember, for instance, the discussion about the Dependency Inversion Principle (DIP) in "Guideline 9: Pay Attention to the Ownership of Abstractions" on page 62), it's often not explained that inheritance also creates coupling. You've seen evidence of that before. While implementing the Visitor design pattern, you experienced that inheritance forces certain implementation details on you. In a classic Visitor, you have to implement the pure virtual functions of a Visitor base class as they are required, even if this is not optimal for your application. You also don't have a lot of choices with respect to the function arguments or return types. These things are fixed.[13]

You also experienced this coupling at the beginning of the discussion on the Strategy design pattern. In this case, inheritance forced a structural coupling that caused a deep(er) inheritance hierarchy, resulted in questionable naming of classes, and impaired reuse.

At this point, you might get the impression that I'm trying to discredit inheritance completely. Well, to be honest, I am trying to make it look just a little bad, but only as much as necessary. To state it clearly: inheritance is not bad, nor is it wrong to use it. On the contrary: inheritance is a very powerful feature, and if used properly you can do incredible things with it. However, of course you remember the Peter Parker Principle:

> With great power comes great responsibility.
>
> —Peter Parker, aka Spider-Man

---

12 According to Sean Parent, there are no polymorphic types, only polymorphic usage of similar types; see "Better Code: Runtime Polymorphism" (*https://oreil.ly/5HwgM*) from the NDC London conference in 2017. My statement supports that opinion.

13 Another example of inheritance creating coupling is discussed in Herb Sutter's *Exceptional C++: 47 Engineering Puzzles, Programming Problems, and Exception-Safety Solutions* (Pearson Education).

The problem is the "if used properly" part. Inheritance has proven to be hard to use properly (definitely harder than we are led to believe; see my previous reasonings), and thus is misused unintentionally. It is also overused, as many developers have the habit of using it for every kind of problem.[14] This overuse appears to be the source of many problems, as Michael Feathers remarks:[15]

> [Programming by difference][16] fell out of favor in the 1990s when many people in the OO community noticed that inheritance can be rather problematic if it is overused.

In many situations, inheritance is neither the right approach nor the right tool. Most of the time it is preferable to use composition instead. You should not be surprised by that revelation, though, because you have already seen it to be true. Composition is the reason the OO form of the Strategy design pattern works so well, not inheritance. It is the introduction of an abstraction and the aggregation of corresponding data members that make the Strategy design pattern so powerful, not the inheritance-based implementation of different strategies. In fact, you will find that many design patterns are firmly based on composition, not on inheritance.[17] All of these enable extension by means of inheritance but are themselves enabled by means of composition.

> Delegate to Services: Has-A Trumps Is-A.
>
> —Andrew Hunt and David Thomas, The Pragmatic Programmer

This is a general takeaway for many design patterns. I suggest you keep this insight close at hand, as it will prove very useful in understanding the design patterns that you will see in the remainder of this book, and will improve the quality of your implementations.

---

14 Are they really to blame for this habit? Since they've been taught that this is the way to go for decades, who can blame them for thinking this way?

15 Michael C. Feathers, *Working Effectively with Legacy Code*.

16 Programming by difference is a rather extreme form of inheritance-based programming, where even small differences are expressed by introducing a new derived class. See Michael's book for more details.

17 See, for instance, the Strategy design pattern in "Guideline 19: Use Strategy to Isolate How Things Are Done" on page 140, the Observer design pattern in "Guideline 25: Apply Observers as an Abstract Notification Mechanism" on page 209, the Adapter design pattern in "Guideline 24: Use Adapters to Standardize Interfaces" on page 198, the Decorator design pattern in "Guideline 35: Use Decorators to Add Customization Hierarchically" on page 348, or the Bridge design pattern in "Guideline 28: Build Bridges to Remove Physical Dependencies" on page 250.

Guideline 21: Use Command to Isolate What Things Are Done

Before we get started with this guideline, let's try an experiment. Open your preferred email client and write an email to me. Add the following content: "I love your book! It keeps me up all night and makes me forget all my troubles." OK, great. Now click Send. Good job! Give me a second to check my emails…No, it's not here yet…No, still not here…Let's try again: Click Resend. No, nothing. Hmm, I guess some server must be down. Or all of my Commands simply failed: the `WriteCommand`, the `SendCommand`, the `ResendCommand`, and so on. How unfortunate. But despite this failed experiment, you now have a pretty good idea of another GoF design pattern: the Command design pattern.

The Command Design Pattern Explained

The Command design pattern focuses on the abstraction and isolation of work packages that (most often) are executed once and (usually) immediately. For that purpose, it recognizes the existence of different kinds of work packages as *variation points* and introduces the corresponding abstraction that allows the easy implementation of new kinds of work packages.

The Command Design Pattern

Intent: "Encapsulate a request as an object, thereby letting you parameterize clients with different requests, queue or log requests, and support undoable operations."[18]

Figure 5-7 shows the original UML formulation, taken from the GoF book.

---

18 Erich Gamma et al., *Design Patterns: Elements of Reusable Object-Oriented Software*.

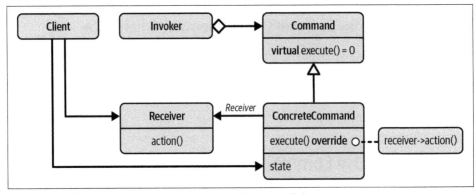

Figure 5-7. The UML representation of the Command design pattern

In this OO-based form, the Command pattern introduces an abstraction in the form of the Command base class. This enables anyone to implement a new kind of ConcreteCommand. That ConcreteCommand can do anything, even perform an action on some kind of Receiver. The effect of a command is triggered via the abstract base class by a particular kind of Invoker.

As a concrete example of the Command design pattern, let's consider the following implementation of a calculator. The first code snippet shows the implementation of a CalculatorCommand base class, which represents the abstraction of a mathematical operation on a given integer:

```
//---- <CalculatorCommand.h> ----------------

class CalculatorCommand
{
 public:
   virtual ~CalculatorCommand() = default;

   virtual int execute( int i ) const = 0;   ❶
   virtual int undo( int i ) const = 0;   ❷
};
```

The CalculatorCommand class expects derived classes to implement both the pure virtual execute() function (❶) and the pure virtual undo() function (❷). The expectation for undo() is that it implements the necessary actions to reverse the effect of the execute() function.

The Add and Subtract classes both represent possible commands for a calculator and therefore implement the CalculatorCommand base class:

```
//---- <Add.h> ----------------

#include <CalculatorCommand.h>
```

```
class Add : public CalculatorCommand
{
 public:
   explicit Add( int operand ) : operand_(operand) {}

   int execute( int i ) const override  ❸
   {
      return i + operand_;
   }
   int undo( int i ) const override  ❹
   {
      return i - operand_;
   }

 private:
   int operand_{};
};


//---- <Subtract.h> ----------------

#include <CalculatorCommand.h>

class Subtract : public CalculatorCommand
{
 public:
   explicit Subtract( int operand ) : operand_(operand) {}

   int execute( int i ) const override  ❺
   {
      return i - operand_;
   }
   int undo( int i ) const override  ❻
   {
      return i + operand_;
   }

 private:
   int operand_{};
};
```

Add implements the execute() function using an addition operation (❸) and the undo() function using a subtraction operation (❹). Subtract implements the inverse (❺ and ❻).

Thanks to the CalculatorCommand hierarchy, the Calculator class itself can be kept rather simple:

```
//---- <Calculator.h> ----------------

#include <CalculatorCommand.h>
#include <stack>
```

```
class Calculator
{
 public:
   void compute( std::unique_ptr<CalculatorCommand> command );   ❼
   void undoLast();   ❽

   int result() const;
   void clear();

 private:
   using CommandStack = std::stack<std::unique_ptr<CalculatorCommand>>;

   int current_{};   ❾
   CommandStack stack_;   ❿
};


//---- <Calculator.cpp> ----------------

#include <Calculator.h>

void Calculator::compute( std::unique_ptr<CalculatorCommand> command )   ❼
{
   current_ = command->execute( current_ );
   stack_.push( std::move(command) );
}

void Calculator::undoLast()   ❽
{
   if( stack_.empty() ) return;

   auto command = std::move(stack_.top());
   stack_.pop();

   current_ = command->undo(current_);
}

int Calculator::result() const
{
   return current_;
}

void Calculator::clear()
{
   current_ = 0;
   CommandStack{}.swap( stack_ );  // Clearing the stack
}
```

The only functions we need for the computing activities are compute() (❼) and undo
Last() (❽). The compute() function is passed a CalculatorCommand instance, immediately executes it to update the current value (❾), and stores it on the stack (❿). The

undoLast() function reverts the last executed command by popping it from the stack and calling undo().

The main() function combines all of the pieces:

```cpp
//---- <Main.cpp> ----------------

#include <Calculator.h>
#include <Add.h>
#include <Subtract.h>
#include <cstdlib>

int main()
{
   Calculator calculator{};   ⓫

   auto op1 = std::make_unique<Add>( 3 );   ⓬
   auto op2 = std::make_unique<Add>( 7 );   ⓭
   auto op3 = std::make_unique<Subtract>( 4 );   ⓮
   auto op4 = std::make_unique<Subtract>( 2 );   ⓯

   calculator.compute( std::move(op1) );  // Computes 0 + 3, stores and returns 3
   calculator.compute( std::move(op2) );  // Computes 3 + 7, stores and returns 10
   calculator.compute( std::move(op3) );  // Computes 10 - 4, stores and returns 6
   calculator.compute( std::move(op4) );  // Computes 6 - 2, stores and returns 4

   calculator.undoLast();  // Reverts the last operation,
                           // stores and returns 6

   int const res = calculator.result();  // Get the final result: 6

   // ...

   return EXIT_SUCCESS;
}
```

We first create a calculator (⓫) and a series of operations (⓬, ⓭, ⓮, and ⓯), which we apply one after another. After that, we revert op4 by means of the undoLast() operation before we query the final result.

This design very nicely follows the SOLID principles.[19] It adheres to the SRP since the *variation point* has already been extracted by means of the Command design pattern. As a result, both compute() and undoLast() do not have to be virtual functions. The SRP also acts as an enabler for the OCP, which allows us to add new operations

---

19 Yes, it follows the SOLID principles, although of course by means of the classic form of the Command design pattern. If you are right now biting your fingernails in frustration or simply wondering if there isn't a better way, then please be patient. I will demonstrate a much nicer, much more "modern" solution in "Guideline 22: Prefer Value Semantics over Reference Semantics" on page 176.

without having to modify any existing code. Last, but not least, if the ownership for the `Command` base class is properly assigned to the high level, then the design also adheres to the DIP (see Figure 5-8).

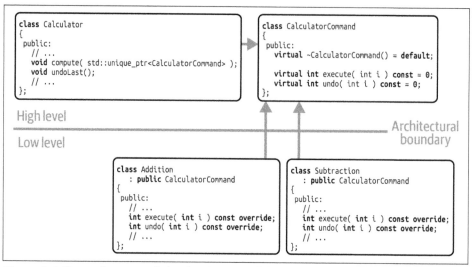

Figure 5-8. Dependency graph for the Command design pattern

There is a second example of the Command design pattern that belongs in the category of classic examples: a thread pool (*https://oreil.ly/jGZd5*). The purpose of a thread pool is to maintain multiple threads waiting for tasks to be executed in parallel. This idea is implemented by the following `ThreadPool` class: it provides a couple of member functions to offload certain tasks to a specific number of available threads:[20]

```
class Command  ⑰
{ /* Abstract interface to perform and undo any kind of action. */ };

class ThreadPool
{
 public:
   explicit ThreadPool( size_t numThreads );

   inline bool   isEmpty() const;
   inline size_t size()    const;
   inline size_t active()  const;
   inline size_t ready()   const;
```

---

20 The given `ThreadPool` class is far from being complete and primarily serves as an illustration for the Command design pattern. For a working, professional implementation of a thread pool, please refer to Anthony William's book *C++ Concurrency in Action*, 2nd ed. (Manning).

```
    void schedule( std::unique_ptr<Command> command );   ⓰

    void wait();

    // ...
};
```

Most importantly, the ThreadPool allows you to schedule a task via the schedule()
function (⓰). This can be *any* task: the ThreadPool is not at all concerned about what
kind of work its threads will have to perform. With the Command base class, it is completely decoupled from the actual kind of task you schedule (⓱).

By simply deriving from Command, you can formulate arbitrary tasks:

```
class FormattingCommand : public Command   ⓲
{ /* Implementation of formatting a disk */ };

class PrintCommand : public Command   ⓳
{ /* Implementation of performing a printer job */ }

int main()
{
    // Creating a thread pool with initially two working threads
    ThreadPool threadpool( 2 );

    // Scheduling two concurrent tasks
    threadpool.schedule(
        std::make_unique<FormattingCommand>( /*some arguments*/ ) );
    threadpool.schedule(
        std::make_unique<PrintCommand>( /*some arguments*/ ) );

    // Waiting for the thread pool to complete both commands
    threadpool.wait();

    return EXIT_SUCCESS;
}
```

One possible example of such a task is a FormattingCommand (⓲). This task would get
the necessary information to trigger the formatting of a disk via the operating system.
Alternatively, you can imagine a PrintCommand that receives all data to trigger a
printer job (⓳).

Also in this ThreadPool example, you recognize the effect of the Command design
pattern: the different kinds of tasks are identified as a *variation point* and are extracted (which again follows the SRP), which enables you to implement different kinds of
tasks without the need to modify existing code (adherence to the OCP).

Of course, there are also some examples from the Standard Library. For instance, you
will see the Command design pattern in action in the std::for_each() (⓴)
algorithm:

```
namespace std {

template< typename InputIt, typename UnaryFunction >
constexpr UnaryFunction
    for_each( InputIt first, InputIt last, UnaryFunction f );  [20]

} // namespace std
```

With the third argument, you can specify *what* task the algorithm is supposed to perform on all of the given elements. This can be any action, ranging from manipulating the elements to printing them, and can be specified by something as simple as a function pointer to something as powerful as a lambda:

```
#include <algorithms>
#include <cstdlib>

void multBy10( int& i )
{
   i *= 10;
}

int main()
{
   std::vector<int> v{ 1, 2, 3, 4, 5 };

   // Multiplying all integers with 10
   std::for_each( begin(v), end(v), multBy10 );

   // Printing all integers
   std::for_each( begin(v), end(v), []( int& i ){
      std::cout << i << '\n';
   } );

   return EXIT_SUCCESS;
}
```

The Command Design Pattern Versus the Strategy Design Pattern

"Wait a second!" I can hear you cry out. "Didn't you just explain that the algorithms of the Standard Library are implemented by means of the Strategy design pattern? Isn't this a complete contradiction of the previous statement?" Yes, you are correct. Just a few pages back, I did explain that the std::partition() and std::sort() algorithms are implemented by means of the Strategy design pattern. And therefore, I admit that it appears as if I am now contradicting myself. However, I did not claim that *all* the algorithms are based on Strategy. So let me explain.

From a structural point of view, the Strategy and Command design patterns are identical: whether you're using dynamic or static polymorphism, from an implementation point of view, there is no difference between Strategy and Command.[21] The difference lies entirely in the intent of the two design patterns. Whereas the Strategy design pattern specifies *how* something should be done, the Command design pattern specifies *what* should be done. Consider, for instance, the std::partition() and std::for_each() algorithms:

```
namespace std {

template< typename ForwardIt, typename UnaryPredicate >
constexpr ForwardIt
    partition( ForwardIt first, ForwardIt last, UnaryPredicate p );    ❷❶

template< typename InputIt, typename UnaryFunction >
constexpr UnaryFunction
    for_each( InputIt first, InputIt last, UnaryFunction f );    ❷❷

} // namespace std
```

Whereas you can only control *how* to select elements in the std::partition() algorithm (❷❶), the std::for_each() algorithm gives you control over *what* operation is applied to each element in the given range (❷❷). And whereas in the shapes example you could only specify *how* to draw a certain kind of shape, in the ThreadPool example you are completely in charge of deciding *what* operation is scheduled.[22]

There are two other indicators for the two design patterns you have applied. First, if you have an object and configure it using an action (you perform *dependency injection*), then you are (most likely) using the Strategy design pattern. If you don't use the action to configure an object, but if instead the action is performed directly, then you are (most likely) using the Command design pattern. In our Calculator example, we did not pass an action to configure the Calculator, but instead the action was evaluated immediately. Therefore, we built on the Command pattern.

Alternatively, we could also implement Calculator by means of Strategy:

```
//---- <CalculatorStrategy.h> ----------------

class CalculatorStrategy
{
 public:
   virtual ~CalculatorStrategy() = default;

   virtual int compute( int i ) const = 0;
```

---

21 This is another example of my statement that design patterns are not about implementation details; see "Guideline 12: Beware of Design Pattern Misconceptions" on page 85.

22 For the complete shape example, see "Guideline 19: Use Strategy to Isolate How Things Are Done" on page 140.

```
};


//---- <Calculator.h> ---------------

#include <CalculatorStrategy.h>

class Calculator
{
 public:
   void set( std::unique_ptr<CalculatorStrategy> operation );   ㉓
   void compute( int value );   ㉔

   // ...

 private:
   int current_{};
   std::unique_ptr<CalculatorStrategy> operation_;  // Requires a default!
};


//---- <Calculator.cpp> ----------------

#include <Calculator.h>

void set( std::unique_ptr<CalculatorStrategy> operation )   ㉓
{
   operation_ = std::move(operation);
}

void Calculator::compute( int value )   ㉔
{
   current_ = operation_.compute( value );
}
```

In this implementation of a `Calculator`, the Strategy is injected by means of a `set()` function (㉓). The `compute()` function uses the injected Strategy to perform a computation (㉔). Note, however, that this approach makes it more difficult to implement a reasonable undo mechanism.

The second indicator to see whether you are using Command or Strategy is the `undo()` operation. If your action provides an `undo()` operation to roll back *what* it has done and encapsulates everything that is needed to perform the `undo()`, then you are—most likely—dealing with the Command design pattern. If your action doesn't provide an `undo()` operation, because it's focused on *how* something is done or because it lacks the information to roll back the operation, then you are—most likely—dealing with the Strategy design pattern. However, I should explicitly point out that the lack of an `undo()` operation is not conclusive evidence of Strategy. It could still be an implementation of Command if the intent is to specify *what* should be done. For instance, the std::for_each() algorithm still expects a Command, despite the fact that there is no need for an undo() operation. The undo() operation should be considered an optional feature of the Command design pattern, not a defining one. In my opinion, undo() is not a strength of the Command design pattern but a pure necessity: if an action has complete freedom to do whatever it desires, then only this action alone will be able to roll the operation back (of course, assuming that you don't want to store a complete copy of everything for every call to a Command).

I admit there is no clear separation between these two patterns and that there is a gray area between them. However, there's no point in arguing about whether something is a Command or a Strategy and losing a couple of friends in the process. More important than agreeing on which one of the two you are using is exploiting their ability to extract implementation details and separate concerns. Both design patterns help you isolate changes and extensions and thus help you follow the SRP and OCP. After all, this ability may be the reason why there are so many examples of these two design patterns in the C++ Standard Library.

Analyzing the Shortcomings of the Command Design Pattern

The advantages of the Command design pattern are similar to those of the Strategy design pattern: Command helps you decouple from the implementation details of concrete tasks by introducing some form of abstraction (for instance, a base class or a concept). This abstraction allows you to easily add new tasks. Thus, Command satisfies both the SRP and the OCP.

However, the Command design pattern also has its disadvantages. In comparison to the Strategy design pattern, the list of disadvantages is pretty short, though. The only real disadvantage is the added runtime performance overhead due to the additional indirection if you implement Command by means of a base class (the classic GoF style). Again, it's up to you to decide whether the increased flexibility outweighs the loss of runtime performance.

In summary, just like the Strategy design pattern, the Command design pattern is one of the most basic and useful ones in the catalog of design patterns. You will encounter implementations of Command in many different situations, both static and dynamic. Thus, understanding the intent, advantages, and disadvantages of Command will prove useful many times.

Guideline 21: Use Command to Isolate What Things Are Done

- Apply the Command design pattern with the intent to abstract and encapsulate an (possibly undoable) action.

- Be aware that the line between the Command and the Strategy design pattern is fluid.

- Use Command for both dynamic and static applications.

Guideline 22: Prefer Value Semantics over Reference Semantics

In "Guideline 19: Use Strategy to Isolate How Things Are Done" on page 140 and "Guideline 21: Use Command to Isolate What Things Are Done" on page 165, I introduced you to the Strategy and Command design pattern, respectively. In both cases, the examples were firmly built on the classic GoF style: they used dynamic polymorphism by means of an inheritance hierarchy. With that classic object-oriented style lacking a modern touch, I imagine that by now all your nail-biting has gotten you in trouble with your manicurist. And you might be wondering: "Isn't there another, better way to implement Strategy and Command? A more 'modern' approach?" Yes, rest assured; there is. And this approach is so important for the philosophy of what we commonly call "Modern C++" that it definitely justifies a separate guideline to explain the advantages. I'm pretty sure your manicurist will understand the reason for this little detour.

The Shortcomings of the GoF Style: Reference Semantics

The design patterns collected by the Gang of Four and presented in their book were introduced as object-oriented design patterns. Almost all of the 23 design patterns described in their book are using at least one inheritance hierarchy and thus are firmly rooted in the realm of OO programming. Templates, the obvious second choice, did not play any part in the GoF book. This pure OO style is what I refer to as the *GoF style*. From today's perspective, that style may appear to be an old, outdated way of doing things in C++, but of course we need to remember that the book was released in October 1994. At that time, templates may already have been a part of the language (at least they were officially described in the *Annotated Reference Manual (ARM)*), but we didn't have template-related idioms, and C++ was still commonly perceived as an OO programming language.[23] Hence, the common way to use C++ was to primarily use inheritance.

---

23 Margaret A. Ellis and Bjarne Stroustrup, *The Annotated C++ Reference Manual* (Addison-Wesley, 1990).

Today we know that the GoF style comes with a number of disadvantages. One of the most important, and usually one of the most-often mentioned, is performance:[24]

- Virtual functions increase the runtime overhead and diminish the compiler's opportunities to optimize.
- Many allocations of small polymorphic objects cost extra runtime, fragment the memory, and lead to suboptimal cache usage.
- The way data is arranged is often counterproductive with respect to data access schemes.[25]

Performance truly is not one of the strong aspects of the GoF style. Without going into a complete discussion about all the possible shortcomings of the GoF style, let's instead focus on one other disadvantage that I consider of particular interest: the GoF style falls into what we today call *reference semantics* (or sometimes also *pointer semantics*). This style got its name because it works primarily with pointers and references. To demonstrate term reference semantics means and why it usually comes with a rather negative connotation, let's take a look at the following code example using the C++20 `std::span` class template:

```cpp
#include <cstdlib>
#include <iostream>
#include <span>
#include <vector>

void print( std::span<int> s )   ❶
{
   std::cout << " (";
   for( int i : s ) {
      std::cout << ' ' << i;
   }
   std::cout << " )\n";
}

int main()
{
   std::vector<int> v{ 1, 2, 3, 4 };   ❷

   std::vector<int> const w{ v };   ❸
   std::span<int> const s{ v };   ❹

   w[2] = 99;  // Compilation error!   ❺
```

---

24 To get an overview of C++ performance aspects in general and performance-related issues with inheritance hierarchies in particular, refer to Kurt Guntheroth's book, *Optimized C{plus}{plus}* (O'Reilly).

25 A possible solution for that is to employ techniques from data-oriented design; see Richard Fabian, *Data-Oriented Design: Software Engineering for Limited Resources and Short Schedules.*

```
    s[2] = 99;  // Works!  ❻

    // Prints ( 1 2 99 4 );
    print( s );  ❼

    v = { 5, 6, 7, 8, 9 };  ❽
    s[2] = 99;  // Works!  ❾

    // Prints ?
    print( s );  ❿

    return EXIT_SUCCESS;
}
```

The print() function (❶) demonstrates the purpose of std::span. The std::span class template represents an abstraction for an array. The print() function can be called with any kind of array (built-in arrays, std::array, std::vector, etc.) without coupling to any specific type of array. In the demonstrated example of std::span with a dynamic extent (no second template argument representing the size of the array), a typical implementation of std::span contains two data members: a pointer to the first element of the array, and the size of the array. For that reason, std::span is considered easy to copy and is usually passed by value. Apart from that, print() simply traverses the elements of the std::span (in our case, integers) and prints them via std::cout.

In the main() function, we first create the std::vector<int> v and immediately fill it with the integers 1, 2, 3, and 4 (❷). Then we create another std::vector w as a copy of v (❸) and the std::span s (❹). Both w and s are qualified with const. Directly after that, we try to modify both w and s at index 2. The attempt to change w fails with a compilation error: w is declared const, and for that reason it's not possible to change the contained elements (❺). The attempt to change s, however, works fine. There will be no compilation error, despite the fact that s is declared const (❻).

The reason for this is that s is not a copy of v and does not represent a value. Instead, it represents a reference to v. It essentially acts as a pointer to the first element of v. Thus, the const qualifier semantically has the same effect as declaring a pointer const:

```
std::span<int> const s{ v };  // s acts as pointer to the first element of v
int* const ptr{ v.data() };   // Equivalent semantical meaning
```

While the pointer ptr cannot be changed and will refer to the first element of v throughout its lifetime, the referenced integer can be easily modified. To prevent an assignment to the integer, you would need to add an additional const qualifier for the int:

```
std::span<int const> const s{v};    // s represents a const pointer to a const int
int const* const ptr{ v.data() };   // Equivalent semantical meaning
```

Since the semantics of a pointer and std::span are equivalent, std::span obviously falls into the category of reference semantics. And this comes with a number of additional dangers, as demonstrated in the remainder of the main() function. As a next step, we print the elements referred to by s (❼). Note that instead, you could also pass the vector v directly, as the std::span provides the necessary conversion constructors to accept std::vector. The print() function will correctly result in the following output:

```
( 1 2 99 4 )
```

Because we can (and because by now, the numbers 1 through 4 probably start to sound a little boring), we now assign a new set of numbers to the vector v (❽). Admittedly, the choice of 5, 6, 7, 8, and 9 is neither particularly creative nor entertaining, but it will serve its purpose. Directly afterward, we again write to the second index by means of s (❾) and again print the elements referred to by s (❿). Of course, we expect the output to be (5 6 99 8 9), but unfortunately that is not the case. We might get the following output:[26]

```
( 1 2 99 4 )
```

Maybe this completely shocks you and you end up with a few more gray hairs.[27] Perhaps you are merely surprised. Or you knowingly smile and nod: yes, of course, undefined behavior! When assigning new values to the std::vector v, we haven't just changed the values but also the size of the vector. Instead of four values, it now needs to store five elements. For that reason, the vector has (possibly) performed a reallocation and has thus changed the address of its first element. Unfortunately, the std::span s didn't get the note and still firmly holds onto the address of the previous first element. Hence, when we try to write to v by means of s, we do not write into the current array of v but to an already discarded piece of memory that used to be the internal array of v. Classic undefined behavior, and a classic problem of reference semantics.

"Hey, are you trying to discredit std::span?" you ask. No, I am not trying to suggest that std::span, and also std::string_view, are bad. On the contrary, I actually like these two a lot since they provide remarkably simple and cheap abstractions from all kinds of arrays and strings, respectively. However, remember that every tool has advantages and disadvantages. When I use them, I use them consciously, fully aware

---

26 Mark my choice of words: "We might get the following output." Indeed, we might get this output but also something else. It depends, as we have inadvertently entered the realm of undefined behavior. Therefore, this output is my best guess, not a guarantee.

27 Now not only your manicurist but also your hairdresser has work to do…

that any nonowning reference type requires careful attention to the lifetime of the value it references. For instance, while I consider both to be very useful tools for function arguments, I tend to not use them as data members. The danger of lifetime issues is just too high.

Reference Semantics: A Second Example

"Well, of course I knew that," you argue. "I also wouldn't store std::span for a longer period of time. However, I'm still not convinced that references and pointers are a problem." OK, if that first example wasn't startling enough, I have a second example. This time I use one of the STL algorithms, std::remove(). The std::remove() algorithm takes three arguments: a pair of iterators for the range that is traversed to remove all elements of a particular value, and a third argument that represents the value to be removed. In particular, note that the third argument is passed by a reference-to-const:

```
template< typename ForwardIt, typename T >
constexpr ForwardIt remove( ForwardIt first, ForwardIt last, T const& value );
```

Let's take a look at the following code example:

```
std::vector<int> vec{ 1, -3, 27, 42, 4, -8, 22, 42, 37, 4, 18, 9 };   ❶

auto const pos = std::max_element( begin(vec), end(vec) );   ❷

vec.erase( std::remove( begin(vec), end(vec), *pos ), end(vec) );   ❸
```

We start with the std::vector v, which is initialized with a few random numbers (❶). Now we are interested in removing all the elements that represent the greatest value stored in the vector. In our example, that is the value 42, which is stored in the vector twice. The first step in performing the removal is to determine the greatest value using the std::max_element() algorithm. std::max_element() returns an iterator to the greatest value. If several elements in the range are equivalent to the greatest element, it returns the iterator to the first such element (❷).

The second step in removing the greatest values is a call to std::remove() (❸). We pass the range of elements using begin(vec) and end(vec), and the greatest value by dereferencing the pos iterator. Last but not least, we finish the operation with a call to the erase() member function: we erase all the values between the position returned by the std::remove() algorithm and the end of the vector. This sequence of operations is commonly known as the *erase-remove idiom* (*https://oreil.ly/fc50R*).

We expect that both 42 values are removed from the vector, and therefore we expect to get the following result:

```
( 1 -3 27 4 -8 22 37 4 18 9 )
```

Unfortunately, this expectation does not hold. Instead, the vector now contains the following values:

```
( 1 -3 27 4 -8 22 42 37 18 9 )
```

Note that the vector still contains a 42 but is now missing a 4 instead. The underlying reason for this misbehavior is, again, reference semantics: by passing the dereferenced iterator to the remove() algorithm, we implicitly state that the value stored in that location should be removed. However, after removing the first 42, this location holds the value 4. The remove() algorithm removes all elements with the value 4. Hence, the next value that is removed is not the next 42 but the next 4, and so on.[28]

"OK, I got it! But that problem is history! Today we don't use the erase-remove idiom anymore. C++20 finally provided us with the free std::erase() function!" Well, I would love to agree with that statement, but unfortunately I can only acknowledge the existence of the std::erase() function:

```
template< typename T, typename Alloc, typename U >
constexpr typename std::vector<T,Alloc>::size_type
    erase( std::vector<T,Alloc>& c, U const& value );
```

The std::erase() function also takes its second argument, the value that is to be removed, by means of a reference-to-const. Therefore, the problem that I just described remains. The only way to resolve this problem is to explicitly determine the greatest element and pass it to the std::remove() algorithm (❶❹):

```
std::vector<int> vec{ 1, -3, 27, 42, 4, -8, 22, 42, 37, 4, 18, 9 };

auto const pos = std::max_element( begin(vec), end(vec) );
auto const greatest = *pos;  ❶❹

vec.erase( std::remove( begin(vec), end(vec), greatest ), end(vec) );
```

"Are you seriously suggesting that we shouldn't use reference parameters anymore?" No, absolutely not! Of course you should use reference parameters, for instance, for performance reasons. However, I hope to have raised a certain awareness. Hopefully, you now understand the problem: references, and especially pointers, make our life so much harder. It's harder to understand the code, and therefore it is easier to introduce bugs into our code. And pointers in particular raise so many more questions: is it a valid pointer or a nullptr? Who owns the resource behind the pointer and manages the lifetime? Of course, lifetime issues are not much of an issue since we have expanded our toolbox and have smart pointers at our disposal. As Core Guideline R.3 (*https://oreil.ly/keyuZ*) clearly states:

A raw pointer (a T*) is non-owning.

---

28 More gray hairs, more work for your hairdresser.

In combination with knowing that smart pointers are taking on the responsibility of ownership, this cleans up the semantics of pointers quite significantly. But still, despite the fact that smart pointers are of course an immensely valuable tool and, for good reasons, are celebrated as a huge achievement of "Modern C++," in the end they are only a fix for the holes that reference semantics has torn in the fabric of our ability to reason about code. Yes, reference semantics makes it harder to understand code and to reason about the important details, and thus is something we would like to avoid.

The Modern C++ Philosophy: Value Semantics

"But wait," I can hear you object, "what other choice do we have? What should we do? And how else should we cope with inheritance hierarchies? We can't avoid pointers there, right?" If you're thinking something along these lines, then I have very good news for you: yes, there is a better solution. A solution that makes your code easier to understand and easier to reason about, and might even have a positive impact on its performance (remember we also talked about the negative performance aspects of reference semantics). The solution is value semantics.

Value semantics is nothing new in C++. The idea was already part of the original STL. Let's consider the most famous of the STL containers, `std::vector`:

```
std::vector<int> v1{ 1, 2, 3, 4, 5 };

auto v2{ v1 };   ⑮

assert( v1 == v2 );   ⑯
assert( v1.data() != v2.data() );   ⑰

v2[2] = 99;   ⑱

assert( v1 != v2 );   ⑲

auto const v3{ v1 };   ⑳

v3[2] = 99;   // Compilation error!
```

We start with a `std::vector` called v1, filled with five integers. In the next line, we create a copy of v1, called v2 (⑮). Vector v2 is a real copy, sometimes also referred to as a *deep copy*, which now contains its own chunk of memory and its own integers, and doesn't refer to the integers in v1.[29] We can assert that by comparing the two vectors (they prove to be equal; see ⑯), but the addresses of the first elements are

---

29 I should explicitly point out that the notion of a "deep copy" depends on the type T of elements in the vector: if T performs a deep copy, then so does the `std::vector`, but if T performs a shallow copy, then semantically `std::vector` also performs a shallow copy.

---

different (**⓱**). And changing one element in v2 (**⓲**) has the effect that the two vectors are not equal anymore (**⓳**). Yes, both vectors have their own arrays. They do not share their content, i.e., they do not try to "optimize" the copy operation. You might have heard about such techniques, for instance, the copy-on-write (*https://oreil.ly/lZae0*) technique. And yes, you might even be aware that this was a common implementation for std::string prior to C++11. Since C++11, however, std::string is no longer allowed to use copy-on-write (*https://oreil.ly/hYbsO*) due to its requirements (*https://oreil.ly/lW1kV*) formulated in the C++ standard. The reason is that this "optimization" easily proves to be a pessimization in a multithreaded world. Hence, we can count on the fact that copy construction creates a real copy.

Last but not least, we create another copy called v3, which we declare as const (**⓴**). If we now try to change a value of v3, we will get a compilation error. This shows that a const vector does not just prevent adding and removing elements but that all elements are also considered to be const.

From a semantic perspective, this means that std::vector, just as any container in the STL, is considered to be a value. Yes, a value, like an int. If we copy a value, we don't copy just a part of the value but the entire value. If we make a value const, it is not just partially const but completely const. That is the rationale of value semantics. And we've seen a couple of advantages already: values are easier to reason about than pointers and references. For instance, changing a value does not have an impact on some other value. The change happens locally, not somewhere else. This is an advantage that compilers heavily exploit for their optimization efforts. Also, values don't make us think about ownership. A value is in charge of its own content. A value also makes it (much) easier to think about threading issues. That does not mean that there are no problems anymore (you wish!), but the code is definitely easier to understand. Values just don't leave us with a lot of questions.

"OK, I get the point about code clarity," you argue, "but what about performance? Isn't it super expensive to deal with copy operations all the time?" Well, you are correct; copy operations can be expensive. However, they are only expensive if they really happen. In real code, we can often rely on copy elision (*https://oreil.ly/Bc4jM*), move semantics, and well...pass-by-reference.[30] Also, we have already seen that, from a performance point of view, value semantics might give us a performance boost. Yes, of course I am referring to the std::variant example in "Guideline 17: Consider std::variant for Implementing Visitor" on page 122. In that example, the use of values of type std::variant has significantly improved our performance because of fewer indirections due to pointers and a much better memory layout and access pattern.

---

30 The best and most complete introduction to move semantics is Nicolai Josuttis's book on the subject, *C++ Move Semantics - The Complete Guide* (NicoJosuttis, 2020).

Value Semantics: A Second Example

Let's take a look at a second example. This time we consider the following `to_int()` function:[31]

```
int to_int( std::string_view );
```

This function parses the given string (and yes, I am using `std::string_view` for the purpose of performance) and converts it to an `int`. The most interesting question for us now is how the function should deal with errors, or in other words, what the function should do if the string cannot be converted to an `int`. The first option would be to return `0` for that case. This approach, however, is questionable, because `0` is a valid return from the `to_int()` function. We would not be able to distinguish success from failure.[32] Another possible approach would be to throw an exception. Although exceptions may be the C++ native tool to signal error cases, for this particular problem, depending on your personal style and preferences, this may appear as overkill to you. Also, knowing that exceptions cannot be used in a large fraction of the C++ community, that choice might limit the usability of the function.[33]

A third possibility is change the signature by a little bit:

```
bool to_int( std::string_view s, int& );
```

Now the function takes a reference to a mutable `int` as the second parameter and returns a `bool`. If it succeeds, the function returns `true` and sets the passed integer; if it fails, the function returns `false` and leaves the `int` alone. While this may seem like a reasonable compromise to you, I would argue that we have now strayed further into the realm of reference semantics (including all potential misuse). At the same time, the clarity of the code has diminished: the most natural way to return a result is via the return value, but now the result is produced by an output value. This, for instance, prevents us from assigning the result to a `const` value. Therefore, I would rate this as the least favorable approach so far.

The fourth approach is to return by pointer:

```
std::unique_ptr<int> to_int( std::string_view );
```

Semantically, this approach is pretty attractive: if it succeeds, the function returns a valid pointer to an `int`; if it fails, it returns a `nullptr`. Hence, code clarity is improved, as we can clearly distinguish between these two cases. However, we gain

---

31 See Patrice Roy's CppCon 2016 talk, "The Exception Situation" (*https://oreil.ly/REqOG*), for a similar example and discussion.

32 Yet this is exactly the approach taken by the `std::atoi()` function (*https://oreil.ly/fByFB*).

33 In his standard proposal P0709 (*https://oreil.ly/E6Qd7*), Herb Sutter explains that 52% of C++ developers have no or limited access to exceptions.

---

this advantage at the cost of a dynamic memory allocation, the need to deal with lifetime management using `std::unique_ptr`, and we're still lingering in the realm of reference semantics. So the question is: how can we leverage the semantic advantages but stick to value semantics? The solution comes in the form of `std::optional`:[34]

```
std::optional<int> to_int( std::string_view );
```

`std::optional` (*https://oreil.ly/6p55b*) is a value type, which represents any other value, in our example, an `int`. Therefore, `std::optional` can take all the values that an `int` can take. The specialty of `std::optional`, however, is that it adds one more state to the wrapped value, a state that represents no value. Thus, our `std::optional` is an `int` that may or may not be present:

```cpp
#include <charconv>
#include <cstdlib>
#include <optional>
#include <sstream>
#include <string>
#include <string_view>

std::optional<int> to_int( std::string_view sv )
{
   std::optional<int> oi{};
   int i{};

   auto const result = std::from_chars( sv.data(), sv.data() + sv.size(), i );
   if( result.ec != std::errc::invalid_argument ) {
      oi = i;
   }

   return oi;
}

int main()
{
   std::string value = "42";

   if( auto optional_int = to_int( value ) )
   {
      // ... Success: the returned std::optional contains an integer value
   }
   else
   {
      // ... Failure: the returned std::optional does not contain a value
   }
}
```

---

34 The experienced C++ developer also knows that C++23 will bless us with a very similar type called `std::expected`. In a few years, this might be the appropriate way to write the to_int() function.

Semantically, this is equivalent to the pointer approach, but we don't pay the cost of dynamic memory allocation, and we don't have to deal with lifetime management.[35] This solution is semantically clear, understandable, and efficient.

Prefer to Use Value Semantics to Implement Design Patterns

"And what about design patterns?" you ask. "Almost all GoF patterns are based on inheritance hierarchies and therefore reference semantics. How should we deal with this?" That is an excellent question. And it provides us with a perfect bridge to the next guideline. To give a short answer here: you should prefer to implement design patterns using a value semantics solution. Yes, seriously! These solutions usually lead to more comprehensive, maintainable code and (often) better performance.

Guideline 22: Prefer Value Semantics over Reference Semantics

- Be aware that reference semantics make it harder to understand code;
- Prefer the semantic clarity of value semantics.

Guideline 23: Prefer a Value-Based Implementation of Strategy and Command

In "Guideline 19: Use Strategy to Isolate How Things Are Done" on page 140, I introduced you to the Strategy design pattern, and in "Guideline 21: Use Command to Isolate What Things Are Done" on page 165, I introduced you to the Command design pattern. I demonstrated that these two design patterns are essential decoupling tools in your daily toolbox. However, in "Guideline 22: Prefer Value Semantics over Reference Semantics" on page 176, I gave you the idea that it's preferable to use value semantics instead of reference semantics. And this of course raises the question: how can you apply that wisdom for the Strategy and Command design patterns? Well, here is one possible value semantics solution: draw on the abstracting power of `std::function`.

Introduction to std::function

In case you have not heard about `std::function`, allow me to introduce you. `std::function` represents an abstraction for a callable (e.g., a function pointer,

---

35 From a functional programming point of view, `std::optional` represents a *monad* (*https://oreil.ly/IowBp*). You'll find much more valuable information on *monad*s and functional programming in general in Ivan Čukić's book, *Functional Programming in C++*.

function object, or lambda). The only requirement is that the callable satisfies a specific function type, which is passed as the only template parameter to std::function. The following code gives an impression:

```cpp
#include <cstdlib>
#include <functional>

void foo( int i )
{
   std::cout << "foo: " << i << '\n';
}

int main()
{
   // Create a default std::function instance. Calling it results
   // in a std::bad_function_call exception
   std::function<void(int)> f{};   ❶

   f = []( int i ){  // Assigning a callable to 'f'   ❷
      std::cout << "lambda: " << i << '\n';
   };

   f(1);  // Calling 'f' with the integer '1'   ❸

   auto g = f;  // Copying 'f' into 'g'   ❹

   f = foo;  // Assigning a different callable to 'f'   ❺

   f(2);  // Calling 'f' with the integer '2'   ❻
   g(3);  // Calling 'g' with the integer '3'   ❼

   return EXIT_SUCCESS;
}
```

In the main() function, we create an instance of std::function, called f (❶). The template parameter specifies the required function type. In our example, this is void(int). "Function type… " you say. "Don't you mean function *pointer* type?" Well, since this is indeed something that you might have rarely seen before, allow me to explain what a function type is and contrast it with the thing you've probably seen more often: function pointers. The following example uses both a function type and a function pointer type:

```cpp
using FunctionType        = double(double);
using FunctionPointerType = double(*)(double);
// Alternatively:
// using FunctionPointerType = FunctionType*;
```

The first line shows a function type. This type represents *any* function that takes a double and returns a double. Examples for this function type are the corresponding overloads of std::sin (*https://oreil.ly/1n7fa*), std::cos (*https://oreil.ly/LuGeK*), std::log (*https://oreil.ly/ZBNt3*), or std::sqrt (*https://oreil.ly/V1XOS*). The second line shows a function pointer type. Note the little asterisk in parentheses—that makes it a pointer type. This type represents the address of *one* function of function type FunctionType. Hence, the relationship between function types and function pointer types is pretty much like the relationship between an int and a pointer to an int: while there are many int values, a pointer to an int stores the address of exactly *one* int.

Back to the std::function example: initially, the instance is empty, therefore you cannot call it. If you still try to do so, the std::function instance will throw the std::bad_function_call exception at you. Better not provoke it. Let's rather assign some callable that fulfills the function type requirements, for instance, a (possibly stateful) lambda (❷). The lambda takes an int and doesn't return anything. Instead, it prints that it has been called by means of a descriptive output message (❸):

```
lambda: 1
```

OK, that worked well. Let's try something else: we now create another std::function instance g by means of f (❹). Then we assign another callable to f (❺). This time, we assign a pointer to the function foo(). Again, this callable fulfills the requirements of the std::function instance: it takes an int and returns nothing. Directly after the assignment, you call f with the int 2, which triggers the expected output (❻):

```
foo: 2
```

That was probably an easy one. However, the next function call is much more interesting. If you call g with the integer 3 (❼), the output demonstrates that std::function is firmly based on value semantics:

```
lambda: 3
```

During the initialization of g, the instance f was copied. And it was copied as a value should be copied: it does not perform a "shallow copy," which would result in g being affected when f is subsequently changed, but it performs a complete copy (deep copy), which includes a copy of the lambda.[36] Thus, changing f does not affect g. That's the benefit of value semantics: the code is easy and intuitive, and you don't have to be afraid that you are accidentally breaking something anywhere else.

At this point, the functionality of std::function may feel a little like magic: how is it possible that the std::function instance can take any kind of callable, including

---

[36] In this example, the std::function object performs a deep copy, but generally speaking, std::function copies the contained callable according to its copy semantics ("deep" or "shallow"). std::function has no way of forcing a deep copy.

things like lambdas? How can it store any possible type, even types that it can't know, and even though these types apparently have nothing in common? Don't worry: in Chapter 8, I will give you a thorough introduction to a technique called *Type Erasure*, which is the magic behind std::function.

Refactoring the Drawing of Shapes

std::function provides everything we need to refactor our shape-drawing example from "Guideline 19: Use Strategy to Isolate How Things Are Done" on page 140: it represents the abstraction of a single callable, which is pretty much exactly what we need to replace the DrawCircleStrategy and DrawSquareStrategy hierarchies, which each contain a single virtual function. Hence, we rely on the abstracting power of std::function:

```
//---- <Shape.h> ----------------

class Shape
{
 public:
   virtual ~Shape() = default;
   virtual void draw( /*some arguments*/ ) const = 0;
};


//---- <Circle.h> ---------------

#include <Shape.h>
#include <functional>
#include <utility>

class Circle : public Shape
{
 public:
   using DrawStrategy = std::function<void(Circle const&, /*...*/)>;   ❽

   explicit Circle( double radius, DrawStrategy drawer )   ❿
      : radius_( radius )
      , drawer_( std::move(drawer) )   ⓫
   {
      /* Checking that the given radius is valid and that
         the given 'std::function' instance is not empty */
   }

   void draw( /*some arguments*/ ) const override
   {
      drawer_( *this, /*some arguments*/ );
   }

   double radius() const { return radius_; }
```

```
  private:
    double radius_;
    DrawStrategy drawer_;    ⓬
};


//---- <Square.h> ----------------

#include <Shape.h>
#include <functional>
#include <utility>

class Square : public Shape
{
 public:
   using DrawStrategy = std::function<void(Square const&, /*...*/)>;   ⓽

   explicit Square( double side, DrawStrategy drawer )    ⓾
     : side_( side )
     , drawer_( std::move(drawer) )    ⓫
   {
      /* Checking that the given side length is valid and that
         the given 'std::function' instance is not empty */
   }

   void draw( /*some arguments*/ ) const override
   {
      drawer_( *this, /*some arguments*/ );
   }

   double side() const { return side_; }

  private:
   double side_;
   DrawStrategy drawer_;    ⓬
};
```

First, in the Circle class, we add a type alias for the expected type of std::function (⓼). This std::function type represents any callable that can take a Circle, and potentially several more drawing-related arguments, and does not return anything. Of course, we also add the corresponding type alias in the Square class (⓽). In the constructors of both Circle and Square, we now take an instance of type std::function (⓾) as a replacement for the pointer to a Strategy base class (Draw CircleStrategy or DrawSquareStrategy). This instance is immediately moved (⓫) into the data member drawer_, which is also of type DrawStrategy (⓬).

"Hey, why are you taking the std::function instance by value? Isn't that terribly inefficient? Shouldn't we prefer to pass by reference-to-const?" In short: no, passing by value is not inefficient, but an elegant compromise to the alternatives. I admit, though, that this may be surprising. Since this is definitely an implementation detail worth noting, let's take a closer look.

If we used a reference-to-const, we would experience the disadvantage that *rvalues* would be unnecessarily copied. If we were passed an rvalue, this rvalue would bind to the (*lvalue*) reference-to-const. However, when passing this reference-to-const to the data member, it would be copied. Which is not our intention: naturally we want it to be moved. The simple reason is that we cannot move from const objects (even when using std::move). So, to efficiently deal with rvalues, we would have to provide overloads of the Circle and Square constructors that would take a DrawStrategy by means of an rvalue reference (DrawStrategy&&). For the sake of performance, we would provide two constructors for both Circle and Square.[37]

The approach to provide two constructors (one for lvalues, one for rvalues) does work and is efficient, but I would not necessarily call it elegant. Also, we should probably save our colleagues the trouble of having to deal with that.[38] For this reason, we exploit the implementation of std::function. std::function provides both a copy constructor and a move constructor, and so we know that it can be moved efficiently. When we pass a std::function by value, either the copy constructor or the move constructor will be called. If we are passed an lvalue, the copy constructor is called, copying the lvalue. Then we would move that copy into the data member. In total, we would perform one copy and one move to initialize the drawer_ data member. If we are passed an rvalue, the move constructor is called, moving the rvalue. The resulting argument strategy is then moved into the data member drawer_. In total, we would perform two move operations to initialize the drawer_ data member. Therefore, this form represents a great compromise: it is elegant, and there is hardly any difference in efficiency.

Once we've refactored the Circle and Square classes, we can implement different drawing strategies in any form we like (in the form of a function, a function object, or a lambda). For instance, we can implement the following OpenGLCircleStrategy as a function object:

```
//---- <OpenGLCircleStrategy.h> ----------------

#include <Circle.h>

class OpenGLCircleStrategy
{
 public:
```

---

37 This implementation detail is explained thoroughly by Nicolai Josuttis in this CppCon 2017 talk, "The Nightmare of Move Semantics for Trivial Classes" (*https://oreil.ly/IbZHb*).

38 One more example of the *KISS* principle (*https://oreil.ly/N7c3B*).

```
    explicit OpenGLCircleStrategy( /* Drawing related arguments */ );

    void operator()( Circle const& circle, /*...*/ ) const;   🔞

  private:
    /* Drawing related data members, e.g. colors, textures, ... */
};
```

The only convention we need to follow is that we need to provide a call operator that takes a `Circle` and potentially several more drawing-related arguments, and doesn't return anything (fulfill the function type `void(Circle const&, /*…*/)`) (🔞).

Assuming a similar implementation for an `OpenGLSquareStrategy`, we can now create different kinds of shapes, configure them with the desired drawing behavior, and finally draw them:

```
#include <Circle.h>
#include <Square.h>
#include <OpenGLCircleStrategy.h>
#include <OpenGLSquareStrategy.h>
#include <memory>
#include <vector>

int main()
{
   using Shapes = std::vector<std::unique_ptr<Shape>>;

   Shapes shapes{};

   // Creating some shapes, each one
   //   equipped with the corresponding OpenGL drawing strategy
   shapes.emplace_back(
      std::make_unique<Circle>( 2.3, OpenGLCircleStrategy(/*...red...*/) ) );
   shapes.emplace_back(
      std::make_unique<Square>( 1.2, OpenGLSquareStrategy(/*...green...*/) ) );
   shapes.emplace_back(
      std::make_unique<Circle>( 4.1, OpenGLCircleStrategy(/*...blue...*/) ) );

   // Drawing all shapes
   for( auto const& shape : shapes )
   {
      shape->draw();
   }

   return EXIT_SUCCESS;
}
```

The `main()` function is very similar to the original implementation using the classic Strategy implementation (see "Guideline 19: Use Strategy to Isolate How Things Are Done" on page 140). However, this nonintrusive, base class–free approach with `std::function` further reduces the coupling. This becomes evident in the

---

dependency graph for this solution (see Figure 5-9): we can implement the drawing functionality in any form we want (as a free function, a function object, or a lambda) and we don't have to abide by the requirements of a base class. Also, by means of std::function we have automatically inverted the dependencies (see "Guideline 9: Pay Attention to the Ownership of Abstractions" on page 62).

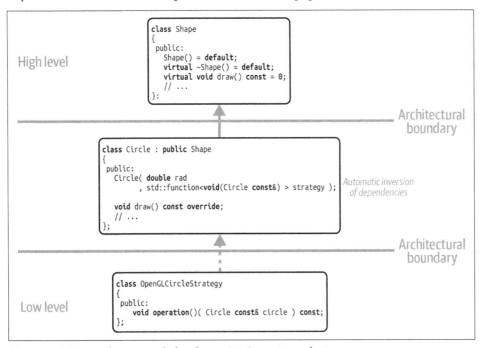

Figure 5-9. Dependency graph for the std::function *solution*

Performance Benchmarks

"I like the flexibility, the freedom. This is great! But what about performance?" Yes, spoken like a true C++ developer. Of course performance is important. Before showing you the performance results, though, let me remind you of the benchmark scenario that we also used to get the numbers for Table 4-2 in "Guideline 16: Use Visitor to Extend Operations" on page 112. For the benchmark, I have implemented four different kinds of shapes (circles, squares, ellipses, and rectangles). Again, I'm running 25,000 translate operations on 10,000 randomly created shapes. I use both GCC 11.1 and Clang 11.1, and for both compilers I'm adding only the -O3 and -DNDEBUG compilation flags. The platform I'm using is macOS Big Sur (version 11.4) on an 8-Core Intel Core i7 with 3.8 GHz, 64 GB of main memory.

With this information in mind, you are ready for the performance results. Table 5-1 shows the performance numbers for the Strategy-based implementation of the drawing example and the resulting solution using std::function.

Table 5-1. Performance results for different Strategy implementations

Strategy implementations	GCC 11.1	Clang 11.1
Object-oriented solution	1.5205 s	1.1480 s
`std::function`	2.1782 s	1.4884 s
Manual implementation of `std::function`	1.6354 s	1.4465 s
Classic Strategy	1.6372 s	1.4046 s

For reference purposes, the first line shows the performance of the object-oriented solution from "Guideline 15: Design for the Addition of Types or Operations" on page 102. As you can see, this solution gives the best performance. This is not unexpected, however: since the Strategy design pattern, irrespective of the actual implementation, introduces additional overhead, the performance is anticipated to be reduced.

What is not expected, though, is that the `std::function` implementation incurs a performance overhead (even a significant one in case of GCC). But wait, before you throw this approach into your mental trash can, consider the third line. It shows a manual implementation of `std::function` using Type Erasure, the technique I will explain in Chapter 8. This implementation performs much better, in fact as good (or nearly as good for Clang) as a classic implementation of the Strategy design pattern (see the fourth line). This result demonstrates that the problem is not value semantics but the specific implementation details of `std::function`.[39] In summary, a value semantics approach is not worse in terms of performance than the classic approach, but instead, as shown before, it improves many important aspects of your code.

Analyzing the Shortcomings of the std::function Solution

Overall, the `std::function` implementation of the Strategy design pattern provides a number of benefits. First, your code gets cleaner and more readable since you don't have to deal with pointers and the associated lifetime management (for instance, using `std::unique_ptr`), and since you don't experience the usual problems with reference semantics (see "Guideline 22: Prefer Value Semantics over Reference Semantics" on page 176). Second, you promote loose coupling. Very loose coupling, actually. In this context, `std::function` acts like a compilation firewall, which protects you from the implementation details of the different Strategy implementations but at the same time provides enormous flexibility for developers on how to implement the different Strategy solutions.

---

[39] A discussion about the reasons for the performance deficiencies of some `std::function` implementations would go beyond the scope and purpose of this book. Still, please keep this detail in mind for performance-critical sections of your code.

Despite these upsides, no solution comes without downsides—even the `std::function` approach has its disadvantages. I have already pointed out the potential performance disadvantage if you rely on the standard implementation. While there are solutions to minimize this effect (see Chapter 8), it's still something to consider in your codebase.

There is also a design-related issue. `std::function` can replace only a single virtual function. If you need to abstract multiple virtual functions, which could occur if you want to configure multiple aspects using the Strategy design pattern, or if you need an `undo()` function in the Command design pattern, you would have to use multiple `std::function` instances. This would not only increase the size of a class due to the multiple data members, but also incur an interface burden due to the question of how to elegantly handle passing multiple `std::function` instances. For this reason, the `std::function` approach works best for replacing a single or a very small number of virtual functions. Still, this does not mean that you can't use a value-based approach for multiple virtual functions: if you encounter that situation, consider generalizing the approach by applying the technique used for `std::function` directly to your type. I will explain how to do that in Chapter 8.

Despite these shortcomings, the value semantics approach proves to be a terrific choice for the Strategy design pattern. The same is true for the Command design pattern. Therefore, keep this guideline in mind as an essential step towards modern C++.

Guideline 23: Prefer a Value-Based Implementation of Strategy and Command

- Consider using `std::function` to implement the Strategy or Command design pattern.
- Take the performance disadvantages of `std::function` into account.
- Be aware that Type Erasure is a generalization of the value semantics approach for Strategy and Command.

CHAPTER 6

The Adapter, Observer, and CRTP Design Patterns

In this chapter, we turn our attention to three must-know design patterns: the two GoF design patterns, Adapter and *Observer*, and the *Curiously Recurring Template Pattern (CRTP)* design pattern.

In "Guideline 24: Use Adapters to Standardize Interfaces" on page 198, we talk about making incompatible things fit together by adapting interfaces. To achieve this, I will show you the Adapter design pattern and its application in both inheritance hierarchies and generic programming. You will also get an overview of different kinds of Adapters, including object, class, and function Adapters.

In "Guideline 25: Apply Observers as an Abstract Notification Mechanism" on page 209, we will deal with how to observe state change and how to get notified about it. In this context, I will introduce you to the Observer design pattern, one of the most famous and most commonly used design patterns. We will talk about the classic, GoF-style Observer, and also how to implement the Observer in modern C++.

In "Guideline 26: Use CRTP to Introduce Static Type Categories" on page 225, we will turn our attention to the CRTP. I will show you how to use CRTP to define a compile-time relationship between a family of related types and how to properly implement a CRTP base class.

In "Guideline 27: Use CRTP for Static Mixin Classes" on page 241, I will continue the CRTP story by showing you how CRTP can be used to create compile-time mixin classes. We will also see the difference between semantic inheritance, where it is used to create an abstraction, and technical inheritance, where it is used as an implementation detail for technical elegance and convenience only.

Guideline 24: Use Adapters to Standardize Interfaces

Let's assume that you have implemented the Document example from "Guideline 3: Separate Interfaces to Avoid Artificial Coupling" on page 24, and that, because you properly adhere to the Interface Segregation Principle (ISP), you're reasonably happy with the way it works:

```
class JSONExportable
{
 public:
   // ...
   virtual ~JSONExportable() = default;

   virtual void exportToJSON( /*...*/ ) const = 0;
   // ...
};

class Serializable
{
 public:
   // ...
   virtual ~Serializable() = default;

   virtual void serialize( ByteStream& bs, /*...*/ ) const = 0;
   // ...
};

class Document
   : public JSONExportable
   , public Serializable
{
 public:
   // ...
};
```

However, one day you're required to introduce the Pages document format.[1] Of course, it is similar to the Word document that you already have in place, but unfortunately, you're not familiar with the details of the Pages format. To make things worse, you don't have a lot of time to get familiar with the format, because you have way too many other things to do. Luckily, you know about a quite reasonable, open source implementation for that format: the OpenPages class:

---

1 The Pages format is Apple's equivalent to Microsoft's Word format.

```
class OpenPages
{
 public:
   // ...
   void convertToBytes( /*...*/ );
};

void exportToJSONFormat( OpenPages const& pages, /*...*/ );
```

On the bright side, this class provides about everything you need for your purposes: a convertToBytes() member function to serialize the content of the document, and the free exportToJSONFormat() function to convert the Pages document into the JSON format. Unfortunately, it does not fit your interface expectations: instead of the convertToBytes() member function, you expect a serialize() member function. And instead of the free exportToJSONFormat() function, you expect the exportToJSON() member function. Ultimately, of course, the third-party class does not inherit from your Document base class, which means that you can't easily incorporate the class into your existing hierarchy. However, there is a solution to this problem: a seamless integration using the Adapter design pattern.

The Adapter Design Pattern Explained

The Adapter design pattern is another one of the classic GoF design patterns. It's focused on standardizing interfaces and helping nonintrusively add functionality into an existing inheritance hierarchy.

The Adapter Design Pattern

Intent: "Convert the interface of a class into another interface clients expect. Adapter lets classes work together that couldn't otherwise because of incompatible interfaces."[2]

Figure 6-1 shows the UML diagram for your Adapter scenario: you already have the Document base class in place (we ignore the JSONExportable and Serializable interfaces for a second) and have already implemented a couple of different kinds of documents (for instance, with the Word class). The new addition to this hierarchy is the Pages class.

---

2 Erich Gamma et al., *Design Patterns: Elements of Reusable Object-Oriented Software.*

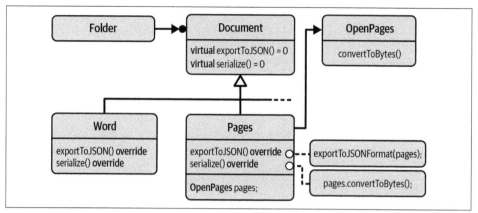

Figure 6-1. The UML representation of the Adapter design pattern

The Pages class acts as a wrapper to the third-party OpenPages class:

```
class Pages : public Document
{
 public:
   // ...
   void exportToJSON( /*...*/ ) const override
   {
       exportToJSONFormat(pages, /*...*/);   ❶
   }

   void serialize( ByteStream& bs, /*...*/ ) const override
   {
       pages.convertToBytes(/*...*/);   ❷
   }
   // ...

 private:
   OpenPages pages;  // Example of an object adapter
};
```

Pages implements the Document interface by forwarding the calls to the corresponding OpenPages functions: a call to exportToJSON() is forwarded to the free exportToJSONFormat() function (❶), and the call to serialize() is forwarded to the convertToBytes() member function (❷).

With the Pages class, you can easily integrate the third-party implementation into your existing hierarchy. *Very* easily indeed: you can integrate it without having to modify it in any way. This nonintrusive nature of the Adapter design pattern is what you should consider one of the greatest strengths of the Adapter design pattern: anyone can add an Adapter to adapt an interface to another, existing interface.

In this context, the `Pages` class serves as an abstraction from the actual implementation details in the `OpenPages` class. Therefore, the Adapter design pattern separates the concerns of the interface from the implementation details. This nicely fulfills the Single-Responsibility Principle (SRP) and blends well with the intention of the Open-Closed Principle (OCP) (see "Guideline 2: Design for Change" on page 11 and "Guideline 5: Design for Extension" on page 35).

In a way, the `Pages` Adapter works as an indirection and maps from one set of functions to another one. Note that it is not strictly necessary to map from one function to exactly one other function. On the contrary, you have complete flexibility on how to map the expected set of functions onto the available set of functions. Thus, Adapter does not necessarily represent a 1-to-1 relationship, but can also support a 1-to-N relationship.[3]

Object Adapters Versus Class Adapters

The `Pages` class is an example of a so-called *object adapter*. This term refers to the fact that you store an instance of the wrapped type. Alternatively, given that the wrapped type is part of an inheritance hierarchy, you could store a pointer to the base class of this hierarchy. This would allow you to use the object adapter for all types that are part of the hierarchy, giving the object adapter a considerable boost in flexibility.

In contrast, there is also the option to implement a so-called *class adapter*:

```cpp
class Pages : public Document
            , private OpenPages  // Example of a class adapter    ❸
{
 public:
   // ...
   void exportToJSON( /*...*/ ) const override
   {
      exportToJSONFormat(*this, /*...*/);
   }

   void serialize( ByteStream& bs, /*...*/ ) const override
   {
      this->convertToBytes(/*...*/);
   }
   // ...
};
```

---

3 If you're an expert on design patterns, you might realize that a 1-to-N Adapter has a certain similarity to the Facade design pattern. See the GoF book for more details.

Instead of storing an instance of the adapted type, you would inherit from it (if possible, nonpublicly) and implement the expected interface accordingly (❸). However, as discussed in "Guideline 20: Favor Composition over Inheritance" on page 162, it is preferable to build on composition. In general, object adapters prove to be much more flexible than class adapters and thus should be your favorite. There are only a few reasons why you would prefer a class adapter:

- If you have to override a virtual function.
- If you need access to a `protected` member function.
- If you require the adapted type to be constructed *before* another base class.
- If you need to share a common virtual base class or override the construction of a virtual base class.
- If you can draw *significant* advantage from the *Empty Base Optimization (EBO)* (*https://oreil.ly/7wLyW*).[4]

Otherwise, and this applies to most cases, you should prefer an object adapter.

"I like this design pattern—it's powerful. However, I just remembered that you recommended using the name of the design pattern in the code to communicate intent. Shouldn't the class be called `PagesAdapter`?" You make an excellent point. And I'm happy that you remember "Guideline 14: Use a Design Pattern's Name to Communicate Intent" on page 97, in which I indeed argued that the name of the pattern helps to understand the code. I admit that in this case, I'm open to both naming conventions. While I do see the advantages of the name `PagesAdapter`, as this immediately communicates that you built on the Adapter design pattern, I don't consider it a necessity to communicate the fact that this class represents an adapter. To me, the Adapter feels like an implementation detail in this situation: I do not need to know that the `Pages` class doesn't implement all the details itself, but uses the `OpenPages` class for that. That's why I said to "consider using the name." You should decide on a case-by-case basis.

Examples from the Standard Library

One useful application of the Adapter design pattern is to standardize the interface of different kinds of containers. Let's assume the following `Stack` base class:

```
//---- <Stack.h> ----------------

template< typename T >
class Stack
```

---

4 In C++20, you achieve a similar effect by applying the [[no_unique_address]] (*https://oreil.ly/H41V8*) attribute to a data member. If the data member is empty, it might not occupy any storage on its own.

```
{
 public:
   virtual ~Stack() = default;
   virtual T& top() = 0;  ❹
   virtual bool empty() const = 0;  ❺
   virtual size_t size() const = 0;  ❻
   virtual void push( T const& value ) = 0;  ❼
   virtual void pop() = 0;  ❽
};
```

This Stack class provides the necessary interface to access the top element of the
stack (❹), check if the stack is empty (❺), query the size of the stack (❻), push an
element onto the stack (❼), and remove the top element of the stack (❽). This base
class can now be used to implement different Adapters for various data structures,
such as std::vector:

```
//---- <VectorStack.h> ----------------

#include <Stack.h>

template< typename T >
class VectorStack : public Stack<T>
{
 public:
   T& top() override { return vec_.back(); }
   bool empty() const override { return vec_.empty(); }
   size_t size() const override { return vec_.size(); }
   void push( T const& value ) override { vec_.push_back(value); }
   void pop() override { vec_.pop_back(); }

 private:
   std::vector<T> vec_;
};
```

You worry, "Do you seriously suggest implementing a stack by an abstract base class?
Aren't you worried about the performance implications? For every use of a member
function, you have to pay with a virtual function call!" No, of course I don't suggest
that. Obviously, you are correct, and I completely agree with you: from a C++ perspective, this kind of container feels strange and very inefficient. Because of efficiency, we usually realize the same idea via class templates. This is the approach taken
by the C++ Standard Library in the form of the three STL classes called Container
adaptors (*https://oreil.ly/RMYzu*): std::stack (*https://oreil.ly/y4cr6*), std::queue
(*https://oreil.ly/LvVNn*), and std::priority_queue (*https://oreil.ly/nTBM8*):

```
template< typename T
        , typename Container = std::deque<T> >
class stack;

template< typename T
        , typename Container = std::deque<T> >
```

```
class queue;

template< typename T
        , typename Container = std::vector<T>
        , typename Compare = std::less<typename Container::value_type> >
class priority_queue;
```

These three class templates adapt the interface of a given Container type to a special purpose. For instance, the purpose of the std::stack class template is to adapt the interface of a container to the stack operations top(), empty(), size(), push(), emplace(), pop(), and swap().[5] By default, you're able to use the three available sequence containers: std::vector, std::list, and std::deque. For any other container type, you are able to specialize the std::stack class template.

"This feels *so* much more familiar," you say, visibly relieved. Again, I absolutely agree. I also consider the Standard Library approach the more suitable solution for the purpose of containers. But it's still interesting to compare the two approaches. While there are many technical differences between the Stack base class and the std::stack class template, the purpose and semantics of these two approaches are remarkably similar: both provide the ability to adapt any data structure to a given stack interface. And both serve as a variation point, allowing you to nonintrusively add new Adapters without having to modify existing code.

Comparison Between Adapter and Strategy

"The three STL classes seem to fulfill the intent of Adapters, but isn't this the same way of configuring behavior as in the Strategy design pattern? Isn't this similar to std::unique_ptr and its deleter?" you ask. And yes, you're correct. From a structural point of view, the Strategy and Adapter design patterns are very similar. However, as explained in "Guideline 11: Understand the Purpose of Design Patterns" on page 80, the structure of design patterns may be similar or even the same, but the intent is different. In this context, the Container parameter specifies not just a single aspect of the behavior, but most of the behavior or even all of it. The class templates merely act as a wrapper around the functionality of the given type—they mainly adapt the interface. So the primary focus of an Adapter is to standardize interfaces and integrate incompatible functionality into an existing set of conventions; while on the other hand, the primary focus of the Strategy design pattern is to enable the configuration of behavior from the outside, building on and providing an expected interface. Also, for an Adapter there is no need to reconfigure the behavior at any time.

---

5 In this context, it's particularly interesting to note that std::stack doesn't allow you to traverse the elements via iterators. As usual for a stack, you're allowed to access only the topmost element.

Function Adapters

Additional examples for the Adapter design pattern are the Standard Library's free functions begin() (*https://oreil.ly/ZP74K*) and end() (*https://oreil.ly/qFeMX*). "Are you serious?" you ask, surprised. "You claim that free functions serve as an example of the Adapter design pattern? Isn't this a job for classes?" Well, not necessarily. The purpose of the free begin() and end() functions is to adapt the iterator interface of any type to the expected STL iterator interface. Thus, it maps from an available set of functions to an expected set of functions and serves the same purpose as any other Adapter. The major difference is that in contrast to object adapters or class adapters, which are based on either inheritance (runtime polymorphism) or templates (compile-time polymorphism), begin() and end() draw their power from function overloading, which is the second major compile-time polymorphism mechanism in C++. Still, some form of abstraction is at play.

 Remember that all kinds of abstractions represent a set of requirements and thus have to adhere to the Liskov Substitution Principle (LSP). This is also true for overload sets; see "Guideline 8: Understand the Semantic Requirements of Overload Sets" on page 56.

Consider the following function template:

```
template< typename Range >
void traverseRange( Range const& range )
{
   for( auto&& element : range ) {
      // ...
   }
}
```

In the traverseRange() function, we iterate through all the elements contained in the given range with a range-based for loop. The traversal happens via iterators that the compiler acquires with the free begin() and end() functions. Hence, the preceding for loop is equivalent to the following form of for:

```
template< typename Range >
void traverseRange( Range const& range )
{
   {
      using std::begin;
      using std::end;

      auto first( begin(range) );
      auto last ( end(range) );
      for( ; first!=last; ++first ) {
         auto&& element = *first;
         // ...
```

```
      }
    }
  }
```

Obviously, the range-based for loop is much more convenient to use. However, underneath the surface, the compiler generates code based on the free begin() and end() functions. Note the two using declarations in their beginning: the purpose is to enable *Argument-Dependent Lookup (ADL)* (*https://oreil.ly/VKcsl*) for the given type of range. ADL is the mechanism that makes sure the "correct" begin() and end() functions are called, even if they are overloads that reside in a user-specific namespace. This means that you have the opportunity to overload begin() and end() for any type and map the expected interface to a different, special-purpose set of functions.

This kind of *function adapter* was called a *shim* by Matthew Wilson in 2004.[6] One valuable property of this technique is that it's completely nonintrusive: it is possible to add a free function to any type, even to types that you could never adapt, such as types provided by third-party libraries. Hence, any generic code written in terms of shims gives you the enormous power to adapt virtually any type to the expected interface. Thus, you can imagine that shims or function adapters are the backbone of generic programming.

Analyzing the Shortcomings of the Adapter Design Pattern

Despite the value of the Adapter design pattern, there is one issue with this design pattern that I should explicitly point out. Consider the following example, which I adopted from Eric Freeman and Elisabeth Robson:[7]

```
//---- <Duck.h> ----------------

class Duck
{
 public:
   virtual ~Duck() = default;
   virtual void quack() = 0;
   virtual void fly() = 0;
};


//---- <MallardDuck.h> ----------------

#include <Duck.h>
```

---

6 Matthew Wilson, *Imperfect C++: Practical Solutions for Real-Life Programming* (Addison-Wesley, 2004).

7 Eric Freeman and Elisabeth Robson, *Head First Design Patterns: Building Extensible and Maintainable Object-Oriented Software* (O'Reilly, 2021).

```
class MallardDuck : public Duck
{
 public:
   void quack() override { /*...*/ }
   void fly() override { /*...*/ }
};
```

We start with the abstract Duck class, which introduces the two pure virtual functions quack() and fly(). Indeed, this appears to be a pretty expected and natural interface for a Duck class and of course raises some expectations: ducks make a very characteristic sound and can fly pretty well. This interface is implemented by many possible kinds of Duck, such as the MallardDuck class. Now, for some reason we also have to deal with turkeys:

```
//---- <Turkey.h> ----------------

class Turkey
{
 public:
   virtual ~Turkey() = default;
   virtual void gobble() = 0;  // Turkeys don't quack, they gobble!
   virtual void fly() = 0;     // Turkeys can fly (a short distance)
};
```

```
//---- <WildTurkey.h> ----------------

class WildTurkey : public Turkey
{
 public:
   void gobble() override { /*...*/ }
   void fly() override { /*...*/ }
};
```

Turkeys are represented by the abstract Turkey class, which of course is implemented by many different kinds of specific Turkeys, like the WildTurkey. To make things worse, for some reason ducks and turkeys are expected to be used together.[8] One possible way to make this work is to pretend that a turkey is a duck. After all, a turkey is pretty similar to a duck. Well, OK, it doesn't quack, but it can gobble (the typical turkey sound), and it can also fly (not for a long distance, but yes, it can fly). So you could adapt turkeys to ducks with the TurkeyAdapter:

```
//---- <TurkeyAdapter.h> ----------------

#include <memory>
```

---

8 Of course, you know better than to try this at home, but let's assume this is one of those strange, Monday-morning management decisions.

```
class TurkeyAdapter : public Duck
{
 public:
   explicit TurkeyAdapter( std::unique_ptr<Turkey> turkey )
      : turkey_{ std::move(turkey) }
   {}

   void quack() override { turkey_->gobble(); }
   void fly() override { turkey_->fly(); }

 private:
   std::unique_ptr<Turkey> turkey_;  // This is an example for an object adapter
};
```

While this is an amusing interpretation of duck typing (*https://oreil.ly/3rGpx*), this example nicely demonstrates that it's way too easy to integrate something alien into an existing hierarchy. A Turkey is simply not a Duck, even if we want it to be. I would argue that likely both the quack() and the fly() function violate the LSP. Neither functions really does what I would expect it to (at least I'm pretty sure that I want a quacking, not gobbling, critter and that I want something that can really fly like a duck). Of course, it depends on the specific context, but undeniably, the Adapter design pattern makes it very easy to combine things that do not belong together. Thus, it's very important that you consider the expected behavior and check for LSP violations when applying this design pattern:

```
#include <MallardDuck.h>
#include <WildTurkey.h>
#include <TurkeyAdapter.h>
#include <memory>
#include <vector>

using DuckChoir = std::vector<std::unique_ptr<Duck>>;

void give_concert( DuckChoir const& duck_choir )
{
   for( auto const& duck : duck_choir ) {
      duck->quack();
   }
}

int main()
{
   DuckChoir duck_choir{};

   // Let's hire the world's best ducks for the choir
   duck_choir.push_back( std::make_unique<MallardDuck>() );
   duck_choir.push_back( std::make_unique<MallardDuck>() );
   duck_choir.push_back( std::make_unique<MallardDuck>() );

   // Unfortunately we also hire a turkey in disguise
```

```
auto turkey = std::make_unique<WildTurkey>();
auto turkey_in_disguise = std::make_unique<TurkeyAdapter>( std::move(turkey) );
duck_choir.push_back( std::move(turkey_in_disguise) );

// The concert is going to be a musical disaster...
give_concert( duck_choir );

return EXIT_SUCCESS;
}
```

In summary, the Adapter design pattern can be considered one of the most valuable design patterns for combining different pieces of functionality and making them work together. I promise that it will prove to be a valuable tool in your daily work. Still, do not abuse the power of Adapter in some heroic effort to combine apples and oranges (or even oranges and grapefruits: they are similar but not the same). Always be aware of LSP expectations.

Guideline 24: Use Adapters to Standardize Interfaces

- Apply the Adapter design pattern with the intent to adapt interfaces so that otherwise incompatible pieces can work together.

- Be aware that Adapter is useful for both dynamic and static polymorphism.

- Distinguish among object adapters, class adapters, and function adapters.

- Understand the differences between the Adapter and Strategy design patterns.

- Pay attention to LSP violations when using the Adapter design pattern.

Guideline 25: Apply Observers as an Abstract Notification Mechanism

Chances are good that you've heard about observers before. "Oh, yes, of course I have—isn't this what the so-called social media platforms are doing with us?" you ask. Well, not exactly what I was going for, but yes, I believe we could call these platforms observers. And yes, there is also a pattern to what they do, even though it is not a design pattern. But I'm actually thinking about one of the most popular GoF design patterns, the Observer design pattern. Even if you are not familiar with the idea yet, you very likely have some experience with helpful observers from real life. For instance, you may have noticed that in some messenger apps the sender of a text message is immediately informed once you've read a new text message. That means that the message is displayed as "read" instead of just "delivered." This little service is essentially the work of a real-life Observer: as soon as the status of the new message changes, the sender is notified, providing the opportunity to respond to the state change.

The Observer Design Pattern Explained

In many software situations it's desirable to get feedback as soon as some state change occurs: a new job is added to a task queue, a setting is changed in some configuration object, a result is ready to be picked up, etc. But at the same time, it would be highly undesirable to introduce explicit dependencies between the subject (the observed entity that changes) and its observers (the callbacks that are notified based on a state change). On the contrary, the subject should be oblivious to the potentially many different kinds of observers. And that's for the simple reason that any direct dependency would make the software harder to change and harder to extend. This decoupling between the subject and its potentially many observers is the intent of the Observer design pattern.

The Observer Design Pattern

Intent: "Define a one-to-many dependency between objects so that when one object changes state, all its dependents are notified and updated automatically."[9]

As with all design patterns, the Observer design pattern identifies one aspect as a *variation point* (an aspect that changes or is expected to change) and extracts it in the form of an abstraction. It thus helps to decouple software entities. In the case of the Observer, the need to introduce new observers—the need to extend a one-to-many dependency—is recognized to be the variation point. As Figure 6-2 illustrates, this variation point is realized in the form of the Observer base class.

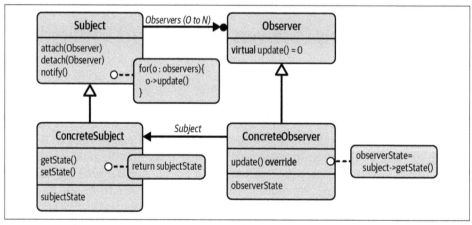

Figure 6-2. The UML representation of the Observer design pattern

---

9 Erich Gamma et al., *Design Patterns: Elements of Reusable Object-Oriented Software.*

The Observer class represents the abstraction for all possible implementations of observers. These observers are attached to a specific subject, represented by the ConcreteSubject class. To reduce the coupling between observers and their subjects, or to simply reduce code duplication by providing all common services to attach() and detach() to different observers, the Subject abstraction can be used. This Subject might also notify() all attached observers about a state change and trigger their corresponding update() functionality.

"Isn't the introduction of the Observer base class another example of the SRP?" you ask. And yes, you're 100% correct: extracting the Observer class, extracting a variation point, is the SRP in action (see "Guideline 2: Design for Change" on page 11). Again, the SRP acts as an enabler for the OCP (see "Guideline 5: Design for Extension" on page 35): by introducing the Observer abstraction, anyone is able to add new kinds of observers (e.g., ConcreteObserver) without the need to modify existing code. If you pay attention to the ownership of the Observer base class and make sure that the Observer class lives in the high level of your architecture, then you also fulfill the Dependency Inversion Principle (DIP).

A Classic Observer Implementation

"Great, I get it! It's nice to see these design principles in action again, but I would like to see a concrete Observer example." I understand. So let's take a look at a concrete implementation. However, I should clearly state the limitations of the following example before we start to look at the code. You might already be familiar with Observer, and therefore you might be looking for help and deeper advice on many of the tricky implementation details of Observer: how to deal with the order of attaching and detaching observers, attaching an observer multiple times, and especially using observers in a concurrent environment. I should honestly state up front that it is not my intention to provide answers to these questions. That discussion would be like opening a can of worms, quickly sucking us into the realm of implementation details. No, although you may be disappointed, my intention is to mostly stay on the level of software design.[10]

---

10 Despite the fact that I don't venture into the thicket of Observer implementation details, I can still give you a few references on how to implement Observers. A good overview on many of the implementation aspects is Victor Ciura's CppCon 2021 talk "Spooky Action at a Distance" (*https://oreil.ly/9TcK6*). A very detailed discussion on how to deal with the concurrency issues of the Observer pattern can be found in Tony Van Eerd's C++Now 2016 talk "Thread-Safe Observer Pattern—You're Doing It Wrong" (*https://oreil.ly/KKU47*).

Like for the previous design patterns, we start with a classic implementation of the Observer design pattern. The central element is the `Observer` base class:

```
//---- <Observer.h> ----------------

class Observer
{
 public:
   virtual ~Observer() = default;

   virtual void update( /*...*/ ) = 0;  ❶
};
```

The most important implementation detail of this class is the pure virtual `update()` function (❶), which is called whenever the observer is notified of some state change.[11] There are three alternatives for how to define the `update()` function, which provide a reasonable implementation and design flexibility. The first alternative is to push the updated state via one or even several `update()` functions:

```
class Observer
{
 public:
   // ...
   virtual void update1( /*arguments representing the updated state*/ ) = 0;
   virtual void update2( /*arguments representing the updated state*/ ) = 0;
   // ...
};
```

This form of observer is commonly called a *push observer*. In this form, the observer is given all necessary information by the subject and therefore is not required to pull any information from the subject on its own. This can reduce the coupling to the subject significantly and create the opportunity to reuse the `Observer` class for several subjects. Additionally, there is the option to use a separate overload for each kind of state change. In the preceding code snippet, there are two `update()` functions, one for each of two possible state changes. And since it's always clear which state changed, the observer is not required to "search" for any state change, which proves to be efficient.

"Excuse me," you say, "but isn't this a violation of the ISP? Shouldn't we separate concerns by separating the `update()` functions into several base classes?" This is a great question! Obviously, you're watching out for artificial coupling. Very good!

---

11 If you're aware of the Non-Virtual Interface (NVI) (*https://oreil.ly/mqwgp*) idiom or the Template Method design pattern, then please feel free to move this virtual function into the `private` section of the class and provide a public, nonvirtual wrapper function for it. You can find more information about NVI in Herb Sutter's Guru of the Week blog (*http://www.gotw.ca*) or in the article "Virtuality" (*https://oreil.ly/GSdnB*) from the *C++ Users Journal*, 19(9), September 2001.

And you are correct: we could separate an `Observer` with several `update()` functions into smaller `Observer` classes:

```
class Observer1
{
 public:
   // ...
   virtual void update1( /*arguments representing the updated state*/ ) = 0;
   // ...
};

class Observer2
{
 public:
   // ...
   virtual void update2( /*arguments representing the updated state*/ ) = 0;
   // ...
};
```

In theory, this approach could help reduce the coupling to a particular subject and more easily reuse observers for different subjects. It might also help because different observers might be interested in different state changes, and therefore it might be a violation of the ISP to artificially couple all possible state changes. And of course this might result in an efficiency gain if a lot of unnecessary state change notifications can be avoided.

Unfortunately, a particular subject is not likely to distinguish among different kinds of observers. First, because this would require it to store different kinds of pointers (which is inconvenient to handle for the subject), and second, because it is possible that different state changes are linked in a certain way. In that case, the subject will expect that observers are interested in *all* possible state changes. From that perspective it can be reasonable to combine several `update()` functions into one base class. Either way, it's very likely that a concrete observer will have to deal with all kinds of state changes. I know, it can be a nuisance to have to deal with several `update()` functions, even if only a small fraction of them are interesting. But still, make sure that you're not accidentally violating the Liskov Substitution Principle by not adhering to some expected behavior (if there is any).

There are several more potential downsides of a push observer. First, the observers are *always* given *all* the information, whether they need it or not. Thus, this push style works well only if the observers need the information most of the time. Otherwise, a lot of effort is lost on unnecessary notifications. Second, pushing creates a dependency on the number and kind of arguments that are passed to the observer. Any change to these arguments requires a lot of subsequent changes in the deriving observer classes.

Some of these downsides are resolved by the second `Observer` alternative. It's possible to only pass a reference to the subject to the observer:[12]

```
class Observer
{
 public:
   // ...
   virtual void update( Subject const& subject ) = 0;
   // ...
};
```

Due to the lack of specific information passed to the observer, the classes deriving from the `Observer` base class are required to pull the new information from the subject on their own. For this reason, this form of observer is commonly called a *pull observer*. The advantage is the reduced dependency on the number and kinds of arguments. Deriving observers are free to query for any information, not just the changed state. On the other hand, this design creates a strong, direct dependency between the classes deriving from `Observer` and the subject. Hence, any change to the subject easily reflects on the observers. Additionally, observers might have to "search" for the state change if multiple details have changed. This might prove to be unnecessarily inefficient.

If you consider only a single piece of information as the changing state, the performance disadvantage might not pose a limitation for you. Still, please remember that software changes: a subject may grow, and with it the desire to notify about different kinds of changes. Adapting the observers in the process would result in a lot of additional work. From that point of view, the *push observer* appears to be a better choice.

Luckily, there is a third alternative, which removes a lot of the previous disadvantages and thus becomes our approach of choice: in addition to passing a reference to the subject, we pass a tag to provide information about which property of a subject has changed:

```
//---- <Observer.h> ----------------

class Observer
{
 public:
   virtual ~Observer() = default;

   virtual void update( Subject const& subject
                        , /*Subject-specific type*/ property ) = 0;
};
```

---

[12] Alternatively, the observer could also remember the subject on its own.

The tag may help an observer to decide on its own whether some state change is interesting or not. It's commonly represented by some subject-specific enumeration type, which lists all possible state changes. This, unfortunately, increases the coupling of the Observer class to a specific subject.

"Wouldn't it be possible to remove the dependency on a specific Subject by implementing the Observer base class as a class template? Take a look at the following code snippet:"

```
//---- <Observer.h> ----------------

template< typename Subject, typename StateTag >   ❷
class Observer
{
 public:
   virtual ~Observer() = default;

   virtual void update( Subject const& subject, StateTag property ) = 0;
};
```

This is a great suggestion. By defining the Observer class in the form of a class template (❷), we can easily lift the Observer to a higher architectural level. In this form, the class does not depend on any specific subject and thus may be reused by many different subjects that want to define a one-to-many relationship. However, you should not expect too much of this improvement: the effect is limited to the Observer class. Concrete subjects will expect concrete instantiations of this observer class, and in consequence, concrete implementations of Observer will still strongly depend on the subject.

To better understand why that is, let's take a look at a possible subject implementation. After your initial comment about social media, I suggest that we implement an Observer for persons. Well, OK, this example may be morally questionable, but it will serve its purpose, so let's go with that. At least we know who is to blame for this.

The following Person class represents an observed person:

```
//---- <Person.h> ----------------

#include <Observer.h>
#include <string>
#include <set>

class Person
{
 public:
   enum StateChange
   {
      forenameChanged,
      surnameChanged,
      addressChanged
```

```
};

using PersonObserver = Observer<Person,StateChange>;  ❺

explicit Person( std::string forename, std::string surname )
   : forename_{ std::move(forename) }
   , surname_{ std::move(surname) }
{}

bool attach( PersonObserver* observer );  ❻
bool detach( PersonObserver* observer );  ❼

void notify( StateChange property );  ❽

void forename( std::string newForename );  ❾
void surname ( std::string newSurname );
void address ( std::string newAddress );

std::string const& forename() const { return forename_; }
std::string const& surname () const { return surname_; }
std::string const& address () const { return address_; }

private:
   std::string forename_;  ❸
   std::string surname_;
   std::string address_;

   std::set<PersonObserver*> observers_;  ❹
};
```

In this example, a Person is merely an aggregation of the three data members:
forename_, surname_, and address_ (❸) (I know, this is a rather simple representation of a person.) In addition, a person holds the std::set of registered observers
(❹). Please note that the observers are registered by pointers to instances of
PersonObserver (❺). This is interesting for two reasons: first, this demonstrates the
purpose of the templated Observer class: the Person class instantiates its own kind of
observer from the class template. And second, pointers prove to be very useful in this
context, since the address of an object is unique. Thus, it is common to use the
address as a unique identifier for an observer.

"Shouldn't this be std::unique_ptr or std::shared_ptr?" you ask. No, not in this
situation. The pointers merely serve as handles to the registered observers; they
should not own the observers. Therefore, any owning smart pointer would be the
wrong tool in this situation. The only reasonable choice would be std::weak_ptr,
which would allow you to check for dangling pointers. However, std::weak_ptr is
not a good candidate for a key for std::set (not even with a custom comparator).
Although there are ways to still use std::weak_ptr, I will stick to raw pointers. But
don't worry, this doesn't mean we are abandoning the benefits of modern C++. No,

using a raw pointer is perfectly valid in this situation. This is also expressed in C++ Core Guideline F.7 (*https://oreil.ly/xS6w6*):

> For the general use, take T* or T& arguments rather than smart pointers.

Whenever you're interested in getting a notification for a state change of a person, you can register an observer via the attach() member function (❻). And whenever you're no longer interested in getting notifications, you can deregister an observer via the detach() member function (❼). These two functions are an essential ingredient of the Observer design pattern and a clear indication of the application of the design pattern:

```
bool Person::attach( PersonObserver* observer )
{
   auto [pos,success] = observers_.insert( observer );
   return success;
}

bool Person::detach( PersonObserver* observer )
{
   return ( observers_.erase( observer ) > 0U );
}
```

You have complete freedom to implement the attach() and detach() functions as you see fit. In this example, we allow an observer to be registered only a single time with a std::set. If you try to register an observer a second time, the function returns false. The same thing happens if you try to deregister an observer that is not registered. Note that the decision to not allow multiple registrations is my choice for this example. In other scenarios, it might be desirable or even necessary to accept duplicate registrations. Either way, the behavior and interface of the subject should of course be consistent in all cases.

Another core function of the Observer design pattern is the notify() member function (❽). Whenever some state change occurs, this function is called to notify all registered observers about the change:

```
void Person::notify( StateChange property )
{
   for( auto iter=begin(observers_); iter!=end(observers_); )
   {
      auto const pos = iter++;
      (*pos)->update(*this,property);
   }
}
```

"Why is the implementation of the notify() function so complicated? Wouldn't a range-based for loop be completely sufficient?" You are correct; I should explain what's happening here. The given formulation makes sure detach() operations can be detected during the iteration. This may happen, for instance, if an observer decides to detach itself during the call to the update() function. But I do not claim that this formulation is perfect: unfortunately it is not able to cope with attach() operations. And don't even start to ask about concurrency! So this is just one example why the implementation details of observer can be so tricky.

The notify() function is called in all three setter functions (❾). Note that in all three functions, we always pass a different tag to indicate which property has changed. This tag may be used by classes deriving from the Observer base class to determine the nature of the change:

```cpp
void Person::forename( std::string newForename )
{
   forename_ = std::move(newForename);
   notify( forenameChanged );
}

void Person::surname( std::string newSurname )
{
   surname_ = std::move(newSurname);
   notify( surnameChanged );
}

void Person::address( std::string newAddress )
{
   address_ = std::move(newAddress);
   notify( addressChanged );
}
```

With these mechanics in place, you are now able to write new kinds of fully OCP-conforming observers. For instance, you could decide to implement a NameObserver and an AddressObserver:

```cpp
//---- <NameObserver.h> ----------------

#include <Observer.h>
#include <Person.h>

class NameObserver : public Observer<Person,Person::StateChange>
{
 public:
   void update( Person const& person, Person::StateChange property ) override;
};


//---- <NameObserver.cpp> ----------------

#include <NameObserver.h>

void NameObserver::update( Person const& person, Person::StateChange property )
{
   if( property == Person::forenameChanged ||
```

```
             property == Person::surnameChanged )
    {
       // ... Respond to changed name
    }
}


//---- <AddressObserver.h> ---------------

#include <Observer.h>
#include <Person.h>

class AddressObserver : public Observer<Person,Person::StateChange>
{
 public:
   void update( Person const& person, Person::StateChange property ) override;
};

//---- <AddressObserver.cpp> ---------------

#include <AddressObserver.h>

void AddressObserver::update( Person const& person, Person::StateChange property )
{
   if( property == Person::addressChanged ) {
      // ... Respond to changed address
   }
}
```

Equipped with these two observers, you are now notified whenever either the name or address of a person changes:

```
#include <AddressObserver.h>
#include <NameObserver.h>
#include <Person.h>
#include <cstdlib>

int main()
{
   NameObserver nameObserver;
   AddressObserver addressObserver;

   Person homer( "Homer"     , "Simpson" );
   Person marge( "Marge"     , "Simpson" );
   Person monty( "Montgomery", "Burns"   );

   // Attaching observers
   homer.attach( &nameObserver );
   marge.attach( &addressObserver );
   monty.attach( &addressObserver );

   // Updating information on Homer Simpson
   homer.forename( "Homer Jay" );  // Adding his middle name
```

```
    // Updating information on Marge Simpson
    marge.address( "712 Red Bark Lane, Henderson, Clark County, Nevada 89011" );

    // Updating information on Montgomery Burns
    monty.address( "Springfield Nuclear Power Plant" );

    // Detaching observers
    homer.detach( &nameObserver );

    return EXIT_SUCCESS;
}
```

After these many implementation details, let's take a step back and look at the bigger
picture again. Figure 6-3 shows the dependency graph for this Observer example.

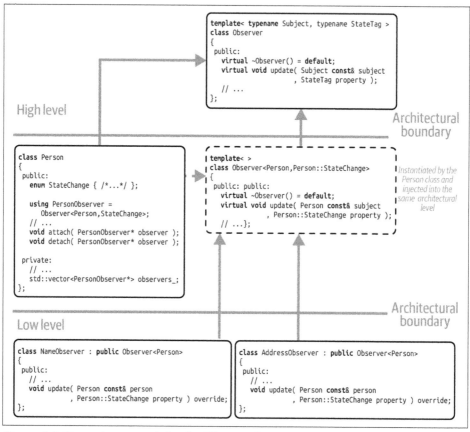

Figure 6-3. Dependency graph for the Observer design pattern

Due to the decision to implement the `Observer` class in the form of a class template, the `Observer` class resides on the highest level of our architecture. This enables you to reuse the `Observer` class for multiple purposes, for instance, for the `Person` class. The `Person` class declares its own `Observer<Person,Person::StateChange>` type and by that injects the code into its own architectural level. Concrete person observers, e.g., `NameObserver` and `AddressObserver`, can subsequently build on this declaration.

An Observer Implementation Based on Value Semantics

"I understand why you've started with a classic implementation, but since you have made the point about favoring value semantics, how would the observer look in a value semantics world?" That is an excellent question, since this is a very reasonable next step. As explained in "Guideline 22: Prefer Value Semantics over Reference Semantics" on page 176, there are a lot of good reasons to avoid the realm of reference semantics. However, we won't entirely stray from the classic implementation: to register and deregister observers, we will always be in need of some unique identifier for observers, and the unique address of an observer is just the easiest and most convenient way to tackle that problem. Therefore, we'll stick to using a pointer to refer to a registered observer. However, `std::function` is an elegant way to avoid the inheritance hierarchy—`std::function`:

```
//---- <Observer.h> ---------------

#include <functional>

template< typename Subject, typename StateTag >
class Observer
{
 public:
   using OnUpdate = std::function<void(Subject const&,StateTag)>;   ❿

   // No virtual destructor necessary

   explicit Observer( OnUpdate onUpdate )   ⓫
      : onUpdate_{ std::move(onUpdate) }
   {
      // Possibly respond on an invalid/empty std::function instance
   }

   // Non-virtual update function
   void update( Subject const& subject, StateTag property )
   {
      onUpdate_( subject, property );   ⓭
   }

 private:
   OnUpdate onUpdate_;   ⓬
};
```

Instead of implementing the `Observer` class as a base class, and thus requiring deriving classes to inherit and implement the `update()` function in a very specific way, we separate concerns and instead build on composition (see "Guideline 20: Favor Composition over Inheritance" on page 162). The `Observer` class first provides a type alias called `OnUpdate` for the `std::function` type for the expected signature of our `update()` function (❿). Via the constructor, you are passed an instance of `std::function` (⓫), and you move it into your data member `onUpdate_` (⓬). The job of the `update()` function is now to forward the call, including the arguments, to `onUpdate_` (⓭).

The flexibility gained with `std::function` is easily demonstrated with an updated `main()` function:

```cpp
#include <Observer.h>
#include <Person.h>
#include <cstdlib>

void propertyChanged( Person const& person, Person::StateChange property )
{
   if( property == Person::forenameChanged ||
       property == Person::surnameChanged )
   {
      // ... Respond to changed name
   }
}

int main()
{
   using PersonObserver = Observer<Person,Person::StateChange>;

   PersonObserver nameObserver( propertyChanged );

   PersonObserver addressObserver(
      [/*captured state*/]( Person const& person, Person::StateChange property ){
         if( property == Person::addressChanged )
         {
            // ... Respond to changed address
         }
      } );

   Person homer( "Homer"     , "Simpson" );
   Person marge( "Marge"     , "Simpson" );
   Person monty( "Montgomery", "Burns"   );

   // Attaching observers
   homer.attach( &nameObserver );
   marge.attach( &addressObserver );
   monty.attach( &addressObserver );

   // ...
```

```
    return EXIT_SUCCESS;
}
```

Thanks to choosing a less intrusive approach and to decoupling with `std::function`, the choice of how to implement the `update()` function is completely up to the observer's implementer (stateless, stateful, etc.). For the `nameObserver`, we build on the free function `propertyChanged()`, which itself is strongly decoupled because it's not bound to a class and might be reused on several occasions. The `addressObserver`, on the other hand, chooses a lambda instead, which could possibly capture some state. Either way, the only convention that these two have to follow is to fulfill the required signature of the required `std::function` type.

"Why do we still need the `Observer` class? Couldn't we just directly use `std::function`?" Yes, it most certainly looks that way. From a functionality point of view, the `Observer` class doesn't add anything by itself. However, as `std::function` is a true child of value semantics, we tend to copy or move `std::function` objects. But this is not desirable in this situation: especially if you use a stateful observer, you don't want a copy of your observer to be called. And although technically possible, it is not particularly common to pass around pointers to `std::function`. Therefore, the `Observer` class may still be of value in the form of an Adapter for `std::function` (see "Guideline 24: Use Adapters to Standardize Interfaces" on page 198).

Analyzing the Shortcomings of the Observer Design Pattern

"This is not quite the value semantics solution I was expecting, but I still like it!" Well, I'm glad you feel this way. Indeed, the value semantics advantages, in combination with the benefits of the Observer design pattern (i.e., decoupling an event from the action taken for that event and the ability to easily add new kinds of observers), work really, really well. Unfortunately, there is no perfect design, and every design also comes with disadvantages.

First, I should explicitly spell out that the demonstrated `std::function` approach works well only for a *pull observer* with a single `update()` function. Since `std::function` can cope with only a single callable, any approach that would require multiple `update()` functions cannot be handled by a single `std::function`. Therefore, `std::function` is usually not the way to go for a *push observer* with multiple `update()` functions, or the potential for a growing number of `update()` functions (remember, code tends to change!). However, it is possible to generalize the approach of `std::function`. If the need arises, the design pattern of choice is Type Erasure (see Chapter 8).

A second (minor) disadvantage, as you have seen, is that there is no pure value-based implementation. While we might be able to implement the update() functionality in terms of std::function to gain flexibility, we still use a raw pointer to attach and detach Observers. And that is easy to explain: the advantages of using a pointer as a unique identifier are just too good to dismiss. Additionally, for a stateful Observer, we don't want to deal with the copy of an entity. Still, this of course requires us to check for nullptr (which takes additional effort), and we always have to pay for the indirection that the pointer represents.[13] I personally would rate this as only a minor point because of the many advantages of this approach.

A far bigger disadvantage is the potential implementation issues with *Observers*: the order of registration and deregistration may matter a lot, in particular if an observer is allowed to register multiple times. Also, in a multithreaded environment, the thread-safe registration and deregistration of observers and handling of events are highly nontrivial topics. For instance, an untrusted observer can freeze a server during a callback if it behaves inappropriately, and implementing timeouts for arbitrary computations is *very* nontrivial. However, this topic is far outside the scope of this book.

What is in the scope of this book, however, is the alleged danger that the overuse of observers can quickly and easily lead to a complex network of interconnections. Indeed, if you are not careful, you can accidentally introduce an infinite loop of callbacks! For that reason, developers are sometimes concerned about using Observers and are afraid that a single notification may result in a huge, global response due to these interconnections. While this danger exists, of course, a proper design should not be severely affected by this: if you have a proper architecture and if you have properly implemented your observers, then any sequence of notifications should always run along a directed, acyclic graph (DAG) toward the lower levels of your architecture. And that, of course, is the beauty of good software design.

In summary, with the intent of providing a solution for notification of state change, the Observer design pattern proves to be one of the most famous and most commonly used design patterns. Aside from the potentially tricky implementation details, it is definitely one of the design patterns that should be in every developer's toolbox.

---

13 You can also choose to build on gsl::not_null<T> from the Guideline Support Library (GSL) (*https://oreil.ly/cx0Jd*).

> ## Guideline 25: Apply Observers as an Abstract Notification Mechanism
>
> - Apply the Observer design pattern with the intent to create a one-to-many relationship between a subject and its observers.
>
> - Understand the trade-offs between push observers and pull observers.
>
> - Utilize the advantages of a value semantics–based Observer implementation.

Guideline 26: Use CRTP to Introduce Static Type Categories

C++ really has a lot to offer. It comes with lots of features, many syntactic curiosities, and a large number of amazing, utterly unpronounceable and (for the uninitiated) plainly cryptic acronyms: RAII, ADL, CTAD, SFINAE, NTTP, IFNDR, and SIOF. Oh, what fun! One of these cryptic acronyms is CRTP, short for the *Curiously Recurring Template Pattern*.[14] If you're scratching your head because the name doesn't make any sense to you, don't worry: as is so often in C++, the name was chosen randomly, but has stuck and has never been reconsidered or changed. The pattern was named by James Coplien in the February 1995 issue of the *C++ Report* after realizing that, curiously, this pattern was recurring in many different C++ codebases.[15] And curiously, this pattern, although building on inheritance and (potentially) serving as an abstraction, does not exhibit the usual performance drawbacks of many other classic design patterns. For that reason, CRTP is definitely worth a look, as it may become a valuable, or should I say *curious*, addition to your design pattern toolbox.

A Motivation for CRTP

Performance is very important in C++. So important in fact, that in several contexts the performance overhead of using virtual functions is considered outright

---

14 If you're wondering what those others stand for: RAII: Resource Acquisition Is Initialization (which is argued to be the most valuable idea of C++, but at the same time is officially the worst acronym; it literally does not make any sense); ADL: Argument Dependent Lookup; CTAD: Class Template Argument Deduction; SFINAE: Substitution Failure Is Not An Error; NTTP: Non-Type Template Parameter; IFNDR: Ill-Formed, No Diagnostic Required; SIOF: Static Initialization Order Fiasco. For an overview of (almost) all C++ acronyms, see Arthur O'Dwyer's blog (*https://oreil.ly/36Gnd*).

15 Ah, the *C++ Report* (*https://oreil.ly/HJIKc*)—such glorious times! However, you may be one of the poor souls who never had an opportunity to read an original *C++ Report*. If so, you should know that it was a bimonthly computer magazine published by the SIGS Publications Group between 1989 and 2002. The original *C++ Report* is hard to come by these days, but many of its articles have been collected in the book edited by Stanley Lippmann *C++ Gems: Programming Pearls from the C++ Report* (Cambridge University Press). This book includes James Coplien's article "Curiously Recurring Template Patterns."

unacceptable. Therefore, in performance-sensitive contexts, such as certain parts of computer games or high-frequency trading, no virtual functions are used. The same is true for high-performance computing (HPC). In HPC, any kind of conditional or indirection, and this includes virtual functions, is banned from the most performance-critical parts, such as the innermost loops of compute kernels. Using them would incur too much of a performance overhead.

To give an example of how and why this matters, let's consider the following DynamicVector class template from a linear algebra (LA) library:

```
//---- <DynamicVector.h> ----------------

#include <numeric>
#include <iosfwd>
#include <iterator>
#include <vector>
// ...

template< typename T >
class DynamicVector
{
 public:
   using value_type    = T;   ❷
   using iterator       = typename std::vector<T>::iterator;
   using const_iterator = typename std::vector<T>::const_iterator;

   // ... Constructors and special member functions

   size_t size() const;   ❸

   T&      operator[]( size_t index );   ❹
   T const& operator[]( size_t index ) const;

   iterator       begin();   ❺
   const_iterator begin() const;
   iterator       end();
   const_iterator end() const;

   // ... Many numeric functions

 private:
   std::vector<T> values_;   ❶
   // ...
};

template< typename T >
std::ostream& operator<<( std::ostream& os, DynamicVector<T> const& vector )   ❻
{
   os << "(";
   for( auto const& element : vector ) {
      os << " " << element;
```

```
    }
    os << " )";

    return os;
}

template< typename T >
auto l2norm( DynamicVector<T> const& vector )   ❼
{
    using std::begin, std::end;
    return std::sqrt( std::inner_product( begin(vector), end(vector)
                                  , begin(vector), T{} ) );
}

// ... Many more
```

Despite the name, DynamicVector does not represent a container but a numerical vector for the purpose of LA computations. The Dynamic part of the name implies that it allocates its elements of type T dynamically, in this example, in the form of std::vector (❶). For that reason, it is suited for large LA problems (definitely in the range of several million elements). Although this class may be loaded with many numerical operations, from an interface point of view you might indeed be tempted to call it a container: it provides the usual nested types (value_type, iterator, and const_iterator) (❷), a size() function to query the current number of elements (❸), subscript operators to access individual elements by index (one for non-const and one for const vectors) (❹), and begin() and end() functions to iterate over the elements (❺). Apart from the member functions, it also provides an output operator (❻) and, to show at least one LA operation, a function to compute the vector's Euclidean norm (*https://oreil.ly/x2a47*) (often also called the *L2 norm*, because it approximates the L2 norm for discrete vectors) (❼).

The DynamicVector is not the only vector class, though. In our LA library, you will also find the following StaticVector class:

```
//---- <StaticVector.h> ----------------

#include <array>
#include <numeric>
#include <iosfwd>
#include <iterator>
// ...

template< typename T, size_t Size >
class StaticVector
{
 public:
    using value_type     = T;   ❽
    using iterator       = typename std::array<T,Size>::iterator;
    using const_iterator = typename std::array<T,Size>::const_iterator;
```

```
    // ... Constructors and special member functions

    size_t size() const;  ❾

    T&        operator[]( size_t index );  ❿
    T const& operator[]( size_t index ) const;

    iterator        begin();  ⓫
    const_iterator begin() const;
    iterator        end();
    const_iterator end() const;

    // ... Many numeric functions

  private:
    std::array<T,Size> values_;  ⓮
    // ...
};

template< typename T, size_t Size >
std::ostream& operator<<( std::ostream& os,      ⓬
                          StaticVector<T,Size> const& vector )
{
   os << "(";
   for( auto const& element : vector ) {
      os << " " << element;
   }
   os << " )";

   return os;
}

template< typename T, size_t Size >
auto l2norm( StaticVector<T,Size> const& vector )  ⓭
{
   using std::begin, std::end;
   return std::sqrt( std::inner_product( begin(vector), end(vector)
                                       , begin(vector), T{} ) );
}
```

"Isn't this almost the same as the DynamicVector class?" you wonder. Yes, these two classes are very similar indeed. The StaticVector class provides the same interface as the DynamicVector, such as the nested types value_type, iterator, and const_iterator (❽); the size() member function (❾); the subscript operators (❿); and the begin() and end() functions (⓫). It also comes with an output operator (⓬) and a free l2norm() function (⓭). However, there is an important, performance-related difference between the two vector classes: as the Static in the name suggests, the StaticVector does not allocate its elements dynamically. Instead, it uses an in-class buffer to store its elements, for instance, with a std::array (⓮). Thus, in contrast to `DynamicVector`, the entire functionality of `StaticVector` is optimized for a small, fixed number of elements, such as 2D or 3D vectors.

"OK, I understand that this is important for performance, but there's still a lot of code duplication, right?" Again, you are correct. If you take a close look at the associated output operator of the two vector classes, you will find that the implementation of these two functions is identical. This is deeply undesirable: if anything changes, for instance, the way vectors are formatted (and remember: change is *the one* constant in software development and needs to be expected; see "Guideline 2: Design for Change" on page 11), then you would have to make the change in many places, not just one. This is a violation of the Don't Repeat Yourself (DRY) principle: it's easy to forget or miss updating one of the many places, thus introducing an inconsistency or even a bug.

"But isn't this duplication easily resolved with a slightly more general function template? For example, I can imagine the following output operator for all kinds of dense vectors:"

```
template< typename DenseVector >
std::ostream& operator<<( std::ostream& os, DenseVector const& vector )
{
   // ... as before
}
```

Although this seems like an adequate solution, I wouldn't accept this code in a pull request. This function template is indeed more general, but I would definitely not call it "slightly" more general; what you are suggesting is the most general output operator one could possibly write. Yes, the name of the function template may suggest that it's written for only dense vectors (including `DynamicVector` and `StaticVector`), but this function template will in fact accept any type: `DynamicVector`, `StaticVector`, `std::vector`, `std::string`, and fundamental types such as `int` and `double`. It simply fails to specify any requirement or any kind of constraint. For that reason it violates Core Guideline T.10 (*https://oreil.ly/bVjjh*):[16]

Specify concepts for all template arguments.

While this output operator will work for all dense vectors and sequence containers, you would get a compilation error for all types that do not provide the expected interface. Or even worse, you might subtly violate the implicit requirements and expectations, and with that the LSP (see "Guideline 6: Adhere to the Expected Behavior of Abstractions" on page 44). Of course, you wouldn't do this consciously, but

---

16 If you can't use C++20 concepts yet, `std::enable_if` provides an alternative formulation. Refer to Core Guideline T.48 (*https://oreil.ly/K2ljM*): "If your compiler does not support concepts, fake them with `enable_if`." See also your preferred C++ templates reference.

likely accidentally: this output operator is a perfect match for any type and might be used even though you don't expect it. Therefore, this function template would be a very unfortunate addition to the output operator overload set. What we need is a totally new set of types, a new type category.

"Isn't this what base classes are for? Couldn't we just formulate a DenseVector base class that defines the expected interface for all dense vectors? Consider the following sketch of a DenseVector base class:"

```cpp
template< typename T >  // Type of the elements
class DenseVector
{
 public:
   virtual ~DenseVector() = default;

   virtual size_t size() const = 0;

   virtual T&       operator[]( size_t index ) = 0;
   virtual T const& operator[]( size_t index ) const = 0;

   // ...
};

template< typename T >
std::ostream& operator<<( std::ostream& os, DenseVector<T> const& vector )
{
   // ... as before
}
```

"This should work, right? I'm just not sure how to declare the begin() and end() functions, as I don't know how to abstract from different iterator types, such as std::vector<T>::iterator and std::array<T>::iterator." I also have a feeling that this could be a problem, and I admit that I also do not have a quick solution for that. But there is something far more concerning: with this base class, we would turn all our member functions into virtual member functions. That would include the begin() and end() functions but, most importantly, the two subscript operators. The consequences would be significant: with every access to an element of the vector, we would now have to call a virtual function. Every single access! Therefore, with this base class, we could wave goodbye to high performance.

Still, the general idea of building an abstraction with a base class is good. We just have to do it differently. This is where we should take a closer look at the CRTP.

The CRTP Design Pattern Explained

The CRTP design pattern builds on the common idea of creating an abstraction using a base class. But instead of establishing a runtime relationship between base and derived classes via virtual functions, it creates a compile-time relationship.

The CRTP Design Pattern

Intent: "Define a compile-time abstraction for a family of related types."

The compile-time relationship between the `DenseVector` base class and the `DynamicVector` derived class is created by upgrading the base class to a class template:

```
//---- <DenseVector.h> ----------------

template< typename Derived >   ⑮
struct DenseVector
{
   // ...
   size_t size() const { return static_cast<Derived const&>(*this).size(); }   ⑰
   // ...
};
```

```
//---- <DynamicVector.h> ----------------

template< typename T >
class DynamicVector : public DenseVector<DynamicVector<T>>   ⑯
{
 public:
   // ...
   size_t size() const;   ⑱
   // ...
};
```

The curious detail about CRTP is that the new template parameter of the `DenseVector` base class represents the type of the associated derived class (⑮). Derived classes, for instance, the `DynamicVector`, are expected to provide their own type to instantiate the base class (⑯).

"Wow, wait a second—is that even possible?" you ask. It is. To instantiate a template, you do not need the complete definition of a type. It is sufficient to use an incomplete type. Such an incomplete type is available after the compiler has seen the `class DynamicVector` declaration. In essence, this piece of syntax works as a forward declaration. Therefore, the `DynamicVector` class can indeed use itself as a template argument to the `DenseVector` base class.

Of course, you can name the template parameter of the base class however you'd like (e.g., simply T), but as discussed in "Guideline 14: Use a Design Pattern's Name to Communicate Intent" on page 97, it helps to communicate intent by using the name of the design pattern or names commonly used for a pattern. For that reason, you could name the parameter CRTP, which nicely communicates the pattern but unfortunately only to the initiated. Everyone else will be puzzled by the acronym. Therefore, the template parameter is often called `Derived`, which perfectly expresses its purpose and communicates its intent: it represents the type of the derived class.

Via this template parameter, the base class is now aware of the actual type of the derived type. While it still represents an abstraction and the common interface for all dense vectors, it is now able to access and call the concrete implementation in the derived type. This happens, for instance, in the `size()` member function (**17**): the `DenseVector` uses a `static_cast` to convert itself into a reference to the derived class and calls the `size()` function on that. What at first glance may look like a recursive function call (calling the `size()` function within the `size()` function) is in fact a call of the `size()` member function in the derived class (**18**).

"So this is the compile-time relationship you were talking about. The base class represents an abstraction from concrete derived types and implementation details but still knows exactly where the implementation details are. So we really do not need any virtual function." Correct. With CRTP, we are now able to implement a common interface and forward every call to the derived class by simply performing a `static_cast`. And there is no performance penalty for doing this. In fact, the base class function is very likely to be inlined, and if the `DenseVector` is the only or first base class, the `static_cast` will not even result in a single assembly instruction. It merely tells the compiler to treat the object as an object of the derived type.

To provide a clean CRTP base class, we should update a couple of details, though:

```
//---- <DenseVector.h> ----------------

template< typename Derived >
struct DenseVector
{
 protected:
   ~DenseVector() = default;   19

 public:
   Derived&        derived()        { return static_cast<Derived&>( *this ); }   20
   Derived const& derived() const { return static_cast<Derived const&>( *this ); }

   size_t size() const { return derived().size(); }

   // ...
};
```

Since we want to avoid any virtual functions, we're also not interested in a virtual destructor. Therefore, we implement the destructor as a nonvirtual function in the `protected` section of the class (**19**). This perfectly adheres to Core Guideline C.35 (*https://oreil.ly/RxGfR*):

A base class destructor should be either public and virtual, or protected and non-virtual.

Keep in mind, though, that this definition of the destructor keeps the compiler from generating the two move operations. Since a CRTP base class is usually empty with nothing to move, this is not a problem; but still, always be mindful about the Rule of 5 (*https://oreil.ly/fzS3f*).

We should also avoid using a `static_cast` in every single member function of the base class. Although it would be correct, any cast should be considered suspicious, and casts should be minimized.[17] For that reason, we add the two `derived()` member functions, which perform the cast and can be used in the other member functions (❷⓪). This resulting code not only looks cleaner and adheres to the *DRY* principle, but it also looks far less suspicious.

Equipped with the `derived()` functions, we can now go ahead and define the subscript operators and the `begin()` and `end()` functions:

```
template< typename Derived >
struct DenseVector
{
   // ...

   ??? operator[]( size_t index )       { return derived()[index]; }
   ??? operator[]( size_t index ) const { return derived()[index]; }

   ??? begin()       { return derived().begin(); }
   ??? begin() const { return derived().begin(); }
   ??? end()         { return derived().end(); }
   ??? end()   const { return derived().end(); }

   // ...
};
```

However, these functions are not as straightforward as the `size()` member function. In particular, the return types prove to be a little harder to specify, as these types depend on the implementation of the `Derived` class. "Well, that shouldn't be too hard," you say. "This is why the derived types provide a couple of nested types, such as `value_type`, `iterator`, and `const_iterator`, right?" Indeed, it appears to be intuitive to just ask nicely:

```
template< typename Derived >
struct DenseVector
```

---

17 Consider any kind of cast (`static_cast`, `reinterpret_cast`, `const_cast`, `dynamic_cast`, and especially the old C-style casts) as adult features: you take full responsibility of your actions and the compiler will obey. Therefore, it is seriously advisable to reduce calls to cast operators (see also Core Guideline ES.48 (*https://oreil.ly/ZEE0P*): "Avoid casts").

```
{
    // ...

    using value_type     = typename Derived::value_type;    ㉑
    using iterator        = typename Derived::iterator;
    using const_iterator  = typename Derived::const_iterator;

    value_type&       operator[]( size_t index )       { return derived()[index]; }
    value_type const& operator[]( size_t index ) const { return derived()[index]; }

    iterator       begin()       { return derived().begin(); }
    const_iterator begin() const { return derived().begin(); }
    iterator       end()         { return derived().end(); }
    const_iterator end()   const { return derived().end(); }

    // ...
};
```

We query for the value_type, iterator, and const_iterator types in the derived class (don't forget the typename keyword) and use these to specify our return types (㉑). Easy, right? You can almost bet that it's not that easy. If you try this, the Clang compiler will complain with a seriously weird and baffling error message:

```
CRTP.cpp:29:41: error: no type named 'value_type' in 'DynamicVector<int>'
using value_type = typename Derived::value_type;
      ~~~~~~~~~~~~~~~~~~~~~~~^~~~~~~~~
```

"No value_type in DynamicVector<int>—strange." The first idea that crosses your mind is that you messed up. It must be a typo. Of course! So you go back to your code and check the spelling. However, it turns out that everything seems to be OK. There is no typo. You check the DynamicVector class again: there it is, the nested value_type member. And everything is public, too. The error message just doesn't make any sense. You reexamine everything, and again, and half an hour later you conclude, "The compiler has a bug!"

No, it isn't a bug in the compiler. Not in Clang or any other compiler. GCC provides a different, still slightly puzzling, but a perhaps little more illuminating error message:[18]

```
CRTP.cpp:29:10: error: invalid use of incomplete type 'class DynamicVector<int>'
   29 |    using value_type = typename Derived::value_type;
      |          ^~~~~~~~~~
```

---

18 This is a great example to demonstrate that it pays off to be able to compile your codebase with several major compilers (Clang, GCC, MSVC, etc.). Different error messages might help you find the source of the problem. Using only one compiler should be considered a risk!

The Clang compiler is correct: there is no `value_type` in the `DynamicVector` class. Not yet! When you query for the nested types, the definition of the `DynamicVector` class hasn't been seen, and `DynamicVector` is still an incomplete type. That's because the compiler will instantiate the `DenseVector` base class before the definition of the `DynamicVector` class. After all, syntactically, the base class is specified before the body of the class:

```
template< typename T >
class DynamicVector : public DenseVector<DynamicVector<T>>
// ...
```

In consequence, there is no way that you can use the nested types of the derived class for the return types of the CRTP class. In fact, you can't use anything as long as the derived class is an incomplete type. "But why can I call the member functions of the derived class? Shouldn't this result in the same problem?" Luckily, this works (otherwise the CRTP pattern would not work at all). But it only works because of a special property of class templates: member functions are only instantiated on demand, meaning when they are actually called. Since an actual call usually happens only after the definition of the derived class is available, there is no problem with a missing definition. At that point, the derived class is not an incomplete type anymore.

"OK, I get it. But how do we specify the return types of the subscript operators and `begin()` and `end()` functions?" The most convenient way to handle this is to use return type deduction. This is a perfect opportunity to use the `decltype(auto)` return type:

```
template< typename Derived >
struct DenseVector
{
   // ...

   decltype(auto) operator[]( size_t index )       { return derived()[index]; }
   decltype(auto) operator[]( size_t index ) const { return derived()[index]; }

   decltype(auto) begin()       { return derived().begin(); }
   decltype(auto) begin() const { return derived().begin(); }
   decltype(auto) end()         { return derived().end(); }
   decltype(auto) end()   const { return derived().end(); }
};
```

"Wouldn't it be enough to just use `auto`? For instance, we could define the return types like this:"

```
template< typename Derived >
struct DenseVector
{
   // ... Note: this doesn't always work, whereas decltype(auto) always works

   auto&      operator[]( size_t index )       { return derived()[index]; }
```

```
      auto const& operator[]( size_t index ) const { return derived()[index]; }

      auto begin()       { return derived().begin(); }
      auto begin() const { return derived().begin(); }
      auto end()         { return derived().end(); }
      auto end()   const { return derived().end(); }
   };
```

It would be enough for this example, yes. However, as I keep emphasizing, code changes. Eventually, there may be another, deriving vector class that does not store its values and returns references to its values but produces values and returns by value. And yes, this is easily conceivable: consider, for instance, a ZeroVector class, which represents the zero element (*https://oreil.ly/DS9FB*) for vectors. Such a vector would not store all of its elements, as this would be wasteful, but would likely be implemented as an empty class, which returns a zero by value every time an element is accessed. In that case, an auto& return type would be incorrect. Yes, the compiler would (hopefully) warn you about that. But you could avoid the entire problem by just returning *exactly* what the deriving class returns. And that kind of return type is represented by the decltype(auto) return.

Analyzing the Shortcomings of the CRTP Design Pattern

"Wow, this CRTP design pattern sounds amazing. So seriously, apart from these slightly-more-complex-than-usual implementation details, isn't this the solution to all performance issues with virtual functions? And isn't this the key, the holy grail for all inheritance-related problems?" I can understand the enthusiasm! At first sight, CRTP most definitely looks like the ultimate solution for all kinds of inheritance hierarchies. Unfortunately, that is an illusion. Remember: every design pattern comes with benefits but unfortunately also with drawbacks. And there are several pretty limiting drawbacks to the CRTP design pattern.

The first, and one of the most restricting, drawbacks is the lack of a common base class. I will repeat this to emphasize the gravity of the repercussions: there is *no* common base class! Effectively, every single derived class has a different base class. For example, the DynamicVector<T> class has the DenseVector<Dynamic Vector<T>> base class. The StaticVector<T,Size> class has the DenseVector<Stati cVector<T,Size>> base class (see Figure 6-4). Thus, whenever a common base class is required, a common abstraction that can be used, for instance, to store different types in a collection, the CRTP design pattern is *not* the right choice.

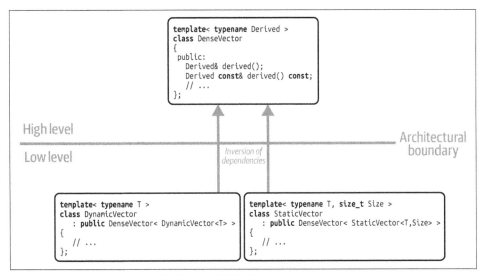

Figure 6-4. Dependency graph for the CRTP design pattern

"Oh, wow, I see that this could be a real limitation. But couldn't we just make the CRTP base class derive from a common base class?" you argue. No, not really, because this would require us to introduce virtual functions again. "OK, I see. What about simulating a common base class using `std::variant`?" Yes, that's an option. However, please remember that `std::variant` is a representation of the *Visitor* design pattern (see "Guideline 16: Use Visitor to Extend Operations" on page 112). And since `std::variant` needs to know about all its potential alternatives, this will limit your freedom to add new types. So you see, even though you might not like it, CRTP really is *not* a replacement for every inheritance hierarchy.

The second, also potentially very limiting drawback is that everything that comes in touch with a CRTP base class becomes a template itself. That is particularly true for all functions that work with such a base class. Consider, for instance, the upgraded output operator and the `l2norm()` function:

```
template< typename Derived >
std::ostream& operator<<( std::ostream& os, DenseVector<Derived> const& vector );

template< typename Derived >
auto l2norm( DenseVector<Derived> const& vector );
```

These two functions should work with all classes deriving from the `DenseVector` CRTP class. And of course they should not depend on the concrete types of the derived classes. Therefore, these two functions must be function templates: the `Derived` type must be deduced. While in the context of a linear algebra library this is usually not an issue because almost all functionality is implemented in terms of templates anyway, this may be a big downside in other contexts. It might be highly undesirable to turn lots of code into templates and move the definitions into header files, effectively sacrificing the encapsulation of source files. Yes, this may be a severe drawback indeed!

Third, CRTP is an intrusive design pattern. Deriving classes have to explicitly opt in by inheriting from the CRTP base class. While this may be a nonissue in our own code, you cannot easily add a base class to foreign code. In such a situation, you would have to resort to the Adapter design pattern (see "Guideline 24: Use Adapters to Standardize Interfaces" on page 198). Thus, CRTP does not provide the flexibility of nonintrusive design patterns (e.g., the Visitor design pattern implemented with `std::variant`, the Adapter design pattern, and so on).

Last but not least, CRTP does not provide runtime polymorphism, only compile-time polymorphism. Therefore, the pattern makes sense only if some kind of static type abstraction is required. If not, it is again not a replacement for all inheritance hierarchies.

The Future of CRTP: A Comparison Between CRTP and C++20 Concepts

"I understand, you're right. CRTP is pure compile-time polymorphism. However, this makes me wonder: wouldn't it be possible to build on C++20 concepts instead of CRTP? Consider the following code. We could use a concept to define the requirements for a set of types, and restrict functions and operators to only those types that provide the expected interface:"[19]

```
template< typename T >
concept DenseVector =
   requires ( T t, size_t index ) {
      t.size();
      t[index];
      { t.begin() } -> std::same_as<typename T::iterator>;
      { t.end() } -> std::same_as<typename T::iterator>;
   } &&
   requires ( T const t, size_t index ) {
      t[index];
      { t.begin() } -> std::same_as<typename T::const_iterator>;
      { t.end() } -> std::same_as<typename T::const_iterator>;
   };

template< DenseVector VectorT >
std::ostream& operator<<( std::ostream& os, VectorT const& vector )
{
```

---

19 If you aren't familiar with the idea or syntax of C++20 concepts yet, you can get a quick and painless introduction in Sándor Dargó's *C++ Concepts*, published at Leanpub (*https://leanpub.com/cppconcepts*).

```
    // ... as before
}
```

You are absolutely correct. I agree, this is a very reasonable alternative. Indeed, C++20 concepts are pretty similar to CRTP but represent an easier, nonintrusive alternative. Especially by being nonintrusive, if you have access to C++20 concepts and it is possible to define the static set of types by a concept, you should prefer the concept over the CRTP.

Still, I'm not entirely happy with this solution. While this formulation of the output operator effectively constrains the function template to only those types that provide the expected interface, it does not completely restrict the function template to our set of dense vector types. It's still possible to pass `std::vector` and `std::string` (`std::string` already has an output operator in the `std` namespace). Therefore, this concept is not specific enough. But if you run into this situation, don't worry: there is a solution using a tag class:

```
struct DenseVectorTag {};  ㉒

template< typename T >
concept DenseVector =
   // ... Definition of all requirements on a dense vector (as before)
   && std::is_base_of_v<DenseVectorTag,T>;

template< typename T >
class DynamicVector : private DenseVectorTag  ㉓
{
   // ...
};
```

By inheriting (preferably nonpublicly) from the `DenseVectorTag` class (㉒), classes like `DynamicVector` can identify as being part of a certain set of types (㉓). Function and operator templates can therefore be effectively limited to accept only those types that explicitly opt in to the set of types. Unfortunately, there's a catch: this approach is no longer nonintrusive. To overcome this limitation, we introduce a compile-time indirection by a customizable type trait class. In other words, we apply the SRP and separate concerns:

```
struct DenseVectorTag {};

template< typename T >
struct IsDenseVector  ㉔
   : public std::is_base_of<DenseVectorTag,T>
{};

template< typename T >
constexpr bool IsDenseVector_v = IsDenseVector<T>::value;  ㉕

template< typename T >
concept DenseVector =
```

```
    // ... Definition of all requirements on a dense vector (as before)
    && IsDenseVector_v<T>;  ㉖

template< typename T >
class DynamicVector : private DenseVectorTag  ㉗
{
    // ...
};

template< typename T, size_t Size >
class StaticVector
{
    // ...
};

template< typename T, size_t Size >
struct IsDenseVector< StaticVector<T,Size> >  ㉘
   : public std::true_type
{};
```

The `IsDenseVector` class template, along with its corresponding variable template, indicates whether a given type is part of the set of dense vector types (㉔ and ㉕). Instead of directly querying a given type, the `DenseVector` concept would ask indirectly via the `IsDenseVector` type trait (㉖). This opens up the opportunity for classes to either intrusively derive from the `DenseVectorTag` (㉗) or to nonintrusively specialize the `IsDenseVector` type trait (㉘). In this form, the concepts approach truly supersedes the classic CRTP approach.

In summary, CRTP is an amazing design pattern for defining a compile-time relationship between a family of related types. Most interestingly, it resolves all performance issues that you may have with inheritance hierarchies. However, CRTP comes with a couple of potentially limiting drawbacks, such as the lack of a common base class, the quick spreading of template code, and the restriction to compile-time polymorphism. With C++20, consider replacing CRTP with concepts, which provide an easier and nonintrusive alternative. However, if you do not have access to C++20 concepts and if CRTP fits, it will prove immensely valuable to you.

Guideline 26: Use CRTP to Introduce Static Type Categories

- Apply the CRTP design pattern to define a compile-time abstraction for a family of related types.

- Be aware of the limited access from the CRTP base class to the derived class.

- Keep in mind the restrictions of the CRTP design pattern, in particular, the lack of a common base class.

- Prefer C++20 concepts to the CRTP design pattern when possible.

Guideline 27: Use CRTP for Static Mixin Classes

In "Guideline 26: Use CRTP to Introduce Static Type Categories" on page 225, I introduced you to the CRTP design pattern. I may also have given you the impression that CRTP is old hat, made obsolete by the advent of C++20 concepts. Well, interestingly it is not. At least not entirely. That's because I haven't told you the complete story yet. CRTP may still be of value: just not as a design pattern but as an *implementation pattern*. So let's take a detour into the realm of implementation patterns and let me explain.

A Strong Type Motivation

Consider the following StrongType class template, which represents a wrapper around any other type for the purpose of creating a unique, named type:[20]

```
//---- <StrongType.h> ----------------

#include <utility>

template< typename T, typename Tag >
struct StrongType
{
 public:
   using value_type = T;

   explicit StrongType( T const& value ) : value_( value ) {}

   T&      get()       { return value_; }
   T const& get() const { return value_; }

 private:
   T value_;
};
```

This class can, for instance, be used to define the types Meter, Kilometer, and Surname:[21]

```
//---- <Distances.h> ----------------

#include <StrongType.h>
```

---

20 This implementation of a StrongType is inspired by Jonathan Boccara's Fluent C++ blog (*https://oreil.ly/Tqafn*) and the associated NamedType library (*https://oreil.ly/F5JO6*). There are several more strong type libraries available, though: alternatively you can use Jonathan Müller's *type_safe* library (*https://oreil.ly/Bju8Z*), Björn Fahller's *strong_type* library (*https://oreil.ly/bxJrf*), or Anthony William's *strong_typedef* library (*https://oreil.ly/q58u6*).

21 The only technical oddity is the declaration of a tag class right in the template parameter list. Yes, this works, and definitely helps create a unique type for the purpose of instantiating distinct strong types.

```
template< typename T >
using Meter = StrongType<T,struct MeterTag>;

template< typename T >
using Kilometer = StrongType<T,struct KilometerTag>;

// ...


//---- <Person.h> ----------------

#include <StrongType.h>

using Surname = StrongType<std::string,struct SurnameTag>;

// ...
```

The use of alias templates for Meter and Kilometer enables you to choose, for instance, long or double to represent a distance. However, although these types are built on fundamental types or Standard Library types, such as std::string in the case of Surname, they represent distinct types (strong types) with semantic meaning that cannot be (accidentally) combined in arithmetic operations, for example, addition:

```
//---- <Main.cpp> ----------------

#include <Distances.h>
#include <cstdlib>

int main()
{
   auto const m1 = Meter<long>{ 120L };
   auto const m2 = Meter<long>{  50L };
   auto const km = Kilometer<long>{ 30L };
   auto const surname1 = Surname{ "Stroustrup" };
   auto const surname2 = Surname{ "Iglberger" };
   // ...

   m1 + km;               // Correctly does not compile!  ❶
   surname1 + surname2;   // Also correctly does not compile!  ❷
   m1 + m2;               // Inconveniently this does not compile either.  ❸

   return EXIT_SUCCESS;
}
```

Although both Meter and Kilometer are represented via long, it isn't possible to directly add Meter and Kilometer together (❶). This is great: it doesn't leave any opening for accidental bugs to crawl in. It's also not possible to add two Surnames, although std::string provides an addition operator for string concatenation (❷).

But this is also great: the strong type effectively restricts undesired operations of the underlying type. Unfortunately, this "feature" also prevents the addition of two Meter instances (❸). This operation would be desirable, though: it is intuitive, natural, and since the result of the operation would again be of type Meter, physically accurate. To make this work, we could implement an addition operator for the Meter type. However, obviously, this would not remain the only addition operator. We would also need one for all the other strong types, such as Kilometer, Mile, Foot, etc. Since all of these implementations would look the same, this would be a violation of the DRY principle. Therefore, it appears to be reasonable to extend the StrongType class template with an addition operator:

```
template< typename T, typename Tag >
StrongType<T,Tag>
   operator+( StrongType<T,Tag> const& a, StrongType<T,Tag> const& b )
{
   return StrongType<T,Tag>( a.get() + b.get() );
}
```

Whereas due to the formulation of this addition operator it is not possible to add two different instantiations of StrongType together (e.g., Meter and Kilometer), it would enable the addition of two instances of the same instantiation of StrongType. "Oh, but I see a problem: while it would now be possible to add two Meters or two Kilometers, it would also be possible to add two Surnames. We don't want that!" You are correct: this would be undesirable. What we need instead is a deliberate addition of operations to specific instantiations of StrongType. This is where CRTP comes into play.

Using CRTP as an Implementation Pattern

Instead of directly equipping the StrongType class template with operations, we provide the operations via *mixin* classes: base classes that "inject" the desired operations. These mixin classes are implemented in terms of the CRTP. Consider, for instance, the Addable class template, which represents the addition operation:

```
//---- <Addable.h> ----------------

template< typename Derived >
struct Addable
{
   friend Derived& operator+=( Derived& lhs, Derived const& rhs ) {   ❹
      lhs.get() += rhs.get();
      return lhs;
   }

   friend Derived operator+( Derived const& lhs, Derived const& rhs ) {   ❺
      return Derived{ lhs.get() + rhs.get() };
```

```
        }
    };
```

The name of the template parameters gives it away: `Addable` is a CRTP base class. `Addable` provides only two functions, implemented as hidden friends (*https://oreil.ly/QmrTG*): an addition assignment operator (❹) and an addition operator (❺). Both operators are defined for the specified `Derived` type and are injected into the surrounding namespace.[22] Thus, any class deriving from this CRTP base class will "inherit" two free addition operators:

```
//---- <StrongType.h> ----------------

#include <stdlib>
#include <utility>

template< typename T, typename Tag >
struct StrongType : private Addable< StrongType<T,Tag> >
{ /* ... */ };


//---- <Distances.h> ----------------

#include <StrongType.h>

template< typename T >
using Meter = StrongType<T,struct MeterTag>;

// ...


//---- <Main.cpp> ----------------

#include <Distances.h>
#include <cstdlib>

int main()
{
    auto const m1 = Meter<long>{ 100 };
    auto const m2 = Meter<long>{  50 };

    auto const m3 = m1 + m2;   // Compiles and results in 150 meters
    // ...
```

---

22 Many years ago, more specifically at the end of the '90s, this kind of namespace injection was called the *Barton-Nackman trick*, named after John J. Barton and Lee R. Nackman. In the March 1995 issue of the *C++ Report*, they used namespace injection as a workaround for the limitation that function templates could not be overloaded at the time. Surprisingly, today this technique has experienced a renaissance as the *hidden friend idiom*.

```
      return EXIT_SUCCESS;
   }
```

"I understand the purpose of the mixin class, but in this form, *all* instantiations of
`StrongType` would inherit an addition operator, even the ones where an addition is
not required, right?" Yes, indeed. Therefore, we aren't finished yet. What we want to
do is to selectively add the mixin class to those `StrongType` instantiations that need
the operation. Our solution of choice is to provide the mixins in the form of optional
template arguments. For that purpose, we extend the `StrongType` class template by a
pack of variadic template template parameters:[23]

```
//---- <StrongType.h> ----------------

#include <utility>

template< typename T, typename Tag, template<typename> class... Skills >
struct StrongType
   : private Skills< StrongType<T,Tag,Skills...> >...   ❾
{ /* ... */ };
```

This extension enables us to individually specify, for each single strong type, which
skills are desired. Consider, for instance, the two additional skills `Printable` and
`Swappable`:

```
//---- <Printable.h> ----------------

template< typename Derived >
struct Printable
{
   friend std::ostream& operator<<( std::ostream& os, const Derived& d )
   {
      os << d.get();
      return os;
   }
};
```

```
//---- <Swappable.h> ----------------

template< typename Derived >
struct Swappable
{
   friend void swap( Derived& lhs, Derived& rhs )
   {
      using std::swap;   // Enable ADL
      swap( lhs.get(), rhs.get() );
```

---

23 In Jonathan Bocarra's blog (*https://oreil.ly/jefQD*), these optional, variadic arguments are aptly called *skills*. I
   very much like this, so I adopt this naming convention.

```
    }
};
```

Together with the `Addable` skill, we can now assemble strong types equipped with the required and desired skills:

```
//---- <Distances.h> ----------------

#include <StrongType.h>

template< typename T >
using Meter =
    StrongType<T,struct MeterTag,Addable,Printable,Swappable>;    ❻

template< typename T >
using Kilometer =
    StrongType<T,struct KilometerTag,Addable,Printable,Swappable>;    ❼

// ...


//---- <Person.h> ----------------

#include <StrongType.h>
#include <string>

using Surname =
    StrongType<std::string,struct SurnameTag,Printable,Swappable>;    ❽

// ...
```

Both `Meter` and `Kilometer` can be added, printed, and swapped (see ❻ and ❼), while `Surname` is printable and swappable, but not addable (i.e., does not receive the `Addable` mixin and therefore does not derive from it) (❽).

"That's great. I understand the purpose of the CRTP mixin class in this context. But how is this CRTP example different from previous examples?" Very good question. You're right, the implementation details are very similar. But there are a couple of distinctive differences. Note that the CRTP base class doesn't provide a `virtual` or `protected` destructor. Hence, in contrast to previous examples, it is not designed as a polymorphic base class. Also note that in this example it is sufficient, and even preferable, to use the CRTP base class as a `private` base class, not a `public` one (❾).

Thus, in this context, the CRTP base class does not represent an abstraction but only an implementation detail. Therefore, the CRTP does not fulfill the properties of a design pattern, and it does not act as a design pattern. It's still a pattern, no question there, but it merely acts as an implementation pattern in this case.

The major difference in the implementation of the CRTP examples is the way we use inheritance. For the CRTP design pattern, we use inheritance as an abstraction according to the LSP: the base class represents the requirements, and thus the available and expected behavior of the derived class. User code directly accesses the operations via pointers or references to the base class, which in turn requires us to provide a `virtual` or `protected` destructor. When implemented this way, CRTP becomes a true element of software design—a design pattern.

In contrast, for the CRTP implementation pattern, we use inheritance for technical elegance and convenience. The base class becomes an implementation detail and does not have to be known or used by calling code. Therefore, it doesn't need a `virtual` or `protected` destructor. When implemented this way, CRTP stays on the level of the implementation details and therefore is an implementation pattern. In this form, however, CRTP does not compete with C++20 concepts. On the contrary: in this form CRTP is unchallenged, as it represents a unique technique to provide static mixin functionality. For that reason, CRTP is still in use today and represents a valuable addition to every C++ developer's toolbox.

In summary, CRTP is not obsolete, but its value has changed. In C++20, CRTP is replaced by concepts and therefore is stepping down as a design pattern. However, it continues to be valuable as an implementation pattern for mixin classes.

Guideline 27: Use CRTP for Static Mixin Classes

- Be aware between the difference between using CRTP as a design pattern and using it as an implementation pattern.

- Understand that CRTP base classes that represent an abstraction act as a design pattern.

- Understand that CRTP base classes that do not represent an abstraction act as an implementation pattern.

CHAPTER 7

The Bridge, Prototype, and External Polymorphism Design Patterns

In this chapter, we will focus on two classic GoF design patterns: the Bridge design pattern and the Prototype design pattern. Additionally, we will study the *External Polymorphism* design pattern. At first glance, this selection may appear as an illustrious, almost random choice of design patterns. However, I picked these patterns for two reasons: first, in my experience, these three are among the most useful in the catalog of design patterns. For that reason, you should have a pretty good idea about their intent, advantages, and disadvantages. Second and equally important: they will all play a vital role in Chapter 8.

In "Guideline 28: Build Bridges to Remove Physical Dependencies" on page 250, I will acquaint you with the Bridge design pattern and its simplest form, the *Pimpl idiom*. Most importantly, I will demonstrate how you can use Bridges to reduce physical coupling by decoupling an interface from implementation details.

In "Guideline 29: Be Aware of Bridge Performance Gains and Losses" on page 266, we will take an explicit look at the performance impact of Bridges. We will run benchmarks for an implementation without Bridge, a Bridge-based implementation, and a "partial" Bridge.

In "Guideline 30: Apply Prototype for Abstract Copy Operations" on page 272, I will introduce you to the art of cloning. That is to say, that we will talk about copy operations and, in particular, abstract copy operations. The pattern of choice for this intent will be the Prototype design pattern.

In "Guideline 31: Use External Polymorphism for Nonintrusive Runtime Polymorphism" on page 279, we continue the journey of separating concerns by extracting the implementation details of a function from a class. To further reduce dependencies, however, we will take this separation of concerns to a whole new level: we will extract not only the implementation details of virtual functions but also the complete functions themselves, with the External Polymorphism design pattern.

Guideline 28: Build Bridges to Remove Physical Dependencies

According to dictionaries, the term *bridge* expresses a time, a place, or a means of connection or transition. If I were to ask what the term *bridge* means to you, I'm pretty certain you would have a similar definition. You might implicitly think about connecting two things, and thus bringing these things closer together. For instance, you might think about a city divided by a river. A bridge would connect the two sides of the city, bring them closer together, and save people a lot of time. You might also think about electronics, where a bridge connects two independent parts of a circuit. There are bridges in music and many more examples from the real world, where bridges help connect things. Yes, intuitively the term *bridge* suggests an increase in closeness and proximity. So naturally, the Bridge design pattern is about the polar opposite: it supports you in reducing physical dependencies and helps to decouple, i.e., it keeps two pieces of functionality that need to work together but shouldn't know too many details about each other, at arm's length.

A Motivating Example

To explain what I have in mind, consider the following `ElectricCar` class:

```
//---- <ElectricEngine.h> ----------------

class ElectricEngine
{
 public:
   void start();
   void stop();

 private:
   // ...
};



//---- <ElectricCar.h> ---------------

#include <ElectricEngine.h>
// ...

class ElectricCar
{
 public:
   ElectricCar( /*maybe some engine arguments*/ );
```

```
    void drive();
    // ...
  private:
    ElectricEngine engine_;  ❶

    // ... more car-specific data members (wheels, drivetrain, ...)
};


//---- <ElectricCar.cpp> ----------------

#include <ElectricCar.h>

ElectricCar::ElectricCar( /*maybe some engine arguments*/ )
   : engine_{ /*engine arguments*/ }
   // ... Initialization of the other data members
{}

// ...
```

As the name suggests, the ElectricCar class is equipped with an ElectricEngine
(❶). However, while in reality such a car may be pretty attractive, the current implementation details are concerning: because of the engine_ data member, the
<ElectricCar.h> header file needs to include the <ElectricEngine.h> header. The
compiler needs to see the class definition of ElectricEngine, because otherwise it
would not be able to determine the size of an ElectricCar instance. Including the
<ElectricEngine.h> header, however, easily results in transitive, physical coupling:
every file that includes the <ElectricCar.h> header will physically depend on the
<ElectricEngine.h> header. Thus, whenever something in the header changes, the
ElectricCar class and potentially many more classes are affected. They might have
to be recompiled, retested, and, in the worst case, even redeployed...*sigh*.

On top of that, this design reveals all implementation details to everyone. "What do
you mean? Isn't it the point of the private section of the class to hide and to encapsulate implementation details?" Yes, it may be private, but the private label is
merely an access label. It is *not* a visibility label. Therefore, everything in your class
definition (and I mean *everything*) is visible to everyone who sees the ElectricCar
class definition. This means that you cannot change the implementation details of
this class without anyone noticing. In particular, this may be a problem if you need to
provide ABI stability, i.e., if the in-memory representation of your class must not
change.[1]

---

1 ABI stability is an important and often debated topic in the C++ community, in particular just before the
  release of C++20. If this sounds interesting to you, I recommend the CppCast interviews with Titus Winters
  (*https://oreil.ly/8rgkm*) and Marshall Clow (*https://oreil.ly/R1XYJ*) to get an impression of both sides.

A slightly better approach would be to only store a pointer to `ElectricEngine` (❷):[2]

```
//---- <ElectricCar.h> ----------------

#include <memory>
// ...
struct ElectricEngine;  // Forward declaration

class ElectricCar
{
 public:
   ElectricCar( /*maybe some engine arguments*/ );

   void drive();
   // ...
 private:
   std::unique_ptr<ElectricEngine> engine_;  ❷

   // ... more car-specific data members (wheels, drivetrain, ...)
};


//---- <ElectricCar.cpp> ---------------

#include <ElectricCar.h>
#include <ElectricEngine.h>  ❸

ElectricCar::ElectricCar( /*maybe some engine arguments*/ )
   : engine_{ std::make_unique<ElectricEngine>( /*engine arguments*/ ) }
   // ... Initialization of the other data members
{}

// ... Other 'ElectricCar' member functions, using the pointer to an
//     'ElectricEngine'.
```

In this case, it is sufficient to provide only a forward declaration to the `ElectricEngine` class, since the compiler doesn't need to know the class definition to be able to determine the size of an `ElectricCar` instance. Also, the physical dependency is gone, since the `<ElectricEngine.h>` header has been moved into the source file (❸). Hence, from a dependency point of view, this solution is much better. What still remains is the visibility of the implementation details. Everyone is still able to see that the `ElectricCar` builds on an `ElectricEngine`, and thus everyone is still implicitly depending on these implementation details. Consequently, any change to these details, such as an upgrade to the new `PowerEngine`, would affect any class that works

---

2 Remember that `std::unique_ptr` cannot be copied. Thus, switching from `ElectricEngine` to `std::unique_ptr<ElectricEngine>` renders your class noncopyable. To preserve copy semantics, you have to implement the copy operations manually. When doing this, please keep in mind that the copy operations disable the move operations. In other words, prefer to stick to the Rule of 5 (*https://oreil.ly/fzS3f*).

with the <ElectricCar.h> header file. "And that's bad, right?" Indeed it is, because change is to be expected (see "Guideline 2: Design for Change" on page 11). To get rid of this dependency and gain the luxury of being able to easily change the implementation details at any time without anyone noticing, we have to introduce an abstraction. The classic form of abstraction is the introduction of an abstract class:

```
//---- <Engine.h> ----------------

class Engine   ❹
{
 public:
   virtual ~Engine() = default;
   virtual void start() = 0;
   virtual void stop() = 0;
   // ... more engine-specific functions

 private:
   // ...
};
```

```
//---- <ElectricCar.h> ----------------

#include <Engine.h>
#include <memory>

class ElectricCar
{
 public:
   void drive();
   // ...
 private:
   std::unique_ptr<Engine> engine_;   ❺

   // ... more car-specific data members (wheels, drivetrain, ...)
};
```

```
//---- <ElectricEngine.h> ----------------

#include <Engine.h>

class ElectricEngine : public Engine
{
 public:
   void start() override;
   void stop() override;

 private:
   // ...
};
```

```
//---- <ElectricCar.cpp> ----------------

#include <ElectricCar.h>
#include <ElectricEngine.h>

ElectricCar::ElectricCar( /*maybe some engine arguments*/ )
   : engine_{ std::make_unique<ElectricEngine>( /*engine arguments*/ ) }  ❻
   // ... Initialization of the other data members
{}

// ... Other 'ElectricCar' member functions, primarily using the 'Engine'
//     abstraction, but potentially also explicitly dealing with an
//     'ElectricEngine'.
```

With the `Engine` base class in place (❹), we can implement our `ElectricCar` class using this abstraction (❺). No one needs to be aware of the actual type of engine that we use. And no one needs to know when we upgrade our engine. With this implementation, we can easily change the implementation details at any time by only modifying the source file (❻). Therefore, with this approach, we've truly minimized dependencies on the `ElectricEngine` implementation. We have made the knowledge about this detail our own, secret implementation detail. And by doing that, we have built ourselves a Bridge.

As stated in the introduction, counterintuitively, this Bridge isn't about bringing the `ElectricCar` and `Engine` classes closer together. On the contrary, it's about separating concerns and about loose coupling. Another example that shows that naming is hard (*https:// oreil.ly/YfDpP*) comes from Kate Gregory's talk at CppCon.

The Bridge Design Pattern Explained

The Bridge design pattern is yet another one of the classic GoF design patterns introduced in 1994. The purpose of a Bridge is to minimize physical dependencies by encapsulating some implementation details behind an abstraction. In C++, it acts as a compilation firewall, which enables easy change:

The Bridge Design Pattern

Intent: "Decouple an abstraction from its implementation so that the two can vary independently."[3]

---

3 Erich Gamma et al., *Design Patterns: Elements of Reusable Object-Oriented Software*.

In this formulation of the intent, the Gang of Four talks about an "abstraction" and an "implementation." In our example, the ElectricCar class represents the "abstraction," while the Engine class represents the "implementation" (see Figure 7-1). Both of these should be able to vary independently; i.e., changes to either one should have no effect on the other. The impediments to easy change are the physical dependencies between the ElectricCar class and its engines. Thus, the idea is to extract and isolate these dependencies. By isolating them in the form of the Engine abstraction, separating concerns, and fulfilling the SRP, you gain the flexibility to change, tune, or upgrade the engine any way you want (see "Guideline 2: Design for Change" on page 11). The change is no longer visible in the ElectricCar class. As a consequence, it is now easily possible to add new kinds of engines without the "abstraction" noticing. This adheres to the idea of the OCP (see "Guideline 5: Design for Extension" on page 35).

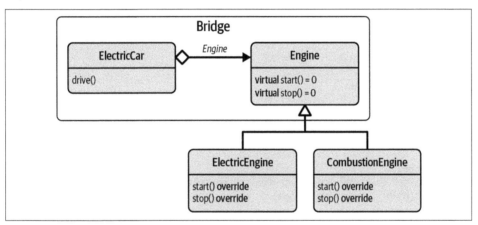

Figure 7-1. The UML representation of the basic Bridge design pattern

While this provides us the ability to easily apply changes, and implements the idea of a Bridge, there is one more step that we can take to further decouple and reduce duplication. Let's assume that we are not just interested in electric cars but also in cars with combustion engines. So for every kind of car that we plan to implement, we are interested in introducing the same kind of decoupling from engine details, i.e., the same kind of Bridge. To reduce the duplication and follow the DRY principle, we can extract the Bridge-related implementation details into the Car base class (see Figure 7-2).

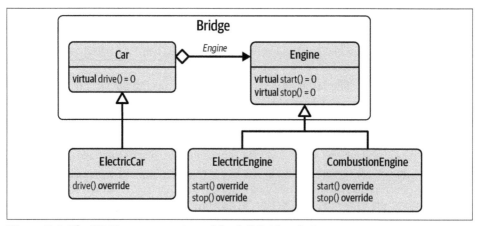

Figure 7-2. The UML representation of the full Bridge design pattern

The Car base class encapsulates the Bridge to the associated Engine:

```
//---- <Car.h> ----------------

#include <Engine.h>
#include <memory>
#include <utility>

class Car
{
 protected:
   explicit Car( std::unique_ptr<Engine> engine )   ❼
     : pimpl_( std::move(engine) )
   {}

 public:
   virtual ~Car() = default;
   virtual void drive() = 0;
   // ... more car-specific functions

 protected:
   Engine*       getEngine()       { return pimpl_.get(); }   ❾
   Engine const* getEngine() const { return pimpl_.get(); }

 private:
   std::unique_ptr<Engine> pimpl_;  // Pointer-to-implementation (pimpl)   ❽

   // ... more car-specific data members (wheels, drivetrain, ...)
};
```

With the addition of the Car class, both the "abstraction" and the "implementation" offer the opportunity for easy extension and can vary independently. While the Engine base class still represents the "implementation" in this Bridge relation, the Car class now plays the role of the "abstraction." The first noteworthy detail about the Car class is the protected constructor (❼). This choice makes sure that only derived classes are able to specify the kind of engine. The constructor takes std::unique_ptr to an Engine and moves it to its pimpl_ data member (❽). This pointer data member is the one pointer-to-*impl*ementation for all kinds of Cars and is commonly called the *pimpl*. This *opaque pointer* represents the Bridge to the encapsulated implementation details and essentially represents the Bridge design pattern as a whole. For this reason, it's a good idea to use the name *pimpl* in the code as an indication of your intentions (remember "Guideline 14: Use a Design Pattern's Name to Communicate Intent" on page 97).

Note that pimpl_ is declared in the private section of the class, despite the fact that derived classes will have to use it. This choice is motivated by Core Guideline C.133 (*https://oreil.ly/99sIG*):

> Avoid protected data.

Indeed, experience shows that protected data members are barely better than public data members. Therefore, to grant access to the pimpl, the Car class instead provides the protected getEngine() member functions (❾).

The ElectricCar class is adapted accordingly:

```cpp
//---- <ElectricCar.h> ----------------

#include <Engine.h>
#include <memory>

class ElectricCar : public Car   ❿
{
 public:
   explicit ElectricCar( /*maybe some engine arguments*/ );

   void drive() override;
   // ...
};


//---- <ElectricCar.cpp> ----------------

#include <ElectricCar.h>
#include <ElectricEngine.h>

ElectricCar::ElectricCar( /*maybe some engine arguments*/ )
   : Car( std::make_unique<ElectricEngine>( /*engine arguments*/ ) )   ⓫
{}

// ...
```

Rather than implementing the Bridge itself, the `ElectricCar` class now inherits from the `Car` base class (❿). This inheritance relationship introduces the requirement of initializing the `Car` base by specifying an `Engine`. This task is performed in the `ElectricCar` constructor (⓫).

The Pimpl Idiom

There is a much simpler form of the Bridge design pattern that has been very commonly and successfully used in both C and C++ for decades. To see an example, let's consider the following `Person` class:

```cpp
class Person
{
 public:
   // ...
   int year_of_birth() const;
   // ... Many more access functions

 private:
   std::string forename_;
   std::string surname_;
   std::string address_;
   std::string city_;
   std::string country_;
   std::string zip_;
   int year_of_birth_;
   // ... Potentially many more data members
};
```

A person consists of a lot of data members: `forename`, `surname`, the complete postal address, `year_of_birth`, and potentially many more. There may be the need to add further data members in the future: a mobile phone number, a Twitter account, or the account information for the next social media fad. In other words, it stands to reason that the `Person` class needs to be extended or changed over time, potentially even frequently. This may come with a whole lot of inconveniences for users of this class: whenever `Person` changes, the users of `Person` have to recompile their code. Not to mention ABI stability: the size of a `Person` instance is going to change!

To hide all changes to the implementation details of `Person` and gain ABI stability, you can use the Bridge design pattern. In this particular case, however, there is no need to provide an abstraction in the form of a base class: there is one, and exactly one, implementation for `Person`. Therefore, all we do is introduce a `private`, nested class called `Impl` (⓬):

```cpp
//---- <Person.h> ----------------

#include <memory>
```

```
class Person
{
 public:
   // ...

 private:
   struct Impl;          ⓬
   std::unique_ptr<Impl> const pimpl_;   ⓭
};

//---- <Person.cpp> ----------------

#include <Person.h>
#include <string>

struct Person::Impl    ⓮
{
   std::string forename;
   std::string surname;
   std::string address;
   std::string city;
   std::string country;
   std::string zip;
   int year_of_birth;
   // ... Potentially many more data members
};
```

The sole task of the nested Impl class is to encapsulate the implementation details of
Person. Thus, the only data member remaining in the Person class is the
std::unique_ptr to an Impl instance (⓭). All other data members, and potentially
some non-virtual helper functions, are moved from the Person class into the Impl
class. Note that the Impl class is only declared in the Person class but not defined.
Instead, it is defined in the corresponding source file (⓮). Only due to this, all details
and all changes that you apply to the details, such as adding or removing data members, changing the type of data members, etc., are hidden from the users of Person.

This implementation of Person uses the Bridge design pattern in its simplest form:
this local, nonpolymorphic form of Bridge is called the *Pimpl idiom* (*https://oreil.ly/
7QULb*). It comes with all the decoupling advantages of the Bridge pattern but,
despite its simplicity, it still results in a bit more complex implementation of the
Person class:

```
//---- <Person.h> ----------------

#include <memory>

class Person
{
 public:
   // ...
```

```
    Person();  ⑮
    ~Person();  ⑯

    Person( Person const& other );  ⑰
    Person& operator=( Person const& other );  ⑱

    Person( Person&& other );  ⑲
    Person& operator=( Person&& other );  ⑳

    int year_of_birth() const;  ㉑
    // ... Many more access functions

 private:
    struct Impl;
    std::unique_ptr<Impl> const pimpl_;
};

//---- <Person.cpp> ---------------

#include <Person.h>
#include <string>

struct Person::Impl
{
    // ...
};

Person::Person()  ⑮
    : pimpl_{ std::make_unique<Impl>() }
{}

Person::~Person() = default;  ⑯

Person::Person( Person const& other )  ⑰
    : pimpl_{ std::make_unique<Impl>(*other.pimpl_) }
{}

Person& Person::operator=( Person const& other )  ⑱
{
    *pimpl_ = *other.pimpl_;
    return *this;
}

Person::Person( Person&& other )  ⑲
    : pimpl_{ std::make_unique<Impl>(std::move(*other.pimpl_)) }
{}

Person& Person::operator=( Person&& other )  ⑳
{
    *pimpl_ = std::move(*other.pimpl_);
    return *this;
}
```

```
int Person::year_of_birth() const   ㉑
{
    return pimpl_->year_of_birth;
}

// ... Many more Person member functions
```

The Person constructor initializes the pimpl_ data member by std::make_unique() (⑮). This, of course, involves a dynamic memory allocation, which means that the dynamic memory needs to be cleaned up again. "And that is why we use std::unique_ptr," you say. Correct. But perhaps surprisingly, although we use std::unique_ptr for that purpose, it's still necessary to manually deal with the destructor (⑯).

"Why on earth do we have to do this? Isn't the point of std::unique_ptr that we don't have to deal with cleanup?" Well, we still have to. Let me explain: if you don't write the destructor, the compiler feels obliged to generate the destructor for you. Unfortunately, it would generate the destructor in the <Person.h> header file. The destructor of Person would trigger the instantiation of the destructor of the std::unique_ptr data member, which in turn would require the definition of the destructor of the Impl class. The definition of Impl, however, is not available in the header file. On the contrary, it needs to be defined in the source file or it would defeat the purpose of the Bridge. Thus, the compiler emits an error about the incomplete type Impl. Fortunately, you do not have to let go of the std::unique_ptr to resolve the issue (and in fact you *should* not let go of it). The problem is rather simple to solve. All you have to do is move the definition of the Person destructor to the source file: you declare the destructor in the class definition and define it via =default in the source file.

Since std::unique_ptr cannot be copied, you will have to implement the copy constructor to preserve the copy semantics of the Person class (⑰). The same is true for the copy assignment operator (⑱). Note that this operator is implemented under the assumption that every instance of Person will *always* have a valid pimpl_. This assumption explains the implementation of the move constructor: instead of simply moving std::unique_ptr, it performs a potentially failing, or throwing, dynamic memory allocation with std::make_unique(). For that reason, it is *not* declared as noexcept (⑲).[4] This assumption also explains why the pimpl_ data member is declared as const. Once it's initialized, the pointer will not be changed anymore, not even in the move operations, including the move assignment operator (⑳).

---

4 Usually, the move operations are expected to be noexcept. This is explained by Core Guideline C.66 (*https://oreil.ly/luKRb*). However, sometimes this might not be possible, for instance, under the assumption that some std::unique_ptr data member is never nullptr.

The last detail worth noting is that the definition of the year_of_birth() member function is located in the source file (❷). Despite the fact that this simple getter function is a great inline candidate, the definition has to be moved to the source file. The reason is that in the header file, Impl is an incomplete type (*https://oreil.ly/wg10k*). Which means that within the header file, you are not able to access any members (both data and functions). This is possible only in the source file, or generally speaking, as soon as the compiler knows the definition of Impl.

Comparison Between Bridge and Strategy

"I have a question," you say. "I see a strong resemblance between the Bridge and the Strategy design pattern. I know you said that design patterns are sometimes structurally very similar and that the only difference is their intent. But what exactly is the distinction between these two?"[5] I understand your question. The similarity between these two is truly a little confusing. However, there is something you can use to tell them apart: how the corresponding data member is initialized is a strong indicator about which one you're using.

If a class does not want to know about some implementation detail, and if for that reason it provides the opportunity to configure the behavior by passing in details from the outside (for instance, via a constructor or via a setter function), then you are most likely dealing with the Strategy design pattern. Because the flexible configuration of behavior, i.e., the reduction of *logical* dependencies, is its primary focus, Strategy falls into the category of a *behavioral design pattern*. For instance, in the following code snippet, the constructor of the Database class is a telltale sign:

```
class DatabaseEngine
{
 public:
   virtual ~DatabaseEngine() = default;
   // ... Many database-specific functions
};

class Database
{
 public:
   explicit Database( std::unique_ptr<DatabaseEngine> engine );
   // ... Many database-specific functions

 private:
   std::unique_ptr<DatabaseEngine> engine_;
};
```

---

5 See "Guideline 11: Understand the Purpose of Design Patterns" on page 80 for my statement about the structural similarity of design patterns.

```
// The database is unaware of any implementation details and requests them
//   via its constructor from outside -> Strategy design pattern
Database::Database( std::unique_ptr<DatabaseEngine> engine )  ❷❷
   : engine_{ std::move(engine) }
{}
```

The actual type of `DatabaseEngine` is passed in from the outside (❷❷), making this a good example of the Strategy design pattern.

Figure 7-3 shows the dependency graph for this example. Most importantly, the `Database` class is on the same architectural level as the `DatabaseEngine` abstraction, thus providing others with the opportunity to implement the behavior (e.g., in the form of the `ConcreteDatabaseEngine`). Since `Database` is depending only on the abstraction, there is no dependency on any specific implementation.

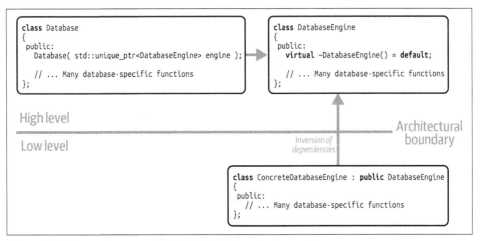

Figure 7-3. Dependency graph for the Strategy design pattern

If, however, a class knows about the implementation details but primarily wants to reduce the *physical* dependencies on these details, then you're most likely dealing with the Bridge design pattern. In that case, the class does not provide any opportunity to set the pointer from outside, i.e., the pointer is an implementation detail and set internally. Since the Bridge design pattern primarily focuses on the physical dependencies of the implementation details, not the logical dependencies, Bridge falls into the category of *structural design patterns*. As an example, consider the following code snippet:

```
class Database
{
 public:
   explicit Database();
   // ...
 private:
   std::unique_ptr<DatabaseEngine> pimpl_;
```

```
};

// The database knows about the required implementation details, but does
//   not want to depend too strongly on it -> Bridge design pattern
Database::Database()
   : pimpl_{ std::make_unique<ConcreteDatabaseEngine>( /*some arguments*/ ) }   ㉓
{}
```

Again, there is a telltale sign for the application of the Bridge design pattern: instead of accepting an engine from outside, the constructor of the `Database` class is aware of the `ConcreteDatabaseEngine` and sets it internally (㉓).

Figure 7-4 shows the dependency graph for the Bridge implementation of the `Database` example. Most notably, the `Database` class is on the same architectural level as the `ConcreteDatabaseEngine` class and does not leave any opportunity for others to provide different implementations. This shows that in contrast to the Strategy design pattern, a Bridge is logically coupled to a specific implementation but only physically decoupled via the `DatabaseEngine` abstraction.

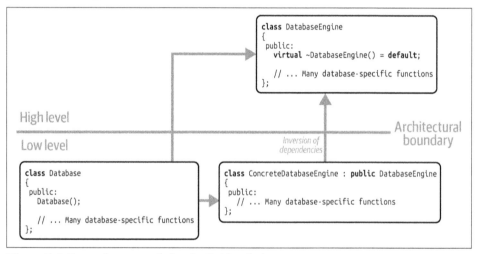

Figure 7-4. Dependency graph for the Bridge design pattern

Analyzing the Shortcomings of the Bridge Design Pattern

"I can totally see why the Bridge design pattern is so popular in the community. The decoupling properties are really great!" you exclaim. "However, you keep telling me that every design has its pros and cons. I expect there is a performance penalty?" Good, you remember that there are always some disadvantages. And of course this includes the Bridge design pattern, although it proves to be very useful. And yes, you're correct to assume that there is some performance overhead involved.

The first of five types of overhead results from the fact that Bridge introduces an additional indirection: the pimpl pointer making all access to the implementation details more expensive. However, how much of the performance penalty this pointer causes is an issue that I will discuss separately in "Guideline 29: Be Aware of Bridge Performance Gains and Losses" on page 266. This is not the only source of performance overhead, though; there are more. Depending on whether you use an abstraction, you also might have to pay for the virtual function call overhead. Additionally, you'll have to pay more due to the lack of inlining of even the simplest function accessing data members. And, of course, you will have to pay for an additional dynamic memory allocation whenever you create a new instance of a class implemented in terms of Bridge.[6] Last but not least, you should also take into account the memory overhead caused by introducing the pimpl pointer. So, yes, isolating the physical dependencies and hiding implementation details is not free but results in a considerable overhead. Still, this shouldn't be a reason to generally discard the Bridge solution: it always depends. For instance, if the underlying implementation performs slow, expensive tasks, such as system calls, then this overhead might not be measurable at all. In other words, whether or not to use a Bridge should be decided on a case-by-case basis and backed up with performance benchmarks.

Furthermore, you have seen the implementation details and realized that the code complexity has increased. Since simplicity and readability of code are a virtue, this should be considered a downside. It's true that this affects only the internals of a class, not the user code. But still, some of the details (e.g., the need to define the destructor in the source file) might be confusing for less-experienced developers.

In summary, the Bridge design pattern is one of the most valuable and most commonly used solutions for reducing physical dependencies. Still, you should be aware of the overhead and the complexity that a Bridge introduces.

Guideline 28: Build Bridges to Remove Physical Dependencies

- Be aware of physical dependencies introduced by data members or includes.
- Apply the Bridge design pattern with the intent to isolate physical dependencies from implementation details.
- Prefer using a pimpl data member to communicate the use of a Bridge.

---

6 If this dynamic allocation turns out to be a severe impediment or a reason not to use a Bridge, you might look into the Fast-Pimpl idiom, which is based on in-class memory. For that, you might refer to Herb Sutter's first book: *Exceptional C++: 47 Engineering Puzzles, Programming Problems, and Exception-Safety Solutions* (Pearson).

- Understand the strengths and the weaknesses of the Bridge design pattern.

- Know the difference between reducing physical dependencies (Bridge) and reducing logical dependencies (Strategy).

Guideline 29: Be Aware of Bridge Performance Gains and Losses

In "Guideline 28: Build Bridges to Remove Physical Dependencies" on page 250, we took a detailed look at the Bridge design pattern. While I imagine the design and decoupling aspect of Bridge left a positive impression on you, I must make you aware that using this pattern may introduce a performance penalty. "Yes, and that worries me. Performance is important to me, and it sounds like a Bridge will create a massive performance overhead," you say. And this is a pretty common expectation. Since performance matters, I really should give you an idea of how much overhead you have to expect when using a Bridge. However, I should also demonstrate how to use Bridges wisely to improve the performance of your code. Sounds unbelievable? Well, let me show you how.

The Performance Impact of Bridges

As discussed in "Guideline 28: Build Bridges to Remove Physical Dependencies" on page 250, the performance of a Bridge implementation is influenced by many factors: access through an indirection, virtual function calls, inlining, dynamic memory allocations, etc. Because of these factors and the huge amount of possible combinations, there is no definitive answer to how much performance a Bridge will cost you. There simply is no shortcut, no substitute for assembling a couple of benchmarks for your own code and running them to evaluate a definitive answer. What I want to demonstrate, though, is that there is indeed a performance penalty of accessing through an indirection, but you can still use a Bridge to actually improve performance.

Let's get started with giving you an idea about the benchmark. To form an opinion on how costly the pointer indirection is, let's compare the following two implementations of a `Person` class:

```
#include <string>

//---- <Person1.h> ----------------

class Person1
{
 public:
   // ...
 private
   std::string forename_;
```

```
    std::string surname_;
    std::string address_;
    std::string city_;
    std::string country_;
    std::string zip_;
    int year_of_birth_;
};
```

The Person1 struct represents a type that is *not* implemented in terms of a Bridge. All seven data members (six std::strings and one int) are directly part of the struct itself. Altogether, and assuming a 64-bit machine, the total size of one instance of Person1 is 152 bytes with Clang 11.1 and 200 bytes with GCC 11.1.[7]

The Person2 struct, on the other hand, is implemented with the Pimpl idiom:

```
//---- <Person2.h> ----------------

#include <memory>

class Person2
{
 public:
   explicit Person2( /*...various person arguments...*/ );
   ~Person2();
   // ...

 private:
   struct Impl;
   std::unique_ptr<Impl> pimpl_;
};


//---- <Person2.cpp> ----------------

#include <Person2.h>
#include <string>

struct Person2::Impl
{
   std::string forename;
   std::string surname;
   std::string address;
   std::string city;
```

---

7 The difference in size of Person1 is easily explained by the different sizes of std::string implementations for different compilers. Since compiler vendors optimize std::string for different use cases, on Clang 11.1, a single std::string occupies 24 bytes, and on GCC 11.1, it occupies 32 bytes. Therefore, the total size of one instance of Person1 is 152 bytes with Clang 11.1 (six 24-byte std::strings, plus one 4-byte int, plus 4 bytes of padding) or 200 bytes with GCC 11.1 (six 32-byte std::strings, plus one 4-byte int, plus 4 bytes of padding).

```
    std::string country;
    std::string zip;
    int year_of_birth;
};

Person2::Person2( /*...various person arguments...*/ )
    : pimpl{ std::make_unique<Impl>( /*...various person arguments...*/ ) }
{}

Person2::~Person2() = default;
```

All seven data members have been moved into the nested `Impl` struct and can be accessed only via the `pimpl` pointer. While the total size of the nested `Impl` struct is identical to the size of `Person1`, the size of the `Person2` struct is only 8 bytes (again, assuming a 64-bit machine).

Via the Bridge design, you can reduce the size of a type, sometimes even significantly. This can prove to be very valuable, for instance, if you want to use the type as an alternative in `std::variant` (see "Guideline 17: Consider std::variant for Implementing Visitor" on page 122).

So let me outline the benchmark: I will create two `std::vectors` of 25,000 persons, one for each of the two `Person` implementations. This number of elements will make certain that we work beyond the size of the inner caches of the underlying CPU (i.e., we will use a total of 3.2 MB with Clang 11.1 and 4.2 MB with GCC 11.1). All of these persons are given arbitrary names and addresses and a year of birth between 1957 and 2004 (at the time of writing, this would represent a reasonable range of ages of employees in an organization). Then we will traverse both person vectors five thousand times, and each time determine the oldest person with `std::min_element()`. The result will be fairly uninteresting due to the repetitive nature of the benchmark. After one hundred iterations, you'll be too bored to watch. The only thing that matters is seeing the performance difference between accessing a data member directly (`Person1`) or indirectly (`Person2`). Table 7-1 shows the performance results, normalized to the performance of the `Person1` implementation.

Table 7-1. Performance results for different Person implementations (normalized performance)

Person implementation	GCC 11.1	Clang 11.1
Person1 (no pimpl)	1.0	1.0
Person2 (complete Pimpl idiom)	1.1099	1.1312

It's fairly obvious that in this particular benchmark, the Bridge implementation incurs a pretty significant performance penalty: 11.0% for GCC and 13.1% for Clang. This sounds like a lot! However, don't take these numbers too seriously: clearly, the result heavily depends on the actual number of elements, the actual number and type of data members, the system we're running on, and the actual computation we perform in the benchmark. If you change any of these details, the numbers will change as well. Thus, these numbers only demonstrate that there is some, and potentially even some more, overhead due to the indirect access to data members.

Improving Performance with Partial Bridges

"OK, but this is an expected result, right? What should I learn from that?" you ask. Well, I admit that this benchmark is fairly specific and does not answer all questions. However, it does provide us with the opportunity to actually use a Bridge to improve performance. If you take a closer look at the implementation of Person1, you might realize that for the given benchmark, the achievable performance is pretty limited: while the total size of Person1 is 152 bytes (Clang 11.1) or 200 bytes (GCC 11.1), respectively, we use only 4 bytes, i.e., a single int, out of the total data structure. This proves to be rather wasteful and inefficient: since in cache-based architectures memory is always loaded as cache lines, a lot of the data that we load from memory is actually not used at all. In fact, almost *all* of the data that we load from memory is not used at all: assuming a cache line length of 64 bytes, we only use approximately 6% of the loaded data. Hence, despite the fact that we determine the oldest person based on the year of birth of all persons, which sounds like a compute-bound operation, we are in fact completely memory bound: the machine simply cannot deliver data fast enough, and the integer unit will idle most of the time.

This setting gives us the opportunity to improve the performance with a Bridge. Let's assume that we can distinguish between data that is used often (such as forename, surname, and year_of_birth) and data that is used infrequently (for instance, the postal address). Based on this distinction, we now arrange the data members accordingly: all data members that are used often are stored directly in the Person class. All data members that are used infrequently are stored inside the Impl struct. This leads to the Person3 implementation:

```
//---- <Person3.h> ----------------

#include <memory>
#include <string>

class Person3
{
 public:
   explicit Person3( /*...various person arguments...*/ );
   ~Person3();
```

```
    // ...

  private:
    std::string forename_;
    std::string surname_;
    int year_of_birth_;

    struct Impl;
    std::unique_ptr<Impl> pimpl_;
};


//---- <Person3.cpp> ----------------

#include <Person3.h>

struct Person3::Impl
{
    std::string address;
    std::string city;
    std::string country;
    std::string zip;
};

Person3::Person3( /*...various person arguments...*/ )
    : forename_{ /*...*/ }
    , surname_{ /*...*/ }
    , year_of_birth_{ /*...*/ }
    , pimpl_{ std::make_unique<Impl>( /*...address-related arguments...*/ ) }
{}

Person3::~Person3() = default;
```

The total size of a Person3 instance is 64 bytes for Clang 11.1 (two 24-byte
std::strings, one integer, one pointer, and four padding bytes due to alignment
restrictions) and 80 bytes on GCC 11.1 (two 32-byte std::strings, one integer, one
pointer, and some padding). Thus, a Person3 instance is only approximately half as
big as a Person1 instance. This difference in size is measurable: Table 7-2 shows the
performance result for all Person implementations, including Person3. Again, the
results are normalized to the performance of the Person1 implementation.

*Table 7-2. Performance results for different Person implementations (normalized
performance)*

Person implementation	GCC 11.1	Clang 11.1
Person1 (no pimpl)	1.0	1.0
Person2 (complete Pimpl idiom)	1.1099	1.1312
Person3 (partial Pimpl idiom)	0.8597	0.9353

In comparison to the `Person1` implementation, the performance for `Person3` is improved by 14.0% for GCC 11.1 and 6.5% for Clang 11.1. And, as stated before, this is only because we reduced the size of the `Person3` implementation. "Wow, this was unexpected. I see, a Bridge is not necessarily all bad for performance," you say. Yes, indeed. Of course, it always depends on the specific setup, but distinguishing between data members that are used frequently and those that are used infrequently, and reducing the size of a data structure by implementing a "partial" Bridge may have a very positive impact on performance.[8]

"The performance gain is huge, that's great, but isn't that running against the intention of a Bridge?" you ask. Indeed, you realize that there is a dichotomy between hiding implementation details and "inlining" data members for the sake of performance. As always, it depends: you will have to decide from case to case which aspect to favor. You hopefully also realize that there is an entire range of solutions in between the two extremes: it is not necessary to hide *all* data members behind a Bridge. In the end, you are the one to find the optimum for a given problem.

In summary, while Bridges in general will very likely incur a performance penalty, given the right circumstances, implementing a partial Bridge may have a very positive effect on your performance. However, this is only one of many aspects that influence performance. Therefore, you should always check to see if a Bridge results in a performance bottleneck or if a partial Bridge is addressing a performance issue. The best way to confirm this is with a representative benchmark, based on the actual code and actual data as much as possible.

Guideline 29: Be Aware of Bridge Performance Gains and Losses

- Keep in mind that Bridges can have a negative performance impact.

- Be aware that a partial Bridge can have a positive impact on performance when separating frequently used data from infrequently used data.

- Always confirm performance bottlenecks or improvements by representative benchmarks; do not rely on your gut feeling.

---

8 You may be aware that we are still *far* away from optimal performance. To move in the direction of optimal performance, we could arrange the data based on how it is used. For this benchmark, this would mean to store all `year_of_birth` values from all persons in one big static vector of integers. This kind of data arrangement would move us in the direction of *data-oriented design*. For more information on this paradigm, see for instance Richard Fabian's book on the subject, *Data-Oriented Design: Software Engineering for Limited Resources and Short Schedules*.

Guideline 30: Apply Prototype for Abstract Copy Operations

Imagine yourself sitting in a fancy Italian restaurant and studying the menu. Oh my, they offer so many great things; the lasagna sounds great. But the selection of pizza they offer is also amazing. So hard to choose…However, your thoughts are interrupted as the waiter walks by carrying this incredible-looking dish. Unfortunately, it's not meant for you but for someone at another table. Oh wow, the smell… At this moment, you know that you no longer have to think about what you want to eat: you want the same thing, no matter what it is. And so you order: "Ah, waiter, I'll have whatever they are having."

The same problem may occur in your code. In C++ terms, what you are asking the waiter for is a copy of the other person's dish. Copying an object, i.e., creating an exact replica of an instance, is a fundamentally important operation in C++. So important that classes are, by default, equipped with a copy constructor and a copy assignment operator—two of the so-called *special member functions*.[9] However, when asking for a copy of the dish, you are unfortunately not aware what dish it is. In C++ terms, all you have is a pointer-to-base (say, a `Dish*`). And unfortunately, trying to copy via `Dish*` with the copy constructor or copy assignment operator usually doesn't work. Still, you want an exact copy. The solution to this problem is another classic GoF design pattern: the Prototype design pattern.

A Sheep-ish Example: Copying Animals

As an example, let's consider the following `Animal` base class:

```
//---- <Animal.h> ----------------

class Animal
{
 public:
   virtual ~Animal() = default;
   virtual void makeSound() const = 0;
   // ... more animal-specific functions
};
```

---

9 The rules when a compiler will generate these two copy operations are beyond the scope of this book, but here is a short summary: *every* class has these two operations, meaning they always exist. They have been generated by the compiler, or you have explicitly declared or even defined them (potentially in the private section of the class or via =delete), or they are implicitly deleted. Note that deleting these functions does not mean that they're gone, but =delete serves as a definition. As these two functions are *always* part of a class, they will *always* participate in overload resolution.

Apart from the virtual destructor, which indicates that `Animal` is supposed to be a base class, the class provides only the `makeSound()` function, which deals with printing cute animal sounds. One example of such an animal is the `Sheep` class:

```
//---- <Sheep.h> ----------------

#include <Animal.h>
#include <string>

class Sheep : public Animal
{
 public:
   explicit Sheep( std::string name ) : name_{ std::move(name) } {}

   void makeSound() const override;
   // ... more animal-specific functions

 private:
   std::string name_;
};
```

```
//---- <Sheep.cpp> ---------------

#include <Sheep.h>
#include <iostream>

void Sheep::makeSound() const
{
    std::cout << "baa\n";
}
```

In the `main()` function, we can now create a sheep and have it make sounds:

```
#include <Sheep.h>
#include <cstdlib>
#include <memory>

int main()
{
    // Creating the one and only Dolly
    std::unique_ptr<Animal> const dolly = std::make_unique<Sheep>( "Dolly" );

    // Triggers Dolly's beastly sound
    dolly->makeSound();

    return EXIT_SUCCESS;
}
```

Dolly is great, right? And so cute! In fact, she's so much fun that we want another Dolly. However, all we have is a pointer-to-base—an `Animal*`. We can't copy via the `Sheep` copy constructor or the copy assignment operator, because we (technically) don't even know that we are dealing with a Sheep. It could be any kind of animal (e.g., dog, cat, sheep, etc.). And we don't want to copy just the Animal part of Sheep, as this is what we call *slicing*.

Oh my, I just realized that this may be a particularly bad example for explaining the Prototype design pattern. Slicing animals. This sounds bad. So let's swiftly move on. Where were we? Ah yes, we want a copy of Dolly, but we only have an Animal*. This is where the Prototype design pattern comes into play.

The Prototype Design Pattern Explained

The Prototype design pattern is one of the five creational design patterns collected by the Gang of Four. It is focused on providing an abstract way of creating copies of some abstract entity.

The Prototype Design Pattern

Intent: "Specify the kind of objects to create using a prototypical instance, and create new objects by copying this prototype."[10]

Figure 7-5 shows the original UML formulation, taken from the GoF book.

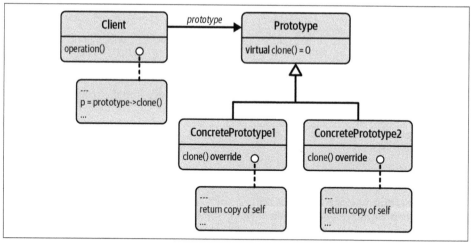

Figure 7-5. The UML representation of the Prototype design pattern

---

10 Erich Gamma et al., *Design Patterns: Elements of Reusable Object-Oriented Software*.

The Prototype design pattern is commonly implemented by a virtual `clone()` function in the base class. Consider the updated `Animal` base class:

```
//---- <Animal.h> ----------------

class Animal
{
 public:
   virtual ~Animal() = default;
   virtual void makeSound() const = 0;
   virtual std::unique_ptr<Animal> clone() const = 0; // Prototype design pattern
};
```

Via this `clone()` function, anyone can ask for an abstract copy of the given (prototype) animal, without having to know about any specific type of animal (`Dog`, `Cat`, or `Sheep`). When the `Animal` base class is properly assigned to the high level of your architecture, it follows the DIP (see Figure 7-6).

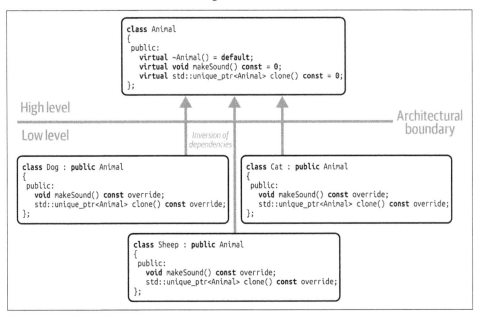

Figure 7-6. Dependency graph for the Prototype design pattern

The `clone()` function is declared as a pure virtual function, which means that deriving classes are required to implement it. However, deriving classes cannot simply implement the function any way they want, but are expected to return an exact copy of themselves (any other result would violate the LSP; see "Guideline 6: Adhere to the Expected Behavior of Abstractions" on page 44). This copy is commonly created dynamically by `new` and returned by a pointer-to-base. This, of course, results not only in a pointer but also in the need to explicitly `delete` the copy again. Since manual cleanup is considered to be very bad practice in Modern C++, the pointer is returned as the std::unique_ptr to Animal.[11]

The Sheep class is updated accordingly:

```
//---- <Sheep.h> ----------------

#include <Animal.h>

class Sheep : public Animal
{
 public:
   explicit Sheep( std::string name ) : name_{ std::move(name) } {}

   void makeSound() const override;
   std::unique_ptr<Animal> clone() const override;   // Prototype design pattern

 private:
   std::string name_;
};


//---- <Sheep.cpp> ----------------

#include <Sheep.h>
#include <iostream>

void Sheep::makeSound() const
{
   std::cout << "baa\n";
}

std::unique_ptr<Animal> Sheep::clone() const
{
   return std::make_unique<Sheep>(*this);   // Copy-construct a sheep
}
```

The Sheep class is now required to implement the clone() function and return an exact copy of the Sheep: Inside its own clone() function, it makes use of the std::make_unique() function and its own copy constructor, which is always assumed to do the right thing, even if the Sheep class changes in the future. This

---

11 Core Guideline R.3 (*https://oreil.ly/YeCHE*) clearly states that a raw pointer (a T*) is nonowning. From this perspective, it would even be incorrect to return a raw pointer-to-base. However, this means that you cannot directly exploit the language feature of covariant return types anymore. If this is desirable or required, a common solution would be to follow the Template Method design pattern and split the clone() function into a private virtual function returning a raw pointer, and a public non-virtual function calling the private function and returning std::unique_ptr.

approach helps avoid unnecessary duplication and thus follows the DRY principle (see "Guideline 2: Design for Change" on page 11).

Note that the Sheep class neither deletes nor hides its copy constructor and copy assignment operator. Hence, if you have a sheep, you can still copy the sheep with the special member functions. That is perfectly OK: the clone() merely adds one more way to create a copy—a way to perform virtual copying.

With the clone() function in place, we can now create an exact copy of Dolly. And we can do this so much easier than we could have back in 1996 when they cloned the first Dolly:

```
#include <Sheep.h>
#include <cstdlib>
#include <memory>

int main()
{
   std::unique_ptr<Animal> dolly = std::make_unique<Sheep>( "Dolly" );
   std::unique_ptr<Animal> dollyClone = dolly->clone();

   dolly->makeSound();        // Triggers the first Dolly's beastly sound
   dollyClone->makeSound();   // The clone sounds just like Dolly

   return EXIT_SUCCESS;
}
```

Comparison Between Prototype and std::variant

The Prototype design pattern really is a classic, very OO-centric design pattern, and since its publication in 1994, it is *the* go-to solution for providing virtual copying. Because of this, the function name clone() can almost be considered a keyword for identifying the Prototype design pattern.

Because of the specific use case, there is no "modern" implementation (except perhaps for the slight update to use std::unique_ptr instead of a raw pointer). In comparison to other design patterns, there is also no value semantics solution: as soon as we have a value, the most natural and intuitive solution would be to build on the two copy operations (the copy constructor and the copy assignment operator).

"Are you sure that there is no value semantics solution? Consider the following example using std::variant:"

```
#include <cstdlib>
#include <variant>

class Dog {};
class Cat {};
class Sheep {};
```

```
int main()
{
   std::variant<Dog,Cat,Sheep> animal1{ /* ... */ };

   auto animal2 = animal1;  // Creating a copy of the animal

   return EXIT_SUCCESS;
}
```

"Aren't we performing an abstract copy operation in this case? And isn't this copy operation performed by the copy constructor? So isn't this an example of the Prototype design pattern but without the clone() function?" No. Although it sounds like you have a compelling argument, this is not an example of the Prototype design pattern. There is a very important difference between our two examples: in your example, you have a closed set of types (typical of the Visitor design pattern). The std::variant animal1 contains a dog, a cat, or a sheep, but nothing else. Therefore, it is possible to perform an explicit copy with the copy constructor. In my example, I have an open set of types. In other words, I haven't the slightest clue what kind of animal I have to copy. It could be a dog, a cat, or a sheep, but it could also be an elephant, a zebra, or a sloth. Anything is possible. Therefore, I can't build on the copy constructor but can only copy using a virtual clone() function.

Analyzing the Shortcomings of the Prototype Design Pattern

Yes, there is no value semantics solution for the Prototype design pattern, but it's a domestic beast from the realm of reference semantics. Hence, whenever the need arises to apply the Prototype design pattern, we have to live with the few drawbacks that come with it.

Arguably, the first disadvantage is the negative performance impact that comes with the indirection due to pointers. However, since we only require cloning if we have an inheritance hierarchy, it would be unfair to consider this a drawback of Prototype itself. It is rather a consequence of the basic setup of the problem. Since it's also hard to imagine another implementation without pointers and the associated indirections, it seems to be an intrinsic property of the Prototype design pattern.

The second potential disadvantage is that, very often, the pattern is implemented by dynamic memory. The allocation itself, and also the possible resulting fragmented memory, causes further performance deficiencies. Dynamic memory is not a requirement, however, and you will see in "Guideline 33: Be Aware of the Optimization Potential of Type Erasure" on page 318 that in certain contexts, you can also build on in-class memory. Still, this optimization applies to only a few special situations, and in most cases, the pattern builds on dynamic memory.

In comparison to the ability to perform an abstract copy operation, the few downsides are easily acceptable. However, as discussed in "Guideline 22: Prefer Value Semantics over Reference Semantics" on page 176, our Animal hierarchy would be simpler and more comprehensible if you could replace it with a value semantics approach and therefore avoid having to apply the reference semantics–based Prototype design pattern. Still, whenever you encounter the need to create an abstract copy, the Prototype design pattern with a corresponding clone() function is the right choice.

Guideline 30: Apply Prototype for Abstract Copy Operations

- Apply the Prototype design pattern with the intent to create copies of abstract entities.

- Prefer building on the two copy operations for value types.

- Keep in mind the performance drawbacks resulting from pointer indirections and memory allocations.

Guideline 31: Use External Polymorphism for Nonintrusive Runtime Polymorphism

In "Guideline 2: Design for Change" on page 11, we saw the enormous benefits of the separation of concerns design principle. In "Guideline 19: Use Strategy to Isolate How Things Are Done" on page 140, we used this power to extract the drawing implementation details from a set of shapes with the Strategy design pattern. However, although this has significantly reduced dependencies, and despite the fact that we modernized the solution in "Guideline 23: Prefer a Value-Based Implementation of Strategy and Command" on page 186 with the help of std::function, some disadvantages remained. In particular, the shape classes were still forced to deal with the draw() operation, although for coupling reasons, it is undesirable to deal with the implementation details. Additionally, and most importantly, the Strategy approach proved to be a little impractical for extracting multiple, polymorphic operations. To further reduce coupling and extract polymorphic operations from our shapes, we are now continuing this journey and taking the separation of concerns principle to a completely new, potentially unfamiliar level: we are separating the polymorphic behavior as a whole. For that purpose, we will apply the External Polymorphism design pattern.

The External Polymorphism Design Pattern Explained

Let's return to our example of drawing shapes and our latest version of our `Circle` class from "Guideline 23: Prefer a Value-Based Implementation of Strategy and Command" on page 186:

```cpp
//---- <Shape.h> ----------------

class Shape
{
 public:
   virtual ~Shape() = default;

   virtual void draw( /*some arguments*/ ) const = 0;   ❶
};
```

```cpp
//---- <Circle.h> ----------------

#include <Shape.h>
#include <memory>
#include <functional>
#include <utility>

class Circle : public Shape
{
 public:
   using DrawStrategy = std::function<void(Circle const&, /*...*/)>;   ❷

   explicit Circle( double radius, DrawStrategy drawer )
     : radius_( radius )
     , drawer_( std::move(drawer) )
   {
     /* Checking that the given radius is valid and that
        the given 'std::function' instance is not empty */
   }

   void draw( /*some arguments*/ ) const override   ❸
   {
     drawer_( *this, /*some arguments*/ );
   }

   double radius() const { return radius_; }

 private:
   double radius_;
   DrawStrategy drawer_;
};
```

With the Strategy design pattern, we have overcome the initial strong coupling to the implementation details of the draw() member function (❶). We've also found a value semantics solution based on std::function (❷). However, the draw() member function is still part of the public interface of all classes deriving from the Shape base class, and all shapes inherit the obligation to implement it (❸). This is a clear imperfection: arguably, the drawing functionality should be separate, an isolated aspect of shapes, and shapes in general should be oblivious to the fact that they can be drawn.[12] The fact that we have already extracted the implementation details considerably strengthens this argument.

"Well, then, let's just extract the draw() member function, right?" you argue. And you're right. Unfortunately, this appears to be a hard thing to do at first sight. I hope you remember "Guideline 15: Design for the Addition of Types or Operations" on page 102, where we came to the conclusion that you should prefer an object-oriented solution when you primarily want to add types. From this perspective, it appears as if we are stuck with the virtual draw() function and the Shape base class, which represents the set of available operations of all shapes, i.e., the list of requirements.

There is a solution, though. A pretty astonishing one: we can extract the complete polymorphic behavior with the External Polymorphism design pattern. The pattern was introduced in a paper by Chris Cleeland, Douglas C. Schmidt, and Timothy H. Harrison in 1996.[13] Its intent is to enable the polymorphic treatment of nonpolymorphic types (types without a single virtual function).

The External Polymorphism Design Pattern

Intent: "Allow C++ classes unrelated by inheritance and/or having no virtual methods to be treated polymorphically. These unrelated classes can be treated in a common manner by software that uses them."

Figure 7-7 gives a first impression of how the design pattern achieves this goal. One of the first striking details is that there is no Shape base class anymore. In the External Polymorphism design pattern, the different kinds of shapes (Circle, Square, etc.) are assumed to be plain, nonpolymorphic types. Also, the shapes are not expected to know anything about drawing. Instead of requiring the shapes to inherit from a Shape base class, the design pattern introduces a separate inheritance hierarchy in the form of the ShapeConcept and ShapeModel classes. This external hierarchy

---

12 See "Guideline 2: Design for Change" on page 11 for a similar example with different kinds of documents.

13 Chris Cleeland, Douglas C. Schmidt, and Timothy H. Harrison, "External Polymorphism—An Object Structural Pattern for Transparently Extending C++ Concrete Data Types," Proceedings of the 3rd Pattern Languages of Programming Conference, Allerton Park, Illinois, September 4–6, 1996.

introduces the polymorphic behavior for the shapes by introducing all the operations and requirements that are expected for shapes.

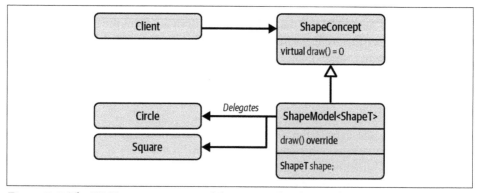

Figure 7-7. The UML representation of the External Polymorphism design pattern

In our simple example, the polymorphic behavior consists of only the draw() function. However, the set of requirements could, of course, be larger (e.g., rotate(), serialize(), etc.). This set of virtual functions has been moved into the abstract ShapeConcept class, which now takes the place of the previous Shape base class. The major difference is that concrete shapes are not required to know about ShapeConcept and, in particular, are not expected to inherit from it. Thus, the shapes are completely decoupled from the set of virtual functions. The only class inheriting from ShapeConcept is the ShapeModel class template. This class is instantiated for a specific kind of shape (Circle, Square, etc.) and acts as a wrapper for it. However, ShapeModel does not implement the logic of the virtual functions itself but delegates the request to the desired implementation.

"Wow, that's amazing! I get the point: this external hierarchy extracts the whole set of virtual functions and, by that, the entire polymorphic behavior of the shapes." Yes, exactly. Again, this is an example of separation of concerns and the SRP. In this case, the complete polymorphic behavior is identified as a *variation point* and extracted from the shapes. And again, SRP acts as an enabler for the OCP: with the ShapeModel class template, you can easily add any new, nonpolymorphic shape type into the ShapeConcept hierarchy. This works as long as the new type fulfills all of the required operations.

"I'm really impressed. However, I'm not certain what you mean by fulfilling all of the required operations. Could you please elaborate?" Absolutely! I think the benefits will become clear when I show you a concrete code example. So let's refactor the complete drawing of the shapes example with the External Polymorphism design pattern.

Drawing of Shapes Revisited

Let's start with the Circle and Square classes:

```cpp
//---- <Circle.h> ----------------

class Circle
{
 public:
   explicit Circle( double radius )
      : radius_( radius )
   {
      /* Checking that the given radius is valid */
   }

   double radius() const { return radius_; }
   /* Several more getters and circle-specific utility functions */

 private:
   double radius_;
   /* Several more data members */
};
```

```cpp
//---- <Square.h> ----------------

class Square
{
 public:
   explicit Square( double side )
      : side_( side )
   {
      /* Checking that the given side length is valid */
   }

   double side() const { return side_; }
   /* Several more getters and square-specific utility functions */

 private:
   double side_;
   /* Several more data members */
};
```

Both classes have been reduced to basic geometric entities. Both are completely non-polymorphic, i.e., there is no base class anymore and not a single virtual function. Most importantly, however, the two classes are completely oblivious to any kind of operation, like drawing, rotating, serialization, etc., that could introduce an artificial dependency.

Instead, all of this functionality is introduced in the ShapeConcept base class and implemented by the ShapeModel class template:[14]

```
//---- <Shape.h> ----------------

#include <functional>
#include <stdexcept>
#include <utility>

class ShapeConcept
{
 public:
   virtual ~ShapeConcept() = default;

   virtual void draw() const = 0;   ❹

   // ... Potentially more polymorphic operations
};


template< typename ShapeT >
class ShapeModel : public ShapeConcept   ❺
{
 public:
   using DrawStrategy = std::function<void(ShapeT const&)>;   ❼

   explicit ShapeModel( ShapeT shape, DrawStrategy drawer )
      : shape_{ std::move(shape) }
      , drawer_{ std::move(drawer) }
   {
      /* Checking that the given 'std::function' is not empty */
   }

   void draw() const override { drawer_(shape_); }   ❾

   // ... Potentially more polymorphic operations

 private:
   ShapeT shape_;   ❻
   DrawStrategy drawer_;   ❽
};
```

---

14 The names Concept and Model are chosen based on the common terminology in the Type Erasure design pattern, where External Polymorphism plays a major role; see Chapter 8.

The ShapeConcept class introduces a pure virtual draw() member function (❹). In our example, this one virtual function represents the entire set of requirements for shapes. Despite the small size of the set, the ShapeConcept class represents a classic abstraction in the sense of the LSP (see "Guideline 6: Adhere to the Expected Behavior of Abstractions" on page 44). This abstraction is implemented within the Shape Model class template (❺). It is noteworthy that instantiations of ShapeModel are the only classes to ever inherit from ShapeConcept; no other class is expected to enter in this relationship. The ShapeModel class template will be instantiated for every desired type of shape, i.e., the ShapeT template parameter is a stand-in for types like Circle, Square, etc. Note that ShapeModel stores an instance of the corresponding shape (❻) (composition, not inheritance; remember "Guideline 20: Favor Composition over Inheritance" on page 162). It acts as a wrapper that augments the specific shape type with the required polymorphic behavior (in our case, the draw() function).

Since ShapeModel implements the ShapeConcept abstraction, it needs to provide an implementation for the draw() function. However, it is not the responsibility of the ShapeModel to implement the draw() details itself. Instead, it should forward a drawing request to the actual implementation. For that purpose, we can again reach for the Strategy design pattern and the abstracting power of std::function (❼). This choice nicely decouples both the implementation details of drawing and all the necessary drawing data (colors, textures, transparency, etc.), which can be stored inside the callable. Hence, ShapeModel stores an instance of DrawStrategy (❽) and uses that strategy whenever the draw() function is triggered (❾).

The Strategy design pattern and the std::function are not your only choices, though. Within the ShapeModel class template, you have complete flexibility to implement drawing as you see fit. In other words, within the ShapeModel::draw() function, you define the actual requirements for the specific shape types. For instance, you could alternatively forward to a member function of the ShapeT shape (which does not have to be named draw()!), or you could forward to a free function of the shape. You just need to make sure that you do not impose artificial requirements on either the ShapeModel or the ShapeConcept abstraction. Either way, any type used to instantiate ShapeModel must fulfill these requirements to make the code compile.

From a design perspective, building on a member function would introduce a more restrictive requirement on the given type, and therefore introduce stronger coupling. Building on a free function, however, would enable you to invert dependencies, similar to the use of the Strategy design pattern (see "Guideline 9: Pay Attention to the Ownership of Abstractions" on page 62). If you prefer the free function approach, just remember "Guideline 8: Understand the Semantic Requirements of Overload Sets" on page 56.

"Isn't `ShapeModel` some kind of generalization of the initial `Circle` and `Square` classes? The ones that were also holding the `std::function` instance?" Yes, this is an excellent realization. Indeed, you could say that `ShapeModel` is kind of a templated version of the initial shape classes. For this reason it helps to reduce the boilerplate code necessary to introduce the Strategy behavior and improves the implementation with respect to the DRY principle (see "Guideline 2: Design for Change" on page 11). However, you gain a lot more: for instance, since `ShapeModel` is already a class template, you can easily switch from the current runtime Strategy implementation to a compile-time Strategy implementation (i.e., policy-based design; see "Guideline 19: Use Strategy to Isolate How Things Are Done" on page 140):

```
template< typename ShapeT
        , typename DrawStrategy >   ❿
class ShapeModel : public ShapeConcept
{
 public:
   explicit ShapeModel( ShapeT shape, DrawStrategy drawer )
      : shape_{ std::move(shape) }
      , drawer_{ std::move(drawer) }
   {}

   void draw() const override { drawer_(shape_); }

 private:
   ShapeT shape_;
   DrawStrategy drawer_;
};
```

Instead of building on `std::function`, you can pass an additional template parameter to the `ShapeModel` class template, which represents the drawing Strategy (❿). This template parameter could even have a default:

```
struct DefaultDrawer
{
   template< typename T >
   void operator()( T const& obj ) const {
      draw(obj);
   }
};

template< typename ShapeT
        , typename DrawStrategy = DefaultDrawer >
class ShapeModel : public ShapeConcept
{
 public:
   explicit ShapeModel( ShapeT shape, DrawStrategy drawer = DefaultDrawer{} )
   // ... as before
};
```

In comparison to applying policy-based design to the `Circle` and `Square` classes directly, the compile-time approach in this context holds only benefits and comes with no disadvantages. First, you gain performance due to fewer runtime indirections (the expected performance disadvantage of `std::function`). Second, you do not artificially augment `Circle`, `Square`, and all the other shape classes with a template argument to configure the drawing behavior. You now only do this for the wrapper, which augments the drawing behavior, and you do this in exactly one place (which again very nicely adheres to the DRY principle). Third, you do not force additional code into a header file by turning a regular class into a class template. Only the slim `ShapeModel` class, which is already a class template, needs to reside in a header file. Therefore, you avoid creating additional dependencies.

"Wow, this design pattern is getting better and better. This seriously is a very compelling combination of inheritance and templates!" Yes, I completely agree. This is an exemplar for combining runtime and compile-time polymorphism: the `ShapeConcept` base class provides the abstraction for all possible types, while the deriving `ShapeModel` class template provides the code generation for shape-specific code. Most impressively, however, this combination comes with huge benefits for the reduction of dependencies.

Take a look at Figure 7-8, which shows the dependency graph for our implementation of the External Polymorphism design pattern. On the highest level of our architecture are the `ShapeConcept` and `ShapeModel` classes, which together represent the abstraction of shapes. `Circle` and `Square` are possible implementations of this abstraction but are still completely independent: no inheritance relationship, no composition, nothing. Only the instantiation of the `ShapeModel` class template for a specific kind of shape and a specific `DrawStrategy` implementation brings all aspects together. However, specifically note that all of this happens on the lowest level of our architecture: the template code is generated at the point where all dependencies are known and "injected" into the right level of our architecture. Thus, we truly have a proper architecture: all dependency connections run toward the higher levels with an almost automatic adherence to the DIP.

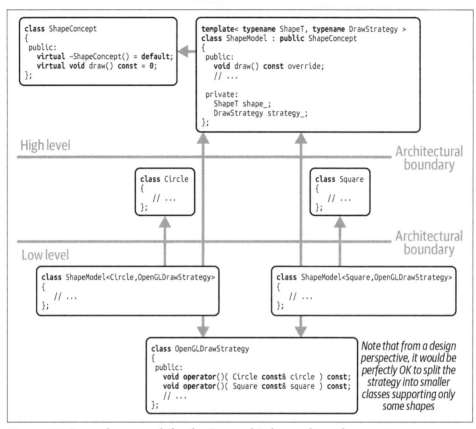

Figure 7-8. Dependency graph for the External Polymorphism design pattern

With this functionality in place, we are now free to implement any desired drawing behavior. For instance, we are free to use OpenGL again:

```
//---- <OpenGLDrawStrategy.h> ----------------

#include <Circle>
#include <Square>
#include /* OpenGL graphics library headers */

class OpenGLDrawStrategy
{
 public:
   explicit OpenGLDrawStrategy( /* Drawing related arguments */ );

   void operator()( Circle const& circle ) const;   ⓫
   void operator()( Square const& square ) const;   ⓬

 private:
```

```
      /* Drawing related data members, e.g. colors, textures, ... */
};
```

Since `OpenGLDrawStrategy` does not have to inherit from any base class, you are free to implement it as you see fit. If you want to, you can combine the implementation of drawing circles and drawing squares into one class. This does not create any artificial dependencies, similar to what we experienced in "Guideline 19: Use Strategy to Isolate How Things Are Done" on page 140, where we combined these functionalities into the base class.

 Note that combining drawing circles and squares in one class represents the same thing as inheriting the class from two Strategy base classes. On that level of the architecture, it does not create any artificial dependencies and is merely an implementation detail.

The only convention you need to follow is to provide a function call operator for `Circle` (❶❶) and `Square` (❶❷), as this is the defined calling convention in the `ShapeModel` class template.

In the `main()` function, we put all of the details together:

```
#include <Circle.h>
#include <Square.h>
#include <Shape.h>
#include <OpenGLDrawStrategy.h>
#include <memory>
#include <vector>

int main()
{
   using Shapes = std::vector<std::unique_ptr<ShapeConcept>>;  ❶❸

   using CircleModel = ShapeModel<Circle,OpenGLDrawStrategy>;  ❶❹
   using SquareModel = ShapeModel<Square,OpenGLDrawStrategy>;  ❶❺

   Shapes shapes{};

   // Creating some shapes, each one
   //    equipped with an OpenGL drawing strategy
   shapes.emplace_back(
      std::make_unique<CircleModel>(
         Circle{2.3}, OpenGLDrawStrategy(/*...red...*/) ) );
   shapes.emplace_back(
      std::make_unique<SquareModel>(
         Square{1.2}, OpenGLDrawStrategy(/*...green...*/) ) );
   shapes.emplace_back(
      std::make_unique<CircleModel>(
         Circle{4.1}, OpenGLDrawStrategy(/*...blue...*/) ) );
```

```
    // Drawing all shapes
    for( auto const& shape : shapes )
    {
        shape->draw();
    }

    return EXIT_SUCCESS;
}
```

Again, we first create an empty vector of shapes (this time a vector of std::unique_ptrs of ShapeConcept) (**⓭**) before we add three shapes. Within the calls to std::make_unique(), we instantiate the ShapeModel class for Circle and Square (called CircleModel (**⓮**) and SquareModel (**⓯**) to improve readability) and pass the necessary details (the concrete shape and the corresponding OpenGLDrawStrategy). After that, we are able to draw all shapes in the desired way.

Altogether, this approach gives you a lot of awesome advantages:

- Due to separating concerns and extracting the polymorphic behavior from the shape types, you remove all dependencies on graphics libraries, etc. This creates a very loose coupling and beautifully adheres to the *SRP*.

- The shape types become simpler and nonpolymorphic.

- You're able to easily add new kinds of shapes. These might even be third-party types, as you are no longer required to intrusively inherit from a Shape base class or create an Adapter (see "Guideline 24: Use Adapters to Standardize Interfaces" on page 198). Thus, you perfectly adhere to the OCP.

- You significantly reduce the usual inheritance-related boilerplate code and implement it in exactly one place, which very nicely follows the DRY principle.

- Since the ShapeConcept and ShapeModel class belong together and together form the abstraction, it's much easier to adhere to the DIP.

- By reducing the number of indirections by exploiting the available class template, you can improve performance.

There is one more advantage, which I consider to be the most impressive benefit of the External Polymorphism design pattern: you can, nonintrusively, equip any type with polymorphic behavior. Really, *any* type, even something as simple as an int. To demonstrate this, let's take a look at the following code snippet, which assumes that ShapeModel is equipped with a DefaultDrawer, which expects the wrapped type to provide a free draw() function:

```
int draw( int i )  ⓰
{
    // ... drawing an int, for instance by printing it to the command line
}
```

```
int main()
{
    auto shape = std::make_unique<ShapeModel<int>>( 42 );   ⑰

    shape->draw();  // Drawing the integer  ⑱

    return EXIT_SUCCESS;
}
```

We first provide a free `draw()` function for an `int` (⑯). In the `main()` function, we now instantiate a `ShapeModel` for `int` (⑰). This line will compile, as the `int` satisfies all the requirements: it provides a free `draw()` function. Therefore, in the next line we can "draw" the integer (⑱).

"Do you really want me to do something like this?" you ask, frowning. No, I do not want you to do this at home. Please consider this a technical demonstration, not a recommendation. But nonetheless, this is impressive: we have just nonintrusively equipped an `int` with polymorphic behavior. Really impressive indeed!

Comparison Between External Polymorphism and Adapter

"Since you just mentioned the Adapter design pattern, I feel like it's very similar to the External Polymorphism design pattern. What is the difference between the two?" Excellent point! You address an issue that the original paper by Cleeland, Schmidt, and Harrison also addresses. Yes, these two design patterns are indeed pretty similar, yet there is a very distinctive difference: while the Adapter design pattern is focused on standardizing interfaces and adapts a type or function to an existing interface, the External Polymorphism design pattern creates a new, external hierarchy to abstract from a set of related, nonpolymorphic types. So if you adapt something to an existing interface, you (most probably) apply the Adapter design pattern. If, however, you create a new abstraction for the purpose of treating a set of existing types polymorphically, then you (most likely) apply the External Polymorphism design pattern.

Analyzing the Shortcomings of the External Polymorphism Design Pattern

"I get the feeling that you like the External Polymorphism design pattern a lot, am I right?" you wonder. Oh yes, indeed, I'm amazed by this design pattern. From my point of view, this design pattern is key to loose coupling, and it's a shame that it is not more widely known. Perhaps this is because many developers have not fully embraced the separation of concerns and tend to put everything into only a few classes. Still, despite my enthusiasm, I do not want to create the impression that everything about External Polymorphism is perfect. No, as stated many times before, every design has its advantages and its disadvantages. The same is true for the External Polymorphism design pattern.

There is only one major disadvantage, though: the External Polymorphism design pattern does not really fulfill the expectations of a clean and simple solution, and definitely not the expectations of a value semantics–based solution. It does not help to reduce pointers, does not reduce the number of manual allocations, does not lower the number of inheritance hierarchies, and does not help to simplify user code. On the contrary, since it is necessary to explicitly instantiate the ShapeModel class, user code has to be rated as slightly more complicated. However, if you consider this a severe drawback, or if you're thinking something along the lines of "This should be automated somehow," I have very good news for you: in "Guideline 32: Consider Replacing Inheritance Hierarchies with Type Erasure" on page 298, we will take a look at the modern C++ solution that will elegantly resolve this issue.

Apart from that, I have only two reminders that you should consider as words of caution. The first point to keep in mind is that the application of External Polymorphism does not save you from thinking about a proper abstraction. The ShapeConcept base class is just as much subject to the ISP as any other base class. For instance, we could easily apply External Polymorphism to the Document example from "Guideline 3: Separate Interfaces to Avoid Artificial Coupling" on page 24:

```cpp
class DocumentConcept
{
 public:
   // ...
   virtual ~Document() = default;

   virtual void exportToJSON( /*...*/ ) const = 0;
   virtual void serialize( ByteStream& bs, /*...*/ ) const = 0;
   // ...
};

template< typename DocumentT >
class DocumentModel : public DocumentConcept
{
 public:
   // ...
   void exportToJSON( /*...*/ ) const override;
   void serialize( ByteStream& bs, /*...*/ ) const override;
   // ...

 private:
   DocumentT document_;
};
```

The DocumentConcept class takes the role of the ShapeConcept base class, while the DocumentModel class template takes the role of the ShapeModel class template. However, this externalized hierarchy exhibits the same problem as the original hierarchy: for all code requiring only the exportToJSON() functionality, it introduces the artificial dependency on ByteStream:

```
void exportDocument( DocumentConcept const& doc )
{
   // ...
   doc.exportToJSON( /* pass necessary arguments */ );
   // ...
}
```

The correct approach would be to separate concerns by segregating the interface into the two orthogonal aspects of JSON export and serialization:

```
class JSONExportable
{
 public:
   // ...
   virtual ~JSONExportable() = default;

   virtual void exportToJSON( /*...*/ ) const = 0;
   // ...
};

class Serializable
{
 public:
   // ...
   virtual ~Serializable() = default;

   virtual void serialize( ByteStream& bs, /*...*/ ) const = 0;
   // ...
};

template< typename DocumentT >
class DocumentModel
   : public JSONExportable
   , public Serializable
{
 public:
   // ...
   void exportToJSON( /*...*/ ) const override;
   void serialize( ByteStream& bs, /*...*/ ) const override;
   // ...

 private:
   DocumentT document_;
};
```

Any function exclusively interested in JSON export can now specifically ask for that functionality:

```
void exportDocument( JSONExportable const& exportable )
{
   // ...
   exportable.exportToJSON( /* pass necessary arguments */ );
```

```
        // ...
}
```

Second, be aware that External Polymorphism, just as the Adapter design pattern, makes it very easy to wrap types that do not fulfill the semantic expectations. Similar to the duck typing example in "Guideline 24: Use Adapters to Standardize Interfaces" on page 198, where we pretended that a turkey is a duck, we also pretended that an int is a shape. All we had to do to fulfill the requirements was provide a free draw() function. Easy. Perhaps too easy. Therefore, keep in mind that the classes used to instantiate the ShapeModel class template (e.g., Circle, Square, etc.) *have* to adhere to the LSP. After all, the ShapeModel class acts just as a wrapper and passes on the requirements defined by the ShapeConcept class to the concrete shapes. Thus, the concrete shapes take the responsibility to properly implement the expected behavior (see "Guideline 6: Adhere to the Expected Behavior of Abstractions" on page 44). Any failure to completely fulfill the expectations may lead to (potentially subtle) misbehavior. Unfortunately, because these requirements have been externalized, it is a little harder to communicate the expected behavior.

However, in the int example it was maybe our own fault to be honest. Perhaps the ShapeConcept base class doesn't really represent an abstraction of a shape. It is reasonable to argue that shapes are more than just drawing. Perhaps we should have named the abstraction Drawable, and the LSP would have been satisfied. Perhaps not. So in the end, it all comes down to the choice of abstraction. Which brings us back to the title of Chapter 2: "The Art of Building Abstractions." No, it isn't easy, but perhaps these examples demonstrate that it is important. Very important. It may be the essence of software design.

In summary, although the External Polymorphism design pattern may not satisfy your expectation in a simple or value-based solution, it must be considered a very important step toward decoupling software entities. From the perspective of reducing dependencies, this design pattern appears to be a key ingredient to loose coupling, and is a marvelous example of the power of separation of concerns. It also gives us one key insight: using this design pattern, you can nonintrusively equip any type with polymorphic behavior, e.g., virtual functions, so *any* type can behave polymorphically, even a simple value type such as int. This realization opens up a completely new, exciting design space, which we will continue to explore in the next chapter.

Guideline 31: Use External Polymorphism for Nonintrusive Runtime Polymorphism

- Apply the External Polymorphism design pattern with the intent to enable the polymorphic treatment of nonpolymorphic types.

- Consider the External Polymorphism design pattern as a key player to achieve loose coupling.

- Exploit the design flexibilities of the externalized inheritance hierarchy.

- Understand the differences between External Polymorphism and Adapter.

- Prefer nonintrusive solutions to intrusive solutions.

CHAPTER 8

The Type Erasure Design Pattern

Separation of concerns and value semantics are two of the essential takeaways from this book that I have mentioned a couple of times by now. In this chapter, these two are beautifully combined into one of the most interesting modern C++ design patterns: Type Erasure. Since this pattern can be considered one of the hottest irons in the fire, in this chapter I will give you a very thorough, in-depth introduction to all aspects of Type Erasure. This, of course, includes all design-specific aspects and a lot of specifics about implementation details.

In "Guideline 32: Consider Replacing Inheritance Hierarchies with Type Erasure" on page 298, I will introduce you to Type Erasure and give you an idea why this design pattern is such a great combination of dependency reduction and value semantics. I will also give you a walkthrough of a basic, owning Type Erasure implementation.

"Guideline 33: Be Aware of the Optimization Potential of Type Erasure" on page 318 is an exception: despite the fact that in this book I primarily focus on dependencies and design aspects, in this one guideline I will entirely focus on performance-related implementation details. I will show you how to apply the *Small Buffer Optimization (SBO)* and how to implement a manual virtual dispatch to speed up your Type Erasure implementation.

In "Guideline 34: Be Aware of the Setup Costs of Owning Type Erasure Wrappers" on page 333, we will investigate the setup costs of the owning Type Erasure implementation. We will find that there is a cost associated with value semantics that sometimes we may not be willing to pay. For this reason, we dare to take a step into the realm of reference semantics and implement a form of nonowning Type Erasure.

Guideline 32: Consider Replacing Inheritance Hierarchies with Type Erasure

There are a couple of recurring pieces of advice throughout this book:

- Minimize dependencies.
- Separate concerns.
- Prefer composition to inheritance.
- Prefer nonintrusive solutions.
- Prefer value semantics over reference semantics.

Used on their own, all of these have very positive effects on the quality of your code. In combination, however, these guidelines prove to be so much better. This is what you have experienced in our discussion about the External Polymorphism design pattern in "Guideline 31: Use External Polymorphism for Nonintrusive Runtime Polymorphism" on page 279. Extracting the polymorphic behavior turned out to be extremely powerful and unlocked an unprecedented level of loose coupling. Still, probably disappointingly, the demonstrated implementation of External Polymorphism did not strike you as a very modern way of solving things. Instead of following the advice to prefer value semantics, the implementation was firmly built on reference semantics: many pointers, many manual allocations, and manual lifetime management.[1] Hence, the missing detail you're waiting for is a value semantics–based implementation of the External Polymorphism design pattern. And I will not keep you waiting anymore: the resulting solution is commonly called *Type Erasure*.[2]

The History of Type Erasure

Before I give you a detailed introduction, let's quickly talk about the history of Type Erasure. "Come on," you argue. "Is this really necessary? I'm dying to finally see how this stuff works." Well, I promise to keep it short. But yes, I feel this is a necessary detail of this discussion for two reasons. First, to demonstrate that we as a community, aside from the circle of the most experienced C++ experts, may have overlooked and ignored this technique for too long. And second, to give some well-deserved credit to the inventor of the technique.

---

1 Yes, I consider the manual use of `std::unique_ptr` manual lifetime management. But of course it could be much worse if we would not reach for the power of RAII.

2 The term Type Erasure is heavily overloaded, as it is used in different programming languages and for many different things. Even within the C++ community, you hear the term being used for various purposes: you might have heard it being used to denote `void*`, pointers-to-base, and `std::variant`. In the context of software design, I consider this a very unfortunate issue. I will address this issue at the end of this guideline.

The Type Erasure design pattern is very often attributed to one of the first and therefore most famous presentations of this technique. At the GoingNative 2013 conference, Sean Parent gave a talk called "Inheritance Is the Base Class of Evil."[3] recapped his experiences with the development of Photoshop and talked about the dangers and disadvantages of inheritance-based implementations. However, he also presented a solution to the inheritance problem, which later came to be known as Type Erasure.

Despite Sean's talk being one of the first recorded, and for that reason probably the most well-known resource about Type Erasure, the technique was used long before that. For instance, Type Erasure was used in several places in the *Boost* libraries (*https://www.boost.org*), for example, by Douglas Gregor for `boost::function` (*https://oreil.ly/XslzJ*). Still, to my best knowledge, the technique was first discussed in a paper by Kevlin Henney in the July-August 2000 edition of the *C++ Report*.[4] In this paper, Kevlin demonstrated Type Erasure with a code example that later evolved into what we today know as C++17's `std::any`. Most importantly, he was the first to elegantly combine several design patterns to form a value semantics–based implementation around a collection of unrelated, nonpolymorphic types.

Since then, a lot of common types have acquired the technique to provide value types for various applications. Some of these types have even found their way into the Standard Library. For instance, we have already seen `std::function`, which represents a value-based abstraction of a callable.[5] I've already mentioned `std::any`, which represents an abstract container-like value for virtually anything (hence the name) but without exposing any functionality:

```
#include <any>
#include <cstdlib>
#include <string>
using namespace std::string_literals;

int main()
{
   std::any a;          // Creating an empty 'any'
   a = 1;               // Storing an 'int' inside the 'any';
   a = "some string"s;  // Replacing the 'int' with a 'std::string'

   // There is nothing we can do with the 'any' except for getting the value back
   std::string s = std::any_cast<std::string>( a );
```

---

3 Sean Parent, "Inheritance Is the Base Class of Evil," GoingNative 2013, YouTube (*https://oreil.ly/COYs2*).

4 Kevlin Henney, "Valued Conversions," *C++ Report*, July-August 2000, CiteSeer (*https://oreil.ly/BPCjV*).

5 For an introduction to `std::function`, see "Guideline 23: Prefer a Value-Based Implementation of Strategy and Command" on page 186.

```
    return EXIT_SUCCESS;
}
```

And then there is std::shared_ptr, which uses Type Erasure to store the assigned deleter:

```
#include <cstdlib>
#include <memory>

int main()
{
   {
      // Creating a 'std::shared_ptr' with a custom deleter
      //   Note that the deleter is not part of the type!
      std::shared_ptr<int> s{ new int{42}, [](int* ptr){ delete ptr; } };
   }
   // The 'std::shared_ptr' is destroyed at the end of the scope,
   //   deleting the 'int' by means of the custom deleter.

   return EXIT_SUCCESS;
}
```

"It appears to be simpler to just provide a second template parameter for the deleter as std::unique_ptr does. Why isn't std::shared_ptr implemented in the same way?" you inquire. Well, the designs of std::shared_ptr and std::unique_ptr are different for very good reasons. The philosophy of std::unique_ptr is to represent nothing but the simplest possible wrapper around a raw pointer: it should be as fast as a raw pointer, and it should have the same size as a raw pointer. For that reason, it is not desirable to store the deleter alongside the managed pointer. Consequently, std::unique_ptr is designed such that for stateless deleters, any size overhead can be avoided. However, unfortunately, this second template parameter is easily overlooked and causes artificial restrictions:

```
// This function takes only unique_ptrs that use the default deleter,
//   and thus is artificially restricted
template< typename T >
void func1( std::unique_ptr<T> ptr );

// This function does not care about the way the resource is cleaned up,
//   and thus is truly generic
template< typename T, typename D >
void func2( std::unique_ptr<T,D> ptr );
```

This kind of coupling is avoided in the design of std::shared_ptr. Since std::shared_ptr has to store many more data items in its so-called control block (that includes the reference count, the weak count, etc.), it has the opportunity to use Type Erasure to literally erase the type of the deleter, removing any kind of possible dependency.

The Type Erasure Design Pattern Explained

"Wow, that truly sounds intriguing. This makes me even more excited to learn about Type Erasure." OK then, here we go. However, please don't expect any magic or revolutionary new ideas. Type Erasure is nothing but a compound design pattern, meaning that it is a very clever and elegant combination of three other design patterns. The three design patterns of choice are External Polymorphism (the key ingredient for achieving the decoupling effect and the nonintrusive nature of Type Erasure; see "Guideline 31: Use External Polymorphism for Nonintrusive Runtime Polymorphism" on page 279), Bridge (the key to creating a value semantics–based implementation; see "Guideline 28: Build Bridges to Remove Physical Dependencies" on page 250), and (optionally) Prototype (required to deal with the copy semantics of the resulting values; see "Guideline 30: Apply Prototype for Abstract Copy Operations" on page 272). These three design patterns form the core of Type Erasure, but of course, keep in mind that different interpretations and implementations exist, mainly to adapt to specific contexts. The point of combining these three design patterns is to create a wrapper type, which represents a loosely coupled, nonintrusive abstraction.

The Type Erasure Design Pattern

Intent: "Provide a value-based, non-intrusive abstraction for an extendable set of unrelated, potentially non-polymorphic types with the same semantic behavior."

The purpose of this formulation is to be as short as possible, and as precise as necessary. However, every detail of this intent carries meaning. Thus, it may be helpful to elaborate:

Value-based
> The intent of Type Erasure is to create value types that may be copyable, movable, and most importantly, easily reasoned about. However, such a value type is not of the same quality as a regular (*https://oreil.ly/aLbCD*) value type; there are some limitations. In particular, Type Erasure works best for unary operations but has its limits for binary operations.

Nonintrusive
> The intent of Type Erasure is to create an external, nonintrusive abstraction based on the example set by the External Polymorphism design pattern. All types providing the behavior expected by the abstraction are automatically supported, without the need to apply any modifications to them.

Extendable, unrelated set of types

Type Erasure is firmly based on object-oriented principles, i.e., it enables you to add types easily. These types, though, should not be connected in any way. They do not have to share common behavior via some base class. Instead, it should be possible to add any fitting type, without any intrusive measure, to this set of types.

Potentially nonpolymorphic

As demonstrated with the External Polymorphism design pattern, types should not have to buy into the set by inheritance. They should also not have to provide virtual functionality on their own, but they should be decoupled from their polymorphic behavior. However, types with base classes or virtual functions are not excluded.

Same semantic behavior

The goal is not to provide an abstraction for all possible types but to provide a semantic abstraction for a set of types that provide the same operations (including same syntax) and adhere to some expected behavior, according to the LSP (see "Guideline 6: Adhere to the Expected Behavior of Abstractions" on page 44). If possible, for any type that does not provide the expected functionality, a compile-time error should be created.

With this formulation of the intent in mind, let's take a look at the dependency graph of Type Erasure (see Figure 8-1). The graph should look very familiar, as the structure of the pattern is dominated by the inherent structure of the External Polymorphism design pattern (see Figure 7-8). The most important difference and addition is the Shape class on the highest level of the architecture. This class serves as a wrapper around the external hierarchy introduced by External Polymorphism. Primarily, since this external hierarchy will not be used directly anymore, but also to reflect the fact that ShapeModel is storing, or "owning," a concrete type, the name of the class template has been adapted to OwningShapeModel.

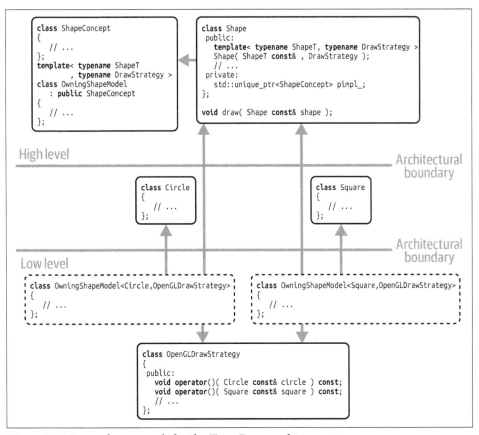

Figure 8-1. Dependency graph for the Type Erasure design pattern

An Owning Type Erasure Implementation

OK, but now, with the structure of Type Erasure in mind, let's take a look at its implementation details. Still, despite the fact that you've seen all the ingredients in action before, the implementation details are not particularly beginner-friendly and are not for the fainthearted. And that is despite the fact that I have picked the simplest Type Erasure implementation I'm aware of. Therefore, I will try to keep everything at a reasonable level and not stray too much into the realm of implementation details. Among other things, this means that I won't try to squeeze out every tiny bit of performance. For instance, I won't use *forwarding references* or avoid dynamic memory allocations. Also, I will favor readability and code clarity. While this may be a disappointment to you, I believe that will save us a lot of headache. However, if you want to dig deeper into the implementation details and optimization options, I recommend taking a look at "Guideline 33: Be Aware of the Optimization Potential of Type Erasure" on page 318.

We again start with the Circle and Square classes:

```
//---- <Circle.h> ----------------

class Circle
{
 public:
    explicit Circle( double radius )
       : radius_( radius )
    {}

    double radius() const { return radius_; }
    /* Several more getters and circle-specific utility functions */

 private:
    double radius_;
    /* Several more data members */
};
```

```
//---- <Square.h> ----------------

class Square
{
 public:
    explicit Square( double side )
       : side_( side )
    {}

    double side() const { return side_; }
    /* Several more getters and square-specific utility functions */

 private:
    double side_;
    /* Several more data members */
};
```

These two classes have not changed since we last encountered them in the discussion of External Polymorphism. But it still pays off to again stress that these two are completely unrelated, do not know about each other, and—most importantly—are non-polymorphic, meaning that they do not inherit from any base class or introduce virtual function on their own.

We have also seen the ShapeConcept and OwningShapeModel classes before, the latter under the name ShapeModel:

```
//---- <Shape.h> ----------------

#include <memory>
#include <utility>

namespace detail {
```

```
class ShapeConcept  ❶
{
 public:
   virtual ~ShapeConcept() = default;
   virtual void draw() const = 0;  ❷
   virtual std::unique_ptr<ShapeConcept> clone() const = 0;  ❸
};

template< typename ShapeT
        , typename DrawStrategy >
class OwningShapeModel : public ShapeConcept  ❹
{
 public:
   explicit OwningShapeModel( ShapeT shape, DrawStrategy drawer )  ❺
      : shape_{ std::move(shape) }
      , drawer_{ std::move(drawer) }
   {}

   void draw() const override { drawer_(shape_); }  ❽

   std::unique_ptr<ShapeConcept> clone() const override
   {
       return std::make_unique<OwningShapeModel>( *this );  ❾
   }

 private:
   ShapeT shape_;  ❻
   DrawStrategy drawer_;  ❼
};

} // namespace detail
```

Next to the name change, there are a couple of other, important differences. For instance, both classes have been moved to the detail namespace. The name of the namespace indicates that these two classes are now becoming implementation details, i.e., they are not intended for direct use anymore.[6] The ShapeConcept class (❶) still introduces the pure virtual function draw() to represent the requirement for drawing a shape (❷). In addition, ShapeConcept now also introduces a pure virtual clone() function (❸). "I know what this is, this is the Prototype design pattern!" you exclaim. Yes, correct. The name clone() is very strongly connected to Prototype and is a strong indication of this design pattern (but not a guarantee). However, although the

---

6 The placement of ShapeConcept and OwningShapeModel in a namespace is purely an implementation detail of this example implementation. Still, as you will see in "Guideline 34: Be Aware of the Setup Costs of Owning Type Erasure Wrappers" on page 333, this choice will come in pretty handy. Alternatively, these two classes can be implemented as nested classes. You will see examples of this in "Guideline 33: Be Aware of the Optimization Potential of Type Erasure" on page 318.

choice of the function name is very reasonable and canonical, allow me to point out explicitly that the choice of the function name for clone(), and also for draw(), is our own: these names are now implementation details and do *not* have any relationship to the names that we require from our ShapeT types. We could as well name them do_draw() and do_clone(), and it would not have any consequence on the ShapeT types. The real requirement on the ShapeT types is defined by the *implementation* of the draw() and clone() functions.

As ShapeConcept is again the base class for the external hierarchy, the draw() function, the clone() function, and the destructor represent the set of requirements for all kinds of shapes. This means that all shapes must provide some drawing behavior—they must be copyable and destructible. Note that these three functions are only requirement choices for this example. In particular, copyability is not a general requirement for all implementations of Type Erasure.

The OwningShapeModel class (❹) again represents the one and only implementation of the ShapeConcept class. As before, OwningShapeModel takes a concrete shape type and a drawing Strategy in its constructor (❺) and uses these to initialize its two data members (❻ and ❼). Since OwningShapeModel inherits from ShapeConcept, it must implement the two pure virtual functions. The draw() function is implemented by applying the given drawing Strategy (❽), while the clone() function is implemented to return an exact copy of the corresponding OwningShapeModel (❾).

 If you're right now thinking, "Oh no, std::make_unique(). That means dynamic memory. Then I can't use that in my code!"—don't worry. std::make_unique() is merely an implementation detail, a choice to keep the example simple. In "Guideline 33: Be Aware of the Optimization Potential of Type Erasure" on page 318, you will see how to avoid dynamic memory with the SBO.

"I'm pretty unimpressed so far. We've barely moved beyond the implementation of the External Polymorphism design pattern." I completely understand the criticism. However, we are just one step away from turning External Polymorphism into Type Erasure, just one step away from switching from reference semantics to value semantics. All we need is a value type, a wrapper around the external hierarchy introduced by ShapeConcept and OwningShapeModel, that handles all the details that we don't want to perform manually: the instantiation of the OwningShapeModel class template, managing pointers, performing allocations, and dealing with lifetime. This wrapper is given in the form of the Shape class:

```
//---- <Shape.h> ----------------

// ...
```

```
class Shape
{
 public:
   template< typename ShapeT
           , typename DrawStrategy >
   Shape( ShapeT shape, DrawStrategy drawer )  ❿
   {
      using Model = detail::OwningShapeModel<ShapeT,DrawStrategy>;  ⓫
      pimpl_ = std::make_unique<Model>( std::move(shape)  ⓬
                                       , std::move(drawer) );
   }

   // ...

 private:
   // ...

   std::unique_ptr<detail::ShapeConcept> pimpl_;  ⓭
};
```

The first, and perhaps most important, detail about the Shape class is the templated constructor (❿). As the first argument, this constructor takes any kind of shape (called ShapeT), and as the second argument, the desired DrawStrategy. To simplify the instantiation of the corresponding detail::OwningShapeModel class template, it proves to be helpful to use a convenient type alias (⓫). This alias is used to instantiate the required model by std::make_unique() (⓬). Both the shape and the drawing Strategy are passed to the new model.

The newly created model is used to initialize the one data member of the Shape class: the pimpl_ (⓭). "I recognize this one, too; this is a Bridge!" you happily announce. Yes, correct again. This is an application of the Bridge design pattern. In the construction, we create a concrete OwningShapeModel based on the actual given types ShapeT and DrawStrategy, but we store it as a pointer to ShapeConcept. By doing this you create a Bridge to the implementation details, a Bridge to the real shape type. However, after the initialization of pimpl_, after the constructor is finished, Shape doesn't remember the actual type. Shape does not have a template parameter or any member function that would reveal the concrete type it stores, and there is no data member that remembers the given type. All it holds is a pointer to the ShapeConcept base class. Thus, its memory of the real shape type has been erased. Hence the name of the design pattern: Type Erasure.

The only thing missing in our Shape class is the functionality required for a true value type: the copy and move operations. Luckily, due to the application of std::unique_ptr, our effort is pretty limited. Since the compiler-generated destructor and the two move operations will work, we only need to deal with the two copy operations:

```
//---- <Shape.h> ----------------

// ...

class Shape
{
 public:
   // ...

   Shape( Shape const& other )      ⑭
      : pimpl_( other.pimpl_->clone() )
   {}

   Shape& operator=( Shape const& other )   ⑮
   {
      // Copy-and-Swap Idiom
      Shape copy( other );
      pimpl_.swap( copy.pimpl_ );
      return *this;
   }

   ~Shape() = default;
   Shape( Shape&& ) = default;
   Shape& operator=( Shape&& ) = default;

 private:
   friend void draw( Shape const& shape )   ⑯
   {
      shape.pimpl_->draw();
   }

   // ...
};
```

The copy constructor (⑭) could be a very difficult function to implement, since we do not know the concrete type of shape stored in the other Shape. However, by providing the clone() function in the ShapeConcept base class, we can ask for an exact copy without needing to know anything about the concrete type. The shortest, most painless, and most convenient way to implement the copy assignment operator (⑮) is to build on the *Copy-and-Swap idiom* (*https://oreil.ly/Pm1uW*).

In addition, the Shape class provides a so-called hidden friend (*https://oreil.ly/ ylXGZ*) called draw() (⑯). This friend function is called a *hidden friend*, since although it's a free function, it is defined within the body of the Shape class. As a friend, it's granted full access to the private data member and will be injected into the surrounding namespace.

"Didn't you say that friends are bad?" you ask. I admit, that's what I said in "Guideline 4: Design for Testability" on page 28. However, I also explicitly stated that hidden friends are OK. In this case, the draw() function is an integral part of the Shape class and definitely a real `friend` (almost part of the family). "But then it should be a member function, right?" you argue. Indeed, that would be a valid alternative. If you like this better, go for it. In this case, my preference is to use a free function, since one of our goals was to reduce dependencies by extracting the `draw()` operation. This goal should also be reflected in the `Shape` implementation. However, since the function requires access to the `pimpl_` data member, and in order to not increase the overload set of `draw()` functions, I implement it as a hidden `friend`.

This is it. All of it. Let's take a look at how beautifully the new functionality works:

```
//---- <Main.cpp> ----------------

#include <Circle.h>
#include <Square.h>
#include <Shape.h>
#include <cstdlib>

int main()
{
   // Create a circle as one representative of a concrete shape type
   Circle circle{ 3.14 };

   // Create a drawing strategy in the form of a lambda
   auto drawer = []( Circle const& c ){ /*...*/ };

   // Combine the shape and the drawing strategy in a 'Shape' abstraction
   // This constructor call will instantiate a 'detail::OwningShapeModel' for
   // the given 'Circle' and lambda types
   Shape shape1( circle, drawer );

   // Draw the shape
   draw( shape1 );   ❶❼

   // Create a copy of the shape by means of the copy constructor
   Shape shape2( shape1 );

   // Drawing the copy will result in the same output
   draw( shape2 );   ❶❽

   return EXIT_SUCCESS;
}
```

We first create `shape1` as an abstraction for a `Circle` and an associated drawing Strategy. This feels easy, right? There's no need to manually allocate and no need to deal with pointers. With the `draw()` function, we're able to draw this `Shape` (❶❼). Directly afterward, we create a copy of the shape. A real copy—a "deep copy," not just the copy of a pointer. Drawing the copy with the `draw()` function will result in the same output (❶❽). Again, this feels good: you can rely on the copy operations of the value type (in this case, the copy constructor), and you do not have to clone() manually.

Pretty amazing, right? And definitely much better than using External Polymorphism manually. I admit that after all these implementation details, it may be a little hard to see it right away, but if you step through the jungle of implementation details, I hope you realize the beauty of this approach: you no longer have to deal with pointers, there are no manual allocations, and you don't have to deal with inheritance hierarchies anymore. All of these details are there, yes, but all evidence is nicely encapsulated within the Shape class. Still, you didn't lose any of the decoupling benefits: you are still able to easily add new types, and the concrete shape types are still oblivious about the drawing behavior. They are only connected to the desired functionality via the Shape constructor.

"I'm wondering," you begin to ask, "Couldn't we make this much easier? I envision a main() function that looks like this":

```
//---- <YourMain.cpp> ----------------

int main()
{
   // Create a circle as one representative of a concrete shape type
   Circle circle{ 3.14 };

   // Bind the circle to some drawing functionality
   auto drawingCircle = [=]() { myCircleDrawer(circle); };

   // Type-erase the circle equipped with drawing behavior
   Shape shape( drawingCircle );

   // Drawing the shape
   draw( shape );

   // ...

   return EXIT_SUCCESS;
}
```

That is a great idea. Remember, you are in charge of all the implementation details of the Type Erasure wrapper and how to bring together types and their operation implementation. If you like this form better, go for it! However, please do not forget that in our Shape example, for the sake of simplicity and code brevity, I have deliberately used only a single functionality with external dependencies (drawing). There could be more functions that introduce dependencies, such as the serialization of shapes. In that case, the lambda approach would not work, as you would need multiple, named functions (e.g., draw() and serialize()). So, ultimately, it depends. It depends on what kind of abstraction your Type Erasure wrapper represents. But whatever implementation you prefer, just make sure that you do not introduce artificial dependencies between the different pieces of functionality and/or code duplication. In other words, remember "Guideline 2: Design for Change" on page 11! That is the reason I favored the solution based on the Strategy design pattern, which you, however, shouldn't consider the true and only solution. On the contrary, you should strive to fully exploit the potential of the loose coupling of Type Erasure.

Analyzing the Shortcomings of the Type Erasure Design Pattern

Despite the beauty of Type Erasure and the large number of benefits that you acquire, especially from a design perspective, I don't pretend that there are no downsides to this design pattern. No, it wouldn't be fair to keep potential disadvantages from you.

The first, and probably most obvious, drawback for you might be the implementation complexity of this pattern. As stated before, I have explicitly kept the implementation details at a reasonable level, which hopefully helped you to get the idea. I hope I have also given you the impression that it is not *so* difficult after all: a basic implementation of Type Erasure can be realized within approximately 30 lines of code. Still, you might feel that it is too complex. Also, as soon as you start to go beyond the basic implementation and consider performance, exception safety, etc., the implementation details indeed become quite tricky very quickly. In these cases, your safest and most convenient option is to use a third-party library instead of dealing with all of these details yourself. Possible libraries include the *dyno* library (*https://oreil.ly/PvVFI*) from Louis Dionne, the *zoo* library (*https://oreil.ly/rB8uj*) from Eduardo Madrid, the *erasure* library (*https://oreil.ly/zKwXF*) from Gašper Ažman, and the *Boost Type Erasure* (*https://oreil.ly/IGNoq*) library from Steven Watanabe.

In the explanation of the intent of Type Erasure, I mentioned the second disadvantage, which is much more important and limiting: although we are now dealing with values that can be copied and moved, using Type Erasure for binary operations is not straightforward. For instance, it is not easily possible to do an equality comparison on these values, as you would expect from regular values:

```
int main()
{
   // ...

   if( shape1 == shape2 ) { /*...*/ }  // Does not compile!

   return EXIT_SUCCESS;
}
```

The reason is that, after all, Shape is only an abstraction from a concrete shape type and only stores a pointer-to-base. As you would deal with exactly the same problem if you used External Polymorphism directly, this is definitely not a new problem in Type Erasure, and you might not even count this as a real disadvantage. Still, while equality comparison is not an expected operation when you're dealing with pointers-to-base, it usually is an expected operation on values.

Comparing Two Type Erasure Wrappers

"Isn't this just a question of exposing the necessary functionality in the interface of Shapes?" you wonder. "For instance, we could simply add an `area()` function to the public interface of shapes and use it to compare two items":

```cpp
bool operator==( Shape const& lhs, Shape const& rhs )
{
   return lhs.area() == rhs.area();
}
```

"This is easy to do. So what am I missing?" I agree that this might be all you need: if two objects are equal if some public properties are equal, then this operator will work for you. In general, the answer would have to be "it depends." In this particular case, it depends on the semantics of the abstraction that the Shape class represents. The question is: when are two Shapes equal? Consider the following example with a Circle and a Square:

```cpp
#include <Circle.h>
#include <Square.h>
#include <cstdlib>

int main()
{
   Shape shape1( Circle{3.14} );
   Shape shape2( Square{2.71} );

   if( shape1 == shape2 ) { /*...*/ }

   return EXIT_SUCCESS;
}
```

When are these two Shapes equal? Are they equal if their areas are equal, or are they equal if the instances behind the abstraction are equal, meaning that both Shapes are of the same type and have the same properties? It depends. In the same spirit, I could ask the question, when are two Persons equal? Are they equal if their first names are equal? Or are they equal if all of their characteristics are equal? It depends on the desired semantics. And while the first comparison is easily done, the second one is not. In a general case, I assume that the second situation is far more likely to be the desired semantics, and therefore I argue that using Type Erasure for equality comparison and more generally for binary operations is not straightforward.

Note, however, that I did not say that equality comparison is impossible. Technically, you can make it work, although it turns out to be a rather ugly solution. Therefore, you have to promise not to tell anyone that you got this idea from me. "You just made me even more curious," you smile whimsically. OK, so here it is:

```cpp
//---- <Shape.h> ----------------

// ...

namespace detail {

class ShapeConcept
{
 public:
   // ...
   virtual bool isEqual( ShapeConcept const* c ) const = 0;
};

template< typename ShapeT
        , typename DrawStrategy >
class OwningShapeModel : public ShapeConcept
{
 public:
   // ...

   bool isEqual( ShapeConcept const* c ) const override
   {
      using Model = OwningShapeModel<ShapeT,DrawStrategy>;
      auto const* model = dynamic_cast<Model const*>( c );   ⓳
      return ( model && shape_ == model->shape_ );
   }

 private:
   // ...
};

} // namespace detail


class Shape
{
   // ...

 private:
   friend bool operator==( Shape const& lhs, Shape const& rhs )
   {
      return lhs.pimpl_->isEqual( rhs.pimpl_.get() );
   }

   friend bool operator!=( Shape const& lhs, Shape const& rhs )
   {
      return !( lhs == rhs );
   }
```

```
    // ...
};


//---- <Circle.h> ---------------

class Circle
{
    // ...
};

bool operator==( Circle const& lhs, Circle const& rhs )
{
    return lhs.radius() == rhs.radius();
}


//---- <Square.h> ---------------

class Square
{
    // ...
};

bool operator==( Square const& lhs, Square const& rhs )
{
    return lhs.side() == rhs.side();
}
```

To make equality comparison work, you could use a dynamic_cast (**❶❾**). However, this implementation of equality comparison holds two severe disadvantages. First, as you saw in "Guideline 18: Beware the Performance of Acyclic Visitor" on page 133, a dynamic_cast does most certainly not count as a fast operation. Hence, you would have to pay a considerable runtime cost for every comparison. Second, in this implementation, you can only successfully compare two Shapes if they are equipped with the same DrawStrategy. While this might be reasonable in one context, it might also be considered an unfortunate limitation in another context. The only solution I am aware of is to return to std::function to store the drawing Strategy, which, however, would result in another performance penalty.[7] In summary, depending on the context, equality comparison may be possible, but it's usually neither easy nor cheap to accomplish. This is evidence to my earlier statement that Type Erasure doesn't support binary operations.

---

7 Refer to "Guideline 31: Use External Polymorphism for Nonintrusive Runtime Polymorphism" on page 279 for the implementation based on std::function.

Interface Segregation of Type Erasure Wrappers

"What about the Interface Segregation Principle (ISP)?" you ask. "While using External Polymorphism, it was easy to separate concerns in the base class. It appears we've lost this ability, right?" Excellent question. So you remember my example with the `JSONExportable` and `Serializable` base classes in "Guideline 31: Use External Polymorphism for Nonintrusive Runtime Polymorphism" on page 279. Indeed, with Type Erasure we are no longer able to use the hidden base class, only the abstracting value type. Therefore, it may appear as if the ISP is out of reach:

```
class Document  // Type-erased 'Document'
{
 public:
   // ...
   void exportToJSON( /*...*/ ) const;
   void serialize( ByteStream& bs, /*...*/ ) const;
   // ...
};

// Artificial coupling to 'ByteStream', although only the JSON export is needed
void exportDocument( Document const& doc )
{
   // ...
   doc.exportToJSON( /* pass necessary arguments */ );
   // ...
}
```

However, fortunately, this impression is incorrect. You can easily adhere to the ISP by providing several type-erased abstractions:[8]

```
Document doc = /*...*/;  // Type-erased 'Document'
doc.exportToJSON( /* pass necessary arguments */ );
doc.serialize( /* pass necessary arguments */ );

JSONExportable jdoc = doc;  // Type-erased 'JSONExportable'
jdoc.exportToJSON( /* pass necessary arguments */ );

Serializable sdoc = doc;  // Type-erased 'Serializable'
sdoc.serialize( /* pass necessary arguments */ );
```

Before considering this, take a look at "Guideline 34: Be Aware of the Setup Costs of Owning Type Erasure Wrappers" on page 333.

"Apart from the implementation complexity and the restriction to unary operations, there seem to be no disadvantages. Well, then, I have to say this is amazing stuff indeed! The benefits clearly outweigh the drawbacks." Well, of course it always depends, meaning that in a specific context some of these issues might cause some

---

8 Many thanks to Arthur O'Dwyer for providing this example.

pain. But I agree that, altogether, Type Erasure proves to be a very valuable design pattern. From a design perspective, you've gained a formidable level of decoupling, which will definitely lead to less pain when changing or extending your software. However, although this is already fascinating, there's more. I've mentioned performance a couple of times but haven't yet shown any performance numbers. So let's take a look at the performance results.

Performance Benchmarks

Before showing you the performance results for Type Erasure, let me remind you about the benchmark scenario that we also used to benchmark the Visitor and Strategy solutions (see Table 4-2 in "Guideline 17: Consider std::variant for Implementing Visitor" on page 122 and Table 5-1 in "Guideline 23: Prefer a Value-Based Implementation of Strategy and Command" on page 186). This time I have extended the benchmark with a Type Erasure solution based on the OwningShapeModel implementation. For the benchmark, we are still using four different kinds of shapes (circles, squares, ellipses, and rectangles). And again, I'm running 25,000 translate operations on 10,000 randomly created shapes. I use both GCC 11.1 and Clang 11.1, and for both compilers, I'm adding only the -O3 and -DNDEBUG compilation flags. The platform I'm using is macOS Big Sur (version 11.4) on an 8-Core Intel Core i7 with 3.8 GHz, 64 GB of main memory.

Table 8-1 shows the performance numbers. For your convenience, I reproduced the performance results from the Strategy benchmarks. After all, the Strategy design pattern is the solution that is aiming at the same design space. The most interesting line, though, is the last line. It shows the performance result for the Type Erasure design pattern.

Table 8-1. Performance results for the Type Erasure implementations

Type Erasure implementation	GCC 11.1	Clang 11.1
Object-oriented solution	1.5205 s	1.1480 s
std::function	2.1782 s	1.4884 s
Manual implementation of std::function	1.6354 s	1.4465 s
Classic Strategy	1.6372 s	1.4046 s
Type Erasure	1.5298 s	1.1561 s

"Looks very interesting. Type Erasure seems to be pretty fast. Apparently only the object-oriented solution is faster." Yes. For Clang, the performance of the object-oriented solution is a little better. But only a little. However, please remember that the object-oriented solution does not decouple anything: the draw() function is implemented as a virtual member function in the Shape hierarchy, and thus you experience heavy coupling to the drawing functionality. While this may come with little performance overhead, from a design perspective, this is a worst-case scenario. Taking this into account, the performance numbers of Type Erasure are truly marvelous: it performs between 6% and 20% better than any Strategy implementation. Thus, Type Erasure not only provides the strongest decoupling but also performs better than all the other attempts to reduce coupling.[9]

A Word About Terminology

In summary, Type Erasure is an amazing approach to achieve both efficient and loosely coupled code. While it may have a few limitations and disadvantages, the one thing you probably cannot ignore easily is the complex implementation details. For that reason, many people, including me and Eric Niebler, feel that Type Erasure should become a language feature:[10]

> If I could go back in time and had the power to change C++, rather than adding virtual functions, I would add language support for type erasure and concepts. Define a single-type concept, automatically generate a type-erasing wrapper for it.

There is more to be done, though, to establish Type Erasure as a real design pattern. I have introduced Type Erasure as a compound design pattern built from External Polymorphism, Bridge, and Prototype. I've introduced it as a value-based technique for providing strong decoupling of a set of types from their associated operations. However, unfortunately, you might see other "forms" of Type Erasure: over time, the term *Type Erasure* has been misused and abused for all kinds of techniques and concepts. For instance, sometimes people refer to a void* as Type Erasure. Rarely, you also hear about Type Erasure in the context of inheritance hierarchies, or more specifically a pointer-to-base. And finally, you also might hear about Type Erasure in the context of std::variant.[11]

The std::variant example especially demonstrates how deeply flawed this overuse of the term *Type Erasure* really is. While External Polymorphism, the main design pattern behind Type Erasure, is about enabling you to add new types, the Visitor design pattern and its modern implementation as std::variant are about adding new operations (see "Guideline 15: Design for the Addition of Types or Operations" on page 102). From a software design perspective, these two solutions are completely

---

9 Again, please don't consider these performance numbers the perfect truth. These are the performance results on my machine and my implementation. Your results will differ for sure. However, the takeaway is that Type Erasure performs really well and might perform even better if we take the many optimization options into account (see "Guideline 33: Be Aware of the Optimization Potential of Type Erasure" on page 318).

10 Eric Niebler on Twitter (*https://oreil.ly/SXeni*), June 19, 2020.

11 For an introduction of std::variant, see "Guideline 17: Consider std::variant for Implementing Visitor" on page 122.

orthogonal to each other: while Type Erasure truly decouples from concrete types and erases type information, the template arguments of `std::variant` reveal all possible alternatives and therefore make you depend on these types. Using the same term for both of them results in exactly zero information conveyed when using the term *Type Erasure* and generates these types of comments: "I would suggest we use Type Erasure to solve this problem." "Could you please be more specific? Do you want to add types or operations?" As such, the term would not fulfill the qualities of a design pattern; it wouldn't carry any intent. Therefore, it would be useless.

To give Type Erasure its well-earned place in the hall of design patterns and to give it any meaning, consider using the term only for the intent discussed in this guideline.

Guideline 32: Consider Replacing Inheritance Hierarchies with Type Erasure

- Apply the Type Erasure design pattern with the intent to provide a value-based, nonintrusive abstraction for an extendable set of unrelated, potentially nonpolymorphic types with the same semantic behavior.

- Consider Type Erasure as a compound design pattern, built from the External Polymorphism, Bridge, and Prototype design patterns.

- Understand the advantages of Type Erasure, but also keep in mind its limitations.

- Use the term Type Erasure only to communicate its intent as a design pattern that allows the easy addition of types supporting a fixed set of operations.

Guideline 33: Be Aware of the Optimization Potential of Type Erasure

The primary focus of this book is software design. Therefore, all this talk about structuring software, about design principles, about tools for managing dependencies and abstractions, and, of course, all the information on design patterns is at the center of interest. Still, I've mentioned a few times that performance is important. *Very* important! After all, C++ is a performance-centric programming language. Therefore, I now make an exception: this guideline is devoted to performance. Yes, I'm serious: no talk about dependencies, (almost) no examples for separation of concerns, no value semantics. Just performance. "Finally, some performance stuff—great!" you cheer. However, be aware of the consequences: this guideline is pretty heavy on implementation details. And as it is in C++, mentioning one detail requires you to also deal with two more details, and so you are pretty quickly sucked into the realm of implementation details. To avoid that (and to keep my publisher happy), I will not elaborate on every implementation detail or demonstrate all the alternatives. I will, however, give additional references that should help you to dig deeper.[12]

In "Guideline 32: Consider Replacing Inheritance Hierarchies with Type Erasure" on page 298, you saw great performance numbers for our basic, unoptimized Type Erasure implementation. However, since we are now in possession of a value type and a wrapper class, not just a pointer, we have gained a multitude of opportunities to speed up performance. This is why we will take a look at two options to improve performance: the SBO and manual virtual dispatch.

Small Buffer Optimization

Let's start our quest to speed up the performance of our Type Erasure implementation. One of the first things that usually comes to mind when talking about performance is optimizing memory allocations. This is because acquiring and freeing dynamic memory can be very *slooowww* and nondeterministic. And for real: optimizing memory allocations can make all the difference between slow and lightning fast.

However, there is a second reason to look into memory. In "Guideline 32: Consider Replacing Inheritance Hierarchies with Type Erasure" on page 298, I might have accidentally given you the impression that we need dynamic memory to pull off Type Erasure. Indeed, one of the initial implementation details in our first `Shape` class was the unconditional dynamic memory allocation in the constructor and `clone()` function, independent of the size of the given object, so for both small and large objects, we would always perform a dynamic memory allocation with `std::make_unique()`. This choice is limiting, not just because of performance, in particular for small objects, but also because in certain environments dynamic memory is not available. Therefore, I should demonstrate to you that there's a lot you can do with respect to memory. In fact, you are in full control of memory management! Since you are using a value type, a wrapper, you can deal with memory in any way you see fit. One of the many options is to completely rely on in-class memory and emit a compile-time error if objects are too large. Alternatively, you might switch between in-class and dynamic memory, depending on the size of the stored object. Both of these are made possible by the SBO.

To give you an idea of how SBO works, let's take a look at a `Shape` implementation that never allocates dynamically but uses only in-class memory:

```
#include <array>
#include <cstdlib>
#include <memory>
```

---

12 You should avoid going too deep, though, as you probably remember what happened to the dwarves of Moria who dug too deep...

```
template< size_t Capacity = 32U, size_t Alignment = alignof(void*) >  ❷
class Shape
{
 public:
   // ...

 private:
   // ...

   Concept* pimpl()  ❸
   {
      return reinterpret_cast<Concept*>( buffer_.data() );
   }

   Concept const* pimpl() const  ❹
   {
      return reinterpret_cast<Concept const*>( buffer_.data() );
   }

   alignas(Alignment) std::array<std::byte,Capacity> buffer_;  ❶
};
```

This Shape class does not store std::unique_ptr anymore, but instead owns an array of properly aligned bytes (❶).[13] To give users of Shape the flexibility to adjust both the capacity and the alignment of the array, you can provide the two nontype template parameters, Capacity and Alignment, to the Shape class (❷).[14] While this improves the flexibility to adjust to different circumstances, the disadvantage of that approach is that this turns the Shape class into a class template. As a consequence, all functions that use this abstraction will likely turn into function templates. This may be undesirable, for instance, because you might have to move code from source files into header files. However, be aware that this is just one of many possibilities. As stated before, you are in full control.

To conveniently work with the std::byte array, we add a pair of pimpl() functions (named based on the fact that this still realizes the Bridge design pattern, just using in-class memory) (❸ and ❹). "Oh no, a reinterpret_cast!" you say. "Isn't this super dangerous?" You are correct; in general, a reinterpret_cast should be considered potentially dangerous. However, in this particular case, we are backed up by the C++ standard (*https://oreil.ly/HKWCv*), which explains that what we are doing here is perfectly safe.

---

13 Alternatively, you could use an array of bytes, e.g., std::byte[Capacity] or std::aligned_storage (*https://oreil.ly/nE5SK*). The advantage of std::array is that it enables you to copy the buffer (if that is applicable!).

14 Note that the choice for the default arguments for Capacity and Alignment are reasonable but still arbitrary. You can, of course, use different defaults that best fit the properties of the expected actual types.

As you probably expect by now, we also need to introduce an external inheritance hierarchy based on the External Polymorphism design pattern. This time we realize this hierarchy in the `private` section of the `Shape` class. Not because this is better or more suited for this `Shape` implementation, but for the sole reason to show you another alternative:

```cpp
template< size_t Capacity = 32U, size_t Alignment = alignof(void*) >
class Shape
{
 public:
   // ...

 private:
   struct Concept
   {
      virtual ~Concept() = default;
      virtual void draw() const = 0;
      virtual void clone( Concept* memory ) const = 0;   ❺
      virtual void move( Concept* memory ) = 0;   ❻
   };

   template< typename ShapeT, typename DrawStrategy >
   struct OwningModel : public Concept
   {
      OwningModel( ShapeT shape, DrawStrategy drawer )
         : shape_( std::move(shape) )
         , drawer_( std::move(drawer) )
      {}

      void draw() const override
      {
         drawer_( shape_ );
      }

      void clone( Concept* memory ) const override   ❺
      {
         std::construct_at( static_cast<OwningModel*>(memory), *this );

         // or:
         // auto* ptr =
         //    const_cast<void*>(static_cast<void const volatile*>(memory));
         // ::new (ptr) OwningModel( *this );
      }

      void move( Concept* memory ) override   ❻
      {
         std::construct_at( static_cast<OwningModel*>(memory), std::move(*this) );

         // or:
         // auto* ptr =
         //    const_cast<void*>(static_cast<void const volatile*>(memory));
```

```
    // ::new (ptr) OwningModel( std::move(*this) );
  }

  ShapeT shape_;
  DrawStrategy drawer_;
};

// ...

  alignas(Alignment) std::array<std::byte,Capacity> buffer_;
};
```

The first interesting detail in this context is the clone() function (❺). As clone() carries the responsibility of creating a copy, it needs to be adapted to the in-class memory. So instead of creating a new Model via std::make_unique(), it creates a new Model in place via std::construct_at(). Alternatively, you could use a placement new (*https://oreil.ly/6G3bn*) to create the copy at the given memory location.[15]

"Wow, wait a second! That's a pretty tough piece of code to swallow. What's with all these casts? Are they really necessary?" I admit, these lines are a little challenging. Therefore, I should explain them in detail. The good old approach to creating an instance in place is via placement new. However, using new always carries the danger of someone (inadvertently or maliciously) providing a replacement for the class-specific new operator. To avoid any kind of problem and reliably construct an object in place, the given address is first converted to void const volatile* via a static_cast and then to void* via a const_cast. The resulting address is passed to the global placement new operator. Indeed, not the most obvious piece of code. Therefore, it is advisable to use the C++20 algorithm std::construct_at(): it provides you with exactly the same functionality but with a significantly nicer syntax.

However, we need one more function: clone() is concerned only with copy operations. It doesn't apply to move operations. For that reason, we extend the Concept with a pure virtual move() function and consequently implement it in the OwningModel class template (❻).

"Is this really necessary? We're using in-class memory, which cannot be *moved* to another instance of Shape. What's the point of that move()?" Well, you are correct that we can't move the memory itself from one object to another, but we can still move the shape stored inside. Thus, the move() function moves an OwningModel from one buffer to another instead of copying it.

---

15 You might not have seen a placement new before. If that's the case, rest assured that this form of new doesn't perform any memory allocation, but only calls a constructor to create an object at the specified address. The only syntactic difference is that you provide an additional pointer argument to new.

The clone() and move() functions are used in the copy constructor (❼), the copy assignment operator (❽), the move constructor (❾), and the move assignment operator of Shape (❿):

```
template< size_t Capacity = 32U, size_t Alignment = alignof(void*) >
class Shape
{
 public:
   // ...

   Shape( Shape const& other )
   {
      other.pimpl()->clone( pimpl() );   ❼
   }

   Shape& operator=( Shape const& other )
   {
      // Copy-and-Swap Idiom
      Shape copy( other );   ❽
      buffer_.swap( copy.buffer_ );
      return *this;
   }

   Shape( Shape&& other ) noexcept
   {
      other.pimpl()->move( pimpl() );   ❾
   }

   Shape& operator=( Shape&& other ) noexcept
   {
      // Copy-and-Swap Idiom
      Shape copy( std::move(other) );   ❿
      buffer_.swap( copy.buffer_ );
      return *this;
   }

   ~Shape()   ⓫
   {
      std::destroy_at( pimpl() );
      // or: pimpl()->~Concept();
   }

 private:
   // ...

   alignas(Alignment) std::array<std::byte,Capacity> buffer_;
};
```

Definitely noteworthy to mention is the destructor of Shape (❶). Since we manually create an OwningModel within the byte buffer by std::construct_at() or a placement new, we are also responsible for explicitly calling a destructor. The easiest and most elegant way of doing that is to use the C++17 algorithm std::destroy_at() (*https://oreil.ly/2FNtm*). Alternatively, you can explicitly call the Concept destructor.

The last, but essential, detail of Shape is the templated constructor:

```cpp
template< size_t Capacity = 32U, size_t Alignment = alignof(void*) >
class Shape
{
 public:
   template< typename ShapeT, typename DrawStrategy >
   Shape( ShapeT shape, DrawStrategy drawer )
   {
      using Model = OwningModel<ShapeT,DrawStrategy>;

      static_assert( sizeof(Model) <= Capacity, "Given type is too large" );
      static_assert( alignof(Model) <= Alignment, "Given type is misaligned" );

      std::construct_at( static_cast<Model*>(pimpl())
                             , std::move(shape), std::move(drawer) );
      // or:
      // auto* ptr =
      //    const_cast<void*>(static_cast<void const volatile*>(pimpl()));
      // ::new (ptr) Model( std::move(shape), std::move(drawer) );
   }

   // ...

 private:
   // ...
};
```

After a pair of compile-time checks that the required OwningModel fits into the in-class buffer and adheres to the alignment restrictions, an OwningModel is instantiated into the in-class buffer by std::construct_at().

With this implementation in hand, we now adapt and rerun the performance benchmark from "Guideline 32: Consider Replacing Inheritance Hierarchies with Type Erasure" on page 298. We run exactly the same benchmark, this time without allocating dynamic memory inside Shape and without fragmenting the memory with many, tiny allocations. As expected, the performance results are impressive (see Table 8-2).

Table 8-2. *Performance results for the Type Erasure implementations with SBO*

Type Erasure implementation	GCC 11.1	Clang 11.1
Object-oriented solution	1.5205 s	1.1480 s
`std::function`	2.1782 s	1.4884 s
Manual implementation of `std::function`	1.6354 s	1.4465 s
Classic Strategy	1.6372 s	1.4046 s
Type Erasure	1.5298 s	1.1561 s
Type Erasure (SBO)	1.3591 s	1.0348 s

"Wow, this is fast. This is…well, let me do the math…amazing, roughly 20% faster than the fastest Strategy implementation, and even faster than the object-oriented solution." It is, indeed. Very impressive, right? Still, you should remember that these are the numbers that I got on my system. Your numbers will be different, almost certainly. But even though your numbers might not be the same, the general takeaway is that there is a lot of potential to optimize performance by dealing with memory allocations.

However, while the performance is extraordinary, we've lost a lot of flexibility: only `OwningModel` instantiations that are smaller or equal to the specified `Capacity` can be stored inside `Shape`. Bigger models are excluded. This brings me back to the idea that we could switch between in-class and dynamic memory depending on the size of the given shape: small shapes are stored inside an in-class buffer, while large shapes are allocated dynamically. You could now go ahead and update the implementation of `Shape` to use both kinds of memory. However, at this point it's probably a good idea to point out one of our most important design principles again: separation of concerns. Instead of squeezing all logic and functionality into the `Shape` class, it would be easier and (much) more flexible to separate the implementation details and implement `Shape` with policy-based design (see "Guideline 19: Use Strategy to Isolate How Things Are Done" on page 140):

```
template< typename StoragePolicy >
class Shape;
```

The `Shape` class template is rewritten to accept a `StoragePolicy`. Via this policy, you would be able to specify from outside how the class should acquire memory. And of course, you would perfectly adhere to SRP and OCP. One such storage policy could be the `DynamicStorage` policy class:

```
#include <utility>

struct DynamicStorage
{
   template< typename T, typename... Args >
   T* create( Args&&... args ) const
   {
```

```
        return new T( std::forward<Args>( args )... );
    }

    template< typename T >
    void destroy( T* ptr ) const noexcept
    {
        delete ptr;
    }
};
```

As the name suggests, `DynamicPolicy` would acquire memory dynamically, for instance via `new`. Alternatively, if you have stronger requirements, you could build on `std::aligned_alloc()` (*https://oreil.ly/oIP3K*) or similar functionality to provide dynamic memory with a specified alignment. Similarly to `DynamicStorage`, you could provide an `InClassStorage` policy:

```
#include <array>
#include <cstddef>
#include <memory>
#include <utility>

template< size_t Capacity, size_t Alignment >
struct InClassStorage
{
    template< typename T, typename... Args >
    T* create( Args&&... args ) const
    {
        static_assert( sizeof(T) <= Capacity, "The given type is too large" );
        static_assert( alignof(T) <= Alignment, "The given type is misaligned" );

        T* memory = const_cast<T*>(reinterpret_cast<T const*>(buffer_.data()));
        return std::construct_at( memory, std::forward<Args>( args )... );

        // or:
        // void* const memory = static_cast<void*>(buffer_.data());
        // return ::new (memory) T( std::forward<Args>( args )... );
    }

    template< typename T >
    void destroy( T* ptr ) const noexcept
    {
        std::destroy_at(ptr);
        // or: ptr->~T();
    }

    alignas(Alignment) std::array<std::byte,Capacity> buffer_;
};
```

All of these policy classes provide the same interface: a `create()` function to instantiate an object of type `T` and a `destroy()` function to do whatever is necessary to clean up. This interface is used by the Shape class to trigger construction and destruction, for instance, in its templated constructor (**12**)[16] and in the destructor (**13**):

```cpp
template< typename StoragePolicy >
class Shape
{
 public:
   template< typename ShapeT >
   Shape( ShapeT shape )
   {
      using Model = OwningModel<ShapeT>;
      pimpl_ = policy_.template create<Model>( std::move(shape) );   12
   }

   ~Shape() { policy_.destroy( pimpl_ ); }   13

   // ... All other member functions, in particular the
   //     special members functions, are not shown

 private:
   // ...
   [[no_unique_address]] StoragePolicy policy_{};   14
   Concept* pimpl_{};
};
```

The last detail that should not be left unnoticed is the data members (**14**): the Shape class now stores an instance of the given StoragePolicy and, do not be alarmed, a *raw* pointer to its Concept. Indeed, there is no need to store std::unique_ptr anymore, since we are manually destroying the object in our own destructor again. You might also notice the [[no_unique_address]] attribute (*https://oreil.ly/5gF5n*) on the storage policy. This C++20 feature gives you the opportunity to save the memory for the storage policy. If the policy is empty, the compiler is now allowed to not reserve any memory for the data member. Without this attribute, it would be necessary to reserve at least a single byte for policy_, but likely more bytes due to alignment restrictions.

In summary, SBO is an effective and one of the most interesting optimizations for a Type Erasure implementation. For that reason, many standard types, such as std::function and std::any, use some form of SBO. Unfortunately, the C++ Standard Library specification doesn't *require* the use of SBO. This is why you can only hope that SBO is used; you can't count on it. However, because performance is so important and because SBO plays such a decisive role, there are already proposals out

---

16 As a reminder, since you might not see this syntax often: the template keyword in the constructor is necessary because we are trying to call a function template on a dependent name (a name whose meaning depends on a template parameter). Therefore, you have to make it clear to the compiler that the following is the beginning of a template argument list and not a less-than comparison.

there that also suggest standardizing the types `inplace_function` and `inplace_any`. Time will tell if these find their way into the Standard Library.

Manual Implementation of Function Dispatch

"Wow, this will prove useful. Is there anything else I can do to improve the performance of my Type Erasure implementation?" you ask. Oh yes, you can do more. There is a second potential performance optimization. This time we try to improve the performance of the virtual functions. And yes, I'm talking about the virtual functions that are introduced by the external inheritance hierarchy, i.e., by the External Polymorphism design pattern.

"How should we be able to optimize the performance of virtual functions? Isn't this something that is completely up to the compiler?" Absolutely, you're correct. However, I am not talking about fiddling with backend, compiler-specific implementation details, but about replacing the virtual functions with something more efficient. And that is indeed possible. Remember that a virtual function is nothing but a function pointer that is stored inside a virtual function table. Every type with at least one virtual function has such a virtual function table. However, there is only one virtual function table for each type. In other words, this table is not stored inside every instance. So in order to connect the virtual function table with every instance of that type, the class stores an additional, hidden data member, which we commonly call the `vptr` and which is a raw pointer to the virtual function table.

When you call a virtual function, you first go through the `vptr` to fetch the virtual function table. Once you're there, you can grab the corresponding function pointer from the virtual function table and call it. Therefore, in total, a virtual function call entails two indirections: the `vptr` and the pointer to the actual function. For that reason, roughly speaking, a virtual function call is twice as expensive as a regular, noninline function call.

These two indirections provide us with the opportunity for optimization: we can in fact reduce the number of indirections to just one. To achieve that, we will employ an optimization strategy that works fairly often: we'll trade space for speed. What we will do is implement the virtual dispatch manually by storing the virtual function pointers inside the `Shape` class. The following code snippet already gives you a pretty good idea of the details:

```
//---- <Shape.h> ----------------

#include <cstddef>
#include <memory>

class Shape
{
 public:
```

```
    // ...

  private:
    // ...

    template< typename ShapeT
            , typename DrawStrategy >
    struct OwningModel  ⓕ
    {
        OwningModel( ShapeT value, DrawStrategy drawer )
           : shape_( std::move(value) )
           , drawer_( std::move(drawer) )
        {}

        ShapeT shape_;
        DrawStrategy drawer_;
    };

    using DestroyOperation = void(void*);    ⓖ
    using DrawOperation    = void(void*);    ⓗ
    using CloneOperation   = void*(void*);   ⓘ

    std::unique_ptr<void,DestroyOperation*> pimpl_;   ⓙ
    DrawOperation*  draw_ { nullptr };                ⓚ
    CloneOperation* clone_{ nullptr };               ⓛ
};
```

Since we are replacing *all* virtual functions, even the virtual destructor, there's no need for a Concept base class anymore. Consequently, the external hierarchy is reduced to just the OwningModel class template (ⓕ), which still acts as storage for a specific kind of shape (ShapeT) and DrawStrategy. Still, it meets the same fate: all virtual functions are removed. The only remaining details are the constructor and the data members.

The virtual functions are replaced by manual function pointers. Since the syntax for function pointers is not the most pleasant to use, we add a couple of function type aliases for our convenience:[17] DestroyOperation represents the former virtual destructor (ⓖ), DrawOperation represents the former virtual draw() function (ⓗ), and CloneOperation represents the former virtual clone() function (ⓘ). Destroy Operation is used to configure the Deleter of the pimpl_ data member (ⓙ) (and yes, as such it acts as a Strategy). The latter two, DrawOperation and CloneOperation, are

---

17 Some people consider function pointers to be the best feature of C++. In his lightning talk, "The Very Best Feature of C++" (*https://oreil.ly/hq15H*), James McNellis demonstrates their syntactic beauty and enormous flexibility. Please do not take this too seriously, though, but rather as a humorous demonstration of a C++ imperfection.

used for the two additional function pointer data members, draw_ and clone_ (❷⓪ and ❷①).

"Oh no, void*s! Isn't that an archaic and super dangerous way of doing things?" you gasp. OK, I admit that without explanation it looks *very* suspicious. However, stay with me, I promise that everything will be perfectly fine and type safe. The key to making this work now lies in the initialization of these function pointers. They are initialized in the templated constructor of the Shape class:

```cpp
//---- <Shape.h> ----------------

// ...

class Shape
{
 public:
   template< typename ShapeT
           , typename DrawStrategy >
   Shape( ShapeT shape, DrawStrategy drawer )
      : pimpl_(        ❷❷
            new OwningModel<ShapeT,DrawStrategy>( std::move(shape)
                                               , std::move(drawer) )
          , []( void* shapeBytes ){        ❷❸
               using Model = OwningModel<ShapeT,DrawStrategy>;
               auto* const model = static_cast<Model*>(shapeBytes);   ❷❹
               delete model;        ❷❺
            } )
      , draw_(     ❷❻
            []( void* shapeBytes ){
               using Model = OwningModel<ShapeT,DrawStrategy>;
               auto* const model = static_cast<Model*>(shapeBytes);
               (model->drawer_)( model->shape_ );
            } )
      , clone_(        ❷❼
            []( void* shapeBytes ) -> void* {
               using Model = OwningModel<ShapeT,DrawStrategy>;
               auto* const model = static_cast<Model*>(shapeBytes);
               return new Model( *model );
            } )
   {}

   // ...

 private:
   // ...
};
```

Let's focus on the pimpl_ data member. It is initialized both by a pointer to the newly instantiated OwningModel (❷❷) and by a stateless lambda expression (❷❸). You may remember that a stateless lambda is implicitly convertible to a function pointer. This language guarantee is what we use to our advantage: we directly pass the lambda as the deleter to the constructor of unique_ptr, force the compiler to apply the implicit conversion to a DestroyOperation*, and thus bind the lambda function to the std::unique_ptr.

"OK, I get the point: the lambda can be used to initialize the function pointer. But how does it work? What does it do?" Well, also remember that we are creating this lambda inside the templated constructor. That means that at this point we are fully aware of the actual type of the passed ShapeT and DrawStrategy. Thus, the lambda is generated with the knowledge of which type of OwningModel is instantiated and stored inside the pimpl_. Eventually it will be called with a void*, i.e., by the address of some OwningModel. However, based on its knowledge about the actual type of OwningModel, it can first of all perform a static_cast from void* to OwningModel<ShapeT,DrawStrategy>* (❷❹). While in most other contexts this kind of cast would be suspicious and would likely be a wild guess, in this context it is perfectly type safe: we can be certain about the correct type of OwningModel. Therefore, we can use the resulting pointer to trigger the correct cleanup behavior (❷❺).

The initialization of the draw_ and clone_ data members is very similar (❷❻ and ❷❼). The only difference is, of course, the action performed by the lambdas: they perform the correct actions to draw the shape and to create a copy of the model, respectively.

I know, this may take some time to digest. But we are almost done; the only missing detail is the special member functions. For the destructor and the two move operations, we can again ask for the compiler-generated default. However, we have to deal with the copy constructor and copy assignment operator ourselves:

```
//---- <Shape.h> ----------------

// ...

class Shape
{
 public:
   // ...

   Shape( Shape const& other )
      : pimpl_( other.clone_( other.pimpl_.get() ), other.pimpl_.get_deleter() )
      , draw_ ( other.draw_ )
      , clone_( other.clone_ )
   {}

   Shape& operator=( Shape const& other )
   {
      // Copy-and-Swap Idiom
      using std::swap;
      Shape copy( other );
      swap( pimpl_, copy.pimpl_ );
      swap( draw_, copy.draw_ );
```

```
    swap( clone_, copy.clone_ );
    return *this;
}

~Shape() = default;
Shape( Shape&& ) = default;
Shape& operator=( Shape&& ) = default;

private:
    // ...
};
```

This is all we need to do, and we're ready to try this out. So let's put this implementation to the test. Once again we update the benchmark from "Guideline 32: Consider Replacing Inheritance Hierarchies with Type Erasure" on page 298 and run it with our manual implementation of virtual functions. I have even combined the manual virtual dispatch with the previously discussed SBO. Table 8-3 shows the performance results.

Table 8-3. Performance results for the Type Erasure implementations with manual virtual dispatch

Type Erasure implementation	GCC 11.1	Clang 11.1
Object-oriented solution	1.5205 s	1.1480 s
std::function	2.1782 s	1.4884 s
Manual implementation of std::function	1.6354 s	1.4465 s
Classic Strategy	1.6372 s	1.4046 s
Type Erasure	1.5298 s	1.1561 s
Type Erasure (SBO)	1.3591 s	1.0348 s
Type Erasure (manual virtual dispatch)	1.1476 s	1.1599 s
Type Erasure (SBO + manual virtual dispatch)	1.2538 s	1.2212 s

The performance improvement for the manual virtual dispatch is extraordinary for GCC. On my system, I get down to 1.1476 seconds, which is an improvement of 25% in comparison to the based, unoptimized implementation of Type Erasure. Clang, on the other hand, does not show any improvement in comparison to the basic, unoptimized implementation. Although this may be a little disappointing, the runtime is, of course, still remarkable.

Unfortunately the combination of SBO and manual virtual dispatch does not lead to an even better performance. While GCC shows a small improvement in comparison to the pure SBO approach (which might be interesting for environments without dynamic memory), on Clang this combination does not work as well as you might have hoped for.

In summary, there is a lot of potential for optimizing the performance for Type Erasure implementations. If you've been skeptical before about Type Erasure, this gain in performance should give you a strong incentive to investigate for yourself. While this is amazing and without doubt is pretty exciting, it is important to remember where this is coming from: only due to separating the concerns of virtual behavior and encapsulating the behavior into a value type have we gained these optimization opportunities. We wouldn't have been able to achieve this if all we had was a pointer-to-base.

> ## Guideline 33: Be Aware of the Optimization Potential of Type Erasure
>
> - Use SBO to avoid expensive copy operations for small objects.
> - Reduce the number of indirections by implementing virtual dispatch manually.

Guideline 34: Be Aware of the Setup Costs of Owning Type Erasure Wrappers

In "Guideline 32: Consider Replacing Inheritance Hierarchies with Type Erasure" on page 298 and "Guideline 33: Be Aware of the Optimization Potential of Type Erasure" on page 318, I guided you through the thicket of implementation details for a basic Type Erasure implementation. Yes, that was tough, but definitely worth the effort: you have emerged stronger, wiser, and with a new, efficient, and strongly decoupling design pattern in your toolbox. Great!

However, we have to go back into the thicket. I see you are rolling your eyes, but there is more. And I have to admit: I lied. At least a little. Not by telling you something incorrect, but by omission. There is one more disadvantage of Type Erasure that you should know of. A big one. One that you might not like at all. *Sigh*.

The Setup Costs of an Owning Type Erasure Wrapper

Assume for a second that Shape is a base class again, and Circle one of many deriving classes. Then passing a Circle to a function expecting a Shape const& would be easy and cheap (❶):

```
#include <cstdlib>

class Shape { /*...*/ };  // Classic base class

class Circle : public Shape { /*...*/ };  // Deriving class

void useShape( Shape const& shape )
{
   shape.draw( /*...*/ );
```

```
   }

int main()
{
   Circle circle{ 3.14 };

   // Automatic and cheap conversion from 'Circle const&' to 'Shape const&'
   useShape( circle );   ❶

   return EXIT_SUCCESS;
}
```

Although the Type Erasure Shape abstraction is a little different (for instance, it always requires a drawing Strategy), this kind of conversion is still possible:

```
#include <cstdlib>

class Circle { /*...*/ };   // Nonpolymorphic geometric primitive

class Shape { /*...*/ };   // Type erasure wrapper class as shown before

void useShape( Shape const& shape )
{
   draw(shape);
}

int main()
{
   Circle circle{ 3.14 };
   auto drawStrategy = []( Circle const& c ){ /*...*/ };

   // Creates a temporary 'Shape' object, involving
   //   a copy operation and a memory allocation
   useShape( { circle, drawStrategy } );   ❷

   return EXIT_SUCCESS;
}
```

Unfortunately, it is no longer cheap. On the contrary, based on our previous implementations, which include both the basic one and optimized ones, the call to the use
Shape() function would involve a couple of potentially expensive operations (❷):

- To convert a Circle into a Shape, the compiler creates a temporary Shape using
  the non-explicit, templated Shape constructor.

- The call of the constructor results in a copy operation of the given shape (not
  expensive for Circle, but potentially expensive for other shapes) and the given
  draw Strategy (essentially free if the Strategy is stateless, but potentially expensive, depending on what is stored inside the object).

- Inside the Shape constructor, a new shape model is created, involving a memory allocation (hidden in the call to std::make_unique() in the Shape constructor and definitely expensive).

- The temporary (rvalue) Shape is passed by reference-to-const to the useShape() function.

It is important to point out that this is not a specific problem of our Shape implementation. The same problem will hit you if, for instance, you use std::function as a function argument:

```
#include <cstdlib>
#include <functional>

int compute( int i, int j, std::function<int(int,int)> op )
{
   return op( i, j );
}

int main()
{
   int const i = 17;
   int const j = 10;

   int const sum = compute( i, j, [offset=15]( int x, int y ) {
      return x + y + offset;
   } );

   return EXIT_SUCCESS;
}
```

In this example, the given lambda is converted into the std::function instance. This conversion will involve a copy operation and might involve a memory allocation. It entirely depends on the size of the given callable and on the implementation of std::function. For that reason, std::function is a different kind of abstraction than, for instance, std::string_view and std::span. std::string_view and std::span are nonowning abstractions that are cheap to copy because they consist of only a pointer to the first element and a size. Because these two types perform a shallow copy, they are perfectly suited as function parameters. std::function, on the other hand, is an owning abstraction that performs a deep copy. Therefore, it is not the perfect type to be used as a function parameter. Unfortunately, the same is true for our Shape implementation.[18]

---

18 At the time of writing, there is an active proposal (*https://oreil.ly/p3cFD*) for the std::function_ref type, a nonowning version of std::function.

"Oh my, I don't like this. Not at all. That is terrible! I want my money back!" you exclaim. I have to agree that this may be a severe issue in your codebase. However, you understand that the underlying problem is the owning semantics of the Shape class: on the basis of its value semantics background, our current Shape implementation will always create a copy of the given shape and will always own the copy. While this is perfectly in line with all the benefits discussed in "Guideline 22: Prefer Value Semantics over Reference Semantics" on page 176, in this context it results in a pretty unfortunate performance penalty. However, stay calm—there is something we can do: for such a context, we can provide a nonowning Type Erasure implementation.

A Simple Nonowning Type Erasure Implementation

Generally speaking, the value semantics–based Type Erasure implementation is beautiful and perfectly adheres to the spirit of modern C++. However, performance is important. It might be so important that sometimes you might not care about the value semantics part, but only about the abstraction provided by Type Erasure. In that case, you might want to reach for a nonowning implementation of Type Erasure, despite the disadvantage that this pulls you back into the realm of reference semantics.

The good news is that if you desire only a simple Type Erasure wrapper, a wrapper that represents a reference-to-base, that is nonowning and trivially copyable, then the required code is fairly simple. That is particularly true because you have already seen how to manually implement the virtual dispatch in "Guideline 33: Be Aware of the Optimization Potential of Type Erasure" on page 318. With this technique, a simple, nonowning Type Erasure implementation is just a matter of a few lines of code:

```
//---- <Shape.h> ----------------

#include <memory>

class ShapeConstRef
{
 public:
   template< typename ShapeT, typename DrawStrategy >
   ShapeConstRef( ShapeT& shape, DrawStrategy& drawer )   ❻
      : shape_{ std::addressof(shape) }
      , drawer_{ std::addressof(drawer) }
      , draw_{ []( void const* shapeBytes, void const* drawerBytes ){
           auto const* shape = static_cast<ShapeT const*>(shapeBytes);
           auto const* drawer = static_cast<DrawStrategy const*>(drawerBytes);
           (*drawer)( *shape );
        } }
   {}

 private:
```

```
   friend void draw( ShapeConstRef const& shape )
   {
      shape.draw_( shape.shape_, shape.drawer_ );
   }

   using DrawOperation = void( void const*,void const* );

   void const* shape_{ nullptr };    ❸
   void const* drawer_{ nullptr };   ❹
   DrawOperation* draw_{ nullptr };  ❺
};
```

As the name suggests, the `ShapeConstRef` class represents a reference to a `const` shape type. Instead of storing a copy of the given shape, it only holds a pointer to it in the form of a `void*` (❸). In addition, it holds a `void*` to the associated `DrawStrategy` (❹), and as the third data member, a function pointer to the manually implemented virtual `draw()` function (❺) (see "Guideline 33: Be Aware of the Optimization Potential of Type Erasure" on page 318).

`ShapeConstRef` takes its two arguments, the shape and the drawing Strategy, both possibly cv qualified, by reference-to-non-const (❻).[19] In this form, it is not possible to pass rvalues to the constructor, which prevents any kind of lifetime issue with temporary values. This unfortunately does not protect you from all possible lifetime issues with lvalues but still provides a very reasonable protection.[20] If you want to allow rvalues, you should reconsider. And if you're really, *really* willing to risk lifetime issues with temporaries, then you can simply take the argument(s) by reference-to-`const`. Just remember that you did not get this advice from me!

This is it. This is the complete nonowning implementation. It is efficient, short, simple, and can be even shorter and simpler if you do not need to store any kind of associated data or Strategy object. With this functionality in place, you are now able to create cheap shape abstractions. This is demonstrated in the following code example by the `useShapeConstRef()` function. This function enables you to draw any kind of shape (`Circles`, `Squares`, etc.) with any possible drawing implementation by simply using a `ShapeConstRef` as the function argument. In the `main()` function, we call use `ShapeConstRef()` by a concrete shape and a concrete drawing Strategy (in this case, a lambda) (❼):

```
//---- <Main.cpp> ----------------

#include <Circle.h>
#include <Shape.h>
```

---

19 The term *cv qualified* (*https://oreil.ly/TGlBO*) refers to the `const` and `volatile` qualifiers.

20 For a reminder about lvalues and rvalues, refer to Nicolai Josuttis's book on move semantics: *C++ Move Semantics - The Complete Guide.*

```
#include <cstdlib>

void useShapeConstRef( ShapeConstRef shape )
{
   draw( shape );
}

int main()
{
   // Create a circle as one representative of a concrete shape type
   Circle circle{ 3.14 };

   // Create a drawing strategy in the form of a lambda
   auto drawer = []( Circle const& c ){ /*...*/ };

   // Draw the circle directly via the 'ShapeConstRef' abstraction
   useShapeConstRef( { circle, drawer } );  ❼

   return EXIT_SUCCESS;
}
```

This call triggers the desired effect, notably without any memory allocation or expensive copy operation, but only by wrapping polymorphic behavior around a set of pointers to the given shape and drawing Strategy.

A More Powerful Nonowning Type Erasure Implementation

Most of the time, this simple nonowning Type Erasure implementation should prove to be enough and fulfill all your needs. Sometimes, however, and only sometimes, it might not be enough. Sometimes, you might be interested in a slightly different form of Shape reference:

```
#include <Cirlce.h>
#include <Shape.h>
#include <cstdlib>

int main()
{
   // Create a circle as one representative of a concrete shape type
   Circle circle{ 3.14 };

   // Create a drawing strategy in the form of a lambda
   auto drawer = []( Circle const& c ){ /*...*/ };

   // Combine the shape and the drawing strategy in a 'Shape' abstraction
   Shape shape1( circle, drawer );

   // Draw the shape
   draw( shape1 );

   // Create a reference to the shape
```

```
// Works already, but the shape reference will store a pointer
// to the 'shape1' instance instead of a pointer to the 'circle'.
ShapeConstRef shaperef( shape1 );   ❽

// Draw via the shape reference, resulting in the same output
// This works, but only by means of two indirections!
draw( shaperef );   ❾

// Create a deep copy of the shape via the shape reference
// This is _not_ possible with the simple nonowning implementation!
// With the simple implementation, this creates a copy of the 'shaperef'
// instance. 'shape2' itself would act as a reference and there would be
// three indirections... sigh.
Shape shape2( shaperef );   ❿

// Drawing the copy will again result in the same output
draw( shape2 );

return EXIT_SUCCESS;
}
```

Assuming that you have a type-erased circle called shape1, you might want to convert this Shape instance to a ShapeConstRef (❽). With the current implementation, this works, but the shaperef instance would hold a pointer to the shape1 instance, instead of a pointer to the circle. As a consequence, any use of the shaperef would result in two indirections (one via the ShapeConstRef, and one via the Shape abstraction) (❾). Furthermore, you might also be interested in converting a ShapeConstRef instance to a Shape instance (❿). In that case, you might expect that a full copy of the underlying Circle is created and that the resulting Shape abstraction contains and represents this copy. Unfortunately, with the current implementation, the Shape would create a copy of the ShapeConstRef instance, and thus introduce a third indirection. *Sigh.*

If you need a more efficient interaction between owning and nonowning Type Erasure wrappers, and if you need a real copy when copying a nonowning wrapper into an owning wrapper, then I can offer you a working solution. Unfortunately, it is more involved than the previous implementation(s), but fortunately it isn't not overly complex. The solution builds on the basic Type Erasure implementation from "Guideline 32: Consider Replacing Inheritance Hierarchies with Type Erasure" on page 298, which includes the ShapeConcept and OwningShapeModel classes in the detail namespace, and the Shape Type Erasure wrapper. You will see that it just requires a few additions, all of which you have already seen before.

The first addition happens in the ShapeConcept base class:

```
//---- <Shape.h> ----------------

#include <memory>
```

```
#include <utility>

namespace detail {

class ShapeConcept
{
 public:
   // ...
   virtual void clone( ShapeConcept* memory ) const = 0;   ⓫
};

// ...

} // namespace detail
```

The ShapeConcept class is extended with a second clone() function (⓫). Instead of returning a newly instantiated copy of the corresponding model, this function is passed the address of the memory location where the new model needs to be created.

The second addition is a new model class, the NonOwningShapeModel:

```
//---- <Shape.h> ----------------

// ...

namespace detail {

// ...

template< typename ShapeT
        , typename DrawStrategy >
class NonOwningShapeModel : public ShapeConcept
{
 public:
   NonOwningShapeModel( ShapeT& shape, DrawStrategy& drawer )
      : shape_{ std::addressof(shape) }
      , drawer_{ std::addressof(drawer) }
   {}

   void draw() const override { (*drawer_)(*shape_); }   ⓮

   std::unique_ptr<ShapeConcept> clone() const override   ⓯
   {
      using Model = OwningShapeModel<ShapeT,DrawStrategy>;
      return std::make_unique<Model>( *shape_, *drawer_ );
   }

   void clone( ShapeConcept* memory ) const override   ⓰
   {
      std::construct_at( static_cast<NonOwningShapeModel*>(memory), *this );

      // or:
```

```
      // auto* ptr =
      //    const_cast<void*>(static_cast<void const volatile*>(memory));
      // ::new (ptr) NonOwningShapeModel( *this );
   }

 private:
   ShapeT* shape_{ nullptr };  ⑫
   DrawStrategy* drawer_{ nullptr };  ⑬
};

// ...

} // namespace detail
```

The NonOwningShapeModel is very similar to the OwningShapeModel implementation, but, as the name suggests, it does not store copies of the given shape and strategy. Instead, it stores only pointers (⑫ and ⑬). Thus, this class represents the reference semantics version of the OwningShapeModel class. Also, NonOwningShapeModel needs to override the pure virtual functions of the ShapeConcept class: draw() again forwards the drawing request to the given drawing Strategy (⑭), while the clone() functions perform a copy. The first clone() function is implemented by creating a new OwningShapeModel and copying both the stored shape and drawing Strategy (⑮). The second clone() function is implemented by creating a new NonOwningShapeModel at the specified address by std::construct_at() (⑯).

In addition, the OwningShapeModel class needs to provide an implementation of the new clone() function:

```
//---- <Shape.h> ----------------

// ...

namespace detail {

template< typename ShapeT
        , typename DrawStrategy >
class OwningShapeModel : public ShapeConcept
{
 public:
   // ...

   void clone( ShapeConcept* memory ) const  ⑰
   {
      using Model = NonOwningShapeModel<ShapeT const,DrawStrategy const>;

      std::construct_at( static_cast<Model*>(memory), shape_, drawer_ );

      // or:
      // auto* ptr =
      //    const_cast<void*>(static_cast<void const volatile*>(memory));
```

```
        // ::new (ptr) Model( shape_, drawer_ );
    }
};

// ...

} // namespace detail
```

The clone() function in OwningShapeModel is implemented similarly to the implementation in the NonOwningShapeModel class by creating a new instance of a NonOwningShapeModel by std::construct_at() (**17**).

The next addition is the corresponding wrapper class that acts as a wrapper around the external hierarchy ShapeConcept and NonOwningShapeModel. This wrapper should take on the same responsibilities as the Shape class (i.e., the instantiation of the NonOwningShapeModel class template and the encapsulation of all pointer handling) but should merely represent a reference to a const concrete shape, not a copy. This wrapper is again given in the form of the ShapeConstRef class:

```
//---- <Shape.h> ----------------

#include <array>
#include <cstddef>
#include <memory>

// ...

class ShapeConstRef
{
 public:
   // ...

 private:
   // ...

   // Expected size of a model instantiation:
   //     sizeof(ShapeT*) + sizeof(DrawStrategy*) + sizeof(vptr)
   static constexpr size_t MODEL_SIZE = 3U*sizeof(void*);   19

   alignas(void*) std::array<std::byte,MODEL_SIZE> raw_;    18
};
```

As you will see, the ShapeConstRef class is very similar to the Shape class, but there are a few important differences. The first noteworthy detail is the use of a raw_ storage in the form of a properly aligned std::byte array (**18**). That indicates that ShapeConstRef does not allocate dynamically, but firmly builds on in-class memory. In this case, however, this is easily possible, because we can predict the size of the required NonOwningShapeModel to be equal to the size of three pointers (assuming that the pointer to the virtual function table, the `vptr`, has the same size as any other pointer) (**❶⑨**).

The `private` section of `ShapeConstRef` also contains a couple of member functions:

```
//---- <Shape.h> ----------------

// ...

class ShapeConstRef
{
 public:
   // ...

 private:
   friend void draw( ShapeConstRef const& shape )
   {
      shape.pimpl()->draw();
   }

   ShapeConcept* pimpl()   ⓴
   {
      return reinterpret_cast<ShapeConcept*>( raw_.data() );
   }

   ShapeConcept const* pimpl() const   ㉑
   {
      return reinterpret_cast<ShapeConcept const*>( raw_.data() );
   }

   // ...
};
```

We also add a `draw()` function as a hidden `friend` and, just as in the SBO implementation in "Guideline 33: Be Aware of the Optimization Potential of Type Erasure" on page 318, we add a pair of `pimpl()` functions (⓴ and ㉑). This will enable us to work conveniently with the in-class `std::byte` array.

The second noteworthy detail is the signature function of every Type Erasure implementation, the templated constructor:

```
//---- <Shape.h> ----------------

// ...

class ShapeConstRef
{
 public:
   // Type 'ShapeT' and 'DrawStrategy' are possibly cv qualified;
   // lvalue references prevent references to rvalues
   template< typename ShapeT
           , typename DrawStrategy >
```

```
    ShapeConstRef( ShapeT& shape
                 , DrawStrategy& drawer )    ㉒
    {
       using Model =
          detail::NonOwningShapeModel<ShapeT const,DrawStrategy const>;   ㉓
       static_assert( sizeof(Model) == MODEL_SIZE, "Invalid size detected" );   ㉔
       static_assert( alignof(Model) == alignof(void*), "Misaligned detected" );

       std::construct_at( static_cast<Model*>(pimpl()), shape_, drawer_ );   ㉕

       // or:
       // auto* ptr =
       //    const_cast<void*>(static_cast<void const volatile*>(pimpl()));
       // ::new (ptr) Model( shape_, drawer_ );
    }

    // ...

 private:
    // ...
};
```

Again, you have the choice to accept the arguments by reference-to-non-const to prevent lifetime issues with temporaries (very much recommended!) (㉒). Alternatively, you accept the arguments by reference-to-const, which would allow you to pass rvalues but puts you at risk of experiencing lifetime issues with temporaries. Inside the constructor, we again first use a convenient type alias for the required type of model (㉓), before checking the actual size and alignment of the model (㉔). If it does not adhere to the expected MODEL_SIZE or pointer alignment, we create a compile-time error. Then we construct the new model inside the in-class memory by std::construct_at() (㉕):

```
//---- <Shape.h> ----------------

// ...

class ShapeConstRef
{
 public:
   // ...

   ShapeConstRef( Shape& other )       { other.pimpl_->clone( pimpl() ); }   ㉖
   ShapeConstRef( Shape const& other ) { other.pimpl_->clone( pimpl() ); }

   ShapeConstRef( ShapeConstRef const& other )
   {
      other.pimpl()->clone( pimpl() );
   }

   ShapeConstRef& operator=( ShapeConstRef const& other )
   {
```

```
    // Copy-and-swap idiom
    ShapeConstRef copy( other );
    raw_.swap( copy.raw_ );
    return *this;
  }

  ~ShapeConstRef()
  {
    std::destroy_at( pimpl() );
    // or: pimpl()->~ShapeConcept();
  }

  // Move operations explicitly not declared  ❷❼

 private:
  // ...
};
```

In addition to the templated ShapeConstRef constructor, ShapeConstRef offers two constructors to enable a conversion from Shape instances (❷❻). While these are not strictly required, as we could also create an instance of a NonOwningShapeModel for a Shape, these constructors directly create a NonOwningShapeModel for the corresponding, underlying shape type, and thus shave off one indirection, which contributes to better performance. Note that to make these constructors work, ShapeConstRef needs to become a friend of the Shape class. Don't worry, though, as this is a good example for friendship: Shape and ShapeConstRef truly belong together, work hand in hand, and are even provided in the same header file.

The last noteworthy detail is the fact that the two move operations are neither explicitly declared nor deleted (❷❼). Since we have explicitly defined the two copy operations, the compiler neither creates nor deletes the two move operations, thus they are gone. Completely gone in the sense that these two functions never participate in overload resolution. And yes, this is different from explicitly deleting them: if they were deleted, they would participate in overload resolution, and if selected, they would result in a compilation error. But with these two functions gone, when you try to move a ShapeConstRef, the copy operations would be used instead, which are cheap and efficient, since ShapeConstRef only represents a reference. Thus, this class deliberately implements the Rule of 3 (*https://oreil.ly/hYYiq*).

We are almost finished. The last detail is one more addition, one more constructor in the Shape class:

```
//---- <Shape.h> ----------------

// ...

class Shape
{
```

```
  public:
    // ...

    Shape( ShapeConstRef const& other )
       : pimpl_{ other.pimpl()->clone() }
    {}

  private:
    // ...
}
```

Via this constructor, an instance of Shape creates a deep copy of the shape stored in the passed ShapeConstRef instance. Without this constructor, Shape stores a copy of the ShapeConstRef instance and thus acts as a reference itself.

In summary, both nonowning implementations, the simple and the more complex one, give you all the design advantages of the Type Erasure design pattern but at the same time pull you back into the realm of reference semantics, with all its deficiencies. Hence, utilize the strengths of this nonowning form of Type Erasure, but also be aware of the usual lifetime issues. Consider it on the same level as std::string_view and std::span. All of these serve as very useful tools for function arguments, but do not use them to store anything for a longer period, for instance in the form of a data member. The danger of lifetime-related issues is just too high.

Guideline 34: Be Aware of the Setup Costs of Owning Type Erasure Wrappers

- Keep in mind that the setup of owning Type Erasure wrappers may involve copy operations and allocations.

- Be aware of nonowning Type Erasure, but also understand its reference semantics deficiencies.

- Prefer simple Type Erasure implementations, but know their limits.

- Prefer to use nonowning Type Erasure for function arguments but not for data members or return types.

CHAPTER 9

The Decorator Design Pattern

This chapter is dedicated to another classic design pattern: the Decorator design pattern. Over the years, Decorator has proven to be one of the most useful design patterns when it comes to combining and reusing different implementations. So it doesn't come as a surprise that it is commonly used, even for one of the most impressive reworks of a C++ Standard Library feature. My primary objective in this chapter will be to give you a very good idea why, and when, Decorator is a great choice for designing software. Additionally, I will show you the modern, more value-based forms of Decorator.

In "Guideline 35: Use Decorators to Add Customization Hierarchically" on page 348, we will dive into the design aspects of the Decorator design pattern. You will see when it is the right design choice and which benefits you're gaining by using it. Additionally, you will learn about differences compared to other design patterns and its potential shortcomings.

In "Guideline 36: Understand the Trade-off Between Runtime and Compile Time Abstraction" on page 367, we will take a look at two more implementations of the Decorator design pattern. Although both implementations will be firmly rooted in the realm of value semantics, the first one will be based on static polymorphism, while the second one will be based on dynamic polymorphism. Even though both have the same intent and thus implement Decorator, the contrast between these two will give you an impression of the vastness of the design space for design patterns.

Guideline 35: Use Decorators to Add Customization Hierarchically

Ever since you solved the design problem of your team's 2D graphics tool by proposing a solution based on the Strategy design pattern (remember "Guideline 19: Use Strategy to Isolate How Things Are Done" on page 140), your reputation as design pattern expert has spread across the company. Therefore, it does not come as a surprise that other teams are seeking you out for guidance. One day, two developers of your companies merchandise management system come to your office and ask for your help.

Your Coworkers' Design Issue

The team of the two developers is dealing with a lot of different Items (see Figure 9-1). All of these items have one thing in common: they have a price() tag. The two developers try to explain their problem by means of two items taken from the C++ merchandise shop: a class representing a C++ book (the CppBook class) and a C++ conference ticket (the ConferenceTicket class).

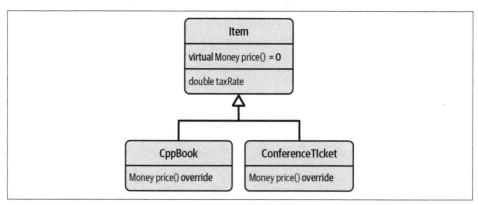

Figure 9-1. The initial Item inheritance hierarchy

As the developers sketch their problem, you start to understand that their problem appears to be the many different ways to modify a price. Initially, they tell you, they only had to take taxes into account. For that reason, the Item base class was equipped with a protected data member to represent the tax rate:

```
//---- <Money.h> ----------------

class Money { /*...*/ };

Money operator*( Money money, double factor );
Money operator+( Money lhs, Money rhs );
```

```
//---- <Item.h> ----------------

#include <Money.h>

class Item
{
 public:
   virtual ~Item() = default;

   virtual Money price() const = 0;
   // ...

 protected:
   double taxRate_;
};
```

This apparently worked well for some time, until one day, when they were asked to also take different rates of discount into account. This apparently required a lot of effort to refactor the large amount of the existing classes for their numerous different items. You can easily imagine that this was necessary because all derived classes were accessing the protected data members. "Yes, you should always design for change…" you think to yourself.[1]

They continue by admitting to their unfortunate misdesign. Of course they should have done a better job of encapsulating the tax rates in the Item base class. However, along with this realization came the understanding that when representing price modifiers by data members in the base class, any new kind of price modifier would always be an intrusive action and would always directly affect the Item class. For that reason, they started to think about how to avoid this kind of major refactoring in the future and how to enable the easy addition of new modifiers. "That's the way to go!" you think to yourself. Unfortunately, the first approach that came to their mind was to factor out the different kinds of price modifiers by means of an inheritance hierarchy (see Figure 9-2).

---

1 Remember "Guideline 2: Design for Change" on page 11 and Core Guideline C.133 (*https://oreil.ly/SrAkz*): "Avoid protected data."

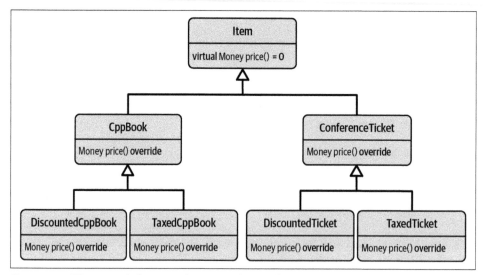

Figure 9-2. The extended Item inheritance hierarchy

Instead of encapsulating the tax and discount values inside the base class, these modifiers are factored out into derived classes, which perform the required price adaptation. "Uh-oh…" you start to think. Apparently your look already gives away that you are not particularly fond of this idea, and so they are quick to tell you that they have already discarded the idea. Obviously they have realized on their own that this would cause even more problems: this solution would quickly cause an explosion of types and would provide only poor reuse of functionality. Unfortunately, a lot of code would be doubled, since for every specific Item, the code for taxes and discounts had to be duplicated. Most troublesome, however, would be the handling of Items that are affected both by tax and some sort of discount: they neither liked the approach to provide classes to handle both, nor did they want to introduce another layer in the inheritance hierarchy (see Figure 9-3).

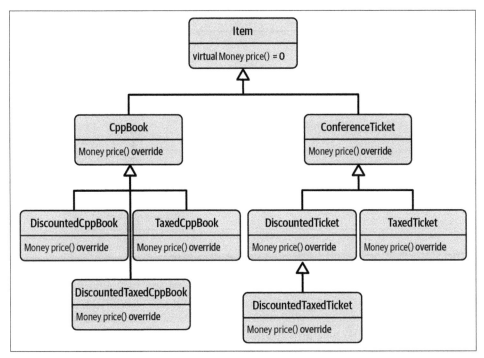

Figure 9-3. The problematic `Item` inheritance hierarchy

Apparently, and surprising for them, they couldn't deal with the price modifiers in the base class or in the derived classes by means of direct inheritance. However, before you have the opportunity to make any comments about separating concerns, they explain that they have recently heard about your Strategy solution. This finally gave them an idea how to properly refactor the problem (see Figure 9-4).

By extracting the price modifiers into a separate hierarchy, and by configuring `Items` upon construction by means of a `PriceStrategy`, they had finally found a working solution to nonintrusively add new price modifiers, which will save them a lot of refactoring work. "Well, this is the benefit of separating concerns and favoring composition over inheritance," you think to yourself.[2] And aloud you ask, "This is great, I'm really happy for you. Everything seems to work now, you've figured it out on your own! Why exactly are you here?"

---

2 See "Guideline 20: Favor Composition over Inheritance" on page 162 for a discussion on why so many design patterns draw their power from composition rather than inheritance.

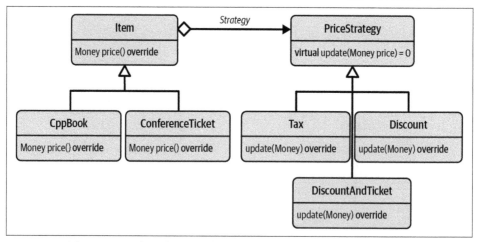

Figure 9-4. The Strategy-based *Item* inheritance hierarchy

They tell you that your Strategy solution is by far the best approach they have (thankful looks included). However, they admit that they are not entirely happy with the approach. From their point of view, two problems remain and, of course, they are hoping that you have an idea how to fix them. The first issue they see is that every Item instance needs a Strategy class, even if no price modifier applies. While they agree that this can be solved by some kind of *null object* (*https://oreil.ly/9RX5N*), they feel that there should be a simpler solution:[3]

```cpp
class PriceStrategy
{
 public:
   virtual ~PriceStrategy() = default;
   virtual Money update( Money price ) const = 0;
   // ...
};

class NullPriceStrategy : public PriceStrategy
{
 public:
   Money update( Money price ) const override { return price; }
};
```

The second problem they have appears to be a little more difficult to solve. Obviously they are interested in combining different kinds of modifiers (e.g., Discount and Tax into DiscountAndTax). Unfortunately, they experience some code duplication in their current implementation. For instance, both the Tax and the DiscountAndTax classes

---

3 A *null object* represents an object with neutral (null) behavior. As such, it can be seen as a default for a Strategy implementation.

contain tax-related computations. And while right now, with only the two modifiers, there are reasonable solutions at hand to cope with the duplication, they are anticipating problems when adding more modifiers and arbitrary combinations of these. Therefore they are wondering if there is another, better solution for dealing with different kinds of price modifiers.

This is indeed an intriguing problem, and you are happy to have taken the time to help them. They are absolutely correct: the Strategy design pattern is not the right solution for this problem. While Strategy is a great solution to remove dependencies on the complete implementation details of a function and to handle different implementations gracefully, it does not enable the easy combination and reuse of different implementations. Attempting to do this would quickly result in an undesirably complex Strategy inheritance hierarchy.

What they need for their problem appears to be more like a hierarchical form of Strategy, a form that decouples the different price modifiers but also allows for a very flexible combination of them. Hence, one key to success is a consequent application of the separation of concerns: any rigid, manually encoded combination in the spirit of a `DiscountAndTax` class would be prohibitive. However, the solution should also be nonintrusive to enable them to implement new ideas at any time without the need to modify existing code. And finally, it should not be necessary to handle a default case by some artificial *null object*. Instead, it would be more reasonable to consequently build on composition instead of inheritance and implement a price modifier in the form of a wrapper. With this realization, you start to smile. Yes, there is just the right design pattern for this purpose: what your two guests need is an implementation of the Decorator design pattern.

The Decorator Design Pattern Explained

The Decorator design pattern also originates from the GoF book. Its primary focus is the flexible combination of different pieces of functionality through composition:

The Decorator Design Pattern

Intent: "Attach additional responsibilities to an object dynamically. Decorators provide a flexible alternative to subclassing for extending functionality."[4]

Figure 9-5 shows the UML diagram for the given `Item` problem. As before, the `Item` base class represents the abstraction from all possible items. The deriving `CppBook` class, on the other hand, acts as a representative for different implementations of

4 Erich Gamma et al., *Design Patterns: Elements of Reusable Object-Oriented Software*.

`Item`. The problem in this hierarchy is the difficult addition of new modifiers for the existing `price()` function(s). In the Decorator design pattern, this addition of new "responsibilities" is identified as a *variation point* and extracted in the form of the `DecoratedItem` class. This class is a separate, special implementation of the `Item` base class and represents an added responsibility for any given item. On the one hand, a `DecoratedItem` derives from `Item` and hence must adhere to all expectations of the `Item` abstraction (see "Guideline 6: Adhere to the Expected Behavior of Abstractions" on page 44). On the other hand, it also contains an `Item` (either through composition or aggregation). Due to that, a `DecoratedItem` acts as a wrapper around each and every item, potentially one that itself can extend the functionality. For that reason, it provides the foundation for a hierarchical application of modifiers. Two possible modifiers are represented by the `Discounted` class, which represents a discount for a specific item, and the `Taxed` class, which represents some kind of tax.[5]

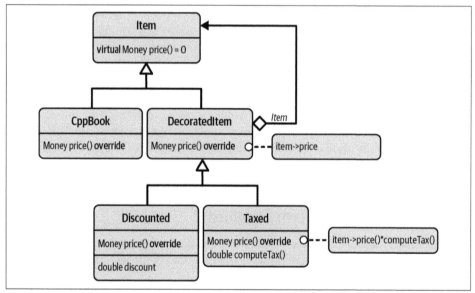

Figure 9-5. The UML representation of the Decorator design pattern

By introducing the `DecoratedItem` class and separating the aspect that's required to change, you adhere to the SRP. By separating this concern and therefore allowing the easy addition of new price modifiers, you also adhere to the *Open-Closed Principle (OCP)*. Due to the hierarchical, recursive nature of the `DecoratedItem` class, and due

---

5 You may be wondering if this is the most reasonable approach for dealing with taxes. No, unfortunately it's not. That's because first, as usual, reality is so much more complex than this simple, educational example, and second, because in this form it's easy to apply taxes incorrectly. While I can't help with the first point (I'm just a mere mortal), I will go into detail about the second point at the end of this guideline.

to the gained ability to reuse and combine different modifiers easily, you also follow the advice of the *Don't Repeat Yourself (DRY)* principle. Last but not least, because of the wrapper approach of Decorator, there's no need to define any default behavior in the form of a *null object*. Any Item that does not require a modifier can be used as is.

Figure 9-6 illustrates the dependency graph of the Decorator design pattern. In this figure, the Item class resides on the highest level of the architecture. All other classes depend on it, including the DecoratedItem class, which resides one level below. Of course, this is not a requirement: it's perfectly acceptable if both the Item and the DecoratedItem are introduced on the same architectural level. However, this example demonstrates that it's always possible (anytime, anywhere) to introduce a new Decorator without needing to modify existing code. The concrete types of Items are implemented on the lowest level of the architecture. Note that there is no dependency between these items: all items, including modifiers like Discounted, can be introduced independently by anyone at any time and, due to the structure of Decorator, be flexibly and arbitrarily combined.

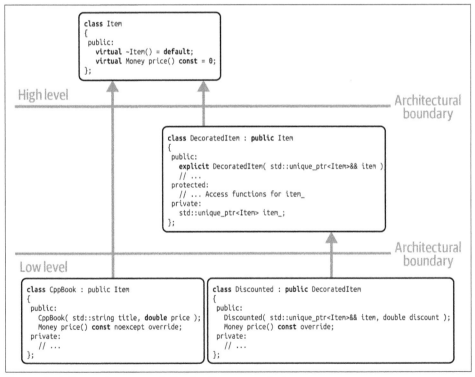

Figure 9-6. Dependency graph for the Decorator design pattern

A Classic Implementation of the Decorator Design Pattern

Let's take a look at a complete, GoF-style implementation of the Decorator design pattern by means of the given Item example:

```cpp
//---- <Item.h> ----------------

#include <Money.h>

class Item
{
 public:
   virtual ~Item() = default;
   virtual Money price() const = 0;
};
```

The Item base class represents the abstraction for all possible items. The only requirement is defined by the pure virtual price() function, which can be used to query for the price of the given item. The DecoratedItem class represents one possible implementation of the Item class (❶):

```cpp
//---- <DecoratedItem.h> ----------------

#include <Item.h>
#include <memory>
#include <stdexcept>
#include <utility>

class DecoratedItem : public Item     ❶
{
 public:
   explicit DecoratedItem( std::unique_ptr<Item> item )     ❸
      : item_( std::move(item) )
   {
      if( !item_ ) {
         throw std::invalid_argument( "Invalid item" );
      }
   }

 protected:
   Item&       item()       { return *item_; }     ❹
   Item const& item() const { return *item_; }

 private:
   std::unique_ptr<Item> item_;     ❷
};
```

A DecoratedItem derives from the Item class but also contains an item_ (❷). This item_ is specified via the constructor, which accepts any non-null std::unique_ptr to another Item (❸). Note that this DecoratedItem class is still abstract, since the pure virtual price() function is not yet defined. DecoratedItem provides only the necessary functionality to store an Item and to access the Item via protected member functions (❹).

Equipped with these two classes, it's possible to implement concrete Items:

```
//---- <CppBook.h> ----------------

#include <Item.h>
#include <string>
#include <utility>

class CppBook : public Item   ❺
{
 public:
   CppBook( std::string title, Money price )
      : title_{ std::move(title) }
      , price_{ price }
   {}

   std::string const& title() const { return title_; }
   Money price() const override { return price_; }

 private:
   std::string title_{};
   Money price_{};
};
```

```
//---- <ConferenceTicket.h> ----------------

#include <Item.h>
#include <string>
#include <utility>

class ConferenceTicket : public Item   ❻
{
 public:
   ConferenceTicket( std::string name, Money price )
      : name_{ std::move(name) }
      , price_{ price }
   {}

   std::string const& name() const { return name_; }
   Money price() const override { return price_; }

 private:
   std::string name_{};
   Money price_{};
};
```

The CppBook and ConferenceTicket classes represent possible specific Item implementations (❺ and ❻). While a C++ book is represented by means of the title of the book, a C++ conference is represented by means of the name of the conference. Most importantly, both classes override the price() function by returning the specified price_.

Both CppBook and ConferenceTicket are oblivious to any kind of tax or discount. But obviously, both kinds of Item are potentially subject to both. These price modifiers are implemented by means of the Discounted and Taxed classes:

```cpp
//---- <Discounted.h> ----------------

#include <DecoratedItem.h>

class Discounted : public DecoratedItem
{
 public:
    Discounted( double discount, std::unique_ptr<Item> item )    ❼
       : DecoratedItem( std::move(item) )
       , factor_( 1.0 - discount )
    {
        if( !std::isfinite(discount) || discount < 0.0 || discount > 1.0 ) {
           throw std::invalid_argument( "Invalid discount" );
        }
    }

    Money price() const override
    {
        return item().price() * factor_;    ❽
    }

 private:
    double factor_;
};
```

The Discounted class (❼) is initialized by passing a std::unique_ptr to an Item and a discount value, represented by a double value in the range of 0.0 to 1.0. While the given Item is immediately passed to the DecoratedItem base class, the given discount value is used to compute a discount factor_. This factor is used in the implementation of the price() function to modify the price of the given item (❽). This can either be a specific item like CppBook or ConferenceTicket or any Decorator like Discounted, which in turn modifies the price of another Item. Thus, the price() function is the point where the hierarchical structure of Decorator is fully exploited.

```cpp
//---- <Taxed.h> ----------------

#include <DecoratedItem.h>

class Taxed : public DecoratedItem
```

```
{
public:
  Taxed( double taxRate, std::unique_ptr<Item> item )    ❾
    : DecoratedItem( std::move(item) )
    , factor_( 1.0 + taxRate )
  {
     if( !std::isfinite(taxRate) || taxRate < 0.0 ) {
        throw std::invalid_argument( "Invalid tax" );
     }
  }

  Money price() const override
  {
     return item().price() * factor_;
  }

private:
  double factor_;
};
```

The Taxed class is very similar to the Discounted class. The major difference is the evaluation of a tax-related factor in the constructor (❾). Again, this factor is used in the price() function to modify the price of the wrapped Item.

All of this functionality is put together in the main() function:

```
#include <ConferenceTicket.h>
#include <CppBook.h>
#include <Discounted.h>
#include <Taxed.h>
#include <cstdlib>
#include <memory>

int main()
{
   // 7% tax: 19*1.07 = 20.33
   std::unique_ptr<Item> item1(    ❿
      std::make_unique<Taxed>( 0.07,
         std::make_unique<CppBook>( "Effective C++", 19.0 ) ) );

   // 20% discount, 19% tax: (999*0.8)*1.19 = 951.05
   std::unique_ptr<Item> item2(    ⓫
      std::make_unique<Taxed>( 0.19,
         std::make_unique<Discounted>( 0.2,
            std::make_unique<ConferenceTicket>( "CppCon", 999.0 ) ) ) );

   Money const totalPrice1 = item1->price();   // Results in 20.33
   Money const totalPrice2 = item2->price();   // Results in 951.05

   // ...
```

```
        return EXIT_SUCCESS;
}
```

As a first `Item`, we create a `CppBook`. Let's assume that this book is subject to a 7% tax, which is applied by means of wrapping a `Taxed` decorator around the item. The resulting `item1` therefore represents a taxed C++ book (❿). As a second `Item`, we create a `ConferenceTicket` instance, which represents CppCon (*https://cppcon.org*). We were lucky to get one of the early-bird tickets, which means that we are granted a discount of 20%. This discount is wrapped around the `ConferenceTicket` instance by means of the `Discounted` class. The ticket is also subject to 19% tax, which, as before, is applied via the `Taxed` decorator. Hence, the resulting `item2` represents a discounted and taxed C++ conference ticket (⓫).

A Second Decorator Example

Another, impressive example that shows the benefits of the Decorator design pattern can be found in the C++17 rework of the STL allocators. Since the allocators' implementation is based on Decorator, it's possible to create arbitrarily complex hierarchies of allocators, which fulfill even the most special of memory requirements. Consider, for instance, the following example using a `std::pmr::mono tonic_buffer_resource` (*https://oreil.ly/UPPxK*) (⓬):

```
#include <array>
#include <cstddef>
#include <cstdlib>
#include <memory_resource>
#include <string>
#include <vector>

int main()
{
    std::array<std::byte,1000> raw;  // Note: not initialized!

    std::pmr::monotonic_buffer_resource
        buffer{ raw.data(), raw.size(), std::pmr::null_memory_resource() }; ⓬

    std::pmr::vector<std::pmr::string> strings{ &buffer };

    strings.emplace_back( "String longer than what SSO can handle" );
    strings.emplace_back( "Another long string that goes beyond SSO" );
    strings.emplace_back( "A third long string that cannot be handled by SSO" );

    // ...

    return EXIT_SUCCESS;
}
```

The `std::pmr::monotonic_buffer_resource` is one of several available allocators in the `std::pmr` namespace. In this example, it's configured such that whenever the `strings` vector asks for memory, it will dispense only chunks of the given byte array `raw`. Memory requests that cannot be handled, for instance because the `buffer` is out of memory, are dealt with by throwing a `std::bad_alloc` exception. This behavior is specified by passing a `std::pmr::null_memory_resource` (*https://oreil.ly/E1t7V*) during construction. There are many other possible applications for a `std::pmr::mon otonic_buffer_resource`, though. For instance, it would also be possible to build on dynamic memory and to let it reallocate additional chunks of memory via `new` and `delete` by means of `std::pmr::new_delete_resource()` (*https://oreil.ly/0oSzS*) (**13**):

```
// ...

int main()
{
   std::pmr::monotonic_buffer_resource
      buffer{ std::pmr::new_delete_resource() };  ⓭

   // ...
}
```

This flexibility and hierarchical configuration of allocators is made possible by means of the Decorator design pattern. The `std::pmr:: mono tonic_buffer_resource` is derived from the `std::pmr::memory_resource` (*https:// oreil.ly/8A1sk*) base class but, at the same time, also acts as a wrapper around another allocator derived from `std::pmr::memory_resource`. The upstream allocator, which is used whenever the `buffer` goes out of memory, is specified on construction of a `std::pmr::monotonic_buffer_resource`.

Most impressive, however, is that you can easily and nonintrusively customize the allocation strategy. That might, for instance, be interesting to enable you to deal with requests for large chunks of memory differently than requests for small chunks. All you have to do is to provide your own, custom allocator. Consider the following sketch of a `CustomAllocator`:

```
//---- <CustomAllocator.h> ----------------

#include <cstdlib>
#include <memory_resource>

class CustomAllocator : public std::pmr::memory_resource  ⓮
{
 public:
   CustomAllocator( std::pmr::memory_resource* upstream )  ⓰
      : upstream_{ upstream }
   {}

 private:
```

```
    void* do_allocate( size_t bytes, size_t alignment ) override;   ❶❼

    void do_deallocate( void* ptr, [[maybe_unused]] size_t bytes,   ❶❽
                        [[maybe_unused]] size_t alignment ) override;

    bool do_is_equal(
        std::pmr::memory_resource const& other ) const noexcept override;   ❶❾

    std::pmr::memory_resource* upstream_{};   ❶❺
};
```

To be recognized as a C++17 allocator, the `CustomAllocator` class derives from the `std::pmr::memory_resource` class, which represents the set of requirements for all C++17 allocators (❶❹). Coincidentally, the `CustomAllocator` also owns a pointer to a `std::pmr::memory_resource` (❶❺), which is initialized via its constructor (❶❻).

The set of requirements for C++17 allocators consists of the virtual functions `do_allocate()`, `do_deallocate()`, and `do_is_equal()`. The `do_allocate()` function is responsible for acquiring memory, potentially via its upstream allocator (❶❼), while the `do_deallocate()` function is called whenever memory needs to be given back (❶❽). Last but not least, the `do_is_equal()` function is called whenever the equality of two allocators needs to be checked (❶❾).[6]

By just introducing the `CustomAllocator` and without the need to change any other code, in particular in the Standard Library, the new kind of allocator can be easily plugged in between the `std::pmr::monotonic_buffer_resource` and the `std::pmr::new_delete_resource()` (❷❿), thus allowing you to nonintrusively extend the allocation behavior:

```
// ...
#include <CustomAllocator.h>

int main()
{
    CustomAllocator custom_allocator{ std::pmr::new_delete_resource() };

    std::pmr::monotonic_buffer_resource buffer{ &custom_allocator };   ❷❿

    // ...
}
```

---

6 If you're wondering about the incomplete implementation: the focus here is entirely on how to *design* allocators, not on how to *implement* an allocator. For a thorough introduction on how to implement a C++17 allocator, see Nicolai Josuttis's *C++17 - The Complete Guide*.

Comparison Between Decorator, Adapter, and Strategy

With the names *Decorator* and *Adapter*, these two design patterns sound like they have a similar purpose. On closer examination, however, these two patterns are very different and hardly related at all. The intent of the Adapter design pattern is to adapt and change a given interface to an expected interface. It is not concerned about adding any functionality but only about mapping one set of functions onto another (see also "Guideline 24: Use Adapters to Standardize Interfaces" on page 198). The Decorator design pattern, on the other hand, preserves a given interface and isn't at all concerned about changing it. Instead, it provides the ability to add responsibilities and to extend and customize an existing set of functions.

The Strategy design pattern is much more like Decorator. Both patterns provide the ability to customize functionality. However, both patterns are intended for different applications and therefore provide different benefits. The Strategy design pattern is focused on removing the dependencies on the implementation details of a specific functionality and enables you to define these details from the outside. Thus from this perspective, it represents the core—the "guts"—of this functionality. This form makes it particularly suited to represent different implementations and to switch between them (see "Guideline 19: Use Strategy to Isolate How Things Are Done" on page 140). In comparison, the Decorator design pattern is focused on removing the dependency between attachable pieces of implementation. Due to its wrapper form, Decorator represents the "skin" of a functionality.[7] In this form, it is particularly well suited to combine different implementations, which enables you to augment and extend functionality, rather than replacing it or switching between implementations.

Obviously, both Strategy and Decorator have their individual strengths and should be selected accordingly. However, it's also possible to combine these two design patterns to gain the best of both worlds. For instance, it would be possible to implement `Items` in terms of the Strategy design patterns but allow for a more fine-grained configuration of Strategy by means of Decorator:

```
class PriceStrategy
{
 public:
   virtual ~PriceStrategy() = default;
   virtual Money update( Money price ) const = 0;
   // ...
};

class DecoratedPriceStrategy : public PriceStrategy
{
```

---

7 The metaphor of Strategy being the guts of an object and Decorator being the skin originates from the GoF book.

```
public:
  // ...
private:
  std::unique_ptr<PriceStrategy> priceModifier_;
};

class DiscountedPriceStrategy : public DecoratedPriceStrategy
{
public:
  Money update( Money price ) const override;
  // ...
};
```

This combination of design patterns is particularly interesting if you already have a Strategy implementation in place: while Strategy is intrusive and requires the modification of a class, it's always possible to nonintrusively add a Decorator such as the DecoratedPriceStrategy class. But of course it depends: whether or not this is the right solution is something you'll have to decide on a case-by-case basis.

Analyzing the Shortcomings of the Decorator Design Pattern

With its ability to hierarchically extend and customize behavior, the Decorator design pattern is clearly one of the most valuable and flexible patterns in the catalogue of design patterns. However, despite its benefits, it also comes with a couple of disadvantages. First and foremost, the flexibility of a Decorator comes with a price: every level in a given hierarchy adds one level of indirection. As a specific example, in the object-oriented implementation of the Item hierarchy, this indirection comes in the form of one virtual function call per Decorator. Thus an extensive use of Decorators may incur a potentially significant performance overhead. Whether or not this possible performance penalty poses a problem depends on the context. You'll have to decide from case to case using benchmarks to determine whether the flexibility and the structural aspects of Decorator outweigh the performance problem.

Another shortcoming is the potential danger of combining Decorators in a nonsensical way. For instance, it's easily possible to wrap a Taxed Decorator around another Taxed Decorator or to apply a Discounted on an already-taxed Item. Both scenarios would make your government happy but still should never happen and therefore should be avoided by design. This rational is nicely expressed by Scott Meyers's universal design principle:[8]

> Make interfaces easy to use correctly and hard to use incorrectly.

---

8 Scott Meyers, *Effective C++*, 3rd ed. (Addison-Wesley, 2005).

Thus the enormous flexibility of Decorators is extraordinary, but can also be dangerous (depending on the scenario, of course). Since in this scenario taxes appear to play a special role, it seems to be very reasonable not to deal with them as Decorator, but differently. Since in reality taxes turn out to be a rather complex topic, it appears to be reasonable to separate this concern via the Strategy design pattern:

```
//---- <TaxStrategy.h> ----------------

#include <Money.h>

class TaxStrategy  ㉑
{
 public:
   virtual ~TaxStrategy() = default;
   virtual Money applyTax( Money price ) const = 0;
   // ...
};


//---- <TaxedItem.h> ----------------

#include <Money.h>
#include <TaxStrategy.h>
#include <memory>

class TaxedItem
{
 public:
   explicit TaxedItem( std::unique_ptr<Item> item
                     , std::unique_ptr<TaxStrategy> taxer )  ㉒
      : item_( std::move(item) )
      , taxer_( std::move(taxer) )
   {
      // Check for a valid item and tax strategy
   }

   Money netPrice() const  // Price without taxes  ㉓
   {
      return item_->price();
   }

   Money grossPrice() const  // Price including taxes  ㉔
   {
      return taxer_->applyTax( item_->price() );
   }

 private:
   std::unique_ptr<Item> item_;
   std::unique_ptr<TaxStrategy> taxer_;
};
```

The TaxStrategy class represents the many different ways to apply taxes to an Item (㉑). Such a TaxStrategy is combined with an Item in the TaxedItem class (㉒). Note that TaxedItem is not an Item itself and therefore cannot be decorated by means of another Item. It therefore serves as a kind of terminating Decorator, which can only be applied as the very last decorator. It also does not provide a price() function: instead, it provides the netPrice() (㉓) and grossPrice() (㉔) functions to enable queries for both the price including taxes and the original price of the wrapped Item.[9]

The only other problem that you might see is the reference semantics–based implementation of the Decorator design pattern: lots of pointers, including nullptr checks and the danger of dangling pointers, explicit lifetime management by means of std::unique_ptr and std::make_unique(), and the many small, manual memory allocations. However, luckily you still have an ace up your sleeve and can show them how to implement Decorators based on value semantics (see the following guideline).

To summarize, the Decorator design pattern is one of the essential design patterns and despite some drawbacks will prove to be a very valuable addition to your toolbox. Just make sure you're not too excited about Decorator and start to use it for everything. After all, for every pattern there is a thin line between good use and overuse.

Guideline 35: Use Decorators to Add Customization Hierarchically

- Understand that inheritance is rarely the answer.
- Apply the Decorator design pattern with the intent to nonintrusively and hierarchically extend and customize behavior.
- Consider Decorators for combining and reusing independent pieces of behavior.
- Understand the difference between the Decorator, Adapter, and Strategy design patterns.
- Utilize the extreme flexibility of Decorators, but know its shortcomings.
- Avoid nonsensical Decorators, but prefer design that is easy to use correctly.

---

9 If you're thinking that the original price() function should be renamed netPrice() to reflect its true purpose, then I agree.

Guideline 36: Understand the Trade-off Between Runtime and Compile Time Abstraction

In "Guideline 35: Use Decorators to Add Customization Hierarchically" on page 348, I introduced you to the Decorator design pattern and hopefully gave you a strong incentive to add this design pattern to your toolbox. However, so far I have illustrated Decorator only by means of classic, object-oriented implementations and again not followed the advice of "Guideline 22: Prefer Value Semantics over Reference Semantics" on page 176. Since I assume that you are eagerly waiting to see how to implement Decorator based on value semantics, it's time to show you two possible approaches. Yes, *two* approaches: I will make up for the deferral by demonstrating two very different implementations. Both are firmly based on value semantics, but in comparison, they are almost on opposite sides of the design space. While the first approach will be an implementation based on static polymorphism, which enables you to exploit all compile-time information you may have, the second approach will rather exploit all the runtime advantages of dynamic polymorphism. Both approaches have their merits but, of course, also their characteristic demerits. Therefore, these examples will nicely demonstrate the broadness of design choices available to you.

A Value-Based Compile Time Decorator

Let's start with the Decorator implementation based on static polymorphism. "I assume that this will again be very heavy on templates, right?" you ask. Yes, I will use templates as the primary abstraction mechanism, and yes, I will use a C++20 concept and even forwarding references. But no, I will try not to make it particularly heavy on templates. On the contrary, the major focus still lies on the design aspects of the Decorator design pattern and the goal to make it easy to add new kinds of Decorators and new kinds of regular items. One such item is the `ConferenceTicket` class:

```
//---- <ConferenceTicket.h> ----------------

#include <Money.h>
#include <string>
#include <utility>

class ConferenceTicket
{
 public:
   ConferenceTicket( std::string name, Money price )
      : name_{ std::move(name) }
      , price_{ price }
   {}

   std::string const& name() const { return name_; }
   Money price() const { return price_; }
```

```
  private:
    std::string name_;
    Money price_;
};
```

The ConferenceTicket perfectly fulfills the expectations of a value type: there is no base class involved and there are no virtual functions. This indicates that items are no longer decorated via pointer-to-base, but instead by means of composition, or alternatively, by means of direct non-public inheritance. Two examples for this are the following implementations of the Discounted and Taxed classes:

```
//---- <PricedItem.h> ----------------

#include <Money.h>

template< typename T >
concept PricedItem =    ❸
  requires ( T item ) {
    { item.price() } -> std::same_as<Money>;
  };


//---- <Discounted.h> ----------------

#include <Money.h>
#include <PricedItem.h>
#include <utility>

template< double discount, PricedItem Item >
class Discounted  // Using composition  ❶
{
 public:
   template< typename... Args >
   explicit Discounted( Args&&... args )
      : item_{ std::forward<Args>(args)... }
   {}

   Money price() const {
      return item_.price() * ( 1.0 - discount );
   }

 private:
   Item item_;
};


//---- <Taxed.h> ----------------

#include <Money.h>
#include <PricedItem.h>
#include <utility>
```

```
template< double taxRate, PricedItem Item >
class Taxed : private Item   // Using inheritance ❷
{
 public:
   template< typename... Args >
   explicit Taxed( Args&&... args )
      : Item{ std::forward<Args>(args)... }
   {}

   Money price() const {
      return Item::price() * ( 1.0 + taxRate );
   }
};
```

Both Discounted (❶) and Taxed (❷) serve as Decorators for other kinds of Items: the Discounted class represents a certain discount on a given item, and the Taxed class represents some kind of tax. This time, however, both are implemented in the form of class templates. The first template argument specifies the discount and the tax rate, respectively, and the second template argument specifies the type of the decorated Item.[10]

Most noteworthy, however, is the PricedItem constraint on the second template argument (❸). This constraint represents the set of semantic requirements, i.e. the expected behavior. Due to this constraint, you can only provide types that represent items with a price() member function. Using any other type would immediately result in a compilation error. Thus PricedItem plays the same role as the Item base class in the classic Decorator implementation in "Guideline 35: Use Decorators to Add Customization Hierarchically" on page 348. For the same reason, it also represents the separation of concerns based on the *Single-Responsibility Principle (SRP)*. Furthermore, if this constraint is owned by some high level in your architecture, then you, as well as anyone else, are able to add new kinds of items *and* new kinds of Decorators on any lower level. This feature perfectly fulfills the *Open-Closed Principle (OCP)*, and due to the proper ownership of the abstraction, also the *Dependency Inversion Principle (DIP)* (see Figure 9-7).[11]

---

10 Note that it is only possible to use floating-point values as non-type template parameters (NTTPs) (*https:// oreil.ly/peHM2*) since C++20. Alternatively, you could store the discount and tax rates in the form of data members.

11 Alternatively, in particular if you cannot use C++20 concepts yet, this is an opportunity to use the *Curiously Recurring Template Pattern (CRTP)*; see "Guideline 26: Use CRTP to Introduce Static Type Categories" on page 225.

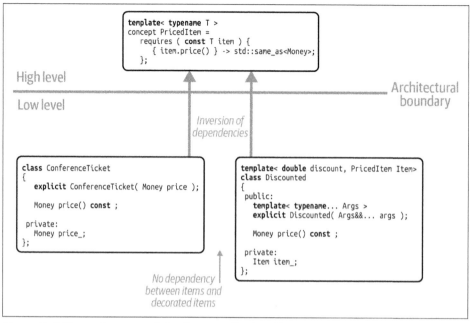

```
                    template< typename T >
                    concept PricedItem =
                        requires ( const T item ) {
                            { item.price() } -> std::same_as<Money>;
                        };
```

High level

Low level

Architectural boundary

Inversion of dependencies

```
class ConferenceTicket
{
    explicit ConferenceTicket( Money price );

    Money price() const ;

private:
    Money price_;
};
```

```
template< double discount, PricedItem Item>
class Discounted
{
 public:
    template< typename... Args >
    explicit Discounted( Args&&... args );

    Money price() const ;

 private:
    Item item_;
};
```

No dependency between items and decorated items

Figure 9-7. Dependency graph for the compile time Decorator

Both the `Discounted` and `Taxed` class templates are very similar, except for the way they handle the decorated `Item`: while the `Discounted` class template stores the `Item` in the form of a data member and therefore follows "Guideline 20: Favor Composition over Inheritance" on page 162, the `Taxed` class template privately inherits from the given `Item` class. Both approaches are possible, reasonable, and have their individual strengths, but you should consider the composition approach taken by the `Discounted` class template as the more common approach. As explained in "Guideline 24: Use Adapters to Standardize Interfaces" on page 198, there are only five reasons to prefer non-`public` inheritance to composition (some of them are *very* rare):

- If you have to override a virtual function
- If you need access to a `protected` member function
- If you need the adapted type to be constructed *before* another base class
- If you need to share a common virtual base class or override the construction of a virtual base class
- If you can draw *significant* advantage from the *Empty Base Optimization (EBO)* (*https://oreil.ly/nvqMn*)

Arguably, for a large number of adapters, *EBO* may be a reason to favor inheritance, but you should make sure that your choice is backed up by numbers (for instance, by means of representative benchmarks).

With these three classes in place, you're able to specify a `ConferenceTicket` with a discount of 20% and a tax of 15%:

```
#include <ConferenceTicket.h>
#include <Discounted.h>
#include <Taxed.h>
#include <cstdlib>

int main()
{
   // 20% discount, 15% tax: (499*0.8)*1.15 = 459.08
   Taxed<0.15,Discounted<0.2,ConferenceTicket>> item{ "Core C++", 499.0 };

   Money const totalPrice = item.price();  // Results in 459.08

   // ...

   return EXIT_SUCCESS;
}
```

The biggest advantage of this compile-time approach is the significant performance improvement: since there are no pointer indirections, and due to the possibility of inlining, the compiler is able to go all out on optimizing the resulting code. Also, the resulting code is arguably much shorter and not bloated with any boilerplate code, and therefore easier to read.

"Could you be a little more specific about the performance results? In C++, developers are bickering about a 1% performance difference and call it *significant*. So seriously: how much faster is the compile-time approach?" I see, you seem familiar with the performance zeal of the C++ community. Well, as long as you promise me, again, that you won't consider my results the definitive answer but only a single example, and if we agree that this comparison won't evolve into a performance study, I can show you some numbers. But before I do, let me quickly outline the benchmark that I will use: I am comparing the classic object-oriented implementation from "Guideline 35: Use Decorators to Add Customization Hierarchically" on page 348 with the described compile-time version. Of course, there is an arbitrary number of decorator combinations, but I am restricting myself to the following four item types:[12]

---

12 To avoid a visit from the tax collection office, I should explicitly state that I'm aware of the questionable nature of the `Discounted<0.2,Taxed<0.19,ConferenceTicket>>` class (see also the list of potential problems of Decorator at the end of "Guideline 35: Use Decorators to Add Customization Hierarchically" on page 348). In my defense: it's an obvious permutation of decorators, which is well suited for this benchmark.

```
using DiscountedConferenceTicket = Discounted<0.2,ConferenceTicket>;
using TaxedConferenceTicket = Taxed<0.19,ConferenceTicket>;
using TaxedDiscountedConferenceTicket =
    Taxed<0.19,Discounted<0.2,ConferenceTicket>>;
using DiscountedTaxedConferenceTicket =
    Discounted<0.2,Taxed<0.19,ConferenceTicket>>;
```

Since in the compile time solution these four types do not have a common base class, I am filling four specific `std::vectors` with these. In comparison, for the classic run-time solution, I use a single `std::vector` of `std::unique_ptr<Item>`s. In total, I am creating 10,000 items with random prices for both solutions and calling `std::accumulate()` 5,000 times to compute the total price of all items.

With this background information, let's take a look at the performance results (Table 9-1). Again, I am normalizing the results, this time to the performance of the runtime implementation.

Table 9-1. Performance results for the compile-time Decorator implementation (normalized performance)

	GCC 11.1	Clang 11.1
Classic Decorator	1.0	1.0
Compile-time Decorator	0.078067	0.080313

As stated before, the performance of the compile-time solution is significantly faster than the runtime solution: for both GCC and Clang, it only takes approximately 8% of the time of the runtime solution, and is therefore faster by more than one order of magnitude. I know, this sounds amazing. However, while the performance of the compile-time solution is extraordinary, it comes with a couple of potentially severe limitations: due to the complete focus on templates, there is no runtime flexibility left. Since even the discount and tax rates are realized via template parameters, a new type needs to be created for each different rate. This may lead to longer compile times and more generated code (i.e., larger executables). Additionally, it stands to reason that all class templates reside in header files, which again increases compile time and may reveal more implementation details than desired. More importantly, changes to the implementation details are widely visible and may cause massive recompilations. However, the most limiting factor appears to be that the solution can only be used in this form if all information is available at compile time. Thus, you may be able to get to this performance level for only a few special cases.

A Value-Based Runtime Decorator

Since the compile time Decorator may be fast but very inflexible at runtime, let's turn our attention to the second value-based Decorator implementation. With this implementation, we will return to the realm of dynamic polymorphism, with all of its runtime flexibility.

As you now know the Decorator design pattern, you realize that we need to be able to easily add new types: new kinds of Item, as well as new price modifiers. Therefore *the design pattern of choice to turn the Decorator implementation from "Guideline 35: Use Decorators to Add Customization Hierarchically" on page 348 into a value semantics–based implementation is Type Erasure*.[13] The following Item class implements an owning Type Erasure wrapper for our priced item example:

```
//---- <Item.h> ----------------

#include <Money.h>
#include <memory>
#include <utility>

class Item
{
 public:
   // ...

 private:
   struct Concept   ❹
   {
      virtual ~Concept() = default;
      virtual Money price() const = 0;
      virtual std::unique_ptr<Concept> clone() const = 0;
   };

   template< typename T >
   struct Model : public Concept   ❺
   {
      explicit Model( T const& item ) : item_( item ) {}
      explicit Model( T&& item ) : item_( std::move(item) ) {}

      Money price() const override
      {
         return item_.price();
      }

      std::unique_ptr<Concept> clone() const override
      {
         return std::make_unique<Model<T>>(*this);
      }

      T item_;
```

---

13 For a thorough overview of Type Erasure, see Chapter 8 and in particular "Guideline 32: Consider Replacing Inheritance Hierarchies with Type Erasure" on page 298.

```
    };

    std::unique_ptr<Concept> pimpl_;
};
```

In this implementation, the Item class defines a nested Concept base class in its
private section (❹). As usual, the Concept base class represents the set of requirements (i.e. the expected behavior) for the wrapped types, which are expressed by the
price() and clone() member functions. These requirements are implemented by
the nested Model class template (❺). Model implements the price() function by forwarding the call to the price() member function of the stored item_ data member,
and the clone() function by creating a copy of the stored item.

The public section of the Item class should look familiar:

```
//---- <Item.h> ----------------

// ...

class Item
{
 public:
   template< typename T >
   Item( T item )   ❻
      : pimpl_( std::make_unique<Model<T>>( std::move(item) ) )
   {}

   Item( Item const& item ) : pimpl_( item.pimpl_->clone() ) {}

   Item& operator=( Item const& item )
   {
      pimpl_ = item.pimpl_->clone();
      return *this;
   }

   ~Item() = default;
   Item( Item&& ) = default;
   Item& operator=( Item&& item ) = default;

   Money price() const { return pimpl_->price(); }   ❼

 private:
   // ...
};
```

Next to the usual implementation of the Rule of 5 (*https://oreil.ly/fzS3f*), the class is
again equipped with a templated constructor that accepts all kinds of items (❻). Last
but not least, the class provides a price() member function, which mimics the
expected interface of all items (❼).

With this wrapper class in place, you are able to add new items easily: neither any intrusive modification of existing code nor any use of a base class is required. Any class that provides a `price()` member function and is copyable will work. Luckily, this includes the `ConferenceTicket` class from our compile-time Decorator implementation, which provides everything we need and is firmly based on value semantics. Unfortunately, this is not true for the `Discounted` and `Taxed` classes, since they expect decorated items in the form of a template argument. Therefore, we re-implement `Discounted` and `Taxed` for use in the Type Erasure context:

```
//---- <Discounted.h> ----------------

#include <Item.h>
#include <utility>

class Discounted
{
 public:
   Discounted( double discount, Item item )
      : item_( std::move(item) )
      , factor_( 1.0 - discount )
   {}

   Money price() const
   {
      return item_.price() * factor_;
   }

 private:
   Item item_;
   double factor_;
};


//---- <Taxed.h> ----------------

#include <Item.h>
#include <utility>

class Taxed
{
 public:
   Taxed( double taxRate, Item item )
      : item_( std::move(item) )
      , factor_( 1.0 + taxRate )
   {}

   Money price() const
   {
      return item_.price() * factor_;
   }
```

```
  private:
    Item item_;
    double factor_;
};
```

It's particularly interesting to note that neither of these two classes are derived from any base class, yet both perfectly implement the Decorator design pattern. On the one hand, they implement the operations required by the `Item` wrapper to count as an item (in particular, the `price()` member function and the copy constructor), but on the other hand, they own an `Item`. Therefore, both enable you to combine Decorators arbitrarily, as demonstrated in the following `main()` function:

```
#include <ConferenceTicket.h>
#include <Discounted.h>
#include <Taxed.h>

int main()
{
    // 20% discount, 15% tax: (499*0.8)*1.15 = 459.08
    Item item(Taxed(0.19, Discounted(0.2, ConferenceTicket{"Core C++",499.0})));

    Money const totalPrice = item.price();

    // ...

    return EXIT_SUCCESS;
}
```

"Wow, this is beautiful: there are no pointers, no manual allocations, and it feels very natural and intuitive. But at the same time, it's extremely flexible. This is too good to be true—there must be a catch. What about the performance?" you say. Well, you sound like you expect a total performance breakdown. So let's benchmark this solution. Of course, I'm using the same benchmark as for the compile-time version of Decorator and just adding the third solution based on Type Erasure. The performance numbers are shown in Table 9-2.

Table 9-2. Performance results for the Type Erasure Decorator implementation (normalized performance)

	GCC 11.1	Clang 11.1
Classic Decorator	1.0	1.0
Compile-time Decorator	0.078067	0.080313
Type Erasure Decorator	0.997510	0.971875

As you can see, the performance is not worse than the performance of the other, classic runtime solution. In fact, the performance even appears to be a tiny bit better, but although this is an average of many runs, I wouldn't put too much emphasis on that. However, remember that there are multiple options to improve the performance of the Type Erasure solution, as demonstrated in "Guideline 33: Be Aware of the Optimization Potential of Type Erasure" on page 318.

While performance may not be the primary strength of the runtime solution(s) (at least in comparison to a compile-time solution), it definitely shines when it comes to runtime flexibility. For instance, it is possible to decide at runtime to wrap any Item in another Decorator (based on user input, based on the result of a computation, …). This, of course, will again yield an Item, which, together with many other Items, can be stored in a single container. It indeed gives you an enormous runtime flexibility.

Another strength is the ability to hide implementation details in source files more easily. While this may result in a loss of runtime performance, it will likely result in better compile times. Most importantly: any modification to the hidden code will not affect any other code and thus save you a lot of recompilations, because the implementation details are more strongly encapsulated.

In summary, both the compile-time and runtime solutions are value based and lead to simpler, more comprehensible user code. However, they also come with individual strengths and weaknesses: while the runtime approach offers more flexibility, the compile-time approach dominates with respect to performance. In reality, you will rarely end up with a pure compile time or runtime approach, but you will very often find yourself somewhere between these two extremes. Make sure you know your options: weigh them against each other and find a compromise that perfectly combines the best of both worlds and fits your particular situation.

Guideline 36: Understand the Trade-off between Runtime and Compile-Time Abstraction

- Be aware of both runtime and compile-time implementations of the Decorator design pattern.

- Understand that compile-time solutions usually perform better but limit runtime flexibility and encapsulation.

- Understand that runtime solutions are more flexible and are good at hiding details but perform worse.

- Prefer a *value semantics* solution to a *reference semantics* solution.

CHAPTER 10

The Singleton Pattern

In this chapter, we take a look at the (in-)famous *Singleton* pattern. I know, you may already be acquainted with Singleton, and you may already have a strong opinion about it. It is even possible that you consider Singleton an antipattern and thus ask yourself how I mustered the courage to include it in this book. Well, I am aware that Singleton is not particularly popular and in many circles has a rather bad reputation, in particular because of the global nature of Singletons. From that perspective, however, it might be very surprising to learn that there are a couple of "Singleton"-like instances in the C++ Standard Library. Seriously! And, honestly, they work fantastically! Therefore, we should seriously talk about *what* a Singleton is, *when* Singleton works, and *how* to deal with Singleton properly.

In "Guideline 37: Treat Singleton as an Implementation Pattern, Not a Design Pattern" on page 380, I will explain the Singleton pattern and demonstrate how it works by a very commonly used implementation, the so-called *Meyers' Singleton*. I will, however, also make a strong argument to *not* treat Singleton as a design pattern but as an *implementation pattern*.

In "Guideline 38: Design Singletons for Change and Testability" on page 385, we accept the fact that sometimes we need a solution to represent the few global aspects in our code. This is what the Singleton pattern is often used for. This also means that we are confronted by the usual problems of Singletons: global state; many strong, artificial dependencies; and an impeded changeability and testability. While these sound like excellent reasons to avoid Singleton after all, I will show you that by proper software design, you can combine the Singleton benefits with excellent changeability and testability.

Guideline 37: Treat Singleton as an Implementation Pattern, Not a Design Pattern

Let me start by addressing the elephant in the room:

> Singleton is *not* a design pattern.

If you haven't heard about Singleton before, then this might not make any sense at all, but bear with me. I promise to explain Singleton shortly. If you *have* heard about Singleton before, then I assume you're either nodding in agreement with a sympathizing "I know" look on your face, or you are utterly stunned and initially don't know what to say. "But why not?" you eventually dare to ask. "Isn't it one of the original design patterns from the Gang of Four book?" Yes, you're correct: Singleton is one of the 23 original patterns documented in the GoF book. At the time of writing, Wikipedia (*https://oreil.ly/jzuFw*) calls it a design pattern, and it is even listed as a design pattern in Steve McConnell's bestseller *Code Complete*.[1] Nevertheless, it still isn't a design pattern, because it doesn't have the properties of a design pattern. Let me explain.

The Singleton Pattern Explained

Sometimes you may want to guarantee that there is only one, and *exactly* one, instance of a particular class. In other words, you have a Highlander situation: "There can be only one."[2] This might make sense for the system-wide database, the one and only logger, the system clock, the system configuration, or, in short, any class that should not be instantiated multiple times, since it represents something that exists only once. That is the intent of the Singleton pattern.

The Singleton Pattern

Intent: "Ensure a class has only one instance, and provide a global point of access to it."[3]

This intent is visualized by the Gang of Four with the UML diagram in Figure 10-1, which introduces the `instance()` function as the global point of access to the unique instance.

---

1 Steve McConnell, *Code Complete: A Practical Handbook of Software Construction*, 2nd ed. (Microsoft Press, 2004).

2 "There can be only one" is the tagline of the 1986 movie *Highlander* (*https://oreil.ly/XT6uF*) featuring Christopher Lambert.

3 Erich Gamma et al., *Design Patterns: Elements of Reusable Object-Oriented Software*.

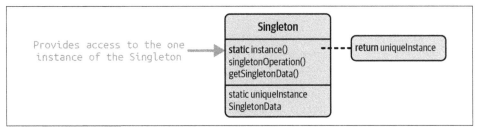

Figure 10-1. The UML representation of the Singleton pattern

There are multiple ways to restrict the number of instantiations to exactly one. Definitely one of the most useful and therefore most commonly used forms of Singleton is the Meyers' Singleton.[4] The following `Database` class is implemented as a Meyers' Singleton:

```
//---- <Database.h> ----------------

class Database final
{
 public:
   static Database& instance()    ❶
   {
      static Database db;  // The one, unique instance
      return db;
   }

   bool write( /*some arguments*/ );
   bool read( /*some arguments*/ ) const;
   // ... More database-specific functionality

   // ... Potentially access to data members

 private:
   Database() {}   ❷
   Database( Database const& ) = delete;
   Database& operator=( Database const& ) = delete;
   Database( Database&& ) = delete;
   Database& operator=( Database&& ) = delete;

   // ... Potentially some data members
};
```

The Meyers' Singleton evolves around the fact that it's possible to access the single instance of the `Database` class only via the `public`, `static instance()` function (❶):

```
#include <Database.h>
#include <cstdlib>
```

---

4 The Meyers' Singleton is explained in Item 4 of Scott Meyers's *Effective C++*.

```
int main()
{
    // First access, database object is created
    Database& db1 = Database::instance();
    // ...

    // Second access, returns a reference to the same object
    Database& db2 = Database::instance();
    assert( &db1 == &db2 );

    return EXIT_SUCCESS;
}
```

Indeed, this function is the only way to get a Database: all functionality that could possibly be used to create, copy, or move an instance is either declared in the private section or is explicitly deleted.[5] Although this appears to be pretty straightforward, one implementation detail is of special interest: note that the default constructor is explicitly defined and not defaulted (❷). The reason is if it were defaulted, up to C++17, it would be possible to create a Database with an empty set of braces, i.e., via *value initialization* (*https://oreil.ly/9h4IB*):

```
#include <cstdlib>

class Database
{
 public:
   // ... As before

 private:
   Database() = default;  // Compiler generated default constructor

   // ... As before
};

int main()
{
    Database db;     // Does not compile: Default initialization
    Database db{};   // Works, since value initialization results in aggregate
                     //   initialization, because Database is an aggregate type

    return EXIT_SUCCESS;
}
```

Up to C++17, the Database class counts as an *aggregate type*, which means that *value initialization* would be performed via *aggregate initialization* (*https://oreil.ly/HSuYl*).

---

5 I know that the explicit handling of the copy and move assignment operators appears to be overkill, but this gives me the opportunity to remind you about the Rule of 5 (*https://oreil.ly/fzS3f*).

Aggregate initialization, in turn, ignores the default constructor, including the fact that it is `private`, and simply performs a *zero initialization* of the object. Thus, value initialization enables you to still create an instance. If, however, you provide the default constructor, then the class does not count as an aggregate type, which prevents aggregate initialization.[6]

The `instance()` function is implemented in terms of a *static local variable* (*https://oreil.ly/mqUoK*). This means that the first time control passes through the declaration, the variable is initialized in a thread-safe way, and on all further calls the initialization is skipped.[7] On every call, the first and all subsequent calls, the function returns a reference to the static local variable.

The rest of the `Database` class is pretty much what you would expect from a class representing a database: there are some `public`, database-related functions (e.g., `write()` and `read()`) and there could be some data members, including access functions. In other words, except for the `instance()` member function and the special members, `Database` is just a normal class.

Singleton Does Not Manage or Reduce Dependencies

Now, with one possible implementation of a Singleton in mind, let's go back to my claim that Singleton is not a design pattern. First, let's remind ourselves of the properties of a design pattern, which I defined in "Guideline 11: Understand the Purpose of Design Patterns" on page 80:

A design pattern:

- Has a name
- Carries an intent
- Introduces an abstraction
- Has been proven

The Singleton pattern definitely has a name, and it definitely has an intent. No question there. I would also claim that it has been proven over the years (although there may be skeptical voices that point out that Singleton is rather infamous). However, there is no kind of abstraction: no base class, no template parameters, nothing. Singleton does not represent an abstraction itself, and it does not introduce an abstraction. In fact, it isn't concerned with the structure of code or with the interac-

---

6 This behavior has changed in C++20, since the declaration of any constructor by the user is now enough to make a type nonaggregate.

7 To be precise and to avoid complaints, if the static local variable is zero or constant initialized, the initialization can happen before the function is entered. In our example, the variable is indeed created in the first pass.

---

tion and interdependencies of entities, and hence it isn't aiming at managing or reducing dependencies.[8] This, though, is what I defined to be an integral part of software design. Instead, Singleton is focused on restricting the number of instantiations to exactly one. Thus, Singleton is not a design pattern but merely an implementation pattern.

"Then why is it listed as a design pattern in so many important sources?" you ask. This is a fair and good question. There may be three answers to that. First, in other programming languages, in particular languages where every class can automatically represent an abstraction, the situation may be different. While I acknowledge this, I still believe that the intent of the Singleton pattern is primarily targeted for implementation details and not for dependencies and decoupling.

Second, Singleton is very commonly used (although often also *mis*used), so it is definitely a pattern. Since there are Singletons in many different programming languages, it does not appear to be just an idiom of the C++ programming language. As a consequence, it appears reasonable to call it a design pattern. This chain of arguments may sound plausible to you, but I feel it falls short of distinguishing between software design and implementation details. This is why in "Guideline 11: Understand the Purpose of Design Patterns" on page 80, I introduced the term *implementation pattern* to distinguish between different kinds of language-agnostic patterns such as Singleton.[9]

And third, I believe that we are still in the process of understanding software design and design patterns. There is no common definition of software design. For that reason, I came up with one in "Guideline 1: Understand the Importance of Software Design" on page 2. There is no common definition of design patterns, either. This is why I came up with one in "Guideline 11: Understand the Purpose of Design Patterns" on page 80. I strongly believe that we must talk more about software design and more about patterns to come to a common understanding of the necessary terminology, especially in C++.

In summary, you do not use a Singleton to decouple software entities. So despite the fact that it is described in the famous GoF book, or in *Code Complete*, or even listed as a design pattern on Wikipedia (*https://oreil.ly/i8lyX*), it does not serve the purpose

---

8 In fact, a naive implementation of Singleton is creating lots of artificial dependencies itself; see "Guideline 38: Design Singletons for Change and Testability" on page 385.

9 Without going into detail, I argue that there are several more so-called "design patterns" that fall in the category of implementation patterns, such as the *Monostate* pattern, the *Memento* pattern, and the *RAII idiom*, which Wikipedia (*https://oreil.ly/qD1L8*) lists as design patterns. While this might make sense in languages other than C++, the intent of RAII is most certainly not to reduce dependencies but to automate cleanup and encapsulate responsibility.

of a design pattern. Singleton is merely dealing with implementation details, and as such you should treat it as an implementation pattern.

> ## Guideline 37: Treat Singleton as an Implementation Pattern, Not a Design Pattern
>
> - The goal of Singleton is not to decouple or manage dependencies, and thus it does not fulfill the expectations of a design pattern.
>
> - Apply the Singleton pattern with the intent to restrict the number of instances of a particular class to exactly one.

Guideline 38: Design Singletons for Change and Testability

Singleton is indeed a rather infamous pattern: there are many voices out there that describe Singleton as a general problem in code, as an antipattern, as dangerous, or even as evil. Therefore, there is a lot of advice out there to avoid the pattern, among others, Core Guideline I.3 (*https://oreil.ly/Mai2n*):[10]

> Avoid singletons.

One of the primary reasons why people dislike Singleton is that it often causes artificial dependencies and obstructs testability. As such, it runs contrary to two of the most important and most general guidelines in this book: "Guideline 2: Design for Change" on page 11 and "Guideline 4: Design for Testability" on page 28. From that perspective, Singleton indeed appears to be a problem in code and should be avoided. However, despite all the good-intentioned warnings, the pattern is persistently used by many developers. The reasons for that are manifold but probably mainly related to two facts: first, sometimes (and let's agree on *sometimes*) it is desirable to express the fact that something exists only once and should be available for many entities in the code. Second, sometimes Singleton appears to be the proper solution, as there *are* global aspects to represent.

So, let's do the following: instead of arguing that Singleton is always bad and evil, let's focus on those few situations where we need to represent a global aspect in our program and discuss how to represent this aspect properly, but still design for change and testability.

---

10 Another such piece of advice is the CppCon 2020 talk by Peter Muldoon's "Retiring the Singleton Pattern: Concrete Suggestions for What to Use Instead" (*https://oreil.ly/su4Xb*), which provides many useful techniques for how to deal with Singletons in your codebase.

Singletons Represent Global State

Singletons are mostly used to represent entities in a program that logically and/or physically exist only once and that should be used by many other classes and functions.[11] Common examples are the system-wide database, logger, clock, or configuration. These examples, including the term *system-wide*, give an indication of the nature of these entities: they commonly represent globally available functionality or data, i.e., global state. From that perspective, the Singleton pattern appears to make sense: by preventing everyone from creating new instances, and by forcing everyone to use *the one* instance, you can guarantee uniform and consistent access to this global state across all using entities.

This representation and introduction of global state, however, explains why Singleton is commonly considered a problem. As Michael Feathers expressed it:[12]

> The singleton pattern is one of the mechanisms people use to make global variables. In general, global variables are a bad idea for a couple of reasons. One of them is opacity.

Global variables are indeed a bad idea, particularly for one important reason: the term *variable* suggests that we are talking about *mutable* global state. And that kind of state can indeed cause a lot of headaches. To be explicit, mutable global state is frowned upon (in general, but especially in a multithreaded environment), as it is difficult, costly, and likely both to control access and guarantee correctness. Furthermore, global (mutable) state is very hard to reason about, as read and write access to this state usually happens invisibly within some function, which, based on its interface, does not reveal the fact that it uses the global state. And last but not least, if you have several globals, whose lifetimes depend on one another and that are distributed over several compilation units, you might be facing the *static initialization order fiasco* (*SIOF*).[13] Obviously, it is beneficial to avoid global state as much as possible.[14]

The problem of global state, however, is a problem that we can't resolve by avoiding Singletons. It's a general problem, unrelated to any particular pattern. The same problem, for instance, also exists for the Monostate pattern, which enforces a single,

---

11 If a Singleton is used for anything else, you should be very suspicious and consider it a misuse of the Singleton pattern.

12 Michael Feathers, *Working Effectively with Legacy Code*.

13 The best summary of SIOF I'm aware of is given by Jonathan Müller in his accordingly named talk "Meeting C++ 2020" (*https://oreil.ly/nvkHT*).

14 "Globals are bad, m'kay?" as stated by Guy Davidson and Kate Gregory in *Beautiful C++: 30 Core Guidelines for Writing Clean, Safe, and Fast Code* (Addison-Wesley).

global state but allows for any number of instantiations.[15] So on the contrary, Singleton can help deal with the global state by constraining access to it. For instance, as Miško Hevery explains in his 2008 article, Singletons that provide a unidirectional data flow to *or* from some global state are acceptable:[16] a Singleton implementing a logger would only allow you to write data but not read it. A Singleton representing a system-wide configuration or clock would only allow you to read the data but not write it, thus representing a global *constant*. The restriction to unidirectional data flow helps avoid many of the usual problems with global state. Or in the words of Miško Hevery (the emphasis being mine):[17]

> *Appropriate* use of "Global" or semi-Global states can greatly simplify the design of applications [...].

Singletons Impede Changeability and Testability

Global state is an intrinsic problem of Singletons. However, even if we feel comfortable with representing global state with a Singleton, there are serious consequences: functions that use Singletons depend on the represented global data and thus become harder to change and harder to test. To better understand this, let's revive the `Database` Singleton from "Guideline 37: Treat Singleton as an Implementation Pattern, Not a Design Pattern" on page 380, which is now actively used by a couple of arbitrary classes, namely `Widget` and `Gadget`:

```
//---- <Widget.h> ----------------

#include <Database.h>

class Widget
{
 public:
   void doSomething( /*some arguments*/ )
   {
      // ...
      Database::instance().read( /*some arguments*/ );
      // ...
   }
```

---

15 The Monostate pattern, to my best knowledge, was first mentioned in the September issue of the 1996 *C++ Report* in the article "Monostate Classes: The Power of One" by Steve Ball and John Crawford (see Stanley B. Lippmann, ed., *More C++ Gems* (Cambridge University Press)). It is also described in Martin Reddy's *API Design for C++* (Morgan Kaufmann). Monostate, in contrast to Singleton, allows any number of instances of a type, but makes sure that there is only a single state for all instances. As such, the pattern should not be confused with `std::monostate`, which is used as a well-behaved empty alternative in `std::variant`.

16 Miško Hevery, "Root Cause of Singletons" (*https://oreil.ly/wQgJC*), *The Testability Explorer* (blog), August 2008.

17 Ibid.

```
};

//---- <Gadget.h> ---------------

#include <Database.h>

class Gadget
{
 public:
   void doSomething( /*some arguments*/ )
   {
      // ...
      Database::instance().write( /*some arguments*/ );
      // ...
   }
};
```

Widget and Gadget both require access to the system-wide Database. For that reason, they call the Database::instance() function and subsequently the read() and write() functions.

Since they use the Database and thus depend on it, we would like them to reside in architecture levels *below* the level of the Database Singleton. That is because, as you remember from "Guideline 2: Design for Change" on page 11, we can call it a proper architecture only if all dependency arrows run toward the high levels (see Figure 10-2).

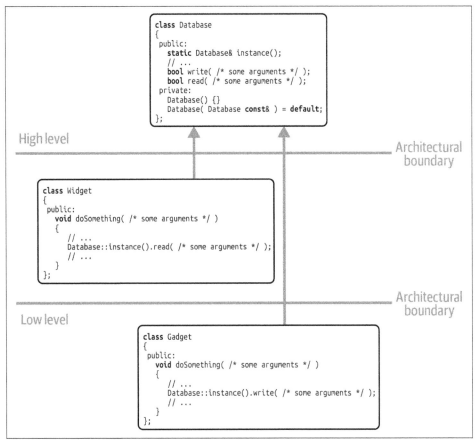

```
class Database
{
 public:
   static Database& instance();
   // ...
   bool write( /* some arguments */ );
   bool read( /* some arguments */ );
 private:
   Database() {}
   Database( Database const& ) = default;
};
```

High level

Architectural boundary

```
class Widget
{
 public:
   void doSomething( /* some arguments */ )
   {
      // ...
      Database::instance().read( /* some arguments */ );
      // ...
   }
};
```

Architectural boundary

Low level

```
class Gadget
{
 public:
   void doSomething( /* some arguments */ )
   {
      // ...
      Database::instance().write( /* some arguments */ );
      // ...
   }
};
```

Figure 10-2. The desired dependency graph for a Database implemented as a Singleton

Although this dependency structure may be desirable, unfortunately it is only an illusion: the Database class is not an abstraction but a concrete implementation, representing the dependency on a very specific database! Therefore, the *real* dependency structure is inverted and looks something like Figure 10-3.

The *actual* dependency structure utterly fails the Dependency Inversion Principle (DIP) (see "Guideline 9: Pay Attention to the Ownership of Abstractions" on page 62): all dependency arrows point toward the lower level. In other words, right now there is no software architecture!

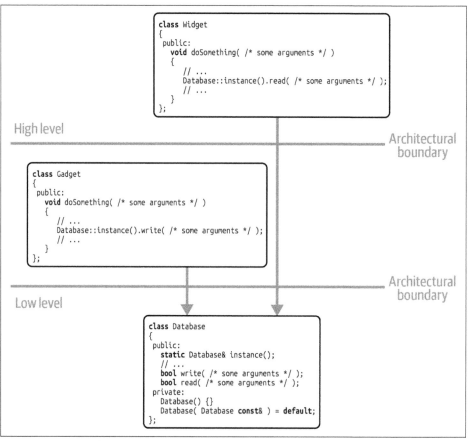

Figure 10-3. The actual dependency graph for a Database implemented as a Singleton

Since the `Database` is a concrete class and not an abstraction, there are strong and unfortunately even invisible dependencies from all over the code to the specific implementation details and design choices of the `Database` class. This may—in the worst case—include a dependency on vendor-specific details that become visible throughout the code, manifest in many different places, and later make changes excruciatingly hard or even impossible. Due to that, the code becomes much more difficult to change.

Also consider how badly tests are affected by this dependency. All tests that use one of the functions depending on the `Database` Singleton become themselves dependent on the Singleton. This means, for instance, that for every test using the `Widget::do Something()` function, you would always have to provide the one and only `Database` class. The unfortunate, but also simple, reason is that none of these functions provide you with a way to substitute the `Database` with something else: any kind of stub, mock, or fake.[18] They all treat the `Database` Singleton as their shiny, precious secret. Testability is therefore severely impeded, and writing tests becomes so much harder that you might be tempted to not write them at all.[19]

This example indeed demonstrates the usual problems with Singletons and the unfortunate artificial dependencies they introduce. These dependencies make the system more inflexible and more rigid, and thus harder to change and test. That, of course, should not be. On the contrary, it should be easy to replace a database implementation with another one, and it should be easy to test functionality that uses a database. For these exact reasons, we must make sure that the `Database` becomes a true implementation detail on the low level of a proper architecture.[20]

"But wait a second, you just said that if the `Database` is an implementation detail, there is no architecture, right?" Yes, I said that. And there is nothing we can do as it is: the `Database` Singleton does not represent any abstraction and does not enable us to deal with dependencies at all. Singleton is just not a design pattern. So in order to remove the dependencies on the `Database` class and make the architecture work, we will have to design for change and testability by introducing an abstraction and using a real design pattern. To achieve that, let's take a look at an example with a good way to deal with global aspects, using Singletons from the C++ Standard Library.

Inverting the Dependencies on a Singleton

I'm returning to a true El Dorado of design patterns, which I have used several times to demonstrate different design patterns: the C++17 polymorphic memory resources:

```cpp
#include <array>
#include <cstddef>
#include <cstdlib>
#include <memory_resource>
#include <string>
#include <vector>
// ...

int main()
{
    std::array<std::byte,1000> raw;  // Note: not initialized!

    std::pmr::monotonic_buffer_resource
        buffer{ raw.data(), raw.size(), std::pmr::null_memory_resource() };  ❶
```

---

18 For an explanation about the different kinds of test doubles, see Martin Fowler's article "Mocks Aren't Stubs" (*https://oreil.ly/K4vR3*). For examples of how to use these in C++, refer to Jeff Langr's *Modern C++ Programming with Test-Driven Development*.

19 But I am sure you won't be deterred from writing the tests anyway, despite it being difficult.

20 This is also one of the strong arguments in Robert C. Martin's *Clean Architecture*.

```
    std::pmr::vector<std::pmr::string> strings{ &buffer };

    // ...

    return EXIT_SUCCESS;
}
```

In this example, we configure the `std::pmr::monotonic_buffer_resource` (*https://oreil.ly/uVQoS*), called `buffer`, to work only with the static memory contained in the given `std::array` raw (❶). If this memory is depleted, `buffer` will try to acquire new memory via its upstream allocator, which we specify to be `std::pmr::null_mem ory_resource()` (*https://oreil.ly/p0V3c*). Allocating via this allocator will never return any memory but will always fail with the `std::bad_alloc()` exception. Thus, `buffer` is restricted to the 1,000 bytes provided by `raw`.

While you should immediately remember and recognize this as an example of the Decorator design pattern, this also serves as an example of the Singleton pattern: the `std::pmr::null_memory_resource()` function returns a pointer to the same allocator every time the function is called and thus acts as a single point of access to the one and only instance of `std::pmr::null_memory_resource`. Thus, the returned allocator acts as a Singleton. Although this Singleton does not provide a unidirectional flow of data (after all, we can both allocate memory and give it back), Singleton still feels like a reasonable choice, as it represents one kind of global state: memory.

It is particularly interesting and important to note that this Singleton does not make you depend on the specific implementation details of the allocator. Quite the opposite: the `std::pmr::null_memory_resource()` function returns a pointer to `std::pmr::memory_resource` (*https://oreil.ly/9wYhs*). This class represents a base class for all kinds of allocators (at least in the realm of C++17), and thus serves as an abstraction. Still, `std::pmr::null_memory_resource()` represents a specific allocator, a specific choice, which we now depend on. As this functionality is in the Standard Library, we tend to not recognize it as a dependency, but generally speaking it is: we are not provided with an opportunity to replace the standard-specific implementation.

This changes if we replace the call to `std::pmr::null_memory_resource()` with a call to `std::pmr::get_default_resource()` (*https://oreil.ly/chMJ7*) (❷):

```
    #include <memory_resource>
    // ...

    int main()
    {
        // ...

        std::pmr::monotonic_buffer_resource
```

```
      buffer{ raw.data(), raw.size(), std::pmr::get_default_resource() };  ❷

   // ...

   return EXIT_SUCCESS;
}
```

The `std::pmr::get_default_resource()` function also returns a pointer to `std::pmr::memory_resource`, which represents an abstraction for the system-wide default allocator. By default, the returned allocator is returned by the `std::new_delete_resource()` (*https://oreil.ly/w4lHB*) function. However, amazingly, this default can be customized by the `std::pmr::set_default_resource()` (*https://oreil.ly/wQBy6*) function:

```
namespace std::pmr {

memory_resource* set_default_resource(memory_resource* r) noexcept;

} // namespace std::pmr
```

With this function, we can define the `std::pmr::null_memory_resource()` as the new system-wide default allocator (❸):

```
// ...

int main()
{
   // ...

   std::pmr::set_default_resource( std::pmr::null_memory_resource() );  ❸

   std::pmr::monotonic_buffer_resource
      buffer{ raw.data(), raw.size(), std::pmr::get_default_resource() };

   // ...

   return EXIT_SUCCESS;
}
```

With `std::pmr::set_default_resource()`, you are able to customize the system-wide allocator. In other words, this function provides you with the ability to inject the dependency on this allocator. Does this ring a bell? Does this sound familiar? I very much hope this makes you think about another, essential design pattern... *drum roll*...yes, correct: the Strategy design pattern.[21]

---

21 For the design pattern experts, I should explicitly point out that the `std::pmr::get_default_resource()` function itself fulfills the intent of another design pattern: the *Facade* design pattern. Unfortunately, I do not go into detail about Facade in this book.

Indeed, this is a Strategy. Using this design pattern is a fantastic choice, because it has an amazing effect on the architecture. While `std::pmr::memory_resource` represents an abstraction from all possible allocators and thus can reside on the high level of the architecture, any concrete implementation of an allocator, including all (vendor-)specific implementation details, can reside on the lowest level of the architecture. As a demonstration, consider this sketch of the `CustomAllocator` class:

```cpp
//---- <CustomAllocator.h> ---------------

#include <memory_resource>

class CustomAllocator : public std::pmr::memory_resource
{
 public:
   // There is no need to enforce a single instance
   CustomAllocator( /*...*/ );
   // No explicitly declared copy or move operations

 private:
   void* do_allocate( size_t bytes, size_t alignment ) override;

   void do_deallocate( void* ptr, size_t bytes,
                       size_t alignment ) override;

   bool do_is_equal(
      std::pmr::memory_resource const& other ) const noexcept override;

   // ...
};
```

Note that `CustomAllocator` publicly inherits from `std::pmr::memory_resource` in order to qualify as a C++17 allocator. Due to that, you can establish an instance of `CustomAllocator` as the new system-wide default allocator with the `std::pmr::set_default_resource()` function (❹):

```cpp
#include <CustomAllocator.h>

int main()
{
   // ...
   CustomAllocator custom_allocator{ /*...*/ };

   std::pmr::set_default_resource( &custom_allocator );   ❹
   // ...
}
```

While the `std::pmr::memory_resource` base class resides on the highest level of the architecture, `CustomAllocator` is logically introduced on the lowest architectural level (see Figure 10-4). Thus, the Strategy pattern causes an inversion of dependencies (see "Guideline 9: Pay Attention to the Ownership of Abstractions" on

---

page 62): despite the Singleton-ness of the allocators, despite representing global state, you depend on an abstraction instead of the concrete implementation details.

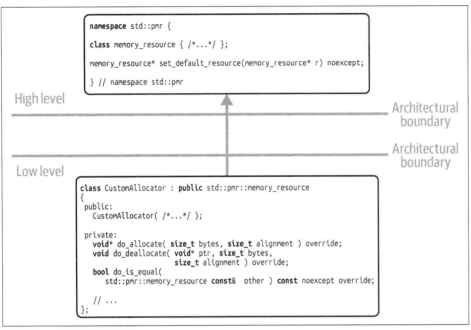

Figure 10-4. The dependency inversion achieved via the std::pmr::memory_resource abstraction

As a side note, it's worth pointing out that with this approach you can trivially avoid any dependency on the order of initialization of globals (i.e., SIOF), since you can explicitly manage the initialization order by creating all Singletons on the stack and in a single compilation unit:

```cpp
int main()
{
    // The one and only system-wide clock has no lifetime dependencies.
    // Thus it is created first
    SystemClock clock{ /*...*/ };

    // The one and only system-wide configuration depends on the clock.
    SystemConfiguration config{ &clock, /*...*/ };

    // ...
}
```

Applying the Strategy Design Pattern

Based on this previous example, you should now have an idea how to fix our Database example. As a reminder, the goal is to keep the Database class as the default database implementation but to make it an implementation detail, i.e., to remove all dependencies on the concrete implementation. All you need to do is apply the Strategy design pattern to introduce an abstraction, alongside a global point of access and a global point for *dependency injection*, on the high level of our architecture. This will enable anyone (and I really mean anyone, as you also follow the Open-Closed Principle (OCP); see "Guideline 5: Design for Extension" on page 35) to introduce a custom database implementation (both concrete implementations as well as test stubs, mocks, or fakes) on the lowest level.

So let's introduce the following PersistenceInterface abstraction (❺):

```cpp
//---- <PersistenceInterface.h> ----------------

class PersistenceInterface   ❺
{
 public:
   virtual ~PersistenceInterface() = default;

   bool read( /*some arguments*/ ) const   ❻
   {
      return do_read( /*...*/ );
   }
   bool write( /*some arguments*/ )   ❼
   {
      return do_write( /*...*/ );
   }

   // ... More database specific functionality

 private:
   virtual bool do_read( /*some arguments*/ ) const = 0;   ❻
   virtual bool do_write( /*some arguments*/ ) = 0;   ❼
};

PersistenceInterface* get_persistence_interface();   ❽
void set_persistence_interface( PersistenceInterface* persistence );   ❾

// Declaration of the one 'instance' variable
extern PersistenceInterface* instance;   ❿
```

The PersistenceInterface base class provides the interface for all possible database implementations. For instance, it introduces a read() and a write() function, split into the public interface part and the private implementation part, based on the example set by the std::pmr::memory_resource class (❻ and ❼).[22] Of course, in reality it would introduce a few more database-specific functions, but let read() and write() be sufficient for this example.

In addition to the PersistenceInterface, you would also introduce a global point of access called get_persistence_interface() (❽) and a function to enable *dependency injection* called set_persistence_interface() (❾). These two functions allow you to access and set the global persistence system (❿).

The Database class now inherits from the PersistenceInterface base class and implements the required interface (hopefully adhering to the Liskov Substitution Principle (LSP); see "Guideline 6: Adhere to the Expected Behavior of Abstractions" on page 44):

```
//---- <Database.h> ----------------

class Database : public PersistenceInterface
{
 public:
   // ... Potentially access to data members

   // Make the class immobile by deleting the copy and move operations
   Database( Database const& ) = delete;
   Database& operator=( Database const& ) = delete;
   Database( Database&& ) = delete;
   Database& operator=( Database&& ) = delete;

 private:
   bool do_read( /*some arguments*/ ) const override;
   bool do_write( /*some arguments*/ ) override;
   // ... More database-specific functionality

   // ... Potentially some data members
};
```

In our special setting, the Database class represents the default database implementation. We need to create a default instance of the database, in case no other persistence system is specified via the set_persistence_interface() function. However, if any other persistence system is established as the system-wide database before Database is created, we must not create an instance, as this would cause unnecessary and unfortunate overhead. This behavior is achieved by implementing the get_persistence_interface() function with two *static local variables* and an *Immediately Invoked Lambda Expression (IILE)* (⓫):

---

22 The separation into a public interface and a private implementation is an example of the Template Method design pattern. Unfortunately, in this book I can't go into detail about the many benefits of this design pattern.

```
//---- <PersistenceInterface.cpp> ----------------

#include <Database.h>

// Definition of the one 'instance' variable
PersistenceInterface* instance = nullptr;

PersistenceInterface* get_persistence_interface()
{
  // Local object, initialized by an
  //   'Immediately Invoked Lambda Expression (IILE)'
  static bool init = [](){  ⓫
    if( !instance ) {
      static Database db;
      instance = &db;
    }
    return true;  // or false, as the actual value does not matter.
  }();  // Note the '()' after the lambda expression. This invokes the lambda.

  return instance;
}

void set_persistence_interface( PersistenceInterface* persistence )
{
  instance = persistence;
}
```

The first time the execution flow enters the get_persistence_interface() function,
the init static local variable is initialized. If, at this point in time, the instance is
already set, no Database is created. However, if it is not, the Database instance is created as another static local variable inside the lambda and bound to the instance
variable:

```
#include <PersistenceInterface.h>
#include <cstdlib>

int main()
{
  // First access, database object is created
  PersistenceInterface* persistence = get_persistence_interface();

  // ...

  return EXIT_SUCCESS;
}
```

This implementation achieves the desired effect: Database becomes an implementation detail, which no other code depends on and which can be replaced at any time
by a custom database implementation (see Figure 10-5). Thus, despite the Singleton-
ness of Database, it does not introduce dependencies, and it can be easily changed
and easily replaced for testing purposes.

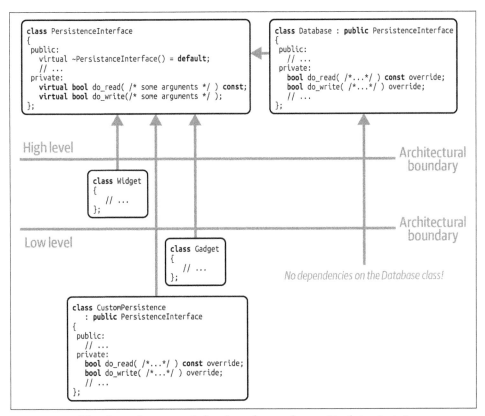

Figure 10-5. The dependency graph for the refactored, non-Singleton Database

"Wow, this is a great solution. I bet I can use that in a few places in my own codebase!" you say, with an impressed and appreciative look on your face. "But I see a potential problem: since I have to inherit from an interface class, this is an intrusive solution. What should I do if I can't change a given Singleton class?" Well, in that case you have two nonintrusive design patterns to choose from. Either you already have an inheritance hierarchy in place, in which case you can introduce an Adapter to wrap the given Singleton (see "Guideline 24: Use Adapters to Standardize Interfaces" on page 198), or you don't have an inheritance hierarchy in place yet, in which case you can put the External Polymorphism design pattern to good use (see "Guideline 31: Use External Polymorphism for Nonintrusive Runtime Polymorphism" on page 279).

"OK, but I see another, more serious problem: is this code truly thread-safe?" Honestly, no, it is not. To give one example for a possible problem: it could happen that during the first call to `get_persistence_interface()`, which may take some time due to the setup of the `Database` instance, the `set_persistence_interface()` is called. In that case, either the `Database` is created in vain or the call to set_persistence_interface() is lost. However, perhaps surprisingly, this is not something that we need to address. Here's why: remember that the instance represents global state. If we assume that set_persistence_interface() can be called from anywhere in the code at any time, in general we can't expect that after calling set_persistence_interface(), a call to get_persistence_interface() would return the set value. Hence, calling the set_persistence_interface() function from anywhere in the code is like pulling the rug from under somebody's feet. This is comparable to calling std::move() on any lvalue:

```
template< typename T >
void f( T& value )
{
  // ...
  T other = std::move(value);  // Very bad move (literally)!
  // ...
}
```

From this perspective, the set_persistence_interface() function should be used at the very beginning of the program or at the beginning of a single test, not arbitrarily.

"Shouldn't we make sure that the set_persistence_interface() function can be called only once?" you ask. We most certainly could do that, but this would artificially limit its use for testing purposes: we would not be able to reset the persistence system at the beginning of every single test.

Moving Toward Local Dependency Injection

"OK, I see. One last question: since this solution involves global state that can be changed, wouldn't it be better to use a more direct and more local dependency injection to the lower-level classes? Consider the following modification of the Widget class, which is given its dependency upon construction:"

```
//---- <Widget.h> ----------------

#include <PersistenceInterface.h>

class Widget
{
 public:
   Widget( PersistenceInterface* persistence )  // Dependency injection
     : persistence_(persistence)
   {}

   void doSomething( /*some arguments*/ )
   {
     // ...
     persistence_->read( /*some arguments*/ );
     // ...
   }
```

```
  private:
    PersistenceInterface* persistence_{};
};
```

I completely agree with you. This may be the next step to address the problem of global state. However, before we analyze this approach, keep in mind that this idea is only an option since we have already inverted the dependencies. Thanks to introducing an abstraction in the high level of our architecture, we suddenly have choices and can talk about alternative solutions. Hence, the first and most important step is to properly manage the dependencies. But back to your suggestion: I really like the approach. The interface of the Widget class becomes more "honest" and clearly displays all of its dependencies. And since the dependency is passed via the constructor argument, the dependency injection becomes more intuitive and more natural.

Alternatively, you could pass the dependency on the Widget::doSomething() function directly:

```
//---- <Widget.h> ----------------

#include <PersistenceInterface.h>

class Widget
{
 public:
   void doSomething( PersistenceInterface* persistence, /*some arguments*/ )
   {
      // ...
      persistence->read( /*some arguments*/ );
      // ...
   }
};
```

While this approach may not be the best for a member function, this may be your only option for free functions. And again, the function becomes a little more "honest" by explicitly stating its dependencies.

However, there is a flip side to this direct dependency injection: this approach may quickly become unwieldy in large call stacks. Passing a dependency through several levels of your software stack to make them available at the point they are needed is neither convenient nor intuitive. Additionally, especially in the presence of several Singletons, the solution quickly becomes cumbersome: passing, for instance, a PersistenceInterface, an Allocator, and the system-wide Configuration through many layers of function calls just to be able to use them on the lowest level truly is not the most elegant approach. For that reason, you may want to combine the ideas of providing a global access point and a local dependency injection, for instance, by introducing a wrapper function:

```
//---- <Widget.h> ----------------

#include <PersistenceInterface.h>

class Widget
{
 public:
   void doSomething( /*some arguments*/ )  ❶❷
   {
      doSomething( get_persistence_interface(), /*some arguments*/ );
   }

   void doSomething( PersistenceInterface* persistence, /*some arguments*/ )  ❶❸
   {
      // ...
      persistence->read( /*some arguments*/ );
      // ...
   }
};
```

While we still provide the previous doSomething() function (❶❷), we now additionally provide an overload that accepts a PersistenceInterface as a function argument (❶❸). The second function does all the work, whereas the first function now merely acts as a wrapper, which injects the globally set PersistenceInterface. In this combination, it's possible to make local decisions and to locally inject the desired dependency, but at the same time it is not necessary to pass the dependency through many layers of function calls.

However, truth be told, while these solutions may work very well in this database example and also in the context of managing memory, it might not be the right approach for every single Singleton problem. So don't believe that this is the only possible solution. After all, it depends. However, it is a great example of the general process of software design: identify the aspect that changes or causes dependencies, then separate concerns by extracting a fitting abstraction. Depending on your intent, you will just have applied a design pattern. So consider naming your solution accordingly, and by that leave traces of your reasoning for others to pick up on.

In summary, the Singleton pattern certainly is not one of the glamorous patterns. It simply comes with too many disadvantages, most importantly the usual flaws of global state. But still, despite the many negative aspects, if used judiciously, Singleton can be the right solution for representing the few global aspects in your code in some situations. If it is, prefer Singletons with unidirectional data flow, and design your Singletons for change and testability by inverting the dependencies and enabling dependency injection with the Strategy design pattern.

Guideline 38: Design Singletons for Change and Testability

- Be aware that Singleton represents global state, with all its flaws.

- Avoid global state as much as possible.

- Use Singleton judiciously and just for the few global aspects in your code.

- Prefer Singletons with unidirectional data flow.

- Use the Strategy design pattern to invert dependencies on your Singleton to remove the usual impediments to changeability and testability.

CHAPTER 11

The Last Guideline

There is only one more guideline, one more piece of advice that I can bestow upon you. So here it is: the last guideline.

Guideline 39: Continue to Learn About Design Patterns

"That's it? This is all you've got? Come on, there are so many more design patterns out there. We barely touched the surface!" you say. Well, honestly, you are completely correct; there is nothing I can add to that. But in my defense, I was planning for many more patterns until reality struck me: there is only so much information that you can fit into a book with 400 pages. But don't fret: in these 400 pages I've taken you on a journey through the most important pieces of advice for any design that you will need anywhere, anytime in your software development career:

Minimize dependencies

Dealing with dependencies is the core of software design. And whatever kind of software you write, if you are seriously interested in making it last, you will have to deal with dependencies: the necessary ones, but primarily the artificial ones. Of course, your major goal is to reduce dependencies and hopefully even minimize them. To achieve this goal, you will inevitably deal with design patterns.

Separate concerns

This may be the most important, central design guideline that you can take away from this book. Separate concerns and your software structures will detangle and become easier to understand, change, and test. All design patterns, without exception, provide you with some way to separate concerns. The major difference between patterns is the way they separate concerns, their *intent*. Although design patterns may be structurally similar, their intent is always unique.

Prefer composition to inheritance

While inheritance is a powerful feature, the true strength of many design patterns stems from building on composition. For instance, the Strategy design pattern, one of the patterns that is used *everywhere* (and hopefully this has become obvious by now), primarily builds on composition to separate concerns, but then also offers you the option to use inheritance to extend the functionality. The same is true for Bridge, Adapter, Decorator, External Polymorphism, and Type Erasure.

Prefer a nonintrusive design

True flexibility and extendibility arise when it isn't necessary to modify existing code but possible to just add new code. Therefore, any design that is nonintrusive is preferable to design that intrusively modifies existing code. Hence, design patterns such as Decorator, Adapter, External Polymorphism, and Type Erasure are such valuable additions to your design pattern toolbox.

Prefer value semantics over reference semantics

To keep code simple, understandable, and away from dark corners such as nullptrs, dangling pointers, lifetime dependencies, etc., you should prefer to employ values instead of pointers and references. And C++ is a wonderful language to use for that purpose, as C++ takes value semantics seriously. It allows you, the developer, to live a happy life in the realm of value semantics. Surprisingly, as we have seen with `std::variant` and Type Erasure, this philosophy does not necessarily have a negative performance impact but may even increase performance.

In addition to these general pieces of advice about software design, you have gained insight into the purpose of design patterns. Now you know what a design pattern is.

A design pattern:

- Has a name
- Carries an intent
- Introduces an abstraction
- Has been proven

Equipped with this information, you will no longer fall for false claims about some implementation detail being a design pattern (as I have been confronted with multiple times in my career), for instance, the claim that smart pointers (`std::unique_ptr`, `std::shared_ptr`, etc.) or factory functions such as `std::make_unique()` are implementations of design patterns. Also, you are now familiar with several of the most important and useful design patterns, which will prove to be useful again and again:

Visitor
> To extend operations on a closed set of types, reach for the Visitor design pattern (possibly realized by `std::variant`).

Strategy
> To configure the behavior and "inject" it from outside, pick the Strategy design pattern (aka policy-based design).

Command
> To abstract from different kinds of operations, possibly undoable operations, utilize the Command design pattern.

Observer
> To observe state change in some entities, choose the Observer design pattern.

Adapter
> To adapt one interface to another one, nonintrusively, without changing code, use the Adapter design pattern.

CRTP
> For a static abstraction, free of virtual functions (and you can't employ C++20 concepts yet), then apply the CRTP design pattern. CRTP might also prove to be useful to create compile-time mixin classes.

Bridge
> To hide implementation details and reduce physical dependencies, make use of the Bridge design pattern.

Prototype
> To create a virtual copy, the Prototype design pattern is the right choice.

External Polymorphism
> To promote loose coupling by adding polymorphic behavior externally, remember the External Polymorphism design pattern.

Type Erasure
> For the power of External Polymorphism in combination with the advantages of value semantics, consider the Type Erasure design pattern.

Decorator
> To nonintrusively add responsibilities to an object, opt for the benefits of the Decorator design pattern.

However, there are more design patterns. Many more! Also a lot of important and useful design patterns. Therefore, you should continue to learn about design patterns. And there are two ways to do that. First is getting to know more patterns: learn about their intent and about their similarities and differences compared to other design patterns. Also, don't forget that design patterns are about a dependency structure, not about implementation details. Second, you should also get a better understanding about each pattern and experience their advantages and shortcomings. For that purpose, keep an eye out for design patterns used in the codebases you work on. I promise you, you will find many of them: any attempt to manage and reduce dependencies is very likely proof of a design pattern. So yes, design patterns are everywhere!

Guideline 39: Continue to Learn About Design Patterns

- Get to know more design patterns and understand their intent.
- Learn more about the advantages and disadvantages of each design pattern.
- Find design patterns in the wild to experience them hands-on.

Index

About the Author

Klaus Iglberger is a freelance C++ trainer and consultant. He completed his PhD in computer science in 2010 and has subsequently concentrated on large-scale C++ software design. He shares his expertise through popular C++ courses, from beginner to advanced, all around the world. He is also the creator and lead designer of the Blaze C++ math library (*https://bitbucket.org/blaze-lib/blaze*), one of the organizers of the Munich C++ user group (MUC++) (*https://www.meetup.com/MUCplusplus*), and the (co-)organizer of the Back-to-Basics (*https://cppcon.org/b2b*) and Software Design (*https://cppcon.org/softwaredesign*) tracks at CppCon (*https://cppcon.org*).

Colophon

The animal on the cover of *C++ Software Development* is is the common crane (*Grus grus*, or "crane crane"). Also known as the Eurasian crane, the common crane is most often found throughout the Paleartic region, which spans northern Europe, northern Asia, and North Africa, though isolated groups have been seen as far east as Ireland and as far west as Japan. The largest nesting populations of common cranes can be found each year in Russia and Scandinavia.

A large, stately bird, the common crane is of medium size among crane species, with a body length of 39–51 inches and a wingspan of 71–94 inches, and weighing 10–12 pounds on average. It has a slate-gray body with a black face, a black-and-white neck, and a red crown. Every two years or so, this migratory bird molts its feathers entirely, remaining flightless for six weeks while new feathers grow in. During migration, flocks of four hundred individuals or more may travel together. These flocks have been observed flying at altitudes of up to 33,000 feet, the second highest of any bird species.

Like all cranes, the common crane is omnivorous, eating plant matter as well as insects, amphibians, rodents, and other small animals. The cranes typically forage in small groups on land or standing in shallow water, probing with their bills for food.

Cranes have featured in human art and iconography since ancient times, appearing in Aesop's Fables, inspiring traditional dances such as one performed in Korea since 646 CE, and having association with gods in ancient South Arabia and Greece, to share just a few examples. Several styles of martial art, particularly kung fu, have taken inspiration from the graceful movements of the crane, as popularized in the 1984 hit film *The Karate Kid*.

With a global population of around six hundred thousand as of 2014, the common crane has been classified by the IUCN as being of least concern, making it one of only four species of crane not considered threatened or dependent on conservation. Many